THE HIGHROAD AROUND MODERNISM

✳ ✳ ✳

SUNY Series in Philosophy
George R. Lucas, Jr., editor

THE HIGHROAD AROUND MODERNISM

* * *

Robert Cummings Neville

* * *

State University of New York Press

Cover by Beth Neville

Published by
State University of New York Press, Albany

For information, address State University of New York Press,
State University Plaza, Albany, N.Y., 12246

Production by Marilyn P. Semerad
Marketing by Fran Keneston

Library of Congress Cataloging-in-Publication Data

Neville, Robert C.
    The highroad around modernism / by Robert Cummings Neville
        p.   cm.—(SUNY series in philosophy)
    Includes bibliographical references and index.
    ISBN 0-7914-1151-6 (hard).—ISBN 0-7914-1152-4 (pbk.)
    1. Philosophy, Modern—20th century.   2. Modernism.
3. Postmodernism.   I. Title.   II. Series.
B791.N45   1992
190′.9′04—dc20   91-47542
                                                                   CIP

        10   9   8   7   6   5   4   3   2

For Naomi Louise Neville

＊

Contents

✳

PREFACE

Postmodernism, with its fierce belief that Western civilization has been defined by a "center," has missed many of that tradition's most interesting parts. Hence it has attacked a fashionably powerful but intellectually dead-ended strand of the Western tradition, namely modernism (understood in certain specific ways). As a result, by its supercalifragilisticexpialidoxic totalizing negation of modernism, breathlessly presented as a rejection of everything from Plato onward, postmodernism has set itself up as the true center of the tradition. The postmodern center is "critique." But in truth, there simply is no center except in fashion. Critique is but one theme, and even then an inconstant one. What counts is finding interesting and suggestive ideas that facilitate saying something truer than the alternatives.

To be sure, the postmodern critique has often been well-aimed. Many of the targets within modernism deserve what they have been given in critique. Perhaps more important, some forms of postmodernism have provided trenchant criticisms of social injustices. These contributions need to be acknowledged in any study of postmodernism. This book slights them, however, because it is a study of an alternative to modernism and postmodernism. In part 2, basic tools of much postmodern critique will themselves be criticized.

The ironic thesis of this book is that the tradition that gets around modernism to something far better is hardly recognized by the postmodern critics and, when it is, it is devastatingly misinterpreted. Though it has many forms, that tradition, I shall argue, runs from Jonathan Edwards through Ralph Waldo Emerson to Charles Sanders Peirce, and from Peirce to William James, John Dewey, George Herbert Mead, and Alfred North Whitehead to Paul Weiss, Charles Hartshorne, John E. Smith, Robert Brumbaugh, Justus Buchler, Stephen David Ross, David

Weissman, William Desmond, David Hall, Irwin Lieb, Carl Vaught and George Allan, to name but a few. These are among the American representatives of the strand. Though not deriving from European modernity at all, the Chinese tradition of Neo-Confucianism bears many similarities to the American pragmatic tradition; some of its main representatives are Chou Tun-i, Chang Tsai, Ch'eng Hao, Ch'eng I, Chu Hsi, Wang Yang-ming, Wang Fu-chih, Anthony Cua, Liu Shu-hsien, Cheng Chung-ying, Tang I-chieh, and Tu Wei-ming. The thinkers in both pragmatic and Neo-Confucian traditions are united by two points: (1) engagement with speculative metaphysics and (2) the necessity to provide alternatives to the interpretation of the Western tradition that was put front and center by Nietzsche and Heidegger and assumed by deconstructionists and postmodernists. The earlier Neo-Confucians were hardly interested in the Western tradition, of course, but our contemporaries in that group are pleased to find the West broad enough to resonate with Chinese practical and speculative concerns. Dialogue with philosophers in the Asian traditions has shown that they too are unbound by the postmodern reading of the West. They have many more points of engagement with the American pragmatic tradition and its progeny than with the recent heroes of wicked "onto-theo-logocentrism."

The postmodernists' ignoration of the American tradition is to be understood partly in terms of the European colonial attitudes toward America; most postmodern ideas have come from Europe. Even such erudite and balanced American postmodernists such as Richard Rorty, however, look at their own tradition with extraordinary blinders. Rorty (1979) interprets Dewey by excluding all the metaphysical speculation, dismisses Whitehead because process philosophy is metaphysics, treats James as a clever observer, and scarcely mentions Peirce the speculative genius. The joke, however, is on the ignorers (or at least I shall argue so).

The title of this book perhaps falls off the subtle balance of irony into polemic parody. That the philosophic line I shall lift up and defend goes "around" modernism, plays on postmodernism's preoccupation with centers and margins. My own career is a personal part of this joke. For years I was told that, as a metaphysician, I was too far from the "mainstream" to be taken seriously by others because everyone knows metaphysics is impossible: metaphysics is of only marginal historical interest. Then around 1970 Americans heard that the French had said that mainstreams and centers are bad and that margins are good: suddenly my kind of philosophy was the evil center that had corrupted the West by its vicious dominance, and right thinking people all lived on happy margins. Well, the kind of philosophy with which I connect goes right around the preoccupation with centers, mainstreams, and margins.

Furthermore, the road around modernism is no footpath (though Heidegger romanticized that too—footpaths are supposed to be more authentic than highways). It is a road of high culture, with readings of both the Western and Eastern traditions that throw both into a new and engaging light. Hence it is a highroad around modernism.

I am tired of being "post" anything. Besides, the whole idea of defining oneself as "post" something requires overdetermining what you are getting beyond so as to be able to negate it totalistically. Hardly any movement is sufficiently unified as to be totalizable except as a matter of fad and fashion. Far better it is to think of that to which one's thought might contribute, to be "pre" something. That cannot be quite right, of course, because we have no guarantee that the future will pay us any mind whatsoever. What is both most modest and yet hopeful is to think of ourselves as something someone later will get over while accepting our contribution. Therefore I advocate thinking of ourselves as paleogalactic.

I wish I could sustain the verbal byplay of this non-postmodern parody of postmodernism, but it would betray the point of this book and indicate an unintended disrespect. The verbal byplay, especially of the deconstructionists, depends on the linearity of the conversation, of the tradition as superText. It has no use in lateral thinking, in sorting and resorting elements within and without the Western resources of ideas. Words make their "differance" less by negations and erasures of the past than by the fact that they come to have meaning by creating their own contexts, sometimes reworking but more often ignoring the story as it has been told so far. Meaning is less negation than it is reconstruction. Reconstructions of course should be true to their components, but this is more likely with self-avowed *re*construction than with the method of negation that projects a hidden coverstory over the past it surmounts. The verbal structure of this book is to create an hypothesis about the way things are, about the ways our history is interestingly read, and about how to conceive the work of philosophy and related cultural enterprises.

Cultural politics is a deep motive of this book. Whereas much postmodernism can be ignorant and silly in what it dismisses, hewing to a rigid party line about what is important enough to dismiss, many of its criticisms of the Western tradition are well taken. John Dewey was no postmodernist in his *Reconstruction in Philosophy* or *Quest for Certainty*, and yet his point is both valid and congenial to postmodernists. Many postmodern achievements, for instance in architecture, are extraordinarily valuable. Why not embrace postmodernism, enlarge it, and go on to better things?

The answer is that the political effect of postmodernism, in philosophy and criticism especially, is to shut down its alternatives. Both in the academy and in art and literary criticism, postmodernism does not engage its alternatives in debate but attempts to delegitimate them, dismiss them from consideration, and then pretend they do not exist. Charles Peirce, for instance, who by a century anticipated the postmodernists in most of their valid points, is dismissed by them in most respects except logic and semiotics because he was also a speculative metaphysician. Perhaps the point is that the postmodernists misunderstand what they oppose and should embrace many of their demons. My counterproposal in cultural politics is to oppose postmodernism so that the traditions that preceded it in so many of its valid points can be allowed to flourish on their own. More particularly, the traditions that continued their own development while modernism was trying to start everything new and then was getting itself deconstructed, should be acknowledged for what they have accomplished on their own in the last one hundred fifty years. We do not need to return to Peirce, although that might not be a bad thing: we need more to attend to Peirce's heirs. Although it is good that analytic modernist philosophers such as Robert Nozick discover that it is possible to do metaphysics (Nozick, 1981), that fact should not be celebrated too much until the new analytic metaphysics grapples with the work of people such as Paul Weiss, Charles Hartshorne, John Findlay, Justus Buchler, Edward Pols, and Leonard Feldstein who produced substantial bodies of metaphysical analysis during the decades when modernists and postmodernists said metaphysics is impossible. It is easy but wicked for the academically well-placed modernists to become postmodernists and celebrate their conversion while still supporting the delegitimation of those who were doing a better (or at least deserving) work all along.

At a deeper level, I am fighting to defend cultural substance against a rule for critique that so easily becomes a clever trick. This is not to say that all cultural substance is valid, nor that the postmodern critiques are always merely clever tricks. But the ambiance of critique fostered by postmodernism alienates people from culture universally; the message undergraduates take from "critical theory" is that they do not need to read books, and that rock music wholly supplants any music written before the Beatles. Postmodernism should recognize the positive culture that it presupposes and that justifies its critical stances. More, our civilization should recognize its need to identify, appropriate, orient, and advance beyond the cultural elements that constitute the substance of human life.

Early versions of most of the chapters here have been tried out as talks and sometimes published; those early versions are quite different from the present progeny. A draft of the section in chapter 1 on Peirce's theory of religion was delivered at the Charles Sanders Peirce Sesquicentennial International Congress in 1989, and may appear in a collection of proceedings. An extremely early version of chapter 2 was given as a talk at Hunter College. Portions of the first sections of chapter 3 appeared in "Metaphysics," *Social Research* 47/4 (Winter 1980). Chapter 4 began as a talk at the American Philosophical Association and had another form with its current title in *Process Studies* 16/4 (Winter, 1987). A version of chapter 5 with its current title was published in *Hegel and Whitehead: Contemporary Perspectives on Systematic Philosophy*, edited by George R. Lucas, Jr. (Albany: State University of New York Press, 1986). Portions of two sections of chapter 6 were given in a talk at the University of Pennsylvania. Chapter 7 contains portions of three talks sponsored by SOPHIA given in conjunction with meetings in 1987, 1988, and 1989 of the American Philosophical Association. Chapter 8 began as a talk in the English Department Lecture Series on Revolution at Boston University and had another form for a talk at Clemson University that might be published in a colloquium series. Portions of the first sections of chapter 9 appeared in "Beyond Production and Class: A Process Project in Economic Theory," in *Economic Life: Process Interpretations and Critical Responses*, edited by W. Widick Schroeder and Franklin I. Gamwell (Chicago: Center for the Scientific Study of Religion, 1988). Chapter 10 began as a talk in the Institute for Philosophy and Religion Series on Freedom, 1988, at Boston University and appeared in a slightly revised form in *On Freedom*, edited by Leroy S. Rouner (Notre Dame: University of Notre Dame Press, 1989). The first version of chapter 11 was my presidential address to the Metaphysical Society of America in March, 1989, and was published in *The Review of Metaphysics* 43/1 (September 1989). An early version of chapter 12 appeared in *Research in Philosophy and Technology*, edited by Frederick Ferre (Greenwich, Conn.: JAI Press, 1990), volume 10. I thank the respective editors for permission to use what remains of the material they published.

The next group of colleagues to be thanked are the contemporary philosophers mentioned in the text, with nearly all of whom I have discussed the issues at hand. This book has repeatedly called to mind the excitement and vigor of our philosophic community. George Allan,

Thomas J. J. Altizer, Robert S. Brumbaugh, Frederick Ferre, Joseph Grange, David L. Hall, Irwin C. Lieb, George R. Lucas, Jr., Robert Mulvaney, Steve Odin, Byron Shafer, John R. Silber, John E. Smith, Mark C. Taylor, Ronald Thiemann, Carl Vaught, Alexander von Schonborn, Paul Weiss, David Weissman, Wu Kuang-ming, and Jon Westling are people who have been attempting to enlighten me about these issues for many years. Jay Schulkin has discussed nearly every part of this book, often having been in attendance when early versions were presented to groups; he has been my most consistent and stringent critic. I have learned much from Lawrence Cahoone, David Rothenberg, and David Strong. Sean Recroft not only has gone over the whole manuscript but even typed the penultimate text. My deep thanks to all. Thanks also to Beth Neville for the cover. Naomi Neville, my daughter, is currently a student of architecture, a postmodern domain, with more than a little of her mother's and father's broader vision of things; I am pleased to dedicate this volume to her.

INTRODUCTION

✳

WHY SPECULATIVE PHILOSOPHY SHOULD
NOT SHUT DOWN

O Creator out of blank nothing of this universe whose immense reality, sublimity and beauty so little thrills me as it should, inspire me
with the earnest desire to make this chapter useful to my brethren!
(Charles S. Peirce, the opening sentence of "The First Chapter
of Logic," unpublished ms. #277, dated 6 October,1907.)

I. The Postmodernist Debate

The loudest debate in contemporary North American intellectual
life surrounds postmodernism. This is not a mere academic philosophical debate, but one that extends across all the humanistic academic disciplines and that takes place as well in the critical discussions of
literature, art, architecture, drama, dance, and the rest of culture.
Whereas once postmodernism was a European phenomenon, quickly
transplanted to American soil in the 1970s and 1980s, it now is hotly de-
bated in East Asia and around the world (Magliola 1984). Strangely
enough, the heat of the debate seems to last only about ten years and
then dissipates, only to rise again with new phenomena in the same
places.

The apparent faddishness of postmodernism is no long-term comfort to its victims, however. To be sure, postmodernism has all the effer-
vescence and evanescence of a "movement." Its main ideas are new and
radically critical, they can be learned in an afternoon and hencefore give
guidance and identity to an undergraduate career, and the movement
itself serves to mark the emancipation of a young generation of writers
and academics from their seniors. In these points, postmodernism is not

1

unique. In fact, it is remarkably like the Sturm und Drang Romanticism of a 170 years ago, or even like the modernist movement of the turn of the last century. Much postmodernism contains another element of timely irrelevance that is perhaps unique to it; namely, that it gives new direction to Marxists at a moment when economic and political Marxism have been discredited. Faddish though it is, there is a deep power in postmodernism. It touches a nerve that runs through many limbs of Western civilization.

This book shall explore postmodernism by attending first to its philosophic limb. Philosophy is less adequately construed as an academic profession than as a cultural process. Hence, philosophy's fate with postmodernism has both a causal and a reflexive relation to much of the rest of culture. Even in its best moments, what postmodernism does with philosophy is to attempt to shut down its speculative, visionary, synoptic, and systematic impulses.

Ironically, postmodernism thinks of itself as liberating and freeing up cultural impulses that had been stifled by modernism. Yet in philosophy, postmodernism functions quite strictly to shut down all forms of philosophy except those consisting in criticism. It engages in the very same academic politics of delegitimation as practised by the modernist philosophies of logical positivism, analysis, and pure phenomenology. So the strategy of this book is not so much to provide an internal analysis and critique of postmodernism itself—that might be construed as nothing more than the ever-turning screw of deconstruction—as to articulate and defend an alternative to modernism and postmodernism at once. Philosophy should be opened truly to its array of alternatives so that they might engage in realistically critical dialogue. The fulcrum for the argument is whether philosophy in its speculative mode should be shut down. In the third section of this chapter, that question will be addressed directly.

Preparatory to questioning the verdict on the end of philosophy, it is necessary to say more about postmodernism and modernism itself.

At one extreme, postmodernism's literary advocates are ecstatic with its iconoclastic "powers." Like a blind inertial force—the rhetoric of "power" and "empowerment" comes from the objectification of nature in early modern physics (see chapter 8 below)—postmodern literary theory overturns and delegitimates any claim for truth or excellence of expression it encounters (Charles Newman 1985). The very definiteness of its object for analysis is the object's undoing, for definiteness excludes alternative ways of lifting up what might be important. What used to be considered "organizing ideas" that give position and direction to participants in cultural and social life now are represented as "dominating onto-theo-logocentric ideas." Instead of criticizing ideas for bad organization, for demeaning or abusing people, for leading to poverty or injustice, the new literary theory criticizes ideas for their very definiteness: because according to other ideas the beggars might be kings, with a new class of beggars, those ideas too should have their day. Or rather, no dominating idea ought to have its day over any other: no dominating ideas, no centering organization, no social or cultural definiteness. Literary theory deconstructs, and deconstructs its deconstruction, on and on without limit until there are no constructs left, for the villain in the piece is construction itself (Culler 1982; Harari 1979; Lentricchia 1980).

At the opposite end of the postmodern spectrum from literary theory is the architecture that gave the movement its popular name. Architectural postmodernism is the rejection of the limiting strictures of specifically modern*ist*, that is, Bauhaus, architecture. Modernist architecture itself was the attempt explicitly to reject all historical reference and reconstruction (Schorske 1980: especially chapters 2 and 5). Postmodern architecture is thus the deliberate attempt to pick up historical references in detailing, though not necessarily to repeat or rework an historical style for the overall integration of a structure. In contrast to most literary postmodernism, which usually takes the form of criticism or of a style explicitly derivative from critical theory, postmodern architecture has produced fine examples of a new style of building, integrating references through a broad stretch of time. Boston is a particularly apt location for appreciating postmodern architecture; a fine postmodern building such as Rowe's Wharf (Skidmore, Owings, and Merrill) is but a short walk from monuments by Bullfinch, Richardson, Cram, McKim, White, Saarinen, and Pei, monuments many of which were themselves "revivals" or reworkings of classical, gothic, or renaissance themes. Unlike the literary extreme of postmodernism that defines itself by negation of modernism and modernist interpretations of history, the architectural extreme defines itself in reaching out and appropriating what modernism itself excluded.

The diversion of one extreme from the other suggests that more attention needs to be paid to the definition of postmodernism.

The term *postmodern* is particularly confusing because it can mean one (or maybe confuse both) of two things: *after modernity*, the modern period, which stretches from the European renaissance in the sixteenth century to the present, or *after modernism*, a particular strain of modernity that arose in the 1880s first among playwrights and then among authors, architects, composers, philosophers, and others, flourishing

through the Bauhaus style and finally generating a reaction against itself in the 1960s, often called "postmodernism" (Bradbury and McFarlane 1974, ch. 1 and *passim;* also Cahoone 1988, Introduction; Harvey
1990). David Ray Griffin, in a significant editorial statement introducing
the volumes in a series entitled *Constructive Postmodern Thought,* defines
postmodern in the former sense, that is, as the cultural movement rejecting and supplanting the entire culture of modernity (Griffin 1988a
or b, ix–xii). He contrasts his sense of *"constructive* or *revisionary"* postmodernism, however, with *"deconstructive* or *eliminative postmodernism,"*
which in its philosophic form he says is "inspired variously by pragmatism, physicalism, Ludwig Wittgenstein, Martin Heidegger, and Jacques
Derrida and other recent French thinkers." With the exception of the
reference to pragmatism, that list sounds very much like modernism,
not modernity, and modernism's deconstruction. Even pragmatism can
be made to fit the list if it is identified with Richard Rorty's reading
rather than with Peirce, James, Royce, Dewey, and Mead (Rorty 1982,
ch. 5). Griffin believes that both kinds of postmodernism reject the
whole of the modern worldview and the social and cultural order reflecting it. Deconstructive postmodernism goes so far, he says, as to reject having a worldview as such; it is an anti-worldview that "issues in
relativism, even nihilism."[1] Griffin's own constructive postmodernism
keeps the goal of a worldview and the hope that a social and cultural
order can be based on such; furthermore, it keeps the main ingredients
of the modern period's worldview—he lists God, self, purpose, meaning, a real world, and truth as correspondence. Constructive postmodernism just changes the modern versions of those ingredients to another
version influenced by Whitehead's philosophy and certain trends in contemporary science and religion.

There is a serious confusion of historical classification here, and
the significance of the classificatory issues has to do with what is recognized in philosophy and culture as important. Francis Bacon is the person usually thought to have first used the word *modern* to describe the
new age he announced. Historians of culture date the beginning of modernity, the modern age, from the scientific, political, and literary revolutions of the sixteenth and seventeenth centuries. That period itself is
rightly called "early modern." Our popular sense of the "modern" refers
to societies that have been transformed by industrial technology and the
economic, educational, military, and communications systems attendent
upon industrialization. Paul Johnson has brilliantly argued in his popular history, *The Birth of the Modern* (1991), that the modern in this sense

took hold in the United States, Britain, and Western Europe in the years 1815 to 1830. The sense of the modern associated with industrial technology and culture is what is at stake in discussions of modernization. Modernization has taken place at different times in different areas and is now the subject of much discussion in contemporary Third World nations. Modern*ism* is a cultural movement arising half a century or more after the period Johnson describes, a movement with a curious blend of intensification of certain aspects of technological development with a violent rejection of much of the bourgeois culture associated with early- and mid-nineteenth century North Atlantic industrialization.

This book will argue that the worldview and culture of the early modern period—the sixteenth and seventeenth centuries—gave rise to a variety of developments, not all consistent and many going off on their own paths. Modernity in its wholeness includes all these, surely Peirce as much as Nietzsche, Wittgenstein, and Heidegger. But modernism, a specific nineteenth- and twentieth-century movement in the arts, letters, and philosophy, is only one development. Modernism in philosophy stands in contrast to pragmatism and process philosophy, to most Latin American philosophy, and to the kinds of philosophy that have evolved in serious interaction with the traditions of China and India. Furthermore, it will be shown that of these, *only* modernist philosophies would totalize whole traditions so as to identify themselves by being *post*something.

Of course, one's characterization of the modern period itself is retrospective and reconstructive. The modernist-postmodernist story, totalizing as it is, must be unified and monolithic in order to make sense; and it gives great place to Kant and Hegel. Those others who identify with pragmatism and process philosophy read the modern period in developmental evolutionary terms, not in terms of negative revolutions in favor of the New. Peirce is thus not a modernist, but surely he is a late modern philosopher who, like Whitehead in the next generation, developed ideas typical of the early modern period so as to overcome some of the difficulties in that early worldview and in aspects of the culture to which early modern philosophy contributed. The genius of the scientific age, Peirce argued, was that it developed principles and a spirit for its own self-correction. A philosophy that improves on the early modern then cannot be postmodern without arbitrariness; it would rather be late or advanced modern, and would expect to be improved upon itself. The historical thesis of this book, defended in chapter 1, is that Peirce is not postmodern. Nor is Whitehead (or Griffin). They are, rather, late modern thinkers building upon and correcting the modern tradition in exactly the modes of critical and experimental argument at the heart of modernity.

As a terminological strategy, then, let us use "modernism" to mean a specific cultural movement of the late ninteenth and early twentieth centuries, and "postmodernism" as the attempt to identify, totalize, and reject that. "Postmodernism" is the movement now associated with deconstruction in literary theory, postmodern architecture, and the "end of philosophy" movement and the redefinition of philosophy as edifying conversation (Rorty 1979, "Introduction" and chapter 8). "Postmodern" means whatever happens in Western culture when "modernity" is over; there is no clue now as to when that shall be or in what it shall consist. "Postmodernist" is surely a dialectical twist on "modernism" within modernity. Far better to wave the flag of paleogalacticism and let future historians decide whether that is part of the modern period or cleanly supersedes it. A modest posture is to admit, all of us, to being "late moderns."

II. Modernity and Modernism

To understand the senses in which there are alternatives to modernism within the array of late modern cultural movements, let us look first at the modernism to which pragmatism and process philosophy are alternatives. Bradbury and McFarlane write:

> The case for Modernism's total dominance has often been put and is easy to see. One of the word's associations is with the coming of a new era of high aesthetic self-consciousness and non-representationalism, in which art turns from realism and humanistic representation toward style, technique, and spatial form in pursuit of a deeper penetration of life. "No artist tolerates reality," Nietzsche tells us; the task of art is its own self-realization, outside and beyond established orders, in a world of abnormally drawn perspectives. (Bradbury and McFarlane 1974, 24–25)

The first element of this characterization is the self-consciousness of rebellion, of the rejection of bourgeois society, and of a commitment to the New, to the new foundation purified of historical liabilities. Carl E. Schorske's brilliant *Fin-de-Siecle Vienna: Politics and Culture* (1980) remains the crispest and most lucid depiction of the negative side of the modernist rebellion.

The second element of the characterization is the intent to turn art in on its own form, to find meaning, significance, and validity solely in itself, without reference to history, context, or biography of the artist. The world created by the artists is intended to be sufficient to itself for meaning, importance, and truth. Modernist emphases on integrity of style for its own sake, and on abstractions of one kind or another, are ways of cutting the artifact off from its situation and giving it intrinsic, foundational justification.

Philosophical modernism shares the twin traits of intrinsic foundationalism and rebellion against bourgeois culture. The roots of analytic philosophy are diverse, but nearly all modernist. The debunking defense of common sense against the pretentious Victorian systems of the idealists sparked the early work of G. E. Moore and Bertrand Russell and played into the Bloomsbury Group, Britain's quintessential modernists.[2] Wittgenstein's early (1922) logical atomism, complementing Russell's, was another root. The two roots grew together in the later (1953) Wittgenstein's language philosophy and that of J. L. Austin (1956). It is a mistake to associate the early Wittgenstein too closely with the logical positivists. But their love of revolutionary ahistorical science, and their view of logic as the form of expression of science, were yet other roots of analytic philosophy.[3] All these forms of analytic philosophy, in addition to their contempt for the larger cultural philosophies, were committed to finding a foundation in mathematics, empirical science, or language on which to build a philosophy without regard for the corrective deliverances of history, religion, normative politics, or other kinds of philosophy. It was as if philosophy has the right style only if in principle it cannot learn from anything else.

The other great modernist philosophy was Husserl's phenomenology, aimed to find a pure empirical base for philosophy and science. The method of leaving the natural standpoint for the transcendental, bracketing all questions of contextual existence in order to make a pure eidetic analysis, had as its ideal a pure foundation resting on no suppositions and uncriticizable by anything except its own continued application. In the author's preface to the English edition of *Ideas,* Husserl quickly described transcendental phenomenology as "the realm of essential structures of transcendental subjectivity immediately transparent to the mind" (1931, 6); calling this the science of pure possibilities, he said "the science of pure possibilites must everywhere precede the science of real facts, and give it the guidance of its concrete logic" (1931, 7). A pure description of the ego can be taken either psychologically and naturalistically, or transcendentally:

And yet this whole content as psychology, considered from the natural standpoint as a positive science, therefore, and related to the world as spread before us, is entirely non-philosophical, whereas "the same" content from the transcendental standpoint, and therefore as transcendental phenomenology, is a philosophical science—indeed, on closer view, *the* basic philosophical science, preparing on descriptive lines the transcendental ground which remains henceforth the exclusive ground for all philosophical knowledge. (1931, 9)

Husserl's was a powerful statement of modernist foundationalism.

Heidegger recognized the practical folly of pure description, and also he sensed the deep cry at the heart of modernism for Being: Why assert the inward turn to self-sufficient form, meaning, significance, and truth, he asked, unless those things seem to be relativized and slipping away in historical and cultural contextualism? Furthermore, the Great War itself seemed to cut the ties of meaningful human existence from the disgraced cultural world of Western civilization. Simultaneously, then, Heidegger, in *Being and Time* (1927), forced the asking of the ontological question, the question of the Being of beings, and invented the onto-theo-logocentric story of Western civilization (see his collection translated into English as *The End of Philosophy,* 1973).

Western civilization, however, Heidegger notwithstanding, contains a great many things competing, overlapping, interweaving, and passing incommensurably. There is no one story of that civilization, but many, and most merely episodes to be chronicled. Heidegger (1959) invented the story of the fall of being, of the grand tragedy of the loss of being in favor of a dominant form. The villain was not the nineteenth-century bourgeoisie, nor the sixteenth-century renaissance scientist, but Plato, the first to think logos rather than being. The brilliance of Heidegger's strategy is that by reducing Western culture to a single story he totalized it and made it possible for the whole thing to be rejected. The irony of Heidegger's strategy is that logocentrism hardly existed in Western culture until Heidegger invented it, following clues from Hegel.[4] His method, like Hegel's, declares all those elements that do not fit the story to be unreal or unimportant. Like Hegel (see chapter 5 below), he defined importance by rational implication in the story, although of course reason is the villain of Heidegger's story, not the hero; the Heideggerian story is of the fall of false gods, not the unfolding of the only true God.

In France, contemporary with Husserl and Heidegger in Germany, de Saussure and Levi-Strauss developed modernist structuralism.

Motivated less by a rejection of bourgeois culture than by a desire to establish social science as science, they developed a science of linguistics as the study of codes (see Culler 1986). This is important for understanding Peirce, who earlier had invented semiotics as the study *of the generation* of codes, not so much as the study of their inner structure. The analogies arising from a study of codes inspired structuralist anthropology and, from that, literary theory (Lentricchia 1980, especially chapter 3). One way of understanding the essential idea of structuralism is to note the point that any definite form (of language, thought, social life, writing), in its very definiteness, excludes its Other and therefore gives that Other a kind of shadow-form (Culler 1982, 89–110, 134–179). By excluding something from importance, it defines that something, and takes its own definition from the exclusion. Suppose we switch sides and reject the form in favor of its Other. Is that not equally legitimate? Any definite cultural form, in its very definiteness, is blind to its Other and unable to reach it. Yet all we need to do is transvalue the forms, adopt the other, and we are blind to the original form. Any form is hostage to its Others, and there is no priority whatsoever save pure convention.

As Marxism, a great nineteenth-century proto-modernist and very modern progressive philosophy, proved to be a failure in the twentieth century in its attempt to lead to a more just world, many academic Marxists switched from left-wing actual politics to right-wing intellectual politics, as noted above, by extending the structuralists' point about the Other.[5] The fault with our civilization, according to the academic and art-critical Marxists, is its logocentrism, its adoption of a dominant form that has alienated, delegitimated, and oppressed all those forms of life that are its Other. Academic Marxism thus can attack any kind of form as dominant if it is adopted, because it must exclude something to be definite. If a worldview is definite enough to have alternatives, it is subject to the attack of logo–centrism, and its Others are as valid as itself. The alternatives cannot be judged inferior to the original worldview except from the blind prejudice of the worldview itself. Therefore all views are equally acceptable. Or, as Griffin notes regarding nihilism, nothing counts more than anything else and, hence, nothing counts. Griffin also notes (1988a, x) that deconstructionist postmodernism can be called "ultramodernism" because it plays out to extreme tendencies in modernism. This is correct. European modernism (in contrast to the British) leads from the positive programs of phenomenology and structuralism to poststructuralism and postmodernist deconstruction. That many commentators have used deconstructive arguments to expose and critique genuinely oppressive conditions does not mitigate the fact the technique can be used to represent any organized conditions whatsoever as oppressive. Chapter 8 below draws out some of the limitations in the ideas of power and narrative that form the basis of much postmodern criticism.

Immanuel Kant is the divide, the response to which separates those strains of modern philosophy and culture that became modernist from those that did not. Kant's intent (1787) was to provide a sure and apodictic foundation for philosophy and, indirectly, for science. His strategy was perhaps the most brilliant innovation in philosophy since Plato and Aristotle, the transcendental turn. Instead of asking what things are and how they can be known, he assumed that some things in mathematics and physics are indeed known with certainty, and asked what the conditions are for that. Having determined the conditions for that knowledge, he then was able to say what the world must be in order to conform to those conditions and what we must be in order to conform as knowers.

The modernist philosophies all attempted variations and improvements on that strategy, trying out logic (Russell, Carnap, Tarski), formal (Wittgenstein) or informal (Wittgenstein, Austin) language, methodic pure description (Husserl), or deep structures (Chomsky) as candidate transcendental conditions. They all sought the foundation Kant claimed is there when the conditions for experience are known. That foundation, they hoped, whatever it might turn out to be, can provide the intrinsic meaning, importance, and validity the modernist philosophers sought.

Not all lines of response to Kant developed into modernism. Many found some way of rejecting Kant's transcendental definition of world and self. Whitehead, for instance, deliberately reverted to pre-Kantian modes of thought and rather simply ignored Kant (and Hegel).[6] Peirce, however, provided a series of arguments against the Kantian transcendental position and thereby defended a genuine alternative to the modernist (see chapter 1 below). He rejected foundationalism of all sorts and gave reasons why nothing is meaningful, important, or true in itself, except perhaps a whole if there be any such thing (which there isn't).

Whereas modernists must totalize the modern period in order to reject it dialectically, the non-modernist pragmatic reading here is historical (and evolutionary) in tracing many strands. The early modern period arose with a suddenly expanded historical and geographic sense on the part of renaissance Europeans, a Platonizing of the common-sense view of reason, and the rise of modern mathematical physics. These together induced an experimental spirit that later came to be formulated as the method of hypothesis and experiment. The sixteenth and seventeenth centuries have been called the "Age of Genius" because of the originality, brilliance, and genuinely fundamental ideas that were developed; some of these are the sources to which Whitehead reverted. But more important than the defense of these ideas was the emergent sense that the ideas need to prove themselves in debate both intellectually and practically. Where they are faulty, they should be amended and improved. The Enlightenment on the one hand and Romantic reaction on the other are part and parcel of the modern heritage. There is no single line of modern doctrine or modern politics or modern sense of self, but many.

Griffin's attempt to construct new categories to do what the early modern period's candidates failed to do is precisely a modern enterprize. That he wants to transcend the current modern world's "individualism, anthropocentrism, patriarchy, mechanization, economism, consumerism, nationalism, and militarism" marks him a disciple of Locke and Leibniz, determined to make good what their own categories could not, insofar as these matters depend on philosophic ideas. Griffin, like Peirce and Whitehead, is a late modern non-modernist, and does not really mean to reject the heritage of the modern period at all. The study of Peirce in chapter 1 below will indicate why this position is a very good one indeed.

Before launching into an exposition of the highroad around modernism, however, it is necessary to grapple more closely with the postmodernist criticism of this very philosophic enterprise. Heidegger's *The End of Philosophy* was cited above: why has philosophy come to an end? Philosophy in what sense?

III. The End of Philosophy

There is a certain strand of philosophy in the West, important in the academic profession, that proclaims the "end of philosophy." Sometimes this has been expressed as the "end of metaphysics," because metaphysics has been central to Western philosophy. But the charge truly is laid against the whole of the critical and rational discipline as developed from Socrates and Plato onward. Karl Marx laid the groundwork for the "end of philosophy" movement with his theory that philosophy is merely the ideology of a class. Friedrich Nietzsche, politically opposite to Marx, directly proclaimed the end of philosophy along with the death of God and the final collapse of the Western culture deriving from Athens and Jerusalem.

In our own century, thinkers such as Edmund Husserl valiantly sought to stave off the end of philosophy, but recognized that there is a "crisis of the European sciences." Husserl wrote (1938, 12),

> Skepticism about the possibility of metaphysics, the collapse of the belief in a universal philosophy as the guide for the new man, actually represents a collapse of the belief in "reason," understood as the ancients opposed *episteme* to *doxa*. It is reason which ultimately gives meaning to everything that is thought to be, all things, values, and ends—their meaning understood as their normative relatedness to what, since the beginnings of philosophy, is meant by the word "truth"—truth in itself—and correlatively the term "what is"—*ontos on*. Along with this falls the faith in "absolute" reason, through which the world has its meaning, the faith in the meaning of history, of humanity, the faith in man's freedom, that is, his capacity to secure rational meaning for his individual and common human existence. (P. 12)

Martin Heidegger was followed by deconstructionists such as Jacques Derrida and neopragmatists such as Richard Rorty who have turned the fatalistic assertion about the state of philosophy into a political and intellectual movement within the profession itself, in both European and North American universities.

Heidegger wrote (1973, 99),

> Philosophy in the age of completed metaphysics is anthropology (cf. *Holzwege,* p. 91 f.) [translator's interpolation]. Whether or not one says "philosophical" anthropology makes no difference. In the meantime philosophy has become anthropology and in this way a prey to the derivatives of metaphysics, that is, of physics in the broadest sense, which includes the physics of life and man, biology and psychology. Having become anthropology, philosophy itself perishes of metaphysics.

Heidegger's general argument is that metaphysics is supposed to mean the playing out of the distinction between the "what" of things and the "that" of things, a distinction with an historical origin in ancient Greek philosophy and that cannot sustain itself historically. Specifically, the question of the "that," of existence, becomes subordinated to the questions of "what," of essence, according to Heidegger. "Existence" becomes reinterpreted as actuality in contrast with potentiality, merely a different "kind" of existence.

Jacques Derrida radicalizes Heidegger by claiming that the entire tradition of Western thought is based on the idea of logos, or a reason which relates to the world as signifier to signified. But the distinction between the signifier and signified cannot be sustained where that suggests that the signified is not also a signifier, that is, a "text." The historical epoch of "logocentrism" thus comes to an end. Derrida writes (1976, 12–13):

> The epoch of the logos thus debases writing considered as mediation of mediation and as a fall into the exteriority of meaning. To this epoch belongs the difference between signified and signifier, or at least the strange separation of their "parallelism," and the exteriority, however extenuated, of the one to the other. This appurtenance is organized and hierarchized in a history. The difference between signified and signifier belongs in a profound and implicit way to the totality of the great epoch covered by the history of metaphysics, and in a more explicit and more systematically articulated way to the narrower epoch of Christian creationism and infinitism when these appropriate the resources of Greek conceptuality.[7]

Richard Rorty, in his most influential book, *Philosophy and the Mirror of Nature* (1979), draws a distinction (beginning on p. 5) between "systematic philosophy," by which he means all attempts to construct a foundational representation or "mirror" of the world, and "edifying philosophy," by which he means conversation with no pretence to be foundational or to ground anything. The former is bad and the latter is good, he says. This does not mean philosophy is at an end, only that it has turned to edifying conversation with an essentially moral bent, usually having the form of criticism. But philosophy in a speculative metaphysical sense also has come to an end, for Rorty. He allows (1979, 394) that "perhaps a new form of systematic philosophy will be found which has nothing whatever to do with epistemology but which nevertheless makes normal philosophical inquiry possible." But because he dismisses the anti-epistemological systems of Peirce, Dewey, and Whitehead, it is difficult to see what he might admit as a candidate systematic philosophy.

For reasons that have little to do with the dynamics of the American tradition in philosophy, Rorty's reinterpretation of pragmatism has become popular under the title of neopragmatism. In comparison with that, the pragmatism defended in this book is paleopragmatism. Because of Rorty's influence as an interpreter, and the power of his thought to delegitimate and shut down what he rejects through dismissal, it is important to collect for the record his views on pragmatism (of the paleopragmatic sort). Rorty writes of Peirce, in an attempt to give what he regards as the correct focus to pragmatism:

> One symptom of this incorrect focus is a tendency to overpraise Peirce. Peirce is praised partly because he developed various logical notions and various technical problems (such as the counterfactual conditional) which were taken up by the logical empiricists. But the main reason for Peirce's undeserved apotheosis is that his talk about a general theory of signs looks like an early discovery of the importance of language. For all his genius, however, Peirce never made up his mind what he wanted a general theory of signs *for,* nor what it might look like, nor what its relation to either logic or epistemology was supposed to be. His contribution to pragmatism was merely to have given it a name, and to have stimulated James. Peirce himself remained the most Kantian of thinkers—the most convinced that philosophy gave us an all-embracing ahistorical context in which every other species of discourse could be assigned its proper place and rank. It was just this Kantian assumption that there was such a context, and that epistemology or semantics could discover it, against which James and Dewey reacted. (1982, 160–161)

Rorty is well known for his positive appreciation of Dewey and, in fact, calls himself a pragmatist, and is called a neopragmatist by others, because of his association with Dewey. But his reading of Dewey is greatly truncated because he insists on purging Dewey's writings of anything like metaphysics. In his essay "Dewey's Metaphysics" (1982, 72–89), he writes:

> Sympathetic expositors of Dewey-as-metaphysician—such as Hofstadter, who describes "the aim of metaphysics, as a general theory of existence" as "the discovery of the basic types of involvements and their relationships"— cannot, I think, explain why we *need* a discipline at that level of generality, nor how the results of such "discoveries" can be anything but trivial. Would anyone—including Dewey himself—really believe that there is a discipline that could somehow do for "the basic types of involvement," something left undone by novelists, sociologists, biologists, poets, and historians? All one might want a philosopher to do is to synthesize the novels, poems, histories, and sociologies of the day into some larger unity. But such syntheses are, in fact, offered us on all sides, in every discipline. To be an intellectual, rather than simply to "do research," is precisely to reach

for some such synthesis. Nothing save the myth that there is something special called "philosophy" that provides the paradigm of a synthetic discipline, and a figure called "the philosopher" who is the paradigm of the intellectual, suggests that the professional philosopher's work is incomplete unless he has drawn up a list of the "generic traits of all existence" or discovers "the basic types of involvements." (1982, 77)

Although this book focuses more on Peirce than on Dewey, it should be known that Dewey developed Peirce's theory of habit and quality, gave quite specific content to Peirce's definition of the Good, and related his metaphysics to history and culture in ways Peirce never did.

Whitehead has generally been recognized as the great speculative genius of the twentieth centry, the truly original representative of the "grand tradition." One would think that in a book such as *Philosophy and the Mirror of Nature* attacking theoretical, systematic, and speculative philosophy, Rorty would have paid Whitehead close attention. The only mentions, however, are in a parenthesis (p. 113) and a footnote (p. 117), both of which dismiss Whitehead as a panpsychist. In *Consequences of Pragmatism* Rorty writes:

> I myself would join Reichenbach in dismissing classical Husserlian phenomenology, Bergson, Whitehead, the Dewey of *Experience and Nature*, the James of *Radical Empiricism*, neo-Thomist epistemological realism, and a variety of other late nineteenth- and early twentieth century systems. Bergson and Whitehead, and the bad ("metaphysical") parts of Dewey and James, seem to me merely weakened versions of idealism—attempts to answer "unscientifically" formulated epistemological questions about the "relation of subject and object" by "naive generalizations and analogies" which emphasize "feeling" rather than "cognition." Phenomenology and neo-Thomism also seem diagnosable and dismissable along Reichenbachian lines. (1982, 213–214)

Well, we'll see.

The argument that philosophy has come to an end, of course, assumes a totalistic assessment of what counts as philosophy. Such attempts to give a total definition of philosophy are nearly always wrong and usually self-serving, as is true in the cases cited here. Although Rorty speaks strongly against wholesale philosophies, his practice is to dismiss whole approaches without careful sifting and weighing of diverse projects (see the quotations above).

Philosophy in the West has at most times in its existence stood in alliance with science and religion but in opposition to the rhetorical tradition. The rhetorical tradition achieved its first great moment under the fifth and fourth century B.C.E. Greek sophists, for instance Protagoras and Isocrates. Cicero represented the cause of rhetoric over against philosophy during Roman antiquity and Bernard of Clairvaux, the great preacher, during the Christian Middle Ages. Voltaire was a rhetorician of the European Enlightenment, and Richard Rorty, declaring the end of Western philosophy in our time, is our most outspoken contemporary rhetorician, while at the same time a philosopher of distinction.

Rorty's totalizing story of philosophy is that, beginning with the modern era, for instance in Descartes, and crystalizing in Kant, Western philosophy has become preoccupied with epistemological foundations. Since Kant, he says, philosophy has turned in on itself in an attempt to be able to "ground" and "criticize" every other cultural enterprize; in doing this it has become specialized, professional, and irrelevant in its groundings and criticisms to those whom it might have thought to address. This neo-Kantian philosophy was essentially religious, according to Rorty:

> "Philosophy" became [in the nineteenth century], for the intellectuals, a substitute for religion. It was the area of culture where one touched bottom, where one found the vocabulary and the convictions which permitted one to explain and justify one's activities *as* an intellectual, and thus to discover the significance of one's life. . . . Further, in the course of the nineteenth century, a new form of culture had arisen—the culture of the man of letters, the intellectual who wrote poems and novels and political treatises and criticisms of other people's poems and novels and treatises. Descartes, Locke, and Kant had written in a period in which the secularization of culture was being made possible by the success of natural science. But by the early twentieth century the scientists had become as remote from most intellectuals as had the theologians. Poets and novelists had taken the place of both preachers and philosophers as the moral teachers of the youth. The result was that the more "scientific" and "rigorous" philosophy became, the less it had to do with the rest of culture and the more absurd its traditional pretensions seemed. The attempts of both analytic philosophers and phenomenologists to "ground" this and "criticize" that were shrugged off by those whose activities were purportedly being grounded or criticized. Philosophy as a whole was shrugged off by those who wanted an ideology or a self-image. (1979, 4–5)

The culture of "letters" was not so new; it was the rhetorical tradition in nineteenth-century form. What Rorty describes quite accurately as the epistemological orientation of the neo-Kantians is simply the modernist philosophies of the twentieth century. Are there any other late modern philosophies that are not like those he describes and procedes to condemn? Are they still truly philosophy and not rhetoric or criticism? The question, in his terms, amounts to asking whether there are any philosophies that are not foundationalist and epistemological.

There are, of course, many differences between Protagoras and Isocrates, Cicero, Bernard, Voltaire, and Rorty; any generalization crossing as many temporal periods as they represent must be taken as a mere approximation. Yet they agree in two points. First, that persuasiveness of argument is the highest excellence of intellect and, second, that philosophers are not only mistaken but deceptive, perhaps even self-deluded, in claiming that the purpose of intellect is to know the truth. According to the rhetorical tradition there is no truth that measures our assertions, only a body of arguments that shape the world of discourse within which assertions take place. Philosophy's deception, according to the rhetoricians, is its suggestion that there is a truth to which it is loyal when in fact any philosophy is only a cluster of arguments expressing the interest of the philosopher.

In contrast to the rhetorical tradition, the philosophical tradition in the West, like that in Asia, believes that there is a truth about which one can be wrong and that philosophical arguments are attempts to state the truth in such a way as to be vulnerable to correction. Philosophers differ widely in their conceptions of truth, in the methods of their arguments, and in the ways of life they claim to follow from the truth as they see it. Philosophers also differ with respect to how language represents truth. For some, such as Aristotle and Peter Strawson, representation is in the form of description; for others, such as Plato, Hegel, and Paul Weiss, it is in a dialectical play of argument; for yet other philosophers, such as Kierkegaard and Nietzsche, representation is not direct at all but is a function of words changing the soul so that truth enters by non-representational means. No less than rhetoricians, philosophers have understood philosophic writing to be an art that need not limit itself to discursive description. One thinks of the dramatic dialogues of Plato, the prayerful confession of Augustine, the pseudonymous works of Kierkegaard, and the aphorisms of Nietzsche. East Asian philosophy includes the verses of Lao Tzu, the stories of Chuang Tzu, the aphorisms of Confucius, as well as the essays of Mencius and Hsun Tzu. In both Western and Eastern philosophic traditions, and in all their forms of expression, there is a dual concern to be faithful to a reality that measures our representations and to let our representations be corrected.[8] Only a few philosophers with this double concern have been "foundationalist" in Rorty's sense.

IV. Ways around Modernism

Is it the case that *all* philosophy, or at least all *Western* philosophy since Kant has developed into modernist philosophy? The alternatives to the modernism-postmodernism development of modernity can be divergences at any place along the line. The particular alternative to be lifted up for consideration here was consolidated in the work of Charles S. Peirce, and the following chapter shall develop the point in detail. Looking backward from Peirce, the earlier European philosophers can be read for their speculative imagination and for their various devices for correcting ideas and learning from experience. The Enlightenment concern for certainty, and Kant's transcendental philosophy appear as interesting deadends. Of particular importance is the development within the Peircean lineage of a concern for value in experience. The early modern conception of physics excluded the appreciation of value in its paradigms for knowledge, and the attempts to correct that appeared early in the philosophies of aesthetics, taste, and common sense. In America the first great philosopher was Jonathan Edwards who brilliantly combined religion, science, and aesthetics. With equal flair, if not equal clarity, Ralph Waldo Emerson and Henry Thoreau continued those themes, adding to them the theme of community. From early in the modern period there had been a fascination with non-European cultures, and in the nineteenth century this came to flower in the development of Transcendentalism (Emerson's romantic philosophy, not Kant's very different transcendental philosophy). In the twentieth century the descendents of Peirce take the philosophers of China and India to be their "tradition" just as much as those of Europe.

Moving down from Peirce are two tightly interwoven lines of descent. The first is the pragmatic tradition of James, Dewey, Mead, and others. The second is the adoptive lineage of Whitehead's process philosophy. George R. Lucas, Jr. (1989), has shown that Whitehead was reacting to the same philosophic and cultural issues as his colleague Bertrand Russell, the quintessential modernist, but without Russell's modernist assumptions. Like Peirce just before him, Whitehead went around modernism. In America, Whitehead called himself a pragmatist and directed the dissertations of the first editors of Peirce's philosophy papers, Charles Hartshorne and Paul Weiss. Although some process philosophers relate themselves more closely to modernism than they need to, and hence to postmodernism, there is a deep affinity between process philosophy and pragmatism.

A century has passed since most of Peirce's groundbreaking work, and it is time for a new reconstruction of his para-modernist project. For one thing, since Peirce modernist philosophies came to dominate academic philosophy with a vengeance, and more recently have rather much died away. Although postmodernism is preoccupied with killing off the modernists, that might not remain interesting very long. Whereas Peirce had only glimmers about philosophies other than the European, we now have had nearly a century of intercultural dialogue in philosophy and theology, with more well-edited texts than can be managed easily.

One more new influence needs to be mentioned to give a clue about the non-modernist–non-postmodernist philosophy to be presented here, namely, the work of Paul Tillich in North America. Although often associated with the early Heidegger, Tillich's real roots were in Cappadocian speculations, German mysticism, and the romanticism of Schelling. The Cappadocians and the German mystics and pietists were the inspiration also of John Wesley whose movement formed much of the religious and popular philosophic culture in America; the mystics and idealistic romantics at the same time were among the principal inspirations of Emerson. Tillich's theology, clearly a non-modernist alternative to modernist Karl Barth, thus found immediate resonance in America with both the highbrow descendents of Emersonian Transcendentalism and the lowbrow Methodists. Although the language has undergone many changes, Tillich's philosophy of religion and theology have made deep connections with pragmatism and process philosophy to form a viable and vigorous philosophic highroad around modernism and postmodernism.

The chapters that follow fall into two groups that appear to be quite different. The first continues the interpretation of the philosophic issues in developing a strand of modern philosophy, late modern philosophy, that is not modernist and that looks in new directions. Chapter 1 is an interpretive exposition of Charles Peirce in terms of which the position regarding modernism and non-modernism is developed in detail. Chapter 2 shifts to Whitehead and his retrieval of the problem of value in Romanticism. Chapter 3 expands the field of vision to provide a brief interpretation of the metaphysics of the twentieth century that both modernism and postmodernism say is impossible. Chapter 4 continues the discussion of process philosophy and chapter 5 connects Whitehead with Hegel and criticizes a modernist theme in both, the idea of totality. Chapter 6 then develops a conception of philosophic system that does not employ the notion of totality. Finally in this group is a reflective chapter on various dimensions of American philosophy insofar as it constitutes itself around but not in and through modernism. These chapters constitute an extended discussion *about* philosophy. But no defense of a philosophy itself is satisfactory without an exhibition of its practice.

The second group of chapters is not about philosophy as much as it is an exercise in philosophy of culture. Postmodernism has defined itself with great brilliance as a philosophy of culture. Here is an alternative. Chapter 8 criticizes central modernist themes deriving from the earliest days of the modern period, those of power and narrative. The arguments here set powerful limits to the moral critique of power often made by postmodernists. Chapter 9 criticizes the modernist polarity of capitalism and Marxism. Chapter 10 rejects the liberal idea of the priority of freedom in favor of the priority of responsibility in political philosophy. Responsibility naturally leads to the problem of leadership, the topic of Chapter 11. Finally, chapter 12 attempts to recapture technology from its interpretation within the modernist-postmodernist line; it is seen here as a theological problem relative to divine creation.

From a philosopher's standpoint, the problem raised by postmodernism is whether speculative systematic philosophy should shut down. That it has been and is being practiced in our time is obvious, a history that will be reviewed in chapter 3 below. But perhaps it is illegitimate. To counter that suspicion it is not enough to give counterarguments in principle. Rather, one must demonstrate, lay out historically—interesting speculative options that are not subject to the criticisms laid against modernism (and having merit). This demonstration requires many parts, among which two are important to mention.

One is to demonstrate that the alternatives to modernism themselves have a history, and that they provide perspectives for rereading much of the rest of the Western tradition and relating productively to other traditions so as to claim filial descendence from much that is good and substantial in civilization. The chapters in part 1 are intended to provide something of a history and place for the non-modernist philosophy of speculative pragmatism (Rosenthal 1986) in its various forms.

The other part of the demonstration is to indicate the merits of the non-modernist philosophies. Speculative vision, of course, is one. The speculators of our time, pragmatic and otherwise, have provided many ways of grasping the world synoptically, each of which allows for the appreciation of things neglected by the others. But beyond this, a speculative vision needs to be helpful in understanding other parts of philosophy, other limbs of culture. From Plato to Whitehead, speculative philosophers have encompassed within their systematic reflections approaches to politics, morals, art, religion, education, and a host of other topics. Only a few speculative philosophers attempt to fit these topics into a tight system (neither Plato nor Whitehead attempted this, although Aristotle and Paul Weiss have). But speculative philosophers think systematically about these topics, and sometimes with great profit. Part 2 is an attempt to think systematically out of a speculative system about topics in politics and culture.[9]

The argument of this book, then, made by many small cases, is that there is at least one highroad around modernism, pointed to in part 1 and traversed some way in part 2. The highroad involves speculative philosophy, and it is broad enough to invite travelers from traditions outside the West.

PART ONE

✻

PHILOSOPHY AROUND MODERNISM

CHAPTER ONE

✳

CHARLES S. PEIRCE AS A NON-MODERNIST THINKER

I. Peirce's Rejection of Foundations: Hypothesis, Habits, and Signs

Can Charles Sanders Peirce (1839–1914), the American genius who invented pragmatism, much modern symbolic logic, and semiotics, be considered a postmodern thinker? Is he a modernist, a typical Kantian epistemologist as Richard Rorty claims (1982, 160–161)? How does Peirce stand with respect to the postmodern movement?

In 1868, in the second number of *The Journal of Speculative Philosophy*, Peirce published two papers that irrevocably steered him and all who followed him away from the program of modernism. In the first, "Questions Concerning Certain Faculties Claimed for Man" (CP 5.213–263), he asked whether there can be any cognition that is immediately or intuitively related to its object, so that it is not itself a sign interpreting something else as a sign.[1] Suppose we have such an intuition. How do we recognize it to be an intuition? By another intuition? If so, we have to determine whether that second intuition is really an intuition, and if that too is by intuition we are heading down an infinite regress from which we can never get back to judge whether the first alleged intuition is really an intuition. Perhaps, on the other hand, the identification of the first intuition is by some kind of discursive, inferential, interpretive process. But that is inherently fallible. Therefore, even if there were an intuitive judgment, or sense datum, or any other allegedly infallible starting point for cognition, the recognition of it as such is either impossible, because of the infinite regress, or itself fallible.

As a result, Pierce pointed out, the quest in knowledge is not to find a starting point but rather to check up on, correct, and improve the process of thinking that is already underway. Admitting, with Locke, that our experience is filled with sensations that physically connect us to our environment, we cannot look to sensation for an incorrigible starting point; rather we should look for better means of discrimination. Admitting, with Descartes, that thorough analysis improves clarity to the point where we cannot ask any more intelligent questions, we cannot treat our eminently clear judgments as the penetration of simples by the natural light; rather, we treat them as assumable truths for belief and action until some new context allows us to ask questions impossible previously. In all, we should recognize that all knowledge is fallible and that the search for an immediate, incorrigible starting point is pointless. So much for the heart of the modernist project; and Peirce beat Richard Rorty to the critique by over 110 years.

In the second paper, "Some Consequences of Four Incapacities," Peirce drew out some lessons for reorienting modern philosophy. First, it is impossible to practice *universal* doubt in Descartes's sense, because even in doubting many habits of mind are assumed; further, to doubt, you have to have reason to doubt, and no reason is universal. Second, whereas Descartes taught that the test of certainty is to be found in the individual consciousness, the fallibility of all thought means there is no certainty, only unquestioned, and at best temporarily unquestionable, habits of thought. Moreover, the questioning is not a matter of the integrity of a specific individual consciousness but of any interpreter who can bring issues to bear upon the fallible judgment. Thinking is thus done by a community, not by an individual except in the sense that one person thinking from many angles can be a mini-community. Third, whereas Cartesianism assumes that the best argument is one that follows along one clear deductive line, the fallibility of all thought requires us to search for a skein of arguments, not a line but a cable made of many strands. Fourth, Descartes was a positivist in the sense that he thought there are things that cannot be explained except by the general postulate that God made them so. On the contrary, if every judgment is an hypothesis, the only reason for asserting any hypothesis is that it explains its topic. Never is there a reason, then, to affirm the hypothesis that something is inexplicable. One may assert, as Peirce does, that God creates things to be the way they are; but that assertion has to be shown to be an explanation, not an evasion (CP 6.494–506).

That every judgment is an hypothesis follows from Peirce's argument that all thinking takes place by means of signs (CP 5.283–317). If there are no immediate intuitive cognitions, then every cognition is a sign standing for its object in a certain respect, as interpreted or interpretable by another sign that links the object and first sign (Peirce called his theory of signs, or semiotic, "speculative grammar," "critic," and "speculative rhetoric"; see CP 2.227–308).[2] Furthermore, every object of a sign is itself taken to be a sign, at least in the sense that it warrants certain signs as capable of standing for it, and others not. Not all objects are mental signs, though all interpretation uses mental signs that are connected with other mental signs involved in semiotic codes with them. Those objects that are "external" to mind still are signs in the sense that they have characters that allow certain signs to represent them in determined respects and others not, as smoke legitimates the inference of fire but not rain. Every sign that interprets another sign as standing for an object is an hypothesis to that effect. Later in his career, Peirce developed a theory explaining the implications of generality in his theory of signs: to take smoke to represent fire requires two kinds of generality, that there is a real general character of fire causing smoke, and that our experience has developed the general habit of noting that fact in particular instances (CP 6.66–286).

Now the polemical target of these early papers of Peirce was Descartes and the view that knowledge needs a starting point. Peirce's answer was that the starting idea is arbitrary and unrecognizable because nothing can be learned from the abrupt jolt from non-knowledge to knowledge. Rather, partly correct cognitive processes already must be underway, and learning amounts to criticizing and improving them. But the theory of hypothesis to which Peirce appealed here and developed at great length throughout his life tells just as strongly against Kant as against Descartes.

Kant had argued that philosophy, in contrast to science, must be certain and apodictic, and that to be this, it must be transcendental. His argument (e.g., 1787, B 797ff.) was that all non-certain and non-apodictic cognition is hypothetical and that hypothetical knowledge presupposes a non-hypothetical definition of hypothesis, of world to which the hypothesis applies, and of the nature of evidence. That is, to say that hypothetical knowledge is knowledge at all presupposes a prior, non-hypothetical, philosophical account of how hypotheses can relate to a real world. According to Kant's complicated but persuasive argument, only a transcendental philosophy, establishing and justifying the conditions for the possibility of knowledge (of hypothetical knowledge in this case), can provide the kind of grounding that legitimates hypothetical knowledge in science and common sense. Edmund Husserl (1931, ch. 3) thematized this argument in his distinction between the natural and transcendental standpoint: for him, a person in only the natural standpoint is ignorant and innocent of the very conditions that give that standpoint the validity it has. Philosophy must move from the natural to the transcendental standpoint in order to reflect on its own nature. For Husserl, the transcendental standpoint is less a deduction of transcendental categories than the development of a method of analysis and the exploration of the basic conditions revealed by the method. For the early Wittgenstein (1922, 61–73, 183–189), the transcendental conditions divided into what logic can show but not say, and those postures that are not in the world but form it. Modernist philosophy (but not all modern philosophy) agrees with Kant, that natural knowing, whether empirical, hypothetical, deductive, or whatever, must be understood and explained from a standpoint that is not itself natural but transcendental and therefore a priori.

Peirce's alternative was simple. The examination of any area of knowing, such as science, common sense, ethics, or the like, must be undertaken from a level of generality that can define its basic elements such as world, evidence, or judgment. But that level itself is hypothetical and is to be in turn examined from whatever levels can objectify its basic suppositions. High level hypotheses are to be checked out by lower level, empirical, even sensible hypotheses: the light is green, not red. Low level hypotheses are to be interpreted by higher ones that articulate their conditions. If a philosophy were looked at as a system, it would be hypotheses from side to side, top to bottom, near and far. Kant would object that there is no standpoint save a transcendental one from which the whole system can be judged. But Peirce's answer (CP 6.498) is that one can never question all the hypotheses at once. Only in "paper doubt" can one ask about the validity of all the interconnected hypotheses. You can ask about the system of highest level categories, but not while doubting the continued existence of the chair on which you sit or the likelihood that lunch will be ready on time. If you do have reason to doubt the continuation of the chair because of its palpable decrepitude, or the likelihood that there will be anything ready for lunch, you are not then doubting the passage of time or the working of your biological organism that will make you hungry soon.

Kant's argument, taken up and carried to consistent extremes by modernist philosophies, is that all hypothetical knowing can be totalized and doubted as a whole. Peirce pointed out two flaws in that. To doubt the whole would require a reason for doubting the whole, and no one has found such a reason except the paper one of imagining that "all knowledge might be wrong." Furthermore, in actual thinking, the work of inventing the conditions to doubt something in particular (even particular categories of great generality) always presupposes or takes for granted much that is not then in question. And if there are no good grounds for questioning them, there may be some beliefs that in actual fact cannot be questioned. At any rate, the dubitability of anything is an empirical matter.

Whereas the modernist philosophies accepted Kant's point that the whole of experiential knowledge must be grounded in something transcendental, or admitted to be groundless, Peirce argued instead that knowing is a kind, or many kinds, of activity. The activity is structured by habits of interacting with the world, and then it reformulates those habits by virtue of the interaction. Knowing for Peirce is not a passive contemplation of truths but a well-guided active life, well-guided because the environment and one's activities are interpreted accurately with good signs. Learning is the modification of one's signs and interpretations so as to correct deficiencies in the guidance of one's activities. Unlike modernist philosophies, Peirce's pragmatism takes knowing to be habitual reflection plus learning; nothing is foundational.

With regard to Kant himself, Peirce was highly complimentary. But he rejected the entire transcendental apparatus of Kant's thinking and adopted instead the primary focus of the Scottish school of common sense. He called himself a "critical commonsensist," critical referring to the laudatory self-referential element in Kant's thought and common sense to the field of habits providing both the context and form for inquiry (CP 5.497–537).

In 1877 and 1878 Peirce published two more seminal papers, "The Fixation of Belief" (CP 5.358–387) and "How to Make Our Ideas Clear" (CP 5.388–410). The first was about truth and the second about meaning. The phrase, "fixation of belief," reflects Peirce's reformulation of the classic problem of knowledge. The problem is not how we know whether we know but rather how we overcome concrete doubt. Our beliefs in most practice are habits that Peirce called "guiding principles." They structure our behavior and experience. For instance, we have beliefs about getting on the subway, to take a trivial example (Peirce's was about getting on a horse-car), and under ordinary circumstances we subliminally think the process as we follow it but do not think much about it. But suppose we discover in reaching for the money that we have a one dollar bill and a twenty; to use the last single might lead to inconvenience later, but it is troublesome to have to break a twenty for a dollar fare. Suddenly doubt has begun to irritate the previously unquestioned belief, and we begin to think *about* getting on the subway. Peirce called this "inquiry," and its purpose is to settle the irritation of doubt, in this case by figuring out whether there is a real advantage to either form of payment, and perhaps by adding to our subway habits a new habit of paying in the larger denomination, or smaller. The activity of boarding the subway involved a great many interpretive habits and cognitive processes. Entering the subway tunnel, for instance, we were actually thinking *about* the viability of epistemological realism because that topic had been made problematic by a book recently read, and by the fact our destination is a philosophy meeting. But we had also paid some attention to the environment, noticed the traffic enough to get into the station, were momentarily distracted by a beautiful person who made our hormones jump, cursed the chewing gum in the way, and were vaguely peeved about the tax situation. The guiding habits that become problematic in the situation determine the focus of attention and inquiry, and these are constantly shifting as our coping mechanisms, more or less intellectual, conduct the inquiries that amend the habits. We ease the sudden pain in the leg by shifting position, never consciously thinking about a muscle cramp; we return again and again to focus on epistemological realism because we cannot find the habits of mind that settle the irritation of *philosophic* doubts.

Peirce's point in "The Fixation of Belief" was to criticize various methods for fixing belief and to suggest his own. Appeals to authority, to what seems a priori true, and to what one has always believed before, are often temporarily successful at setting aside doubt. But they are disconnected from the realities with which the relevant belief-habits deal, and the doubt will be triggered again. The best way to get a belief which there are no good reasons to doubt is to make the belief true in the sense of corresponding to its objects. Therefore, the best method for fixing beliefs is to make them vulnerable to correction by the realities themselves. Our activities are structured by habits that interpret the world; where those interpretations are mistaken, the habits will be interrupted. The experimentalist's method, as Peirce called it, turns as quickly as possible to finding ways of making nature say No to those aspects of the habits that are mistaken (CP 5.574–604). Peirce derived this method from science and spent most of his life trying to refine it (CP 5.411–412). Of course, he had to generalize it far beyond science; his use of it in religion will be considered shortly. But it was science that he took to be the hallmark of the modern age. And the experimental method is the hope for the correction of any of the specific mistakes of science, metaphysics, religion, or culture that the modern period has developed. In this central sense, Peirce solidly affirmed modernity: it is the period that thematized learning from experience. Insofar as Kant could be read to say that knowledge is to be gained from experience, Peirce thought of himself as a Kantian, though a critical commonsensist Kantian, not a transcendental one. And he completely rejected a priori foundationalism.

II. Reality: Generality and the Habits of Nature

The reference to truth of course pushed Peirce into the problem of reality (CP 5.549–573). He himself had no qualms about epistemological realism. The real is the object of a well-founded hypothesis. Since all hypotheses are fallible, "well-foundedness" has to be defined in terms of the community of inquirers who criticize the hypothesis in all respects, testing it in all ways, which requires an infinite amount of time because at no finite stage of probation is it ever infallible. So he defined reality as the object of the opinion ultimately fated to be believed by the community of investigators in the infinite long run (CP 5.405–410). The infinite long run never comes, and therefore we will not be able ever to give a completely determined identification of reality. Furthermore, Peirce's youthful enthusiasm for the scientific community quickly faded in the face of historical realities. Perhaps mistakes will be covered up rather than exposed; perhaps the community of inquirers will get killed off by disease or war. Perhaps no one is honest enough to carry on very long, let alone for an infinite long run. So he gave up the view that the opinion defining reality was "fated." But reality, he thought, is what a genuinely honest and critical community would discover if it investigated infinitely.

In order to be very specific about the experimentalist's method Peirce had to raise the question of meaning. In his early papers such as "How to Make Our Ideas Clear," he wrote in a positivistic vein, attempting to eliminate as meaningless those kinds of ideas for which no experimental situation could be imagined. Later he realized that the philosophic burden lies in imagining ever more sensitive experimental situations, not in using some reductive idea of experiment to eliminate candidate ideas. But even the early papers contained the germs of his theory.

Precisely because ideas are signs that shape actions, we should define their meaning in terms of the difference they make to actions. This is a dangerous idea, easily misunderstood. Peirce formulated it exactly as follows: "Consider what effects, that might conceivably have practical bearings, we conceive the object of our conception to have. Then, our conception of these effects is the whole of our conception of the object." (CP 5.402) William James and most European commentators on pragmatism have read that quickly to say that the meaning of an idea is the practical effects of its object. Peirce is very clear, by virtue of the repetition of "conception" and its cognates, that the meaning of an idea is the sum of the *conceptions* of the effects. The meaning of an idea, for Peirce, is entirely intellectual. The truth of an idea, however, has to do with causal interpretive activities that connect the intellectual knower with the realities that include the object of the idea. It should be obvious that we can have many meaningful but false ideas. The cheap pragmatism that identifies meaning with practical effects conflates meaning and truth and, thus, is unable to account for meaningful but false ideas. If there were no meaningful false ideas, there would be no contrasts for meaningful true ones, and experiment would be impossible. The pragmatic maxim has to do with meaning, not truth. The pragmatic method of experimentation sets up criteria for truth. Truth itself, Peirce says again and again, is correspondence of our ideas or judgments with reality (CP 5.549–573).

It has been customary in modernist thought to distinguish sharply between judgments, which can be true or false, and ideas, which can only be meaningful or meaningless. Modernism also, since Frege, distinguishes sharply between the order of ideas, to which many modernist philosophers give a Platonistical interpretation, and the order of reality signified by ideas, to which many give a materialist interpretation.[3] Neither of these distinctions is very trustworthy for Peirce, and an exploration of his theory of signs will indicate why.

Peirce's theory of signs is metaphysically grounded in his theory of reality. Metaphysics, he thought, should develop the simplest categories for classifying all things. His candidates were so simple as to be called Firstness, Secondness, and Thirdness (CP 8.327–379; 1.203–520). Firstness is anything that is what it is without any reference to anything else; it thus has no character that distinguishes it from anything else, it is not different, it cannot be thought or discriminated. Secondness is anything that is what it is precisely by being other than something else; Secondness is sheer otherness, mere difference that is not difference-in-some-respect. Like Firstness, Secondness cannot be thought or discriminated, although it can be felt as an aspect of something else, such as the sheer effort in pushing against a door when someone is pushing back on the other side. Thirdness is that which is what it is by virtue of relating something to something else; it is difference in a respect, a character that distinguishes its object from others, a mediator. Pushing against the door, we know the Thirdness in the fact of the door, the pushing, and the opposing person. The Secondness is in the mere effort.

Anything we know or deal with in our world is at least a Third, something determinate with respect to something else. It also has aspects of Secondness, whereby it is sheerly different, and of Firstness, whereby it is in itself. Insofar as it can be known, however, it is Firstness and Secondness integrated and related to other things by Thirdness.

This holds of signs themselves. As Thirds they relate objects to other signs as interpretants. But they also have an existence of their own that differentiates them from other things. The differentia, of course, are Thirds; but the fact of difference is their Secondness. Furthermore, they have an immediate material quality of their own that bears the mediating function; this is their Firstness. Peirce used the threefold analysis of the categories to provide classifications of signs. The most important is that into icons, indices, and symbols. An icon represents its object just by virtue of its own character (the Thirdness of Firstness). A picture is an iconic sign, and it represents regardless of whether a real object exists; fictions thus are mainly iconic. An indexical sign represents strictly by virtue of being in causal relation with its object (the Thirdness of Secondness). That is, the real character of the object determines the indexical thing to be a sign, as smoke is an index of fire, or your finger an index of its object because the physical location of its object is that at which it points (when your finger is not in an indexical relation to some object, it is not pointing, although it always goes in some direction). A symbol represents by virtue of a character conventionally established to relate object and interpretant in some respect (the Thirdness of Thirdness).

These are not the only classifications, however. A sign functions as a sign only when it is interpreted by another sign. Interpretants, which can be parsed as judgments or what Peirce called "arguments," are signs that can have icons, indices, or symbols either as their objects or as the signs they relate to other objects. They themselves always represent iconically, indexically, or symbolically. The code of signs consists of all the possible combinations of these three categorial classifications for signs, objects, and interpretants. In a causal stream of interpretation or interpretive interaction, each object is itself a sign of something else, is interpreted by signs that are also objects, by interpretants that themselves can be further interpreted as objects and as signs representing objects.

With respect to classification and analysis according to their interdefinition in codes, signs can be treated as logical entities. In this respect, they are meanings that can be defined sheerly logically, that is, in terms of their potentials for interpretation. They are subjunctive realities, if you will, signs with meanings such that *if* they were involved in an

interpretation they *would* mean such and so. Their logical nature, however, is an abstraction of a dimension of Thirdness from the much more
concrete processes of actual interpretive activity. That activity has a material reality of its own, in unique time and place. It has a singular existence. And it also has many forms, including the logical ones of the
signs involved.[4]

The true punch of Peirce's analysis of activity is that it is not merely
singularly located but also general by virtue of having the logical forms
of interpretation. Insofar as an activity is structured by a general sign, by
a Third, its reality involves being an instance of a more general habit.
The significance of the interpretive activity includes the fact of tendency, the tendency or habit of the general meaning in its signs. Nominalism, against which Peirce argued throughout his career, treats
activities as singular in their place and time, and the general signs within
them are treated as imposed from without by further interpretation that
reduces them to general abstractions. Peirce's "scholastic realism" (CP
5.93–107), by contrast says that the reality of an activity is not exhausted
in its spatio-temporal singular existence but actually includes generality
and tendency. An interpretation is not just the actual *instance* of a play of
habits of symbolizing, but the habits themselves in singular exercize.
Thus no particular thing, no particular interpretation (or anything else
for that matter) is only particular; it includes the general within it as
formed tendency and habit.

The most interesting question for the theory of signs, then, for
semiotic, is not what the codes are but how signs get formed into codes.
How do the generalities get determined? Suppose there is an activity
whose habits are formed such that one has the specific signs for interpreting a door with a knob on one side that is to be turned and pulled
or pushed, depending on which side of the jam the door is near. Then
one encounters a sliding door with no knob but a niche for fingers. One
first generalizes the sign of "door to be opened and closed," and then
finds a new specification of how to do it. Then one encounters an au-
tomatic door that needs to be opened by pressing a hand plate, and another that opens and closes by a person's step on a floor plate, and yet
another that works by an electric eye. The notion of "door" becomes
more abstract and vague: vagueness is when the sign can be specified by
incompatible subspecies, and does not apply to particulars until it is so
specified. A door, for instance, has to be either hinged or sliding (or
some other kind); those are contradictories—the door can't be both. But
the door has to be some one specific kind of door to be actual. Not only

that, the door has to be wholly determined to be actual, a Scotistic haecceity. Thus, a door of the ordinary knob *kind* has to have the knob exactly somewhere at the lock, either engaging it with $^{15}/_{16}$ths or with $^{17}/_{18}$ths inch play (or some other dimension). In fact, anything we can measure reasonably is an approximation and really defines a somewhat general class. Any number of doors can locate the knob relative to the lock with $^{15}/_{16}$ths inches of play. But only this actual door can have just this play. The lesson Peirce draws from this is opposite to the nominalist's. Though actual particularity makes things wholly unique in their secondness, in nearly all practical matters, what is important about the things is some general class character, not the details of haecceity. That the door has a knob that works is more important than whether its play is $^{15}/_{16}$ths or $^{17}/_{18}$ths of an inch. Only when something goes wrong and a locksmith finds the knob a problem does the measurable degree of play become important.

Notice that the argument has been about reality, about doors and locks. The realities are the things that have both absolutely specific haecceity and various general traits. That people possess the general traits of humanity is often far more important than whether they possess a snub nose or some other shape. Yet, if they are Socrates or Cleopatra, the nose might be historically important whereas their humanity is to be taken for granted. That which can be interpreted about the world, and thus that which our signs pick out and our habits negotiate through, is all general. Peirce's Scotistic realism consists in the doctrine of common natures (Neville 1989, 140–145).

The interesting problem in the development of codes of signs, therefore, becomes that of adjusting the generalities in our signs to the generalities in reality as they become relevant, while becoming more specific about alternative instantiations. Our signs regarding doors change, becoming vaguer so as to be inclusive of many new types, as our environment suddenly has new opening mechanisms for doors. In contrast to the European semiotic theory that has been taken up and developed by structuralism, Peirce's theory of signs is embedded in a larger theory of human action and a metaphysical theory of what makes reality significant. Whereas the European preoccupation with codes can legitimately take the interpretation of texts as its paradigm for interpretation in general, because that is like breaking a code, Peirce's theory takes the investigation of nature to be the paradigm. What are the general traits of nature that again and again show themselves in controlled experiments and their less formal commonsense analogues? Those are the

ones that control the development of signs as those traits become relevant to human activity. The theory of signs is thus part of systematic historical studies, not merely of synchronic studies.

Like the theory of signs, all forms of philosophy have specific
objects but reach out into the whole range of human activity and inquiry. For Peirce, philosophy cannot be sharply distinguished from the
sciences, nor from artistic and belletristic work, nor from moral life,
nor from religious reflection. It calls upon all these in the making of
its arguments from many strands. Therefore, philosophy could never
be grounded on something self-grounding, or self-contained in its
meaning, importance, or value. Peirce would reject modernism for its
opposite suppositions. Philosophy is rather a highly reflective and synoptic part of intellectual life, responsive to curiosity and opportunity
for inquiry.

Peirce, in fact, elaborated a theory of the divisions of philosophy,
based on his three categories (CP 5.120–150). The first division is phenomenology, which examines the phenomena of the world with respect
to their illustrating the categories of Firstness, Secondness, and Thirdness. The second division is normative science, and consists of logic, ethics, and aesthetics; these three all have to do with the relation of
phenomena to ends or goods. Logic is the study of the ethics of thinking,
which, like most other acting, is subject to control and therefore can be
controlled for the better or worse. Ethics is the control of actions in general relative to what is worthwhile. Aesthetics is the study of what is
worthwhile in itself and therefore justifies ethical and logical judgments
as good or bad relative to their ends. The third great division is metaphysics, the endeavor to comprehend the reality of phenomena (CP
5.121); reality, said Peirce, is an affair of "Thirdness as Thirdness," that
is, in its mediation between Secondness and Firstness. Phenomenology,
in sum, deals with the Thirdness of Firstness, normative science with the
Thirdness of Secondness, the right or wrongness of procedures relative
to ends, and metaphysics with the Thirdness of Thirdness. What more
could there be?

The exposition here has moved back and forth between Thirdness
in reality and Thirdness in signs. Peirce was explicit about the importance of this, and it shapes his Scotistic realism. He argued for the reality
of generality or Thirdness with what he called an "experiment." In a lecture (CP 5.93–101), he told his audience he was going to drop a stone
from his hand to see whether it would fall to the floor. But of course he
didn't have to because everyone knew in advance it would fall, and to
actually drop it would seem silly: without the slightest reason to doubt,

there is no judicious sense to experiment. Now is it the case that, whereas the habits of mind are solidly general, there is no generality in the stone and the earth's mass? If we can form solidly settled habits of expecting the stone to drop, can the dropping stone be a bare particular without the habit of falling toward a center of gravity? Not at all, said Peirce. To suppose that habits are not in nature is to suppose that every lawlike operation of realities is a miracle or accident; it is to suppose either that our predictions are made to come true by a God who makes the universe look lawlike when it is not, or that the appearance of lawlikeness in things is only a frame imposed on accident. But that latter can be only an hypothesis, and no hypothesis ought to be believed that says its object cannot be explained. In the very nature of the case, an hypothesis supposes that it explains something of its object. Therefore, the only worthwhile metaphysical hypothesis is that, if our habits of thought are fixed and appropriately reinforced in recognizing certain regularities, then reality is more or less regular in the ways we recognize. There are always problems of insufficient, overdetermined or underdetermined interpretation. But if we are led through experimental experience, looking to every possible strand of argument, to represent realities as having regularities, then we should say that realities are regular. Because at least some realities are also actual, and wholly definite as individuals with haecceity, they have the Secondness of being themselves and not any other thing. That they are wholly individual, however, does not preclude them from having regular characters or Scotistic "common natures" that make them classifiable and regularly connectible with other things.

The usual picture of nature in early modern physics and now in our common sense is that it consists of particular atoms or particles that are governed in their changes by universal laws that apply deterministically. As Whitehead (1933, ch. 7) and others have observed, this picture has great difficulty understanding how independent and universal general laws can relate to bare individuals so as to govern them. Peirce has argued that individuality, by including Firstness, Secondness, and Thirdness, thereby makes law, modelled on habit, a character of generality in things (CP 5.45–58). The modern position has often included the claim that universal determinism also is true, the doctrine, namely, that nothing exists or changes except insofar as some universal law determines it to do so. Peirce, in his essay, "The Doctrine of Necessity Examined" (CP 6.35–65) radically transformed the issue of determinism.

Why consider determinism a postulate that must be presupposed for science to be possible? Why assume it to be contradictory that some things happen without a law connecting them to other conditions? Why not instead treat it as an empirical question: How much regularity is there in the world? Common sense had discovered a great many regularities, such as the stone's habit of falling, long before science developed a theory that articulated the conditions under which falling takes place as regular behavior of two bodies toward each other. There is, in fact, an historical interaction between the regularities we notice as relevant to our activities and the development of theories and instruments to pick up new regularities. But, if we think experimentally, surveying our experience, there are also many areas where regularities are lacking. There is no regularity between changes in the Library of Congress catalogue system and the price of eggs in Bankok, nor between my pocketbook and my financial needs, nor between my recognition of the good and my performance relative to it. If one puts universal determinism forward as an hypothesis about nature, it is clearly false, so false as to be silly. At best what might be true is that everything is determined in certain respects.

But should one reformulate the question the following way, interesting results might follow: where is nature determined by regularities, and in what respects? All science can do is find regularities, or fail to find them. The empirical approach to nature's habits, to regularity or lawlikeness, could never deny any regularity science (or other inquiry) might discover. But it would not generalize to a universal claim unless, contrary to historical fact, we found every sample of our survey of changes to exhibit regularity: at that point, the probability of universal determinism would approach 1.0.

Contrary then to the modernist and postmodern conception of nature as a machine, from which human life must be rescued or acknowledged to be meaningless, or entirely self-creative of meaning, Peirce conceived nature as a creature of habit. Not every behavior is rigidly fixed. But those that do exhibit regularity can be known to do so.

III. Speculative Metaphysics

To draw out the implications of these last points it is necessary to develop Peirce's mature speculative metaphysics. Contrary to Rorty and others who have focused on Peirce's theory of science and dismissed his speculations, his most interesting contributions are in metaphysics. In this Peirce is like Descartes, Locke, Spinoza, and Leibniz, modern philosophers whose work is not predominately epistemology. He is not like the strain within modernity running from Hume and Kant to modernism. He intended his own speculative metaphysics to realize and articulate correctly the vision of experimentation in the early modern period, a vision that previous speculative metaphysicians rendered incorrectly.

The place to begin is Peirce's claim that speculative metaphysics does not find final explanation to consist in first principles. Order itself is the great mystery of the universe. Chaos alone does not need an explanation, for there is nothing to explain. To attempt to explain order by appealing to some first orders, such as the law of non-contradiction or a principle of determinism, amounts to asserting the hypothesis that order cannot be explained, only specialized orders. Of course, never should an hypothesis be asserted that claims its subject matter is inexplicable. As a result, metaphysical speculations must give an account of order itself.

Peirce's brilliant suggestion was that the simplest explanation of the universe has to be an evolutionary one, beginning with nothing (CP 6.287–317).[5] The next simplest step is to suppose chaos, a swarm of "Firsts," each itself with no bearing upon anything other. The next simplest step is to suppose difference, "Secondness," the sheer not-thisness, not-thatness of things. With the final step, the supposition of relation, "Thirdness," continuity and connection, the elementary categories are in hand for developing any other specific things, differences, and relations. Peirce's radical beginning point is instructive:

> Metaphysics has to account for the whole universe of being. It has, therefore, to do something like supposing a state of things in which that universe did not exist, and consider how it could have arisen. However, this statement needs amendment. For time is itself an organized something, having its law or regularity; so that time itself is part of the universe whose origin is to be considered. We have therefore to suppose a state of things before time was organized. Accordingly, when we speak of the universe as "arising" we do not mean that literally. We mean to speak of some kind of sequence, say an objective logical sequence; but we do not mean in speaking of the first stages of creation before time was organized, to use "before," "after," "arising," and such words in the temporal sense. (CP 6.214)

Given the elementary orders of evolution, Firstness, Secondness, and Thirdness, Peirce then characterized principles within evolution, Chance, Necessity, and Continuity. (With his love of neologisms, he sometimes characterized these as tychism, anancism, and synechism; proliferating distinctions he labeled his special versions of chance, necessity, and continuity as tychasm, anancasm, and agapasm (CP 6.302).

To deploy these categories he employed a many-strand set of arguments, mathematical and empirical as well as philosophically dialectical. In this sketch only the briefest summary can be given.

The doctrine of chance (see generally CP 6.7–101) says that certain things can occur that are not determined by other things. Insofar as these are within an otherwise ordered temporal flow, they appear as spontaneous. Chance bespeaks the irreducibility of Firstness. Of course, Secondness is also present in chance in that the spontaneous occurrences are different from the rest; and the noting of the difference involves Thirdness. But chance is the occurrence of things just on their own.

In experimentalist fashion, Peirce put forward the doctrine of chance as an hypothesis. The main things chance would explain are the various kinds of variety and specificity in the universe. One might hypothesize, contrarily, that the multiplicity of things was created all at some "beginning." But it is difficult to make sense of "beginning" in that usage. Furthermore, it requires appeal to an extraordinary miracle to get not only vast diversity but such coordination and continuity that the universe has. The simpler hypothesis is to say that variations sport out bit by bit. No matter how complexly organized a system is, random variations will produce novelties, and these might become further integrated to form continuing new characters. Chance variation is small and does not require us to believe that the whole ordered world noted by common sense might suddenly shift its major characters. Determinism presents another contrary hypothesis; as noted above, Peirce insists that determinism itself be considered an hypothesis, and when it is, it is seen to have limited applicability. There is much order in the world, but then again also much lack of connection. Even on the large scale of events noticed in daily life, amidst the interweaving regularities are chance happenings, some of which can be subsequently integrated to provide interesting novelty.

The doctrine of chance is important for Peirce also because it allows him to account for specificity. A specific thing is itself and not some other thing. It cannot be vaguely continuous with other things. And its differences cannot be the exclusive consequence of its own nature. Specificity requires a metaphysical counterpart to epistemic surprise at the Other. This is Secondness in chance, and it makes reference to necessity.

Necessity, in the strict sense for Peirce, is the obdurate character of the Other. It is that which conditions and must be taken into account by a thing. Natural law is a combination of generality and necessity. A thing might be of a type such that, if there is an antecedent condition of another type, the law prescribes the thing a specific character. The actual antecedent condition is the necessity in causation, the Secondness that cannot be gainsaid. Peirce once (CP 5.48) called it the long arm of the sheriff that enforces the law. Considered in abstraction from concrete things, laws of nature are mere hypothetical conditions. Embodied in concrete things, they have the force of necessity.

Peirce interpreted the Darwinian theory of evolution to acknowledge a combination of chance and necessity, mechanical systems plus sports. Peirce considered this to be insufficient for a variety of reasons and argued that, on the metaphysical scale if not the natural history of living things, Lamarck was closer to the point. To put the issue dialectically: How can chance plus necessity account for the fact that truly random sports are incorporated into the ecosystem? The system grows out to reach them, it generalizes beyond the specific order of necessity to a more flexible law that incorporates the novelties.

The doctrine of continuity thus does not mean mechanical repetition plus irrelevant chance variations. It means an extension of character to include new components and tolerate greater internal variation. Peirce's model was mind, and the example given above of the growth of the habit of opening doors to include sliding and electric eye doors is a case in point. There is a tendency in mind always to generalize, to interpret a sign as standing for not just one kind of object but for its cousins as well. The obdurate character of things exerts necessitarian limitations on generalizations. A habit that leads to conflict with reality will be instantly frustrated and perhaps corrected. But the interpretive process follows a principle of generalization and growth just as much as chance and necessitarian elements. Things in the universe have an elementary property of taking on habits, of coming to behave with a continuous character, of being, at a moment, not only particularly actual but generally potential. Peirce wrote:

> Now, those who insist on the doctrine of necessity will for the most part insist that the physical world is entirely individual. Yet law involves an element of generality. Now to say that generality is primordial, but generalization not, is like saying that diversity is primordial but diversification not. It turns logic upside down. At any rate, it is clear that nothing but a principle of habit, itself due to the growth by habit of an infinitesimal chance tendency toward habit-taking, is the only bridge that can span the chasm between the chance-medley of chaos and the cosmos of order and law. (CP 6.262)

The metaphysical reach of the doctrine of continuity leads Peirce to say that the law of the universe is "evolutionary love," or his principle of agapasm (CP 6.272–317). The picture of the universe it displays is a process of chance variations within an otherwise regulated and ordered universe, with things defined in part by the habits of reaching out to relate to novelties and to otherwise unordered elements, creating a new and more subtle order; all this to be continuously repeated so that the universe in all its parts can be conceived to be growing.

Although many scholars have claimed that Social Darwinism was a political philosophy derived from Darwin and justifying greed, Peirce claimed that the attractiveness of Darwin's theory of evolution in the first place was that it appealed to greed. He counterposed it to the Christian tradition for which he spoke:

> The *Origin of Species* of Darwin merely extends politico-economical views of progress to the entire realm of animal and vegetable life. The vast majority of our contemporary naturalists hold the opinion that the true cause of those exquisite and marvelous adaptations of nature for which, when I was a boy, men used to extol the divine wisdom, is that creatures are so crowded together that those of them that happen to have the slightest advantage force those less pushing into situations unfavorable to multiplication or even kill them before they reach the age of reproduction. Among animals, the mere mechanical individualism is vastly reenforced as a power making for good by the animal's greed. As Darwin puts it on his title-page, it is the struggle for existence; and he should have added for his motto: Every individual for himself, and the Devil take the hindmost! Jesus, in his sermon on the Mount, expressed a different opinion.
>
> Here, then, is the issue. The gospel of Christ says that progress comes from every individual merging his individuality in sympathy with his neighbors. On the other side, the conviction of the nineteenth century is that progress takes place by virtue of every individual's striving for himself with all his might and trampling his neighbor under foot whenever he gets a chance to do so. This may accurately be called the Gospel of Greed. (CP 6.293–294)

Peirce, of course, did not give the political consequence of Darwinism as a reason for rejecting it as an hypothesis, nor the salubrious consequence of agapasm as a reason for acceptance. Instead, he reviewed countless details of natural knowledge to provide arguments for his hypothesis.

In his American experimentalist way, Peirce was a grand systematic metaphysician. His full-scale metaphysics compares with Hegel's, which he said was almost right save for the fact it diminished the full force of Secondness and therefore gave the Hegelian equivalent of Thirdness the force of necessity. Peirce's system owes much of its thematic content to the German and British idealists who were his contemporaries. Yet it shared none of their concerns to achieve deductive certainty or to have the shape of a totality. Philosophical systems, for Peirce, including his own, are to be construed as hypothetical, and therefore he completely lacked the foundationalism characteristic of modernist philosophies. Like Whitehead, he thought that thinking takes place for the purpose of better guiding life, especially toward better goals. And like Whitehead he believed that the abstractions of such generality as metaphysics are important for preserving our perception of concrete phenomena from reductive hypotheses.

By virtue of his reconstruction of science and his imaginative systematic metaphysics, Peirce surely must be considered a modern philosopher. But not a modernist one. His pragmatism was a parallel development to modernism, one that is not touched by the critiques of postmodernism and that, in its theory of signs, anticipated certain of the postmodernist critiques of "logocentrism." Peirce would point out, however, that logocentrism no more defines the whole of the Western philosophic tradition than does nominalism.

Before summing up the case regarding Peirce and postmodernism, it is instructive to see how his treatment of religion brings together the major themes of his thought.

IV. Religion

Peirce's contribution to the understanding of religion looks like a paradox.[6] The main line of its development is governed by the logic of philosophy of science, dealing first with the nature of experimental argument about divine matters and then about the divine evolution of the universe. But this line is prefaced with a rejection of the *religious* importance of such concerns, and it is to this preface that we must first attend.

In a wonderful 1898 essay, "Detached Ideas on Vitally Important Topics," Peirce sharply contrasted vitally important topics, such as one's salvation or how to live life, from philosophic reflection on those topics. Philosophy will not guide us through these topics: indeed, "all sensible talk about vitally important topics must be commonplace, all reasoning about them unsound, and all study of them narrow and sordid." Rather, philosophy does quite well with the matters that we find or can put at a distance.[7] Vitally important topics should be approached by the heart, not the mind.[8]

The reason for preferring the reasons of the heart in vitally important matters, of course, is that the heart is the repository of our deepest habits, those that have been developed through what Dewey called "the funded wisdom of the race," those least likely to be in touch with fads and false starts, those that over time have been sensitive to the most enduring and obdurate realities unclouded by clever coping. In fact, given Peirce's observation that thinking always arises in the middle of ongoing activity as a corrective device, the heart is the middlemost of evolved human activities, trained by and attuned to the most massive accumulations of evidence. Whereas intellectual science intends to reduce its considerations to the fewest variables and control for finite experiments, the learning of the heart proceeds by assembling the greatest range of evidence, relatively unprejudiced by screening devices save those that have been reinforced through countless variations in time and situation. In a practical sense, then, as a vitally important topic religion requires learning to listen to the heart.

It is with this in mind that Peirce constructed his famous "Humble Argument" in "A Neglected Argument for the Reality of God." The argument begins by noting that there are "three universes," those analyzed as Firstness, Secondness, and Thirdness. In this essay, in fact, Peirce treated them as three universes of experience: Ideas, Brute Actuality, and Sign. Peirce's particular analysis of the universe is far too specialized for the Humble Argument as such. His point could just as well be illustrated by the elements in Whitehead's Category of the Ultimate: Unity, Disjunctive Multiplicity, and Creativity connecting the multiplicity into one (Whitehead 1929, chapter 2). The issue is that *any* view of the universe notes a multiplicity connected into a complex interrelation. Pure unity, as Parmenides observed and Bradley concurred, allows for none of the distinctions of experience. Pure multiplicity could not be recognized as such for there would be no common ground to note diversity. There is rather a one in many or many in one. How can this be so?

Though perhaps not a vitally important topic, musing on one or another form of the problem of the one and the many seems to be recorded in the literature of nearly all cultures in civilized times. Peirce observed that "musement" is a free and easy reflective play that, when unhindered by the bias of urgency or special purpose, can solve just about any problem with "forty or fifty minutes of vigorous and unslackened analytic thought (CP 6.461). And sure enough, the consensus of musement is that the three universes, or any other complex plurality of elements, are possible together because they are created that way *ex nihilo*. There is nothing coercive about this argument. It seems like a blatant appeal to the *consensus gentium*. And surely there are historical exceptions to it. But Peirce defended it as an argument of the heart, and that defense of the Humble Argument is itself the Neglected Argument.

There is an important distinction to be drawn, said Peirce, between an argument and an argumentation. An argument is any line of reasoning that gets you from a problem or set of premises to a conclusion. An argumentation does that according to a set of rules; it therefore requires that the terms of the problem, or the premises, be set in what logicians call well-formed formulae. Now, the Humble Argument, the inference of the creator God from complex multiplicity, is an argument, not an argumentation. It concludes in an extraordinarily vague idea of God, so vague, for instance, as to allow that ideas, purposes, temporal activity, and the rest that traditional theology likes to attribute to God, are among the things of the three universes said to be created (CP 6.466). But the hypothesis of God is not vague with respect to the claim that the three universes are mutually created. Furthermore, the hypothesis becomes more and more specific as one muses on the characters of the universes; like Thirdness itself, the hypothesis grows in range and specificity. The Humble Argument is just the vague hypothesis: there is a God that creates the universes. Peirce said that musing theologians get in trouble as soon as they begin to make the hypothesis of God specific, and then lose the near unanimity of musement (CP 6.496). Even to say there is "a" God suggests an individuality and separateness to the creator that is a great move toward specification beyond the Humble Argument.

The core of the Neglected Argument is Peirce's general theory of hypothesis and explanation, a theory that will give weight to the Humble Argument by itself. As is well known, Peirce analyzed inquiry into three stages: Abduction (or Retroduction), Deduction, and Induction. Abduction is simply a guess, the musing formulation of an hypothesis that might work as an answer. It is an argument, not an argumentation. The Humble Argument is exclusively at the stage of Abduction. Unless some special cogency can be given to Abduction in general, the hypothesis must still be tested. Deduction begins the test and has two stages of its own. First, the hypothesis constructed by the musing guess must be "explicated," or rendered clear in categories that allow for logical inferences to be made from it. Like Abduction, Explication of the Hypothesis is an argument, not an argumentation; it works by analogy, by further guesses, most particularly by importing categories from other areas of inquiry. In the case of the Humble Argument, the creation hypothesis is explicated by employing categories descriptive of one's view of the world: Firstness, Secondness, Thirdness in Peirce's case. Thus Peirce cites purpose and growth as elements of the hypothesis about God, even though they cannot be applied in a univocal sense to the creator of those very characters. Theology falls into endless controversy at the stage of Explication; cultural differences bring such different analogical suppositions to the explicative process.

Having explicated an hypothesis, inquirers can make logical deductions or predictions from it that would make a pragmatic difference in experience. This part of Deduction is an argumentation and proceeds according to logical rules; it is the first part of inquiry that does so. That logical deductions can be made does not prove the hypothesis true; there must be an inductive process to examine experience in light of the deductions from the explicated hypothesis.

Unlike many subsequent philosophers of science, Peirce did not believe that inquirers just check experience to ascertain whether the predictions are valid. Rather, he distinguished three steps in the Inductive process. First, and most important, is classification, the analysis of experience to see whether and how it falls into the categories derived from the explicated hypothesis. Not begging the question, Classification is an argument, not an argumentation. The degeneration of genuine inquiry into scientism occurs precisely at the point where the separate step of Classification is omitted. It is entirely questionbegging to assume that the categories or well-formed formulae employed in the deductions from the explicated hypothesis are the obvious terms of experience. This was the mistake of the determinists against whom Peirce so frequently argued: they assumed that the characterization of events that follows from the determinist hypothesis in fact characterizes the contents of experience, and thus refused to see or admit into evidence any contrary traits.

In theology, the omission of the step of classification, separate from deduction, is the point at which theology has been reductive and dogmatic. The relevant experience against which the intellectual muser's hypothesis about God is to be tested is the vast array of religions in their historical depth and interactions, including the various cultural forms of theoretical analysis. Although Peirce did not draw out the point because history of religions as a discipline was barely being formulated in his time, his analysis of the logic of the hypothesis of God suggests that the discipline is essential for the process of classification. But the present form of history of religions is inadequate to the task precisely because of its common rejection of theology and other intellectual elements in religion. This rejection is understandable in light of the frequently imperial procedure of theology that skips classification entirely and slices experience according to its hypothesized categories. But theology ought not do that, Peirce taught, and history of religions ought to include theology and be theological in criticizing its own categories.

Induction involves two steps after Classification. The first Peirce called "Probation," and it involves ascertaining the empirical facts regarding the reality of the classifications and relating these to the deduced predictions. The second, which Peirce called the "Sentential" part, summarizes the probations relative to the hypothesis and declares the overall judgment on the hypothesis—where it is strong and where weak, where it is responsive to actual classes of experience and where off the point, where it is multiply reinforced and where its success hangs by a slender thread of evidence. The Sentential step thus pushes the hypothesis to further growth, eliciting new corrective Abductive arguments. Probation and Sentential induction involve many argumentations in addition to arguments, said Peirce, who analyzed them according to the mathematics of induction. In theology today, given the state of the discipline, only dialogue among religious traditions could provide a context for the whole of Induction.

Given that the Humble Argument is but the first hypothesis, a mere argument in the whole texture of inquiry, is it entirely untested? According to Peirce, it is untested in the strict sense. Especially, it is untested in any explicated form that might be superimposed, such as the Christian or Saivite notions of divinity. But it has a standing on its own in the following sense. If our Abductive faculties were wholly random, with no veracious connection between problem and guessed hypothesis, the likelihood that anyone ever would abduce an hypothesis about anything that could be explicated, tried, and found worthwhile in experience would be almost zero. The range of propositions that could function as hypotheses is infinite, and the accidental relevance to any finite situation would be overwhelmingly unlikely if there were no intrinsic connection in argument between problem and guess. From this Peirce concluded that there has evolved an affinity between human habits of mind and the universe. Although an abductive hypothesis is not itself as such tested out in experience, its very occurrence carries some likelihood that it is true. Better yet, the vaguer the hypothesis, the more likely it is. And the degree to which a specification of the hypothesis is true does indeed depend on importing explicative categories, logical systems, and inductive classifications, probations and assessments that have independent support. Upon first meeting a door that opens with an electronic button, one wouldn't rehearse a whole repertoire of activities designed to get one's way, such as shouting, dancing, twitching, and praying, but would look, by analogy with doorknobs, for something to manipulate.

The Humble Argument, then, is to be trusted, at least in vague outline, because it arises from habits of the heart, from evolutionary adaptations to inquiry that have attuned our musement to reality. The argument is particularly good when there are no alternative hypotheses. Nothing, said Peirce, besides creation in a vague sense, makes sense of the three universes.

The alternate strategy to Peirce's, of course, is not an alternate explanation of why there is complexity in the universe, but the claim that such complexity does not need to be explained. It can be argued that the question of why there is something definite, hence complex, is meaningless. But that argument is itself an hypothesis, Peirce would say, and it is never worth asserting because it says that what it is supposed to explain cannot be explained. Such an argument from meaninglessness either is a covert voluntarism that decides issues by mere will or an importation of a criterion for meaningfulness that is the very question at issue in explaining the existence of meaningfulness in the universe. Another argument against the creation explanation is that most complexities can be explained as illustrations of some first principles and that the first principles, by virtue of being first, cannot be explained further. This argument assumes that only principles explain. But Peirce argued that divine creation explains by accounting for the evolution of principles. That evolution can be described in terms of principles, such as Firstness, Secondness, and Thirdness, but the reason for them, each particularly, is that it is made to be itself in relation to the others.

Peirce thus laid out a path that would have helped Whitehead had he known of it. Whitehead formulated his "ontological principle" of explanation to say that any complexity needs to be explained in terms of actual decisions that compose it (Whitehead 1929, chapter 2 and passim). He applied this to the practice of science, but was ambivalent about its use at the metaphysical level. Whitehead did say that the metaphysical structures of the universe are the product of the Prime Created Fact (this sounds like Peirce), but he also insisted that God exemplify the categories and not be an exception. God thus was depicted by Whitehead as an actual entity subject to the Category of the Ultimate. The complexity in the Category of the Ultimate then cannot be accounted for by anything, either by God or by a higher principle. Peirce, on the other hand, would not have been reluctant to say that God is an exception to the categories, since the categories are the very things God is hypothesized to explain as their creator. The only limitation Peirce recognized is that the *hypothesis* of God must exemplify the created logical strictures.[9]

To the point, then, is a consideration of some of Peirce's concrete theological views that arise from the defense of the Neglected Argument and their bearing on the study of religion.

First we should note that, although the hypothesis of God arises from an abductive argument, it should not be thought to be thereby non-experiential. Human beings, on the contrary, according to Peirce, "can know nothing except what we *directly* experience. All the creations of our mind are but patchworks from experience. So that all our ideas are but ideas of real or transposed experiences" (CP 6.492). Our reasonings only contextualize experiences by making them signs in interpretive processes. "Where would such an idea, say as that of God, come from, if not from direct experience? Would you make it a result of some kind of reasoning, good or bad? Why, reasoning can supply the mind with nothing in the world except an estimate of the value of a statistical ratio. . . . No: as to God, open your eyes—and you see him" (CP 6.493). True, many people don't identify the experience of God to be such, because they fail to muse or engage in other meditations on the vast vague ordering of the universe; thus they fail to contextualize the experience of God in the interpretive connections that give it its significance. As soon as we try to make the idea of God very precise, the universality of the experience evaporates, because people's contexts on the general level differ so greatly. But, said Peirce, if any individual continues to muse on the idea, working out its significance in the context important for and definitive of that person's life, the vague hypothesis will elaborate itself into an idea the person can hardly doubt and that frames the individual's love.[10]

Here lies Peirce's answer to the criticism inevitably raised against his appeal to the heart, namely that it leads to syrupy fideism. On the contrary, the vague instincts of the heart tend, like all basic ideas, to generalize and ramify in many directions. Thus the people of Israel understood the vague creator of the universe to be specifically present in the dilemma of existing between the Egyptians and the Babylonians. In this sense of the growth of an idea, it is connected to the things with which one is concerned and that punctuate one's corporate world. Generalization, for Peirce, does not necessarily mean being made more abstract but rather being connected increasingly to more things.[11] In his writings on aesthetics, Peirce defined intrinsic goodness as concrete reasonableness, that is, as an idea ranging over a wide scope of things, yet articulating details and making dense connections. The idea, of course, is not a mere representation but a real sign actually making the connections and thus including the connected elements within it. This density of God-world is what we come increasingly to feel as we think through the idea of God in the concrete terms of our world. So Peirce knew we live not by instinct alone but by instinct embodied in and densely ramified throughout the texture of our life. That ramification is the intellectual task that Peirce practised and urged upon us.

In many respects, Peirce's theory is the theoretical background for theories of religious understanding such as Wilfrid Cantwell Smith's (1981) that require it to combine objective knowledge with intersubjective communication, reading all in the densest possible historical context that trivializes apparent lacunae between traditions and persons. Peirce himself liked to meditate upon the vast intricacy of the universe, filled with intelligent creatures on countless other planets (CP 6.501); he also recognized that the religious embodiment of the idea of God is the religious life itself, the life framed by habits of practice and belief that pervasively take one's world to be created. From Peirce we thus can take direction for the empirical development of religious studies.

But equally we can thank him for reconstructive abstract speculative theology. As he put the point in terms of the theory of signs, it is impossible to experience an object directly as such without an interpretant with which to grasp it. The interpretant itself is part of the direct experience. But the semiotic system elaborating the parts of experience into complex significant meaning must be developed to give the interpretant sharp shape. Although the danger is run here of falling into error by virtue of mis-specifying the vague concept, experientially the gain to be won is concrete experience of God and of the world in relation to its creator. The price of remaining with the initial guess of the Humble Argument is that one has only the vaguest *experience* of God. As Peirce would put it, the corrective for my particularity and bias in explicating, demonstrating, and inductively probating the vague hypothesis is the inclusion of your particularity, and everyone else's. Wilfrid Cantwell Smith (1981, ch. 1) makes the point by saying that there is only one history of religions, though there are many religions, each practiced uniquely by its members. To understand any one particularity in depth requires dense reference to the others.

Peirce's contribution to the study of religion, then, is to combine the speculative adventure of hypothesis-expanding philosophy and theology with the need to flesh that out in concrete empirical studies. That is an important lesson for a time such as ours where empirical students of religion and theologians and philosophers see each other as the diminution of their own work.

Peircean Postscript: Postmodernism Again

For Peirce, the hallmark of the modern period, distinguishing it from the preceding scholastic period, is its insistence on learning through an engagement with nature. This began with the development of early modern mathematical physics, and Peirce claimed to have understood its inner truth in his theory of interpretation and experimental pragmatism. He was correct in this.

Because inquiry takes place by experiential engagement—by the deliberate placing of hypotheses or habits in jeopardy—no inquiry has boundaries. Philosophy bleeds off in all direction. Or, better put, philosophy needs to learn from and incorporate all other inquiries. In building his arguments with many strands, Peirce ranged far beyond the narrowly philosophical observations with which he has been summarized in the above. Engaging reality from as many interpretive perspectives as possible, it is impossible to think that the paradigm of interpretation is the reading of texts. It is almost as difficult to think of interpretation as laboratory science with controlled experiments, although that is closer to the mark. Rather, interpretation is the many-pronged inquiry that uses any means that might have bearing on the subject. Peirce, of course, would suppose that interpretation is like the structure of agapastic reality in this regard.

In this light, modernism, that special movement in late modernity from the end of the last century to the middle of this, is a dwarfing of modernity, an impoverishment. Peirce could say of it, as he did of other reductionist philosophies, that it is like passing a law that everything has to be made out of paper: you discover many inventive uses of paper but still have a needlessly impoverished world. The development of parts of modernity to modernism, in the quest for certainty, has been traced above. Peirce and his pragmatism, then, stand out as the more robust late development of the modern period.

We are now in a position to ask whether Peirce could be a postmodern thinker. He surely anticipated many themes and positions later taken up by postmodernism. An arbitrary periodization of cultural history could make that seem possible. But in the organic sense of cultural development, a "post-" movement requires the negating of what it comes after. Furthermore, that negation requires a totalizing of the situation negated: the "modern" must be a unified something for "post-modernism" to get beyond it. Declining to totalize, one works in the mode of Peirce, rejecting some things (e.g. nominalism), accepting others (e.g. experimentation), modifying yet others (e.g. the metaphysical categories). In this mode, one might move beyond certain aspects of the past, but by building on other aspects; one is never "post" the definitive character of the past. Peirce would have thought postmodernism is absurd and arrogant because no one is smart enough to identify a whole culture and definitively negate it.

There are many aspects of modern culture that Peirce rejected, including the hypocrisy of official religion and the shallowness of the perception technological filters give us of the world. Like Griffin, he advocated the fulfillment of the early modern dream of living effectively in harmony with the earth, but without the dominance that the early moderns thought was required to cure disease and feed the hungry. Like Griffin, he advocated freedom for all classes of people, part of Francis Bacon's dream, but through the concrete development of cultural forms that foster the habits of freedom, not through the wholesale destruction of social structures associated with the habits of oppression and servitude. Peirce would have found the postmodernist critique of logocentrism a wickedness, not because of its complaints about rationalism—reason always needs polishing—but because of its substitution of the problematic of power for that of truth.

There is, of course, an issue of power in the debate about nomenclature. A postmodernism that totalizes in order to negate inevitably tells a biased story. Heidegger, who supplied the main reading for postmodernism of what is supposed to be the tradition of the West, read Peirce and his antecedents out of the story. He distorted and perverted the modern approach to experiment and experience and filtered the vast melange of thinkers and ideas through a sieve that passes only the quest for certainty. Rorty follows Heidegger in this, dismissing Peirce and Whitehead and reading Dewey with a clean excision of his metaphysical ideas. A simple piety toward the past, far more variegated and rich than any single (logocentric) story, requires a resolute refusal to totalize or represent one's work as definitively rejecting and succeeding the whole of a valuable past. In order for reconstructive thinkers, in Griffin's usage, to protect their antecendents it is necessary to decline the self-understanding of the New Age.

CHAPTER TWO

✳

ALFRED NORTH WHITEHEAD AND ROMANTICISM

I. Nature: Mechanism and Freedom

Whitehead's philosophy can be approached *sub specie aeternitatis* and it can also be appreciated as an extraordinary cultural artifact of the first third of our century.[1] Whatever its very considerable external merits, in the second regard its historical locus is different from our own. Our own philosophy is responsible for situating problems and responses in our own time, with respect to which Whitehead's time was an antecedent. This point of historical concreteness is to be stressed, first, because Whitehead himself did, especially in *Science and the Modern World* (1925), second, because too many of us have succumbed to reiterating Whitehead's thought as if it were true regardless of history, and third, because there are very specific differences between Whitehead's situation and ours that need to be discussed. In particular, the situation in which he appealed to romantic poetry, in his famous lecture on the Romantic Reaction (1925, chapter 5), is not paralleled exactly by our own situation although we may feel the need for at least an analogous appeal. For reasons beyond those Whitehead knew, we are drawn like him to art for wholeness, to religion, and to philosophic system.

Whitehead's general approach to romantic poetry is set within this statement whose elegance merits full quotation:

I hold that philosophy is the critic of abstractions. Its function is the double one, first of harmonising them by assigning to them their right relative status as abstractions, and secondly of completing them by direct comparison with more concrete intuition of the universe, and thereby promoting

53

the formation of more complete schemes of thought. It is in respect to this comparison that the testimony of great poets is of such importance. Their survival is evidence that they express deep intuitions of mankind penetrating into what is universal in concrete fact. Philosophy is not one among the sciences with its own little scheme of abstractions which it works away at perfecting and improving. It is the survey of sciences, with the special objects of their harmony, and of their completion. It brings to this task, not only the evidence of the separate sciences, but also its own appeal to concrete experience. It confronts the sciences with concrete fact. (1925, 126–127)

Whitehead's is not a crude empiricism of the arts. Although he sometimes appealed to "naive experience," he never suggested that the great poets have an uninterpreted privileged access to concrete reality against which abstractions are to be measured. Rather, he argued that the poets themselves were historically situated. They reacted, he said, against the misplaced abstractions of their time, uncovering dimensions of concrete fact in the countervalence of those abstractions. It is worthwhile summarizing his analysis.

The abstractions facilitating the development of natural science up to the nineteenth century included a materialistic mechanism. Yet the moral intuitions of even those who were mechanists, for instance Kant, included the importance of teleological behavior and responsibility. The contradition between these two sets of claims—mechanisms *vs.* teleology—undermines the force of the culture believing both. Whitehead wrote:

A scientific realism, based on mechanism, is conjoined with an unwavering belief in the world of men and of the higher animals as being composed of self-determining organisms. This radical inconsistency at the basis of modern thought accounts for much that is half-hearted and wavering in our civilization. It would be going too far to say that it distracts thought. It enfeebles it, by reason of the inconsistency lurking in the background. (1925, 110)

In reaction to the abstractions of materialistic mechanisms the romantic poets discerned and celebrated the solidarity of nature, the felt presence of all things in each standpoint. Wordsworth's theme, said Whitehead, "is nature *in solido*, that is to say, he dwells on that mysterious presence of surrounding things, which imposes itself on any separate element that we set up as individual for its own sake. He always grasps the whole of nature as involved in the tonality of the particular instance. That is why he laughs with the daffodils, and finds in the primrose thoughts 'too deep for tears' " (1925, 121).

Shelley, more enthusiastic about science than Wordsworth, still rejected the distinction between primary and secondary qualities presupposed by materialism. "Shelley's nature," said Whitehead, "is in its essence a nature of organisms, functioning with the full content of perceptual experience" (1925, 124). After quoting lines from Shelley's *Mont Blanc* Whitehead remarked that, however you construe him, Shelley is here an emphatic witness to a prehensive unification as constituting the very being of nature" (1925, 125).

The mention of prehension reminds us of Whitehead's own agenda of reconstructing the concept of nature. Feeling the solidarity of the universe from the standpoint of a unifying event was conceived by Whitehead through the rejection of the notion of simple location. His categories of change, value, eternal objects, endurance, organism, and interfusion were put forward in *Science and the Modern World* to explain his new philosophy of "organic mechanism." These conceptions were refined and systematized in *Process and Reality* and perhaps constitute Whitehead's contributions to philosophy *sub specie aeternitatis*. But they are not to the point of the present discussion.[2]

The point is that both aesthetic intuitions of the romantic poets and the categories of Whitehead's philosophical system demonstrate how we can be free and responsible in comporting ourselves toward the whole. The problem with materialistic mechanism is not that an allegedly free human action is determined but that it is determined too narrowly to be free and responsible. It is determined by an immediate and local past, and therefore, like the stars, "blindly runs." A free and responsible action is determined in part by its role within a larger organic whole, including a future; if the action is to be justified, it may make reference to its determination relative to a whole background of past, present, and future. This remark does not intend to address many of the most important questions of freedom, such as diversity of real alternatives, indetermination with respect to the force of the past, the discernment of merit in options, and the like. Whitehead did address these and other issues in various writings (see also Neville 1974). The remark does address Whitehead's thesis about nature and freedom: if nature is materialistic, freedom is impossible; the poets saw that nature is not materialistic but organic and, therefore, philosophy should construct a system conceiving how this is so.

For Whitehead in the first third of this century, the problem of re-conciling the philosophical suppositions of his culture with its intuitions of freedom and responsibility came from misplaced abstractions about nature. Between the decades of the romantic poets and Whitehead's flourishing, those misplaced scientific abstractions had been jostled loose from their obviousness. Whitehead's own work was to reconstruct a conception of nature that incorporated the new theories of relativity and quantum mechanics, while at the same time building upon the his-torical criticisms of the modern abstractions which had been lodged by their own dialectic and by the independent but reactive visions of the poets. Only perhaps in the sciences, surely not in the arts or in letters, has the twentieth century found a revolutionary genius at reconstruc-tion equal to Whitehead, transcending the decay of the modern world from its own inconsistencies by envisioning a new world from its decom-posed elements. Even if his view is finally unacceptable *sub specie aeter-nitatis*, it is a cultural artifact of consummate genius.

II. Modernism and Fragmentation

The problem of our own time, in contrast to Whitehead's, is not primarily the reconception of nature. Whitehead or his alternatives have done that. Rather the problem is a fragmentation deeper than he envisioned, one resulting from the decay of modernism. Before dis-cussing modernism in more detail it is appropriate to remark that Whitehead seems simply to have missed it. Contemporary with the arch-modernist philosophers Russell, Wittgenstein (in his early years), and Husserl, Whitehead apparently did not know that he was supposed to be doing what they did, that modernism had defined philosophy as a pro-fessional in-group affair. In this respect, as much as in doctrinal affini-ties, Whitehead stands with Peirce, James, and Dewey as philosophers who simply found their way around modernism rather than through it.

Modernism is a large-scale phenomenon of European culture within which philosophy's modernist adventures play but a small part. Except for those who escaped modernism, it is the cultural conscious-ness that brings to an end the period of the "modern" which began with the European renaissance. Perhaps the epitome of the rise of modern-ism, as the coda on the modern according to the postmodernists, is re-counted in Carl Schorske's (1980) discussion of Vienna's Ringstrasse, its critics and the birth of urban modernism. When the liberal bourgeoisie came to power in Vienna in the 1860s with a new constitutional govern-ment, the area where the wall had stood ringing the old city lay open for development. Over the next three decades colossal public buildings were erected in scattered positions around the monumental new Ringstrasse. The buildings were colossal not only in scale but in their aggrandisement of the bourgeois ego and its accomplishments. Most particularly, these buildings were required to be "historical-style architecture," (1980, 40) reflecting styles of the past, mainly Gothic or renaissance. In fact, advanced architectural students at the Viennese Academy of Fine Arts were required to choose to enter either a program in Renaissance or one in Gothic architecture (1980, 82). The grandiosity of nineteenth-century liberal bourgeois architecture was not limited to Vienna, as those of us know who go to the the New York City Post Office at 8th Avenue and 34th Street or to City Hall, or to the bank in nearly any small town across America's midwest. Against this grandiosity the modernist architects launched their reforms that come to perfection in the International style, the Bauhaus school, in our Lever Brothers, Seagrams, Hancock, and Citicorp buildings. The pioneering modernist architectural theorist was Otto Wagner who prefaced his 1895 textbook, *Modern Architecture*, with this remark:

> One idea inspires the whole book; namely, that the whole basis of the views of architecture prevailing today must be displaced by the recognition that the only possible point of departure for our artistic creation is modern life. (Quoted in Schorske 1980, 74)

To determine the content of "modern life" Wagner was joined by Gustaf Klimt the artist and, subsequently, by the whole tradition of modernist abstraction down to Ad Reinhardt. All of the sciences, arts, and letters have been affected by modernism, which may now be characterized more generally, building on the discussion in the introduction above.

Modernism is the cultural style that attempts to integrate things so that they have self-contained intelligibility and worth. It is anti-historical, then, because historical reference moves beyond the artifact. It is obsessed with being grounded, certain, self-justifying. This is possible when things are abstracted from their ongoing context of life and treated in themselves. Abstraction generally is characteristic of modernism, as in abstract art. The New Critics (for instance Cleanth Brooks, William Wimsatt) produced the ideology for modernist literature. Political economy (Keynes) became the construction of reductive economic models and systems. Understanding of human character, previously thought to be worked out in the tumble of history, became psychology (Watson, Freud). Structural-functionalism and other forms of what has become known as systems theory (Parsons, Isard) dominated the social sciences. The modernist development in the social sciences was fed by the older modern appreciation of mathematics as a tool for order and explanation, and the physical sciences carried this even further. The explosion in knowledge since the European renaissance combined with modernism to produce specialization in knowledge and skill to the point of redefining professionalism. From early times the professions have been service vocations such as law, medicine, or divinity, in which excellence of performance needs to be judged by peers rather than by the clients served; convicted felons, for instance, are not fair judges of whether their lawyers have done the best for them in the circumstances. The proliferation of specialized scientific knowledge produces a somewhat similar need to be judged by peers because non-specialists just do not know enough. What modernism did to this specialization was to legitimate its boundaries. Since the intelligibility and worth of one's specialty is supposed to be self-contained, not only are non-specialists incapable of judging it, their judgments would be irrelevant or perverse even if they should come to know enough. Because professional excellence in the modernist sense is self-contained and results from specialization, it is taught through an emphasis on discipline or method and in fact is defined as "what the method produces." Changes in method tend to be small or to be intelligible in terms of difficulties or opportunities relative to the older method.

Long before postmodernists identified modernism as such, Whitehead recognized the decisive importance of professional specialization in the modernist period. He wrote:

> Professionals are not new to the world. But in the past, professionals have formed unprogressive castes. The point is that professionalism has now been mated with progress. The world is now faced with a self-evolving system, which it cannot stop. There are dangers and advantages in this situation. It is obvious that the gain in material power affords opportunity for social betterment. If mankind can rise to the occasion, there lies in front a golden age of beneficent creativeness. But material power in itself is ethically neutral. It can equally well work in the wrong direction. The problem is not how to produce great men, but how to produce great societies. The great society will put up the men for the occasions. (1925, 294–295)

Whitehead's solution to the problem was not to cultivate the generalist but to couple specialized training, which is limited to thorough understanding of a few abstractions, with an artistic and aesthetic education that places the abstractions within the whole of things. His suggestion has great merit if it can be accomplished; modernist education works by the functional unit of information or skill, which is the contradictory of Whitehead's sense of aesthetic vision. The point here is that Whitehead identified and appreciated the fact that modernist specialization and professionalization diminish society. It does not take a postmodernist to make that point. Indeed, Whitehead rejected the postmodernist antithesis of generalization to specialization and reconceived the problem as abstraction relative to discernment and appreciation of context.[3]

To summarize the general account: modernism is the cultural style that seeks self-contained intelligibility, significance, and worth; in a diverse world this leads to professional specialization; its self-consciousness involves making a self-contained new start, significantly discontinuous with the past; and the methodological self-definition of a specialty allows, indeed encourages, a practitioner to declare those who follow other methods to fall outside the specialty.

This last point is a hallmark of modernist philosophy for which it counts as a refutation to call one's opponent "not really a philosopher."[4] As in architecture and art, Vienna was a breeding ground for modernist philosophy. Toulmin and Janik's *Wittgenstein's Vienna* (1973) is a splendid companion piece to Schorske's *Fin-De-Siecle Vienna*. Like Wittgenstein and the Vienna Circle, Moore and Russell in England launched their philosophies as revolutionary rejections of the past, intelligible in terms of their own language and notation. Husserl studied with Brentano in Vienna and launched his own modernist attempt to ground all science in a philosophical certainty obtained by a transcendental-phenomenological method resulting in the possibility of pure description. As the revolutionary ferver of the early modernists cooled and their views became nuanced and qualified, their schools became institutionalized around an internal dialectic of methods and issues that were intelligible and prized in and only in the schools.

Western philosophers became modernist or not depending on their response to Kant in light of absolute idealism. From a cultural point of view, Kant's theory of knowledge attempted to do two things: first, to carry out the Cartesian project of establishing certainty as the proper mode of scientific knowing and, second, to define the world in terms of the conditions of its being known. The absolute idealists, for instance Bradley, Bowne, and Blanshard, embraced this double project with imagination and verve, declaring both knowers and the world to be a great knower, outside of which there could be nothing to upset the certainty of its self-identity; certainty, for the absolute idealists, applied less

to judgments than to being. The modernists rejected the absolute idealists' grand synthesis because it required philosophical identification
with the whole world which, baldly put, is preposterous. But they sustained both of Kant's projects by retreating to something that they
thought humbly could be made intelligible, significant, and valuable in
itself. Some found certainty in pure description, methodologically controlled. Others found it in language, formal or otherwise. Both description and language use are important and finitely manageable functions
of human experience. But they are also fragments.

The non-modernist response to Kant in light of absolute idealism
was simply to abandon the search for certainty to embrace, as we have
seen, what Kant, at the end of the *Critique of Pure Reason,* called "the
method of hypothesis" and condemned as untranscendental. Thus
Peirce called himself a "critical commonsensist," where "critical" means
what is left of Kant after the removal of the dialectic of certainty and the
transcendental constitution of the world. Absolute idealism, for Peirce,
was not an object of rebellion but simply an interesting, though inadequate, hypothesis held by his friend Josiah Royce and others. With
Kant's critical philosophy, Peirce defined the world in terms of knowing
it. But Peirce conceived of knowing as hypothetical inquiry guiding action and habit, and as meaningful only in the context of community; this
conception of knowledge was a far larger fragment of human life than
the modernists' employment of Kant. James and Dewey followed Peirce
in this, and Whitehead somewhat independently developed the idea of
speculative philosophy as hypothetical and as concerned to be a natural
tool for living better rather than for knowing with certainty (Whitehead
1929a). Both for the pragmatists and for Whitehead, philosophy is not
self-contained but essentially moves off to history, science, and the arts
and literature.

Marxism is a highly diverse tradition relative to modernism. Doc-
trinaire dialectical materialism, on the one hand, is a kind of inverted
absolute idealism. Absolute idealism is the Ringstrasse of philosophy,
and much of the pre-Gorbachev Soviet sensibility seems to be like Ringstrasse Vienna. Marxism has on the other hand become a tool of academic analysis with modernist concerns for purity and wholeness of
intelligibility in Marxian frames. Yet again Marxist humanism seems to
have abandoned the requirement of certainty and interprets itself as an
hypothesis needing warrant from diverse spheres of inquiry and life.

For all the non-modernists, Kant is diminished in importance, and
so is the enterprize of epistemology, as Rorty would require. Rather,
non-modernist epistemology is a function of practical, ethical, aesthetic,

and social concerns that make up philosophy proper. A series of remarks from Whitehead's *Function of Reason* (1929a) reveals his non-modernistic understanding of philosophy.

> The higher forms of life are actively engaged in modifying their environment. . . . The explanation of this active attack in the environment is a three-fold urge: (I) to live, (II) to live well, (III) to live better. In fact the art of life is *first* to be alive, *secondly* to be alive in a satisfactory way, and *thirdly* to acquire an increase in satisfaction. . . .
>
> The primary function of Reason is the direction of the attack on the environment. (8) . . . The speculative Reason is in its essence untrammelled by method. Its function is to pierce into the general reasons beyond limited reasons, to understand all methods as coordinated in a nature of things only to be grasped by transcending all method. . . . Reason which is methodic is content to limit itself within the bounds of successful method. It works in the secure daylight of traditionally practical activity. (65–66) . . . The proper satisfaction to be derived from speculative thought is elucidation. It is for this reason that fact is supreme over thought. . . . Thus the supreme verification of the speculative flight is that it issues in the establishment of a practical technique for well-attested ends, and that the speculative system maintains itself as the elucidation of that technique. In this way there is a progress from thought to practice, and regress from practice to the same thought. This interplay of thought and practice is the supreme authority. It is the test by which charlatanism of speculation is restrained. (80–81)

III. Modernism: A Non-Postmodernist Critique

The culture of the modernist style is now in trouble. One need not be a postmodernist to agree to that. We should consider, however, how a non-postmodernist critique of modernism might look. The place to begin is with an analysis of "language games," the notion invented out of modernism to critique modernism.

The conception of language games was developed in the philosophy of the later Wittgenstein (1953). Recall the motive that led Wittgenstein to this conception. His early philosophy (1922) was designed to establish a wholly public and logically perspicuous theory of knowledge oriented to grounding natural science. He came to reject the picture theory in this early philosophy because it was inattentive to the actual uses of language that were far more multifarious than picturing. In fact, analyzing the nature of language in its use, the conception of picturing an external given reality found little if any use. The truly public nature of language rests in the activities of a community of people developing and moulding a language game in the context of their form of life. Epistemological suggestions of picturing, like metaphysical problems about the nature of reality, arise only when we forget that our language is an instrument of use and wrench it from its context in the form of life, claimed Wittgenstein. Wittgenstein's motive in developing the conception of language games, it should be stressed, was to acknowledge the greater publicity of meaning in use than that which accrues to special justifications and proofs. Richard Rorty (1979) has credited Wittgenstein, among others, with rediscovering the true publicity of intellectual conversation.

There is a tragic irony here, nevertheless. For, although a language game is public to those within it, it is closed to those without. To those without it is private, alien speech. And to those within, relative to those without, it is a private club. Of course a person can learn several language games; most people who work away from home have at least two. Furthermore, research in the social sciences depends upon the capacity of the researcher to enter skillfully into the language games of those studied. Wittgenstein's devastating criticism of Frazer's *Golden Bough* was on target in condemning the analysis of primitive cultures in Western terms that made them look superstitious; all cultures should be understood on their own terms. Similarly, in the arts, each poem or story establishes a language or voice of its own, to be understood on its own terms. Each work of art has its own vocabulary and style, to be appreciated from the inside. Each religion is a whole way of life, a way of having a world, and is not to be judged true or false, good or bad, on extrinsic criteria. By eliminating the reductionism of understanding all things by one's own preferred language, Wittgenstein greatly enhanced the diversity of worlds to which we can have public access. But the untranslatability of languages into each other and the very moving from one language game into another testify to the fact that on this conception the connections between the language games are not public. Not being a part of any language game, the activities of moving in and out are private matters. They are perhaps privately intelligible to will and to aesthetic taste; truly, one's decisions and adventures from one language game to another are among the most important parts of life. But on Wittgenstein's theory they must be private to the extent they are not functions of yet a larger language game. That tragedy is the legacy of modernism, a point akin to Whitehead's critique of specialization.

Although perhaps extreme, there is a great truth in calling our academic specialties "language games." Each modernistically defines a world for its practitioners, with an initiatory learning process and self-contained intelligibility, significance, and worth. Individuals can step into yet other worlds of recreation which may in turn be other specialties. But the specialties are insulated from one another as a language game needs to be protected from imposed external judgments that are irrelevant on its own terms.

The analogical move from language game to academic specialty is not great. May we not extend the analogy farther to the worlds of enterprise? The business world is a language game with notorious deviations from other games. Perhaps there are diverse business worlds, from the local grocery to the multinational corporation, each relatively unintelligible to the other—the far distant ones almost wholly so. There is also the world of government. Of the creative and performing arts. Of local neighborhoods. Of religion. The list could be extended. An individual may participate serially in several or all of these worlds. (Making this point counts on a kind of sophistication among the readers because understanding the point requires their experience of being able to participate in many worlds.) But the individual who participates is private. The more each world is objectified as its own language game, the more alien it seems to those who participate in it. And should we think to find our true selves in our home life, in our self-chosen recreation or creative work, those too now appear as mini-public language games into which we move on occasion. The legacy of modernism is anonymity. We have lost our proper names and are known by the definite descriptions of our language games.

This complaint about the legacy of modernism has been couched in personal, psychological terms, and we cannot make too much of that. After all, there is the special language of self-realization therapies designed especially to turn anonymity into a practical language game of its own. And we may think of ourselves in the Protean rather than Anonymous Age and feel better for it.

The depth of the tragedy of modernism's legacy is not psychological but actually historical and cultural. The self-containedness of the language games of life ruins our institutions and impoverishes our culture. Our communities and cities do not run well because government is a language game divorced from the other things that go on in society. Our schools and universities do not run well because the expectations of teachers and students are in different worlds, because there are few visible connections between specialties taught, because both students and teachers are locked within their own language games and can find no motivations there to engage the other language games that make up the institution. Family life is crumbling (among other reasons) because language games define the borders of generation gaps. The list of institutional harms could be extended at length. Perhaps the greatest cultural harm in modernism's legacy is exhibited in the encounter of Western culture with non-Western cultures. Fragmented as it is, some seem to think that Western culture has an integrity of its own so tight that the other cultures are separate and alien language games. So we either impose our culture's interests on the others, if we tend toward conservatism, or we collapse in a swoon of self-rejecting fawning on the interests of the others if our sympathies are leftist. Thus a truly public cultural world is impossible for modernism without imperialism or homogenization.

One could not conclude from this litany of ills that modernism had no virtues. Indeed its cultural achievements rank with those of any style, for it discovered and created many worlds of great self-contained intelligibility, significance, and worth. But now *our* culture requires *our* responses, and our problems are in large measure the legacy of modernism. Note that this is not the critique postmodernism would make of modernism; the problem here is not the oppression of domineering categories but, rather, that there are no categories or social habits that can knit things together enough even to pretend to dominate. The question is, do the non-modernist cultural movements provide resources for meeting those problems? This brings us back to non-modernist Whitehead, specifically to three points, the last of which recurs to romantic poetry.

IV. System's Way around Modernism

Whitehead's own specific contribution to philosophy was his invention, or perhaps rediscovery, of speculative systematic philosophy. Such philosophy has been spurned or ignored by modernist philosophies, but that speaks all the better for it in the present context. To conceive the specialties of intellectual life, and the different domains of practical life, as language games virtually insures their fragmentation. To conceive them from a systematic perspective is a possibility that suggests at least one kind of important integration. The phrase 'systematic philosophy' conjures up many connotations that are incompatible with Whitehead's conception of the enterprise, however, and they need to be distinguished from his intention.

The first conception of systematic philosophy to be rejected is the one associated with Aristotle and expressed in the nineteenth century by John Henry Newman in his educational views (1852). According to the Aristotelian conception, the various branches of philosophy are distinguished by their objects and are fit together systematically in the ways in which their objects fit together. As soul is related to personal virtue and in turn to social virtue, so psychology is related to ethics and to politics; as the universal principles of reality are related to the principles of nature in this cosmos and in turn to the specific kinds of natural beings, so metaphysics is related to physics or cosmology and in turn to biology and the specific sciences. The difficulty with the conception of system is that the identification of the objects in the modern world is at least partially dependent on methods of investigation; because the methods are not commensurate among the sciences and even among branches of academic philosophy, the objects are not commensurate enough simply to fit together. Whitehead did not suggest that a systematic classification and organization of all knowledge would ever be possible. The Encyclopedia of the Unified Sciences movement was the last gasp of this conception of system, and it died with the demise of simple positivism.

A second conception of system to be rejected derives from Kant, was perfected by Hegel, and was developed with variations by the absolute idealists. It was actually a version of the ontological argument applied to the world and it involves finding some moving principle by which things in the world are construed as parts of an inferred totality. The system is the totality presupposed by parts of the world. In Hegel the moving principle is the extraordinarily subtle conception of negation and dialectic, a conception that charts a way through concrete historical material. In other idealists such as Bradley, Royce, or Blanshard, the moving principle is more akin to a logical conception of intelligibility: the possibility of knowing anything, even the possibility that one might be mistaken, presupposes a norm of total intelligibility. The dialectical difficulty with this conception of system is that it has a logical alternative, namely the method of hypothesis according to which it becomes an empirical or at least piecemeal question to determine just how much integration of intelligibility there is in the world; faced with a wholesale alternative, the "ontological totality" conception of system itself becomes a mere hypothesis and the forces of self-reference then all support its alternative. The practical difficulty with this conception is that it is liable to distort the local areas of life and investigation by forcing them to conform to the pattern of the whole system. Ironically, system in this sense becomes reductionistic, and it evokes legitimate defenses of the pristine integrity of local domains. In fact, the importance of the conception of language games is that it provides a counterbalance to the conception of system as ontological totality (see chapter 5 below).

In contrast to these conceptions of system, Whitehead's is that of a perspective that can be taken on things in the formal unity of which the indefinite number of variety of elements of the world can be comprehended (see Whitehead 1929, part 1, chapter 1). Those familiar with Whitehead's own cosmology will recognize his theory of system to be an instance of his more general claim that the integration of separate actual entities into a world is always located in specific perspectives; a perspective, in fact, is the actualization of an entity that integrates what it prehends in a way unique to itself (Whitehead 1929, part 3; Ross 1983). Whereas, for Whitehead, every entity integrates all its conditions at least at some dumb, dull level that homogenizes and trivializes most of them, organisms with higher phases of experience can select out certain items for high discrimination in conscious awareness while trivializing the rest. Systematic philosophy is a coordinate pattern aimed to lift what is important in all experienceable data into a high level of conscious awareness. It forms a perspective of high awareness on the multifariousness of the world. Whitehead's requirements are well known (from 1929, part 1, chapter 1), that a system be consistent and coherent formally and that as an hypothesis it must be adequate to illustrate all things, and in all of its assertions applicable to something. Three points are implicit but too little developed in Whitehead's conception of system.

The first is that a system is a set of formal categories that is supposed to provide access to any domain or item that might be mentioned. The system itself is so abstract that by itself it contains nothing concrete. But if the system is a good one, any item one might want to consider can be interpreted as a specification of the system. Systematic thinking then, in contrast to contemplating the system, is the interpretive process of seeing how various local domains of life and understanding are specific versions of the systemative categories. If one's particular system is Whitehead's, for instance, one can ask how the diverse elements of human freedom are functions of actual occasions, prehensions, and the like. Through interpretive processes, the system itself is a formal means of access to any local domain. In contrast to both the Aristotelian and Hegelian senses of system in which system contains the parts of the world, in Whitehead's sense the system contains only its formal categories and provides access to intelligent encounter with any mentionable domain in the world. Because the specifications of the system come not from the system but from the specifying of it, there should be no fear that the system distorts or biases any local domain to make it fit in. Thus the integrity and local idiosyncrasy of domains are not only protected: this conception of system calls explicit attention to diversity. The various local domains become commensurate with one another only after all have been rendered as diverse specifications of the same system of abstract categories. Thus system is one tool for surmounting fragmentation, without imperialism.

The second point is that philosophic systems of Whitehead's sort are not only abstract but vague. Vagueness and generality are two species of abstraction, as Peirce argued. Whereas a general category applies immediately without further interpretation to all its instances, a vague category requires further interpretation before it applies. Because, from the standpoint of the vague category itself, the needed additional interpretations can be many, various, and even contradictory to one another, the law of excluded middle does not apply to the vague. This was a major point of Charles Peirce's philosophy.

The importance of the point regarding philosophical systems is that they allow for being specified by contradictory interpretive theories. Suppose for instance, we wanted to explain the psychological mechanism of freedom in terms of actual occasions. The model of psychological mechanisms might be Freud's, or Skinner's, or Sartre's. All of these can be interpreted as specifications of Whitehead's system. Probably they contradict one another and thus cannot all be true. The vagueness of the system allows all to be specifications of its terms, and after the specifications are made it is possible to discern just where they are overlapping, complementary, and contradictory. The system itself makes no claim as to the truth of any of its specifying domains; they must be justified on their own terms. It only gives access to how they relate. This feature of system again calls attention to idiosyncrasy and in addition guarantees against misplacing the locus of inquiry and justification. Furthermore, it provides a logical alternative to the claim that the world must be a total whole (see chapter 6 below); the nature and degree of coherence and connection is an empirical question. The system when specified can even demonstrate the mutual irrelevance of local domains.

The third point is that philosophical system has a kind of human substance of its own, despite its hypothetical, abstract, and vague character. Whitehead expressed the principle for this when he wrote:

We are told by logicians that a proposition must either be true or false, and that there is no middle term. But in practice, we may know that a proposition expresses an important truth, but that it is subject to limitations and qualifications which at present remain undiscovered. It is a general feature of our knowledge, that we are insistently aware of important truths; and yet that the only formulations of these truths which we are able to make presuppose a general standpoint of conceptions which may have to be modified. (1925, 262f)

Although a philosophical system by itself requires modification by the specifications of the local domains to which it applies, the system itself can be appreciated as picking out and relating principles of genuine importance as potentials for a unified mode of systematic understanding. Coupled with practice at specifying it, in either personal practice or the intellectual habits of a culture, a system is a means toward a special kind of experience of wholeness. It is a cultural achievement of great worth, not only practically in overcoming fragmentation but aesthetically in providing unity of experience. The justification of a particular system comes from many sources, of course, from dialectical tussel with other systems, from finding reinforcement in the domains that specify it, from providing vague categories that allow recalcitrantly idiosyncratic local domains to become part of a large view. Systematic philosophy also moves the commonsense habits of thought to become less dogmatic, for it provides a non-reductive tool for allowing any one perspective to be interpreted in terms of others, always providing different angles of vision.

The helpfulness of Whitehead's conception of philosophic system in this age of the legacy of modernism is that it provides a sophisticated intellectual strategy for coping with the diversity noted by specialties. But it does not give a modernist interpretation to diversity that would guarantee mutual insulation of the fragments from each other. Nor does it give a postmodernist deconstruction of all principles of organization and connection. Instead it provides a non-reductive pattern for thinking that allows for apprehending the world as a whole from the thinker's standpoint. The whole is not an objective totality but a formal unity of categories for gaining access to things.

The limitation to the helpfulness of system, of course, is its very intellectual sophistication. A system is accessible only to those who work at it as a specialty in its own right. And even then, the wholeness it provides is *only* at the higher philosophic phases of experience, and the wholeness needed by persons and society is feeling in the gut.

If a sense of wholeness is felt in the gut, that is the work of religion. Religion is that dimension of culture where the images forming certain of the higher phases of experience penetrate down to the lower phases of experience and organize them so as to enable a concrete, though mostly unconscious, registering of the outer reaches of the world in a unified, feeling response. Although religion has its undeniable intellectual elements, and for the last two thousand years has been rightly associated with systematic thinking, its main embodiments are in ritual and spiritual practices that translate its imagery into visceral orientations (Neville 1991a, chapter 10).

It is commonplace to say that there is no genuinely authentic religion nowadays, that religions with fundamentalistic effectiveness of ritual and spiritual practice are much too narrow to respond to the true breadth of the world and that the liberal religions that are intellectually responsive fail to move their imagery to the heart. Without gainsaying that, it can still be pointed out that religion may therefore be the true locus of the problems left by modernism. It is very difficult to do anything about bad or inadequate religion. Although systematic philosophy allows us to take responsibility for our intellectual responses to things, its categories are not the images that move the heart, nor should they, for that would pervert their hypothetical lightness. How can we take responsibility for religion?

Art, however, is the critical human endeavor that does create heart-moving images (Neville 1981, part 2). This brings us round again to Whitehead's discussion of romantic poetry. He may be read as saying that the romantic poets created an imagery for giving expression to a felt failure of science to express the solidarity of permanence and flux in nature. That is, their imagery both formed and gave voice to gut feelings of nature that had been diminished or silenced by the reigning ideas of science. May we look to romantic poetry now for a similar protest and enlightenment?

Probably not. Whitehead's perception of the nineteenth century was of an easier time than ours. In a relative sense, the solidarity and interfusion of nature were already there, already influencing human feeling and, thus, crying out for expression. The task of the romantic poets was thus representational in a way, although we cannot underestimate the creativity required for inventing images that effectively articulate. What is disjoint in our own situation is not a secretly whole nature but an actually fragmented culture. So far as it appears, there is no unity to our cultural experience waiting for an imagery to express it. Rather, what unity there might be will have to be created by the very imagery we await. Works of imagination today must be genuinely promethean. To risk overstatement, our imaginative tasks are not those of a romantic recovery of lost unity but, rather, those of an axial age, an age for the birthing of something new, not even to be named negatively as "the postmodern." Our poet rightly fears the great beast slouching toward Bethlehem to be born.

If systematic philosophy as described is at least a viable task on the purely intellectual level, it suggests certain crucial limitations or requirements for poetic imagination. First, poetry must not only respect but also give expression to the diversity of idioms with which modernism achieved its excellences. That is, it must flourish with specialization and local differences. Second, it must find some imaginative equivalent of the vague, of broad feelings tolerant of contradiction; since art thrives on the focal and specific, this is a conundrum. And finally, the poetic imagination must find a moving place for human life in a pluralized cosmos, for it is only in movement that the unity of vague feelings results in concrete experienced access to things. An embodied gut orientation to the pluralistic world left by modernism would not be a stance but a habit. Romantic poetic images of humankind at home, lost, or wandering, belie the synthetic creative task of being human now. One wonders if there can be other ways of humanity and awaits poesis. Postmodernism is not poesis but reactive power.

CHAPTER THREE

✳

METAPHYSICS IN THE TWENTIETH CENTURY

In the Western tradition the twentieth century ranks with the seventeenth and thirteenth, and with the fourth century B.C., in the originality and daring of its metaphysics. This despite the eclipse of metaphysics in the formation of academic philosophy.

I. Whitehead and the Basic Ideas

Despite the obviously original genius of Peirce, James, Royce, Bradley, and Alexander, the first brilliant crystallization of the twentieth-century revolution in metaphysics was achieved by Alfred North Whitehead. For philosophy as a profession in the North Atlantic community, Whitehead was significant for demonstrating that a conceptual system, in the sense described in chapter 2, arising out of the dominant intellectual and historical adventures of the age and enjoying the latest techniques of demonstration, can address the whole of reality as exhibited in experience (Whitehead 1925, 1929, 1933). Whitehead was the greatest master of this model of thinking since Leibniz and Spinoza.

But for metaphysical thinking itself, Whitehead contributed two revolutionary conceptions. The first is a distinction between what he called "coordinate" and "genetic" analysis and their unification in an integrated theory. The second, following from the first, is a wholly original theory of causation.

Coordinate analysis is the analysis of a thing or state of affairs in terms of the orders within which it falls from the standpoint of the analyst (Whitehead 1929, part 4, chapter 1). Two points are significant about this. First, it expresses the perspectivalism that has emerged as a dominant theme in our century from its beginning in Descartes, namely, that the character that a thing presents in the world is relative to the subject to whom it is presented. A thing may be analyzed or experienced according to an indefinite number and variety of orders, depending on the position of the analyst (Ross 1983). This is not an epistemological conception, as Rorty might believe, that would say that the analyst imposes matrices of orders over things to which the orders are external. It is rather a metaphysical conception according to which the objective reality of a thing in the world is its variously matrixed orders for the diverse positions of analysts.[1]

The second point of significance is that this conception gives a metaphysical interpretation of scientific inquiry as the construction of access to various modes of order through instruments and conceptual means. One test of a scientific theory-plus-instruments is whether things in fact can be ordered in the world that way. But other tests are pragmatic ones having to do with the merits of that way of ordering the world.

With the conception of coordinate analysis Whitehead thus removed all threats that a science might pose to any other orders for appreciating the world, to any experiential insights, or to metaphysics itself. Contrary to the modernist and postmodernist *conflict* between science and the humanities, between Snow's "two cultures," science cannot inhibit, distort, or dismiss any domain of life or reality except by being bad science. "Orders" for any analysis must prove their merits on their own terms, not on those of a metaphysical view. Reductive or eliminative materialisms may make their cases, but the result would still be only an assertion of the importance of the analytical perspectives from which those orders locate things. Justus Buchler has developed the conception of coordinate analysis into a systematic and foundational metaphysical system (see Buchler 1955, 1966, 1974).

Genetic analysis is the analysis of the coming-into-being or genesis of things (Whitehead 1929, part 3, chapter 1). Whitehead sharply distinguished causation in the sense of genesis from causation in the sense of change. Whereas change from one time to another is registered by coordinate analysis, genetic analysis accounts for the coming-into-being of a new state of affairs. Genetic analysis logically begins with the state of affairs prior to the new state and shows how, according to principles of combination and exclusion, the prior state is modified to yield a new one. What a genetic analysis exhibits, however, is existential power, the spontaneous creativity in the arising occasion that drives toward the satisfaction of the logical demands of concrete definiteness in the occasion's character, demands that are regulative of many phases of indefinite combinations and exclusions of the past. "Mentality" was Whitehead's word for the process of genesis, subjectively structured as the intentional drive toward a satisfactory integration of the multitude of conditions out of which the occasion arises. This provides the cosmological rudiments for a theory of human subjectivity involving intentionality, spontaneity, and feeling. In a stroke Whitehead thereby brought within his metaphysical framework the concerns for subjectivity that have found expression in the anti-scientific literature of the nineteenth century and in the phenomenology and existentialism of our day.

Like all great metaphysical conceptions, Whitehead's distinction between coordinate and genetic analysis provides a language for stating with simple generality some basic themes that thinkers have been attempting to express from partial standpoints for generations. But more important, it reunites the philosophic interests sundered by Descartes. Whereas Descartes handed over science and other coordinate concerns to the language of corporeality, which could be understood quite without reference to mind, and whereas Descartes secured the interiority and intensity of human subjectivity and intentionality by reference to mental substance that could not be corporeal, Whitehead captured each side, even in its extreme forms, through a distinction integrated in his theory of process.

Without asserting that Whitehead's distinction between coordinate and genetic analysis is completely or even largely successful, it can be said to determine the situation in metaphysics as follows. Without directly showing the inadequacy of that distinction, other attempts to do metaphysics within only one side or the other of the distinction are fundamentally incomplete as components of the metaphysical dialogue, except for the nonsystematic contributions they may make incidentally. One may mention Heidegger as an extraordinary systematic philosopher who addressed the entire scope of metaphysical issues with a sophisticated version of the subjective or genetic side alone. But his philosophy has not deepened our understanding of nature or of science's inquiry into nature except insofar as they are mapped onto the articulation of *Dasein* as the subjective focus of human affairs (Heidegger 1927). The other side of the coin is the explicitly metaphysical philosophy of Justus Buchler, whose "ordinal metaphysics" is coordinate analysis alone. Despite the noteworthy advances beyond Whitehead in sophistication regarding the nature of complexes of things within orders, Buchler registers the elements of human subjectivity as merely one or several orders among others.[2] One historical test of the validity of Whitehead's distinction between genetic and coordinate analysis will be whether Heidegger's fundamental ontology will be forced eventually to recognize alien claims of nature and whether Buchler's ordinal metaphysics will be forced to acknowledge alien subjectivity.

The real test of Whitehead's distinction, however, consists in the viability of his conception of causation, his second major contribution. For it is through this conception that he presents a unified theory of genesis and coordination in process. Prior to Whitehead, causality anciently had been visualized as a power in the actual to actualize potentialities. With Descartes's sundering of body from mind, no "power" could be visualized in bodily changes and causality in corporeal matters was restricted to regularities of changes. "Power" could be "felt" in mental life as will or intentionality, but such power produced no changes, except perhaps in mental life itself, and did not embody the passage of time in its exercise. Whitehead's genius was to reverse the roles of the active and passive in causation. Action is the creative emergence of a new occasion; it is not exercised by an agent but creates the occasion as its agent. What is already actual is past, no longer active but passive. Nevertheless the passive past is the set of givens or conditions out of which the novel occasion emerges. A thing's "present" is genetic process or arising that finishes with giving itself a date; it is subjectively located in that present. But once having achieved its actual character, it can enter into any other subsequent occasion, subject to compatibility with other things, in the location of that new occasion's present.

A given causal process therefore requires two analyses for complete understanding. It requires a coordinate analysis of the various changes within the relevant orders, as in a scientific account, for instance. And it requires a genetic analysis of the existential arising of the components of the process. Time with causation thus has both a successive and an eternal aspect. Successively, time is the order of changes. Eternally, time is the creative synthesis within each occasion whereby the occasion arises from the chaos of previous actualities to definite existence with its own date relative to past and future. As passive conditions, actualized elements in the past do not exercise power but set limits on what can arise; and insofar as the past is organized into lines of conditions conditioning conditions, it provides limits in the character of vectors of forces. The subjectivity of the present is the locus of the exercise of power and, within human experience, the reality of intentionality; but it has no temporal date in succession of past and future until it has come into being fully; and then it is no longer becoming but actual being, past and passive, which is why physicists and sociologists find no powers but only vectors of force.

A final point needs to be made about Whitehead's general contribution to metaphysics, and it concerns aesthetics and value. In his philosophy, each occasion is intrinsically nested in the world, not an isolated substance or individual. The technical rendering of this has to do with coordinate division. Not only is an occasion itself analyzable by coordinate division, its own constitution is a kind of coordination of all the past elements so as to make for itself a definite and individual perspective within the environing past. According to Whitehead's system, a thing must make itself up by relating (positively or negatively, mainly negatively) to absolutely everything actual; hence the actual coordination of occasion-within-world is extraordinarily dense, though finite and definite. Intellectual reconstructions of this coordination are necessarily far more abstract.

In constituting its own perspective, an occasion gives each past thing a value within its perspective. So, to note that hot sun is "good" for corn in July is to say that growing corn finds the sun important; without the hot sun the corn itself would be less good. The occasion is the sum of the values of the things it positively incorporates and thus has an intrinsic value. Each of the things in its past also has an intrinsic value, for the same reason as the valuable things in its own arising. Therefore, not only is Whitehead able to represent our common sense that things have worth, but he is able to exhibit how a thing constitutes itself as having a kind of aesthetic field. Its perspective on all things notes their individual worths and coordinates them with what, for beings complex enough to be conscious, is a kind of subjective immediacy of nuanced coordinated values.

When Whitehead urged that specialists' training in narrow abstractions be supplemented with fine-tuned aesthetic sensibilities, he was making implicit reference to the fact that the abstractions, no matter how narrow, are representations of a vast actual field of aesthetically coordinated values. The values in the things neglected by abstractions force themselves upon experience, insisting upon themselves, when we attend to the aesthetic rather than the analytical elements of experience. So, like Dewey, Whitehead developed a metaphysical system that surmounts the distinction between fact and value just as it does the distinction between mind and body.

Whitehead's metaphysics deals directly with the metaphysical problems of late modernity, including those that brought rigor mortis to modernism. He dealt with those problems not by totalizing and denying them, or by turning to postmodernism, but by returning to the ideas of early modernity and reorganizing them. He would be the first to say that he was only helping modernity straighten out the strengths of its own resources. Of course, his originality in this was a spectacular advance within modernity itself. We shall return in the next chapter to a more systematic evaluation of his contribution.

II. Weiss and the Problematic of Metaphysics

Although Whitehead has been treated here as a metaphysician, he sometimes called himself a "cosmologist," and for good reason.[3] His categories are empirical generalizations, imaginative leaps tested in experience.[4] Whitehead did not ask why the categories should be the way they are. He did not ask whether he had the simplest explanation (although he tried to have such). Nor did he consider what could be known of things simply as determinate things, characteristics that would hold in any world. All of these crucial metaphysical questions and their consideration push the metaphysical discussion beyond Whitehead's original contributions to the crucial contributions of Paul Weiss, Whitehead's student and one of the editors, with Charles Hartshorne, of the Peirce papers.

Early on in *Nature and Man* (1947, chapter 3), Weiss articulated the nature and relations of things in terms of what he called the "inside" and the "outside." He was thinking there mainly of natural substances and was trying to reassert an Aristotelian notion of substance over against Whitehead's category of occasion. But as his later *Modes of Being* (1958) made clear, the significance of that distinction is to provide an account of determinate being that is wholly general with respect to whatever kinds of things might be under discussion: natural objects, changes, mental objects, abstract forms, categories themselves, or whatever. As Weiss argues, a thing has essential features (its inside) and nonessential features (its outside). The nonessential features are as necessary to a thing as its essential ones because they are the ones a thing has that make it determinate with respect to other things (Weiss 1958, 280–281). To be determinate at all is to be determinate with respect to something else. The essential features are those a thing has that give it an integrity of its own, that integrate its nonessential connections into a reality with its own depth. There are thus two fundamental kinds of relations between determinate things, on Weiss's view. First there are connections, the continuities, the mergings constituted by the network of nonessential features. Second, there are relations between the essential features of one thing and the essential features of the others, the context in which they are mutually disjoined.[5]

Even Whitehead's cosmology illustrates Weiss's categories as a special case. An actual occasion prehends past data as nonessential features and integrates them with an essential creativity producing essential subjective form. Or consider a Whiteheadian eternal object, nonessentially related to other eternal objects when graded in God's primordial envisagement but essentially a pure potential for determinateness in the aboriginal multiplicity united in God's creativity.

Weiss, of course, has not concretized his metaphysical abstractions with Whitehead's cosmology but rather with his own explorations of various domains of reality. His ostensible method of what might be called "applied metaphysics" is to articulate a field first on its own terms and then, when those terms are inadequate for making complete sense, to introduce modifications, special categories, and the like. But in practice what Weiss looks for is the nonessential features by which a thing relates to its environment, and also for the essential features it brings to the environment. And then its essential features have nonessential connections and also essential ones, and so on down. The full elegance and integrity of this mode of applied analysis first flowered in *The World of Art* (1961). But with increasing degrees of success Weiss had used this analysis from the first, beginning with the analysis of metaphysical issues in *Reality* (1939), *Modes of Being* (1958), *Beyond All Appearances* (1974), and *First Considerations,* (1977), human nature in *Nature and Man* (1947), *You, I, and the Others* (1980), and *Privacy* (1983), ethics in *Man's Freedom* (1950), politics in *Our Public Life* (1950) and *Toward a Perfected State* (1986), history in *History: Written and Lived* (1962), religion in *The God We Seek* (1964), sports in *Sport* (1969).

Weiss's practice of applied philosophy is a second major determinant of twentieth-century metaphysics, namely, the development of a system that includes not only the system of metaphysical categories but also its embodiment in various domains of life. The list of topics and books in the paragraph above makes this abundantly clear. Whereas Whitehead's system was his categories, with an informal sporadic interpretation of life and history, most developed in books other than *Process and Reality,* Weiss's system includes the explicit articulation of major domains of life under the leading strings of his metaphysical vision. In this Weiss addresses the challenge of John Dewey to bring philosophy to the problems of people rather than to the problems of philosophers alone. Because of Weiss, if we were not convinced by Dewey, we can no longer

conceive metaphysics as a special domain of philosophy that can be practiced as an isolated speciality. It is not a modernist profession. Rather, it
is a disciplined center of perspectives from which the rest of life can be
engaged.

The cultural significance of Weiss's distinction between the essential and nonessential, coupled with its relevant application in the study
of the rest of experience, is that it offers a metaphysically general conceptual mode for grasping, appreciating, and protecting pluralism. On
the abstract level alone, Weiss's account of the one and the many in
terms of the two kinds of relation mentioned above constitutes the century's most important theory of metaphysical pluralism. William James
was a worthy predecessor, but he took insufficient delight in abstractions. Weiss has set the standard for articulating the pluralism which the
twentieth century has come so much to prize. Justus Buchler is an
equally vigorous champion of pluralism, but for him it consists in the
absolute integrity of the indefinitely diverse orders according to which
things can be analyzed. It does not include an existential account of the
essential features of things over and beyond their location in orders.

Although Weiss presented a more general metaphysical conception than Whitehead, it may still not be general enough. Suppose it is
true that any determinate thing contains essential and non-essential features. Why are there any determinate things at all?

Some would argue that this is a meaningless question on the
ground that metaphysics begins with the assumption of the world and
does not have to explain the existence of what it merely makes comprehensible. But the presumption of the existence of determinate things is
only the beginning of inquiry, not the first premise in explanation. Furthermore, what provokes questioning in any field is complexity: why are
these components conjoined this way? If determinate things as such are
combinations of essential and nonessential features, they are complex.
Therefore we can meaningfully ask why there are determinate things at
all, just as we ask why the sea is salty, what causes inflation, and what
metaphysical identity consists in. What alone does not provoke questioning is utter simplicity, complete lack of regularity or order; chaos, in
other words. Charles Peirce pointed out that "law is *par excellence* the
thing that wants a reason" (CP. 6. 12).

Other philosophers, including Weiss, would argue that the question, Why are there determinate things?, is not meaningless but mis-
stated. Whitehead would probably have agreed with this point of view.
The proper way to get at the issue is by asking, Why is there this particular, or sort of, determinate thing? The answer to any such specific

question could then be given in terms of other things. Weiss, for instance, in *Modes of Being*, held that things are to be accounted for in terms of at least two other things, other modes of being, one of which is the medium in which their nonessential features connect and the other of which provides the ground for the disjunction of their essential features. In his later writings (1974, 1977) Weiss calls these "Finalities" and argues that anything is what it is by virtue of all the Finalities, not only two. But on Weiss's own argument the essential features of anything are precisely what stand over against any of the other things with which the thing may be related. So it is impossible for a third thing to relate the disjoined essential feature of any two. This holds for Finalities as well as modes of being or any other determinate thing. Of course there must be a context in which essential features of different things are mutually relevant. Otherwise the things as combinations of their essential and nonessential features could not be related even through the nonessential features. But the context of mutual relevance cannot be another determinate thing. What could it be, some metaphysicians ask, but a creative power of being that brings determinate things to existence in connection with each other?[6] The being of a determinate thing is its being created to exist in connection with other things. The connections themselves consist in the network of nonessential features.

Yet other metaphysicans—for example, Hartshorne (1948, 1962, 1970) and Weissman (1965, 1977, 1987, 1989)—would say that it is meaningless to ask for an explanation of first principles, even if they are complex, because as "first" they can have no explanation. The root argument here is that explanation must be in terms of principles. But what explains complex principles? Complexity is explained by decisive action, and ultimate explanation is a locating of an ultimate decision; hence the emphasis on creation. Perhaps, however, appeal to locating decisive action as ultimate explanation is only an empiricist bias, set over against rationalistic comfort in first principles. Whether empiricist or rationalist, the debate about the ultimate reference of explanation is a vital part of the conversation.

Weiss has brought metaphysics to the brink of posing once again the classical question of ontology: Why is there something rather than nothing? The very abstractness of his conception of essential and nonessential features is an extraordinary stimulus for mobilizing metaphysical thought from a host of traditions. Put in the language of creation, the ontological question arouses a theistic response from Thomism; consider the outstanding logical work of James F. Ross (1969). It can move process philosophy from the cosmological divine entity of Whitehead and Hartshorne to a primordial ground for process itself, as in the work of Lewis S. Ford (1978, 1987). Expressed in the terms of the One and the Many, the question can arouse metaphysical interest in the Heideggerians and phenomenologists. Even more remarkable, the abstractness of the problem makes responses from Eastern philosophy as relevant as those from the West. Stressing the context of mutual relevance ontologically connecting determinate things, Buddhist and Taoist conceptions of interrelation and interpenetration provide fertile resources (Neville 1982, chapters 6–10; 1991a, chapters 3–5). Stressing the contingency of the determinate on the nondeterminate, Indian conceptions of *atman, maya, cit,* and the distinction between Saguna and Nirguna Brahman are of obvious importance. Because of this, metaphysics is no longer helpfully considered as a discipline of Western philosophy alone but as a field of intercultural endeavor.

On the one hand, Weiss's conception of essential and nonessential features needs to be pressed to a more general ontology. But on the other hand, it needs to be mined for its implications concerning value. If to be determinate is to have essential and nonessential features, those features must be harmonized. The heart of twentieth-century pluralism, expressed in Peirce's theory of Thirdness, Whitehead's theory of contrasts, Dewey's theory of quality and consummatory experience, and Weiss's theory of the one and the many, is that "togetherness" is not accomplished by components being contained or related within some third thing, which would be the monistic idealist solution. Rather, components are together because they just fit, because they harmonize. Harmony is an intrinsically normative notion. There are degrees of harmony as there are ways by which components fit together that differ according to better and worse.[7]

The metaphysical pluralism pioneered by Weiss opens the way for reexploring the ancient theme that to be is to be valuable. Maintained in related ways by both Plato and Aristotle, as well as by Confucius and Mencius, Christian thinkers took the goodness of being and beings to follow from their divine creation. The theme has been implausible, however, for most of the metaphysical theories dominating the modern period, for the moderns have tended to assert either that values are functions of mind alone and are only imposed upon objects by mind, or that the value one thing has relative to another is really a function of some higher reality that relates them, in a hierarchy of higher realities on up to the Absolute that can be characterized only in terms of thought.[8] Contemporary metaphysics takes a decisive step in being able to exploit the normative aspects of the conception of pluralities of harmonies.

Whitehead (1929, part 2, chapter 4; 1938) recognized that value is a transcendental property of all actual things, but failed to give more than a few hints as to the metaphysical character of this. Weiss developed a detailed and sophisticated account, but one which treats value as one mode of being or Finality among others, influencing or infecting others but not intrinsic to them (Weiss 1958, chapter 2; 1974, part 3); this misses, perhaps, the potential profundity of his conception of togetherness, which has to do equally with all the modes.[9] The problematic for metaphysics is to develop an axiological dimension.

Harmonies can helpfully be understood according to what varies when they are altered.[10] If the components that are harmonized are exchanged, then the harmony varies in complexity. If the ways by which the components are arranged together are altered, the harmony varies in order or simplicity. If harmonies are the basic metaphysical character of things, something like intuition must be the basic act of cognitive and appreciative intellect in which actuality, structure, and normative achievement of beauty are entertained. But an intuition of harmony cannot be analogous to those modern conceptions of intuition that were supposed to provide certainty, because what is intuited in any instance is the set of elements noticed as contributing to complexity and simplicity, and what is noticed therein is always fallible and subject to further revision. In fact, if things can be analyzed in an indefinite number of orders, as Whitehead suggested in his conception of coordinate division, any given intuition is always partly a function of the contingent and fallible position of the intuiter, a point made well by Buchler (1966) and Stephen David Ross (1983).

A theory of experience acknowledging intuition in the sense used here, finds inspiration in the work of Peirce and Dewey, for their related doctrines of "quality" were experiential approaches to the problems of harmony.[11] But it would involve a much more far-reaching reconstruction than anything they attempted of the conceptions of imagination, interpretation, theorizing, and moral reasoning that have dominated modern philosophy. For each one of those modes of thinking or experience, and perhaps others, metaphysics would have to understand how the values in harmonies are taken up, registered, and responded to.

Although the root of value may be in the harmony constituting the metaphysical character of any determinate thing, and intuition may be the root knowledge of value, the claim that this is the case is a theoretical proposition. Part of its metaphysical support comes from the extent to which it clarifies, elaborates, and reinforces other metaphysical conceptions for which there are other good justifications. But much of its support comes from its fruitfulness for interpreting our diverse experiences of value. This aspect of the pragmatic theory of quality has been a consistent theme in the writings of John E. Smith (1961, 1968, 1970, 1973, 1978, and 1983). On the one hand, the theory of harmony surmounts the cultural separation of fact and value that has come to be seen as spurious in the twentieth century. On the other hand, it provides an abstract unifying perspective on our diverse experiences of immediate appreciation, enjoyment, or repulsion, as well as on our experience in morals, politics, and the arts, in deliberation and critical evaluation. Deliberation and critical evaluation have to do with imaginatively altering the factors of complexity and simplicity in the field for valuation to discover what they really are, how they harmonize, and what their alternatives are. A metaphysical axiology therefore promises a powerful new resource for reconceiving the normative elements in the professions and in the subject studied by the social sciences.

III. Metaphysics as Philosophy

The emergence of ontology and axiology to commanding positions in metaphysics can be linked as well to a new conception of the place of metaphysics relative to other forms of inquiry. Two models of metaphysics' place were current at the beginning of this century. One, the Aristotelian and Thomistic, distinguished metaphysics by its subject matter—for example, Being and the transcendentals—and set it alongside other subject matters; this view could not sustain itself as compatible with the widespread belief that divisions of subject matters depend in large part on the perspective or method of the inquirer. The other, the idealist model, depicted metaphysics as the most general or inclusive study, containing all other knowledge but not attending to their differentia. This conception, as well, foundered on conceptual relativity.

The new conception, deriving from Peirce's theory of vagueness, says that metaphysics is abstract, prescinding from inquiries of lesser abstraction by virtue of singling out what is hypothetically most important and abandoning the trivial, not inclusively general. Such abstract metaphysics thus does not itself directly refer to the world or any part of it, or impose an empirical unity upon it. Rather, its reference and applicability require intermediate studies to add specificity to its abstractions. *Any* intermediate study would do, as long as it does specify the metaphysical abstractions and as long as it stands on its own merits. *Some* intermediate studies are necessary in order for the metaphysical abstractions to have applicability, and *all* plausible intermediate studies must be capable of being specifications of the abstractions if the metaphysics is to be adequate (see the discussion in chapter 7 below). Philosophical cosmology is useful for the special function of orienting abstract metaphysics to empirical studies, for cosmology is a general organization of categories and principles reflecting pertinence to this world; cosmology in turn depends on more specific forms of inquiry. Metaphysics, on this conception, is nevertheless incorrigibly hypothetical, in terms of both its internal plausibility and its experiential fruitfulness. Yet metaphysics cannot dictate to the intermediate studies, leaving them to make their own cases, empirically or otherwise. Consequently, metaphysics in this sense is not subject to difficulties lodged by deconstructionists, for example, Foucault (1972) and Derrida (1976). Metaphysics as theoretical hypothesis is a way around the metaphysics of modernism that they attack.

If all this is positive, why then has metaphysics been eclipsed in the firmament of academic philosophy? Several reasons may be cited.

First, because of the rise of Nazism there was a great influx into Britain and the United States of positivists or logical empiricists. These philosophers were attractive in their adopted countries both because they seemed to carry the authority of science and because they sounded themes inspiring even metaphysicians. But by turning philosophy to epistemology, as well as by their extreme nominalistic doctrines, the positivists read metaphysics out of philosophy. The enthusiasm for Vienna Circle logical empiricism, however, is over.

Second, there was a sea change in British philosophy from the presumption that philosophy aims to create access to new problems and new understanding to the presumption that philosophy simply aims to solve problems present in prephilosophic or mistakenly philosophic modes of thinking. The view that philosophy's job is to solve problems, or more narrowly "puzzles," is inimical to metaphysics in any but its most defensive postures. It bespeaks a kind of scholasticism of formal and informal language. Unless this sea change had taken place, the early antimetaphysical writings of Moore, Russell, and Wittgenstein would have been dismissed as not yet having arrived at the starting position.

Third, one of the chief reasons for the sea change was the academic professionalization of philosophy, as argued in the last chapter. Philosophy can become an academic profession if and only if it can be taught by the end of graduate school. Locke, Berkeley, and Hume did not become philosophers this way, nor did Descartes, Spinoza, or

Leibniz. Kant's formal education was in physics. But if philosophy is to be strictly an academic profession, it cannot be defined by any broad cultural paideia. It must rather be defined as a set of techniques for solving problems. And this is precisely what happened. Analytic philosophy especially defines itself as a set of techniques for analysis and rejects metaphysics, because metaphysics seems so often foolish when reduced to what can be understood through those techniques. Through its commitment to philosophy as a technique, anti-metaphysical analysis backs itself into a kind of positivism where science or some other field provides the positive data for analysis. Because analytical philosophy has concentrated so much on doing what is necessary for professionalization, it has come to control the profession of philosophy in America. Because the good metaphysicians in America tend to be "fringy" types—and not only because they have been excluded from the center of the profession— there is considerable power in the observation that, *if* philosophy is mainly an academic profession, then it had better concentrate on technique rather than novel concepts leading to deeper perspectives.

Fourth, both analytic philosophy and phenomenology have been concerned to dig down to a trustworthy starting point for philosophy, a conceptually certain foundation. Metaphysics, however, has discovered just how hypothetical it is, depending on experience as probated by many other disciplines. But if it is assumed that philosophy *must* build on certain foundations, metaphysics often mistakenly appears as arrogating an extraordinary certainty to itself, contrary to its claim to a hypothetical status.

Fifth, and paradoxically in light of the above, both analytic philosophy and phenomenology have developed a sense of security in staying very close to the field under investigation, learning its language game, attending to the data, and avoiding abstractions that distance one from the field. A metaphysician's concern, therefore, to invent an abstract neutral language that can be specified in two or more concrete field languages is incomprehensible to these schools. Why would anyone want to do that when the risk of distortion of the original purity of field language is so great? The metaphysical answer is: Because a unifying perspective in addition to the various field language is an enlightening, interesting, and worthwhile experience to attain on its own.

The situation in philosophy today seems far less dominated by the intellectual ideologies and political games of a generation ago. Analytic philosophy itself has begun to acknowledge the name "metaphysics" (or "ontology") as its study of the kinds of things referred to in logic, science, or ordinary speech. Saul Kripke (1980) has made some strong claims for metaphysical realism within the ambiance of analytic philosophy (see also Putnam 1978). Although metaphysicians who consort with White-head or Weiss take analytic metaphysics to be altogether innocent in its uncritical assumption that the problem of reference is a real problem, there is a potential for serious mutual learning.

IV. The American Highroad of Metaphysics

The worth of metaphysics is in the quality of metaphysical work, not in its academic fortunes. That the twentieth century has been so revolutionary in metaphysics will be remembered long after it is forgotten that metaphysicians in the grand tradition were without honor in their own country. Indeed, with an appreciation of these great figures and the problematic they have unfolded, it will be possible to read back through the twentieth century and find a very rich group of travelers who have taken the metaphysical highroad around modernism. These are thinkers who used that systematic angle to comment philosophically on the array of human culture first brought to philosophic reflection by Confucius, Plato, Mencius, and Aristotle.

We should begin by noting the stature in metaphysics of Peirce's great contemporaries who dominated the American philosophical scene in Dewey's youth. William James was the most famous of the group and currently the most influential because of his recovery by Richard Rorty and the neopragmatists. The irony of that current fame is that James's most important metaphysical works—*Essays in Radical Empiricism, A Pluralistic Universe,* and *Some Problems of Philosophy*—are the very ones Rorty excizes from the helpful Jamesian corpus.[12] True, James lacked the technical flair in systematic metaphysics of Peirce or Whitehead. But he had seminal ideas that helped pave the way around modernism and post-modernism, and these are being taken up again to be developed in a sophisticated reaction to Whiteheadian process philosophy by Nancy Frankenberry (1987; see also William Dean 1986, 1988). Frankenberry's project is indebted as well to that of Henry Nelson Wieman (1946) whose sources were James and Whitehead in about equal measure.

George Santayana is known now mainly as an essayist and commentator; surely that is his most brilliant genre. Yet he took seriously the task of showing the way around the modernist preoccupation with certainty and the positivist concern with the scientist's rendition of matter, with a thoroughly materialist metaphysics. At the same time his great *Realms of Being* trilogy was perhaps the most developed aesthetic theory of any of his contemporaries, most of whom based their value-theories on aesthetics. It is possible to read Santayana's aesthetic concerns, particularly in criticism, as a part of the New Critics' modernism; but it is not possible to do so if one joins that with his naturalistic metaphysics. The philosopher most influenced by Santayana is Justus Buchler who develops the naturalistic philosophy (1966) with a clear orientation to the aesthetic (1974). Through Buchler, David Weissman's systematic naturalism owes much to Santayana, as does Stephen David Ross's.

Josiah Royce was Peirce's one contemporary to develop a system of comparable depth, breadth, and imagination.[13] Royce failed to appreciate the hypothetical character of metaphysics, and like Blanshard after him, and many British idealists, sought for absolute realities and absolute knowledge that could not be denied. Yet he believed that action is more real than thought and that concreteness is attained by the individuation of will in purpose rather than by intellectual comprehension; he called himself an "absolute pragmatist." Moreover, he came to accept Peirce's theory of signs and interpretation and believed that the interpreting, purposing community, rather than the philosopher grounded in some foundation, is the locus of truth.[14] Royce's student William Ernest Hocking, though appreciative of some aspects of idealism, was clearly on the road of American philosophy around modernism. His explorations of experience, religion, human personality, society, and politics are models of the reflective American philosopher carrying out a modern agenda in a new time and place with an eye to a world far wider than that embraced by European philosophy. Brand Blanshard, John Findlay, and Errol Harris have carried out impressive studies of the main problems of twentieth-century philosophy within the general tradition stemming from Kant, Hegel, and the British and American idealists; yet all three have interpreted dialectic in ways that steer quite wide of foundationalism, and they have been able to be acute commentators on the range of cultured life. Charles Sherover (1989) has developed Royce's social philosophy in outstanding ways.

Whitehead was influential in many directions. Not counting his influence on logic with Russell, perhaps his greatest impact has been on theology, and this in four waves. The first was his stimulation of the "empirical theologians," Henry Nelson Wieman, Bernard Meland, Bernard Loomer, and their students; these people responded to the themes of process and the immanence of creativity in Whitehead, not to his technical apparatus. But it is one thing, a very kind and liberal thing, to say that everything is in process and creative because that suggests anything is possible; it is quite another to *show* that is possible, and the next wave of Whitehead's influence involved an extremely technical approach to metaphysics. Charles Hartshorne at the University of Chicago competes with Weiss in his generation (both are alive in their nineties as of this writing) as a "compleat" systematic philosopher; though far narrower than Weiss in the range of topics systematically explored, he has been extraordinarily thorough in his approach to God and certain other metaphysical problems from many angles. Balancing the empirical theologians at Chicago, Hartshorne trained John B. Cobb, Jr., Schubert Ogden, and many others, and their students in philosophical theology such as Delwin Brown, David R. Griffin, and Gene Reeves. In the persons of William Christian and Robert S. Brumbaugh, Yale University fostered an alternate approach to Whitehead's legacy, less theological than Chicago's but equally demanding of technical mastery. Of the students of that Yale department, Lewis S. Ford has made outstanding contributions and is perhaps the most original of the Whiteheadean theologians in moving beyond Whitehead's and Hartshorne's conceptions.

The third wave of Whitehead's influence consists of those who have been stimulated to original speculative metaphysics by Whitehead's example and by the liberating power of some of his ideas. These people could not be called "Whiteheadians" in any strict sense but they self-consciously work within a field he opened in the twentieth century and legitimated. Weiss, of course, is the first and still the most outstanding example, and he was at Yale with Brumbaugh and Christian. Christian is a careful interpreter of Whitehead, with a theological interest. Brumbaugh, by contrast, is a daring and imaginative user of Whitehead for his outstanding interpretations of Plato (Brumbaugh 1961, 1962, 1989), his philosophy of education (1982), and his metaphysics (1961, chapter 3; 1984). His originality relative to Whitehead is shown in the title of his major work in metaphysics, *Unreality and Time* (1984). Among the metaphysical students of the Yale Department at this time were George Allan, Lewis S. Ford as mentioned, David Hall, John Lachs (whose leanings have been more toward Santayana than Whitehead), Irwin C. Lieb, Donald Sherburne, and Carl Vaught.[15] Yale, of course, was not the only place for metaphysicians aiming to be as systematic and original as Whitehead. One thinks of the extensive work of Edward Pols whose first major work (1967) was a solid criticism of *Process and Reality* and who, since then, has elaborated his own system. Justus Buchler has already been mentioned. Then there is a large group of younger metaphysicians, some trained by the people mentioned and others educated through the literature, including William Desmond, Leonard Feldstein, Jorge Gracia, Elizabeth Kraus, David Leahy, George R. Lucas, Jr., Brian Martine, John Post, Stephen David Ross, Richard Dien Winfield, Robert E. Wood, and many others. Each has been stimulated by Whitehead, but has not conformed to his work.

The fourth wave of Whitehead's influence, perhaps too far from the source even to be named by it, consists of those people who have used Whitehead's approaches to things, if not always his categories, to write philosophy that self-consciously relates Western to East Asian philosophy. Among the first to do this was John B. Cobb, Jr., who initiated and continues to lead a theological dialogue with Buddhism (1975). David Hall, whose first book, *The Civilization of Experience* (1973) was on Whitehead's philosophy of culture, has put Taoism (1982, 1982a) and now Confucianism (1987, with Roger Ames) at the center of systematic reflection. Steve Odin (1982), Thomas P. Kasulis, and John Berthrong (1993) have done important studies that contribute to the context of world philosophy, rather than Western philosophy, as the ambiance for original and relevant speculation.[16] From the Asian side, Cheng Chung-ying, Anthony Cua, and Tu Wei-ming have brought Confucian thinking into connection with Whitehead, and Chang Chung-yuan has done the same for Taoist thinking. Whitehead's philosophy, along with pragmatism, has the effect of opening up the entire Western tradition, making it permeable by ideas and arguments from other traditions.

A review of metaphysical philosophers in America who found ways around, not through, modernism (and now postmodernism) needs to mention the Boston personalists. Bordon Parker Bowne, the founder of that movement, was an absolute idealist pure and simple, with a strictly European, mainly Kantian, orientation. His disciple, Edgar Sheffield Brightman, however, was far more oriented to the American problematic of experience and defended, like William James and Alfred North Whitehead, a doctrine of a finite God limited by recalcitrant evil. The third generation personalist, Peter A. Bertocci, understood metaphysics to be hypothetical and defended the personalist theory of personhood in God and individuals on dialectical, hypothetical grounds. The effect of the personalist metaphysics was to direct attention to experience and to relate a conception of God to the history of philosophy and to the problems of the mid-century world in ways that embraced the popular imagination and the intellectual elite together. Neither pragmatism nor process philosophy had a set of conceptions that engaged the whole American community the way personalism did; Martin Luther King, Jr., is the best-known of the public personalists. For paradoxical reasons, the experiential orientation of personalism resonates with the existential theology of Paul Tillich, with the result that their union is important for the metaphysical elements in philosophy of religion today.

John Dewey's signposts around modernism are polyvalent. It has been argued above that, contrary to Richard Rorty's attempt to purge his writings of metaphysics, Dewey's metaphysics were central to his own vision and highly influential in subsequent philosophy. Yet Dewey was also an instrumentalist, and it is quite possible to hold to an anti-intellectual, anti-metaphysical instrumentalism. This surely happened in the development of educational theory from his philosophy, and it is what appeals in a strange way to Rorty and the neopragmatists. The split between instrumentalism and pragmatic metaphysics is not a necessary one, however. It has to do with keeping in mind at once many levels of abstraction in reflection, some having to do with concrete problem solving, others having to do with the identification of enjoyments and satisfactions, yet others having to do with reflection of a metaphysical level of abstraction. If Dewey influenced instrumentalists such as Sidney Hook at Columbia, he also influenced abstract metaphysicians such as Justus Buchler and, through Buchler, David Weissman. Dewey did not enjoy the happy fate of the personalists who, when their doctrines were popularized in the prairies, were only understood less subtly. When Dewey's thought was popularized, it was misunderstood as anti-intellectual. Rorty is entirely right when he lifts up Dewey's subtle critiques of much of the Western tradition of philosophy. But the other side of Dewey's subtlety is that he combined those critiques with instrumentalism and a broad-ranging metaphysics of experience.

The intent of this section has been to illustrate the claim that the American philosophers' road around modernism was not a small trail taken by flakey eccentrics, but indeed a highroad down which many distinguished people have walked. A review of those thinkers mentioned above who are still writing, illustrates how vital and busy that road is and how many intersections it has with other important traffic. The argument here has emphasized, doubtless overemphasized, the *American* character of this highroad, even while pointing out the connections. Surely thinkers such as the British philosopher Austin Farrer ought to be mentioned as distinguished metaphysicians who meet the other characteristics of the group discussed here. The chauvinism of this argument, however, has a polemical intent.

One of the earliest chroniclers of the recent "American scene" in philosophy was Richard Bernstein. He offered in 1966 an interpretation of Dewey that gave proper acknowledgment of the metaphysical character of pragmatism (see also Rosenthal, 1986). Yet his works, beginning with *Praxis and Action* (1971) and including *The Restructuring of Social and Political Theory* (1976), *Beyond Objectivism and Relativism* (1983), and *Philosophical Profiles* (1986), have all had the point of justifying or legitimating the American tradition by showing that it is rather like, or at least can be put in dialogue with, the analytic and European traditions. This is as if to say that analytic and European philosophy define the real thing and that the American approach is justified to the extent it resembles it, or can help it or supplement it. As a result, Bernstein anticipates Rorty in neglecting Whitehead and downplaying the plainly metaphysical contributions to the American tradition. Even worse, Bernstein's arguments have the effect of suggesting that the Americans can be just as modernist as the analytic philosophers and the Europeans. That is exactly the wrong conclusion to draw. By neglecting the metaphysical problematic in American philosophy, he fails to see just what a clearcut alternative the American traditions have to the narrowing of modernity in modernism and its deserved rejection in postmodernism of Rorty's sort.

Far better to follow the lead of John E. Smith, a pivotal figure in the formation of recent American philosophy. Although he has worked in many fields and commented on many philosophers in different dimensions, his critical idea was to distinguish what he called the "classical" from the "reformed" sense of empiricism. The classical form was British empiricism, which represents the problem as passive minds needing to be impressed with external data. The reformed conception of experience was the pragmatic one according to which mind is not to be separated from body but to be understood as the guiding element of people in action, corrected by experience and given to imaginative reflection and even to metaphysics in the form of hypotheses. More, even, than the influence of Whitehead at Yale, Smith's interpretation of the freshness and originality of American roots empowered generations of students to undertake metaphysics with freedom from the modernist problematic. His philosophy is an entry point for reading backward to the golden age of pragmatic and process philosophers and forward to the current age of speculative American metaphysicians.[17]

CHAPTER FOUR

※

CONTRIBUTIONS AND LIMITATIONS OF PROCESS PHILOSOPHY

Despite its obvious importance for recent speculative metaphysics, process philosophy enjoys a paradoxical position in the history of twentieth century thought. In the work of Alfred North Whithead, its primary text, it gave felicitous and thorough expression to the insights of several philosophers in France, Great Britain, and the United States who were persuaded of the neglected importance of time, change, feeling, value, and transition. One thinks of Henri Bergson, Samuel Alexander, and the pragmatists Charles Peirce, William James, John Dewey, and George Herbert Mead. In this positive role, process philosophy has been developed by an extremely vigorous group of thinkers with specialized professional societies and a journal.[1] Despite this, and despite the prominence of process philosophy within the American highroad around modernism detailed in the previous chapter, process philosophy virtually has been ignored by both continental philosophy and Anglo-American philosophy, which consider themselves to be mainstream. Consequently, most accounts of twentieth century philosophy relegate process thought to a corner where it is acknowledged but not understood or addressed.[2]

The purpose of this chapter is to set forth several of the major contributions of process philosophy that make it a decisive part of twentieth century thought. This continues the discussion begun in the previous chapter concerning its place in stimulating the metaphysical dimensions of the broad American highroad. Yet Whitehead's position is not entirely satisfactory, and so it should be understood in terms of certain limitations.[3] Hence the contributions are presented in conjuction with limitations. The limitations are not so much criticisms of

Whitehead as indications that the speculative philosophy he initiated
has wider vistas than even he knew.

I. Speculative Philosophy and the Ontological Question

Perhaps the most important and surely the most liberating contribution of Whitehead has been the construction and legitimation of speculative philosophy. Whitehead's most extended discussion of speculative
philosophy is the notable first chapter of *Process and Reality* (1929; see
also 1929a and 1938, chapter 4). For Whitehead speculative philosophy
is the attempt to create a conceptual vision of the world through which
all things might be seen in their mutual bearings of value and causation.
In this, his systematic goals were comparable to the great philosophers
of the past. The method he most often employed was empirical generalization, spread by imaginative analogy across an expanse of topics and
checked by internal logic and external application. For Whitehead a
speculative system has the status of grand hypothesis, vulnerable to correction as are all hypotheses, and its work in part is to balance philosophy in its more analytical and piecemeal phases. In the Preface to *Process
and Reality* Whitehead wrote:

> In putting out these results, four strong impressions dominate my
> mind: First, that the movement of historical, and philosophical, criticism
> of detached questions, which on the whole has dominated the last two cen-
> turies, has done its work, and requires to be supplemented by a more sus-
> tained effort of constructive thought. Secondly, that the true method of
> philosophical contruction is to frame a scheme of ideas, the best that one
> can, and unflinchingly to explore the interpretation of experience in
> terms of that scheme. Thirdly, that all constuctive thought, on the various
> special topics of scientific interest, is dominated by some scheme, unac-
> knowledged, but no less influential in guiding the imagination. The im-
> portance of philosophy lies in its sustained effort to make such schemes
> explicit, and thereby capable of criticism and improvement. (1929, xiv)

Whitehead had a true sense of Platonic irony: any system is a mere
construction, inadequate to its task, yet absolutely essential for attaining
the cultural position of philosophic wisdom, namely the humbling contrast between the constructed wholeness of culture and the finally un-
encompassable plenitude of reality.[4]

Whitehead did not talk *about* speculative philosophy as much as he
actually created one. Unlike the intuitive leaps and biased emphases of

so many of his early twentieth century predecessors, Whitehead's system was developed with such thoroughness that it makes a legitimate claim to comprehensiveness. Furthermore, the detail of its technical internal development is so fine as to put aside once and for all the complaint that speculative philosophy is fuzzy, unclarified thinking. So the first and most important way by which process philosophy legitimates speculative thinking is by presenting a beautiful, thoroughgoing, actual instance of it. The argument from actuality to possibility, from *esse* to *posse,* is scarcely assailable.

The second way in which Whitehead's work legitimates speculative philosophy comes from his analysis of what went wrong with the European tradition. In brief, his analysis was that it got stuck on bad ideas. The solution is not to abandon philosophy's task but to get better ideas, which Whitehead claimed to supply in part. More particularly, the problem for modern philosophy has been to understand the world with mathematical science in it. The seventeenth century was a cauldron of interesting attempts at this, but in the cooling down of the tradition the ideas which became dominant were the wrong ones, or were generalized beyond due measure. Whitehead returned to that period to pick up other notions with which he fashioned a system he thought appropriate even to twentieth century physics and world affairs (Whitehead 1925; 1929, part 2).

The third way in which Whitehead's work legitimates speculative philosophy is by providing an alternative to philosophical modernism, as has been argued. Modernism harbors two requirements for philosophy: that philosophy be foundationalist and that it be intelligible and valuable in a self-contained manner. These two requirements have been addressed in the twentieth century philosophies that have focused pre-emptive attention on symbolic logic, on language, on phenomenological descriptions, and on various existential versions of Kierkegaard's thesis that truth is subjectivity. Like modernism in literature and art, philosophical modernism has claimed the title of mainstream and rejected non-modernist philosophies, not so much as false but as not properly philosophical.

Speculative philosophy for Whitehead cannot be modernist, any more than it could be for Peirce. It cannot be foundationalist if it always has the status of an hypothesis subject to further revision. It cannot be intelligible in a self-contained manner because it necessarily makes external reference to the fields it envisions and unifies, both being informed by them and informing them. Philosophy thus necessarily bleeds off referentially into science, politics, religion, art, history, and practical affairs. The value of speculative philosophy in part resides in the insights and wisdom it provides for those engaged in other fields, not just for philosophers. This pragmatic strain is one of the reasons process philosophy and pragmatism are such close, mutually reinforcing, movements.

The objections to non-modernist philosophy as such have little weight once there is a real alternative to the modernist requirements. Like its near neighbor pragmatism, process philosophy presents a highly developed non-modernist alternative, newly to be appreciated in these days of postmodernism. To the ear of non-modernist traditions, the dire modernist and postmodernist laments about the end of philosophy, about the need to build upon some non-philosophic ground such as science or a pre-philosophic culture, sound like overdramatizations based on an insufficient reading of the alternatives. Freed from the false requirement to live up to modernist conditions, process philosophy can offer itself as a more or less successful attempt to provide breadth of vision and wisdom about what is important in life, a prosaic but perennial task for thinking.

For all its brilliance and legitimating force, Whitehead's conception of systematic philosophy is limited by its inability to ask the basic ontological question, why is there something rather than nothing? What accounts for the being of things? The "ontological question" of course is Heidegger's phrase. Josiah Royce (1899, chapter 2) formulated the question with his distinction between "what" things are—the cosmological or metaphysical question—and "that" things are, the ontological one (see John E. Smith 1961, chapter 6; Neville 1991a, chapter 9).

Some thinkers, of course, take this to be a meaningless question, and therefore believe it to be no limitation to Whithead's system to be unable to answer or even to raise it. But Peirce was right, as quoted above, in believing that what needs explanation most of all is order or regularity. The only thing that does not require explanation is chaos, for nothing is there to explain. Whitehead's system, like Aristotle's, explains by developing a set of basic categories or orders, but it does not explain that basic order itself.

Whitehead did in fact recognize the problem. According to his "ontological principle," anything definite or complex needs to be explained by reference to various decision points that determine it to be the way it is rather than no way or some other way. He stated (1929, 24) the ontological principle as follows: "That every condition to which the process of becoming conforms in any particular instance has its reason *either* in the character of some actual entity in the actual world of that concrescence, *or* in the character of the subject which is in process of concrescence" (his italics). When Whitehead applied the principle to the metaphysical categories, he speculated that they are determined by the primordial envisagement of God. But God's nature and activity must exemplify those very categories. In particular, God must exemplify the Category of the Ultimate, namely, the principle that creativity unifies any many by creating a new unifying perspective which then becomes another one among the many (see 1929, 31–34, 342–351). What accounts for the complex identity of the category of the Ultimate? Nothing within Whitehead's scheme, which limits itself to empirical generalizations about what the structures of things are. Empirical generalizations simply cannot express the peculiar combination of necessity and contingency required of a treatment of the ontological question.[5]

The difficulty in Whitehead's failure to approach ontology consists in his neglect of dialectic in the sense of Plato's practice of creating elaborate systematic hypotheses and then climbing upon them to see their own genesis and assmptions (see Plato's *Republic:* Books 5–7; Brumbaugh 1961; Neville 1992, chapter 7). Whitehead was the master of creating novel philosophic hypotheses and then relating them to the modes of experience they are intended to explain. What the ontological question needs, however, is a method for approaching the ground of definiteness represented by the hypothesis itself. The method of course *uses* hypotheses, as Plato did, but in a way different from their employment as hypothetico-deductive systems. Without a cosmological hypothesis on the scale of Whitehead's, it is difficult to frame ontological dialectic. But we must do more with that hypothesis than Whitehead did.

The Platonic dialectical tradition in the West is a rich supplement to Whitehead's conception of philosophy. But it has an unfortunate bias against which Whitehead can defend us. Beginning with Plato, dialecticians have believed they need to account for order; the reference earlier to Peirce's claim that order is what needs to be explained is an instance of the bias. But what truly needs to be explained is definiteness and complexity. Complexity is a mixture, to use Plato's language in the *Philebus,* of order and the unordered. A complex thing without its order dissolves into its component parts, each of which without its order further dissolves, all the way down. The ontological question then is not just how some chaos gets ordered but also how there gets to be a chaos that could sustain order. The ontological question is two sided: the being of a thing is both its harmonizing order and its particular diversity of components harmonized, its oneness and its manyness, its implicit references to higher unification and also to the multifarious, quasi-independent careers of its components. In ontological matters, the principle of order needs to be balanced by the principle of plenitude. Whitehead's ingenious Category of the Ultimate (1929, 21ff.) is the twentieth century's most succinct reminder of this, balancing the one and the many in the process of creativity.[6]

One reason for harping here on the ontological question is its vast cultural importance. The early Wittgenstein (1922) recognized the question clearly because of the sharpnesss of his understanding of hypothetico-deductive systems as worlds whose explanation is beyond them. But he had to regard the ontological as non-philosophical because of the modernist limitation of his philosophy. Heidegger even more clearly recognized the importance of the ontological question, but found that the limitations of his philosophic method prevented him from addressing it directly: hermeneutics is no closer to dialectic than is hypothetico-deductive system analysis. Both philosophers, as well as most of the monuments of imagination in twentieth century art, music, literature, and theology, despised our age because it lost touch with the ontological question. The failure is not one of mere curiosity but of taking responsibility for our own existence. Not to ask the question is to forsake the true center, home, and meaning of existence. The result is that we are forced to what the Hebrew scriptures called "idolatry," that is, the attempt to make some cosmological part of the world play those ontolgical roles. Among the idols of Whitehead's time were nationalism, progress, status, and social order, to which we have added at least economic and political dominance, professionalism, and psychotherapeutic fulfillment. Philosophy's role in treating the ontological question may not be to package the experience of the ontological question, but, as in most things, it is to frame hypotheses that point out the important rather than the trivial paths to take. What a sad irony that Whitehead, unlike his modernist contemporaries, provided the splendid speculative hypothesis that makes the dialectic of the ontological question possible, but failed to ask it as seriously as they.

II. Whitehead's Model of Nature

Turn now from Whitehead's conception of philosophy to his main philosophic conception, namely, his revolutionary model of nature. The difficulties with modern philosophy, he thought, stem from the fact that its main conceptions are incompatible both with the emerging findings of science and with the span and plumb of human experience. A model of nature should be able to illustrate what it is to be a thing, causation, conditioning relations, and enduring identity through time, particularity the continuous identity of an acting agent. The center of Whitehead's revolution is his conception of causation, which stemmed from a critical observation he made about the dominance of substance philosophy in the modern period. He thought that the moderns construed substances to be units of matter, corporeal extensiveness, that are "simply located" (1925, 71–82). To be simply located is to exist within one's own place and time, and nowhere and never anywhere else. To act, a simply located thing might alter its self-contained nature (if even that is intelligible) but cannot act on others; transfer of force can be a property only of the external relations of things in an existential medium, for only the medium would be common to two things. Hence an agent cannot be said to act on others in any direct way; yet the action of agents on others is what the substance theory is supposed to be good for.[7] Furthermore, a thing cannot enter into another as an object of knowledge; only another thing, a simply located part of the knower, can represent the object known, and all the attendant problems of representative perception and knowledge are born. The cultural result of the philosophy of simple location is personal solipsism and an exaggeration of the importance of the conceptual media we impose on things to connect them; within contemporary philosophy, one thinks of these results in the work of Stanley Cavell, for instance, in his *The Claim of Reason* (1979).

Whitehead's solution was to say that existential causation consists in a thing's coming-to-be by grasping or "prehending" previously actualized things to integrate them into a new actualized thing, its own self (1929, part 3; see also Christian 1959, and Kraus 1979). The raw materials for actualizing are previously actualized things. But they can no longer act. The activity of actualizing is a function of the emergent process of resolving indeterminacies regarding how the previously actualized things can be altered so as to fit together in a wholly definite way. When a thing has resolved those indeterminacies it has come to be as a definite fact and is ready to be prehended by subsequent emerging things. Although paradoxical to thinkers wedded to simple location, Whitehead speculated that things have multiple locations: a proper subjective place in an extensive continuum as determined by their processes of coming to be, and objective functional places in all subsequent things that prehend them. The content of a prehension is not a representation of a past thing but the real presence of that thing as a potential determinant of the emergent. (A representation is a rare, complicated construct that by substitution allows a real thing to be eliminated.) Modernity has come to accept as common sense that it takes an agent to act. Whitehead proposed a contrary hypothesis, that agents are the result of acts, and that the degree of continuity through time is not guaranteed metaphysically by some supposed substantiality but rather is a function of the continuity of developmental patterns embodied in successive acts.

The boldness of Whitehead's hypothesis is revealed in the way it treats actuality and determinateness. From Aristotle to Heidegger, with residues in our common sense, determinateness of form has been taken to be the mark of actuality. To be is to be something, and to be actual is to have attained determinateness out of a relatively indeterminate array of potential possibilities; see, for instance, Aristotle's discussion in *Metaphysics* IX, 1048 ff. Yet there is obviously something wrong with this doctrine, for it slides invincibly into the doctrine that actuality is form, a view Aristotle thought false and liked to impute to Plato. Yet if actuality is form, then the fact of existence is hidden and philosophical truths become mere intellectualisms, as Heidegger complained (Heidegger 1973, chapter 4). Whitehead met this problem with a revolutionary strategy. He argued that definiteness and determinateness are marks of potentiality and that decision is the mark of actuality. Thus eternal objects or forms are potentials for ingression into occasions; and the objectivity of occasions that have reached their "complete reality" is to be potentials for prehension by later occasions. Actuality is the deciding that takes place within concrescence, the process of becoming concrete, whereby the indeterminately arrayed determinate potentials are harmonized so as to constitute the complete determinateness of the satisfied occasion. With the completion of the actual deciding, the occasion slips from self-actuality into potentiality for affecting subsequent processes, for being in the "matter."

Furthermore, decisiveness is what accounts for or acknowledges the "subjective reality" of things. "Subjective reality" does not mean conscious or pre-conscious awareness, and it does not refer to anything epistemological. Rather, as its meaning was fixed in the Medieval period, subjective reality is the reality a thing has for or in itself, as contrasted with its "objective" reality for another. A present actual thing, as opposed to a mere quality, for instance, has subjective reality. Whitehead's contribution was to account for subjective reality in terms of the decisiveness of an occasion: decision orders otherwise merely objective elements for the sake of the ordering occasion's own determinateness. Although only some actualities, for Whithead, have conscious awareness, all have the subjective immediacy of deciding their own being; deciding one's own being is being actual. Whitehead sometimes called things "actual occasions" to highlight his claim that the actual existence of things in and for themselves is a subjective process of decision, of eliminating ambiguities regarding how to integrate prehended objects. He also often called things "actual entities" in order to indicate that, as having subjective reality, those very same things once having achieved definiteness can be themselves the objects of subsequent prehensions, thus multiply located.

Part of Whitehead's genius can be seen in the potential his metaphysical hypothesis has for the mind-body problem. As a finished fact, every occasion is an objective state of affairs integrated with other states of affairs so as to be what we read as physical. In its subjective coming-to-be, however, each occasion has the decisiveness and the intention toward becoming definite that we associate with mentality (Whitehead 1933, chapter 11; see chapter 3 above). It remains a deep problem of course to specify which complex structures of decision making, which nests of complex occasions, which kinds of continuity, deserve to be called "mentality"; Whitehead by no means meant to say that all things have minds. But his philosophy presents the place of mind directly in the center of nature, not in a separate substance or ideal spectator. Because every occasion once finished is physical, there is no limitation to the domain of physical science. Because human occasions can be as mental as we may construe, there is no reduction of mind to matter. Descartes's two substances both have full embodiment in Whitehead's hypothesis, but as integrated aspects of the multiple location of things, not as disjoint and incommunicable. Whitehead thus provided an integrated hypothesis that allows for the full range of physical scientific claims and also for the full range of mentalistic and phenomenolgical claims, insofar as each can be made out according to its own explanatory power.

Two important limitations to Whitehead's main speculative hypothesis about causation and the kinds of things that cause are worth noting here. The first is that the hypothesis cannot account for personal continuity through time, and the second is that it fails to provide a nuanced account of the texture of human life.

III. Enduring Personal Identity and the Texture of Life

The first limitation concerns the viability of his hypothesis for accounting for an agent's identity through time. According to Whitehead (1929, part 1, chapter 3), a personal agent is a complex society of actual occasions, each prehending and thereby including its predecessors, at least with respect to important reiterations of pattern whatever else is eliminated from subsequent integrations. In addition to the overall continuities of inherited pattern, Whitehead said that a *living* personal society has a range of relevant decisive options broad enough that it can be called "free." That is, within the context of inherited character a person can initiate new actions not wholly determined by the inheritance. Further, the ways a personal society determines itself moment by moment (some of them free) initiate chains of events that extend beyond the person; to the extent the events in those external chains are limited in their own options as to how to respond to the person, the person has control over long-range effects.

The chief difficulty in this account is that it can render no clear distinction, among the decisive moments with which the person is connected in tight causal or dialogical ways, between those within the person and those outside the person. Such a distinction is needed for at least two reasons. A person is responsible for past actions intitated by his or her own doings and is not responsible for past actions of others that may in fact be tightly causally connected. Conversely, a person in the present acts with moral consequence for his or her *own* future in ways his or her acts cannot have for the future of *others*, even when the person is more influential on others than on his or her own future. Whitehead's view can account for aggregates and it can account for uniquely configured harmoniously integrated causal chains. But it cannot account for a difference between the aggregative quality of continuous human identity and the aggregative quality of a person's imbeddedness in an environment. It also cannot account for the difference between the harmonious continuities of a person's developing career, including moral commitments to past and furture, and the continuities of causal actions that enter a person from beyond or extend from the person far into the environment.

Whitehead needs to be supplemented by a model that embodies the following distinction between essential and conditional elements (see Neville 1974, chapters 2, 4–6; the distinction derives from Weiss's between essential and non-essential features as explained in chapter 3, section 3, above). An occasion within a person's life is conditioned by all antecedent occasions; but those conditions that are its own past are *essential* to it whereas occasions which are not itself are only *conditional*, however important they might be. Similarly, what a person does at a moment conditions all subsequent moments; but the subsequent moments which are its own future self are *essential* to its present character whereas future occasions not itself are *only conditions* to be influenced, however important they are. The distinction is that occasions within the life of a discursive individual are *essentially* connected while occasions outside the individual are *conditionally* connected; occasions in an individual's own past and future can be conditionally as well as essentially connected (see Neville 1989, chapters 5, 10, 12). Whitehead was correct, over against Aristotle, to see the causal relations between a thing and its past to be of a piece with the causal relations between it and its external environment; nature and nurture are both causal inheritances. Similarly, he was right to see a person's causal effects on the person's own self to be of a piece with the effects on other things. But he was shortsighted in not seeing the need for a further distinction between essential connections and conditional ones.

Paul Weiss was among the first to see this need, and the language of essential and conditional features is borrowed, with modifications, from him (Weiss 1958, chapters 10, 12).[8] Weiss treated the distinction in substantialist terms, however, and a preferable view is that the essential connections have to do with the ways that norms bind the temporally distinct occasions of people. Because the notion of norms is crucial for a discussion of value to come below, let us pursue the axiological claim that norms are the key to continuity in personal identity. Consider the following observation. The conditions of a person's world provide the *content* of his or her obligations, and morally weighted actions might affect anything in that world. But only a person's own earlier occasions can provide moral commitments for the person's own later occasions, and only that person's later occasions can be guilty or praiseworthy because of that person's earlier actions. Why is this? In a given moment of decision, many conditions enter for resolution, each with its own values, its own claims on how the outcome should be structured. Insofar as there is lattitude for deciding various ways, the free contribution of the person is the establishment of the value priorities that order the various claims of the initial conditions. Whereas each initial condition might be a motive for decision, the decision itself is the ordering of the multitude of motives into a definite pattern of priorities which then constitutes the reason for acting. With this much Whitehead would agree, and he would give not just a human-scale moral account but a thoroughgoing cosmological rendition of this situation.

But we ask what it is within the decisive moments that is or produces the value selections. Whitehead's answer is twofold. First, God presents a general pattern of priorities that the emerging entity prehends and uses as the subjective aim guiding the rest of the concrescence or decision making. But second, because the divinely originated subjective aim is just one motive among the many initial motivating conditions, the

entity can pay more or less attention to it, and thus uses its own spontaneous creativity to grade it up or down. By saying thus that God provides the direction but creatures can do with it what they will within
limits, Whitehead sought to defend creatures' freedom from God. The
idea of each entity prehending a divinely presented lure is not intuitively
plausible, however. Moreover it is superfluous. If the creature has the
need to integrate the divine lure with all the other initially presented
conditions with their value claims, then the divine lure is no particular
help. In fact, the more dominant the divine lure and the more binding
the subjective aim, the less free the creature can be from a God who
causes in just the same way other external things cause. It is better simply to say that the person, or occasion, provides a valuational hierarchy
of competing claims so as to resolve ambiguities in what will be important for the outcome, leaving God out altogether. Whitehead may be
right that the actual resolution of value priorities is a function of spontaneous creativity within a decisive occasion. Referring to the earlier distinction, the ordering of priorities is a matter of essential features, and
the competing conditions so ordered are conditional features (see Neville 1989, chapter 5–12)

The discussion here has not yet reached the point of addressing the
problem of personal continuity, for the essential features resulting from
spontaneity treat all conditions as if they were external to the essential
deciding process; the conditions are potential contents but not essential
determinants of the value priorities. In order to account for enduring
personal identity we have to supplement Whitehead's account by saying
that one's own past states enter the emerging present, not merely as conditions to be integrated but also as essential determinants of the value
priorities. Essential features from the past do not determine value priorities in the same way that spontaneous ones in the present do. Spontaneous present essential features are the mark of actuality, making,
creating. Those from the past are ineffective in the actualizing sense;
but among other things they determine the moral worth of the decision
according to how the decision responds to them. If I have made a past
promise and decide now not to keep it, an essential part of my decision
is guilt contributed by the promise; no one else's past promise could
make me so guilty. In this sense, the past state plays an essential role of
determining the value priorites of the present. By converse reasoning
we can say that future states of a person play essential roles in priority
setting because present decisions derive some of their value from how
they oblige or morally affect the future; I can make myself but no one
else guilty. Essential features then are of three sorts: the active sponta-

neous ones of the present, those derived from the past, and those derived from the future, both the latter determining crucial elements in the value of the outcome of a decision.

Admittedly, this is a very abstract account, one generalizing wildly from the metaphors of moral life. The true continuity of a person would stem from those specific norms having to do with the obligations to develop an appreciative and responsible self. The norms most relevant are those governing the obligations to develop and act representatively toward universal personal structures. Promise keeping is a highly refined instance of personhood. Even at this abstract stage, however, it is possible to contrast this view of personal identity both with substantialist views which refer to identity of underlying physical structure and with Whitehead's functionalist account.

Substantialist accounts would have personal identity collapse after a person's body has been replaced by enough artificial limbs and organs; replacement of parts would not affect the axiological account except insofar as they might prevent an essential past moment from conditioning a present one, which would be the death of the person though not of the repaired body. Whitehead's account of identity as reiteration of common patterns is an advance upon the substantialist account, but it fails to distinguish continuities of the individual from continuities of environment. A metabolic pattern relative to an environment is likely to be far more stable than the personal identities of individuals, generation after generation, within that environment. The weakness of the axiological account lies in the infancy of any serious theory of value and norms.[9]

The second limitation to Whitehead's main speculative hypothesis is its failure to develop a nuanced sense of the texture of human life. This should be said with some hesitation, because Whitehead is the most adept philosopher after Hegel in articulating and paying homage to depth and breadth of "civilized experience." Furthermore, it is a customary but unfair criticism of Whitehead to say that he read the nuance of human experiences downward into clearly non-human things. The criticism here is simply that the technical cosmology developed in *Process and Reality* does not go far enough in providing the categories for a nuanced account of the texture of human life. Whitehead did, however, make two signal contributions to such a theory, contributions setting him above the competition of his time.

First, he developed a technical account of a person as an organism containing many different internally coherent chains of causal process, some integrated to form tissues, integrated further to form organs, and so forth; and on the side of subjective inheritance there are chains of language ability, metaphoric development, of interrelating purposes, and so forth. In addition, there are causal chains that enter a person's make-up, that affect it, and that then extend beyond the person; metabolic and communicative processes are examples. Whitehead also pointed out that there are orders of dominance of some causal chains over others; neural affairs dominate the body because the causal information coming to them is exquisitely sorted and because neural actions have precise and significant distant effects. The upshot of this contribution is that Whitehead can model how a given high level occasion of human experience can inherit coherently from a wide range of organized bodily occasions and from other neuro-mental occasions, and can have a physical and communicative consequences far from itself.

Whitehead's second contribution was to give a beautiful and detailed account of the internal structure of a highly complex intellectual and passionate human occasion of experience (1929, part 2, chapters 8–9; part 3, chapters 3–4). The process of integrating prehensions can include abstractions from prehended objects so as to form propositions with reference and prediction, propositions that can be connected with the theory of *Principia Mathematics* on the one hand and with the "propositions" in a sexual advance on the other, those that "lure." Within concrescence, a proposition is a pattern for possible integration of the intitially given objects. It functions as a lure for the feeling at definiteness and as an object of the appetite to eliminate ambiguity in the ways given things can fit together. A proposition is a pattern of priorities, and it lures by virtue of the values potentially achieved by that pattern. With the structure of proposition upon propositions, Whitehead modeled perception, consciousness, imagination, purpose, and other high level human functions. In this he proved the power of his speculative vision to be anti-reductionistic at the same time that its elements are atomic micro-moments.

What Whitehead failed to do in this regard, however, was to provide an account of the structures that link the vast patterns of moments necessary for the highly developed structure embodied in a moment. To speak a sentence intelligently, for instance, requires having acquired a language, a ready and appropriate audience, something to say, and a sense of how to participate in conversation. These in turn are based within a matrix of social, historical, and cultural structures. Although Whitehead acknowledged all these, he did not tie them to his model which thus appears as an atomism too dependent on promissory notes about connective tissues.

Whereas Paul Weiss was one of Whitehead's earliest critics concerning agency, he is also one of the most recent to present a detailed account of nuanced structures of human life that might provide a context for what Whitehead said happens in an occasion. Weiss provides an account of privacy, in his book of the same name (1983), for which Whitehead's closest equivalent is a continuity of high level concrescences each prehending its predecessors with a reiterated mental hybrid physical prehension. Beginning in the womb, a person's privacy develops structured "epitomizations" that Weiss details as sensitivity, sensibility, need, desire, orientation, sociality, mind, resolution, and personhood; beyond those is the structured self with autonomy, responsible action, the I, and a personal locally individuated identity he calls the "idios." One of his most important ideas is that people are obliged to structure themselves as representatives of anyone under moral obligation. Not to structure ourselves as so representative is to fail to be human at a certain stage of development. These are but suggested ideas, briefly summarized, and Weiss's book as a whole is highly recommended. Nevertheless the ideas suggest at least some of the contextual structures Whitehead's theory requires but does not provide.[10]

A proper account of the structures of processive human life needs to show how structures of the sort Weiss has analyzed arise as the result of norms being made binding to and ingredient in the web of causal and mental process Whitehead modeled. The temporally thick structures of personality, for instance, should be modeled in terms of the ways essential features from both past and future impact on essential present action so as to give a value to the enduring person that arcs across time. To act "in character" is to act a certain way because that way reflects the value implications of one's past and future as bearer of that character. To be *forced* to act regularly is not to be in character but to be merely mechanical. Habits need to be distinguished into those that are merely mechanical and those that we exercise because they carry forward a value implication from the past. Although the developmental learning of norm-determined structures may be largely unconscious, the meaning of those structures as defining "the human" consists in their embodiment of the norms involved in the essential features. The structures of friendship, family, economy, war, government, and history are even more complex and exhibit essential and conditional connections (see Neville 1989, chapter 12). Although Whitehead paid comparatively more attention to these than to personal structures, for instance in *Adventures of Ideas*, the topic is still undeveloped. With these sketchy

remarks about what Whitehead failed to do regarding the nuanced texture of human life and what no one else has done to supplement his
model, let us now turn to his contribution to the theory of value.

IV. Value

Like Peirce, James, and Dewey, Whitehead saw human experience
to be thoroughly valuational, affective, shot through with enjoyments,
pains, purposes, and moving episodes (see John E. Smith 1963). But
whereas the pragmatists all testified to the pervasiveness and objectivity
of value, they did not give sufficient accounts of their supposition that
being a thing is ipso facto being valuable. Whitehead did. And the sig-
inificance of his contribution is that it shows a way to get behind the in-
sufferable distinction between facts and values that seems endemic to
modern modes of thought. If his account is plausible, and if it both sustains the respect for scientific thinking that science has so well earned
and lends itself to the experiential hermeneutics, it might be a philosophic inspiration for much of the way around modernism and
postmodernism.

A satisfactory understanding of value requires at least two kinds of
account, how value functions in nature and experience, and what it is
that makes something valuable. Whitehead has a thoroughly functional
account of value relative to his cosmology, and a brilliant but brief and
only suggestive account of what makes something valuable. His functional account already has been alluded to in part. A thing prehended
has a value of its own, which claims importance in the prehender; propositions are patterns for integrating valued things according to priorities; the aim at definiteness in an emerging occasion is an intention to
actualize some definite value. Whitehead's functional account is more
elaborate than this by far, but it may be put aside for the moment to focus instead on his account of what makes something valuable.

In repudiating the fact-value distinction, Whitehead understood
that he would have to show how any fact has a worth. In terms of his
cosmology this means that the process of concrescence in any occasion is
the achievement of some value. Value is connected with definiteness
and, as mentioned above, definiteness is a harmony of order and
chaos.[11] Whitehead said (1929, 112) "harmony requires the due coordination of chaos, vagueness, narrowness, and width." Chaos for him is a
group of actual entities that are not perceived as having any elements in
common. Vagueness is a group of actual entities perceived so much in
terms of a common characteristic that the differences between them are

neglected. Narrowness is the massive reinforcement of a particular characteristic by a wealth of entities so as to produce simplicity of integration. Width is the diversity of functioning entities. The kind and degree of value in a harmony is thus a function of the ways and degrees in which that order maximizes narrowness and width, thus combining a maximum number of different things with the maximum reinforcement of the simple uniting characteristics. A highly valuable order would involve intense contrasts between diverse things held in tension in the foreground, while the background is a chaos of entities vaguely united by overall orienting characteristics.

The apprehension of the figure-foreground distinction, with narrowness and width in the foreground, is aesthetic in two senses. It is aesthetic in that it apprehends the immediate value presented in the situation, not just an instrumental value for something else. And it is aesthetic in the sense that it is a function of basic perception or appreciation: to grasp a harmony as the value it is, however much that perception might be distorted when integrated with other elements in experience. It was in this context that Whitehead called his philosophy of organism a "critique of pure feeling" which supersedes the other Kantian critiques (1929, 113).

Whitehead's characterization of the nature of value is highly suggestive and has much intuitive plausibility. It follows in the tradition of Plato, Leibniz, and Peirce. But Whitehead hardly developed it beyond the elements mentioned above. It needs much further elucidation and, then, as an empirical hypothesis, it needs to be tested for exemplification in a host of areas where we have obvious cases of evaluation. In morals, for instance, do we imaginatively vary the width of components and the simplifications in order to project alternatives with different apparent values? If so, that is a partial confirmation of Whitehead's suggestion. Whitehead's suggestions provide a fruitful first step in unraveling the philosophic complexities having to do with value, a good beginning for value theory. No one can complain that Whitehead did not complete the job. More than a century may be required before a fair assessment of his intuitions can be made.

Whitehead failed to recognize the radical extent of his suggestions regarding value, however. The occasion for the origin of modern philosophy was the invention of mathematical science, an invention that integrated qualitative classificatory thinking with quantitative thinking. The paradigms of mathematical science nevertheless completely excluded valuational thinking from any cognitive status. And therefore Whitehead's suggestion that the perception of a thing includes the perception of its value is paradigmatically incompatible with modern philosophy. His cosmology is not merely an elegant reworking of the ideas of modernity, as he thought, but a radical fresh start that integrates valuative thinking with quantitative and qualitative (see Neville 1981, chapter 1).

Whitehead's process philosophy is an inspired beginning for a new era in philosophy, not a finished achievement to be defended as such. The directions to be urged for its development can be stated in the form of a glossed summary, in reverse order, of the points made here.

1. Recovery from the modern period's separation of cognizable fact from value requires a thoroughgoing discussion of axiology, as applied particularly to thinking. The scientific and imaginative gains of modernity do not need to be abandoned but rather set within a new philosophic context—one, incidentally, which might also befriend the philosophic contributions of thinkers and traditions outside the European and North American pale. Whitehead's brief value theory is an extraordinary but undeveloped beginning.

2. Philosophy in the modern period has failed to deal adequately with the subtle textures of human life because thinkers have followed one or the other but not both of Descartes's identifications of reality: corporeal substance or mental substance. Materialists have tried to reduce mind to matter and have lost the living waters of mind. Idealists have tried to render body from the perspective of mind and have lost the body's perspective. Whitehead's brilliant response was to present a naturalistic account of life in which the physical and mental are different, but intrinsically related in the larger whole of process. Whitehead, however, did not press far beyond the general cosmological statement to develop an account of the nuances of life with the use of his natualistic model. Beyond an axiology of thinking we need extensive naturalistic explorations of the structures of personal and social affairs.

3. Whitehead achieved his naturalistic integration of Descartes's bifurcated substances with a new cosmological model that emphasizes the rhythmic pulse of actualized, objective, physical facts on the one hand and actualizing, subjective (mental in higher forms) concrescing occasions. The rhythmic pulse militates against subjective continuities from one occasion to the next, and it renders the continuities of personal identity difficult to distinguish from continuities with other things. A supplementary account of personal identity thus is called for, something in the direction of the distinction between essential and conditional features.

4. The entire enterprise of philosophy that Whitehead initiated is speculative, and he contrasted speculative philosophy with critical philosophy (1938, 173 f.). The latter, according to him, limits itself to a verbal analysis of what is known, whereas the former seeks to extend what is known by speculating larger interpretive contexts for it. Given the sea-changes in the world's cultures, speculative philosophy is needed more than ever. But Whitehead did not delve deep enough in this instance. Useful as far as it goes, his model of speculative philosophy stops short of the dialectic needed to address the ontological question, a question by which, in many diverse and often incompatible ways, all the major traditions of the world measure spiritual vitality, a question by which contemporary Western culture finds itself lacking. The ontological question, in practical cultural terms, is about a spritiual or religious dimension to things. Whitehead was one of the few recent philosophers to recognize that philosophy's affiliation with religion is as close as, though different from, its affiliation with science. His own strength was in exploiting the scientific connection, for that was the source of his revolutionary cosmological model. His approach to theology, however, also was controlled by scientific conceptions of the use of hypothesis and for this reason was undialectical. Without dialectic, ontology is impossible. So speculative philosophy needs to be enhanced with the critical modes of dialectic appropriate for the ontological question.

CHAPTER FIVE

✳

HEGEL AND WHITEHEAD ON TOTALITY

The concept of totality seems to be central to systematic philosophy. Rightly or wrongly, both modernists and postmodernists take it to be central when they reject metaphysics, speculation, and system. The concept of totality marks the scale or domain of things to be understood and is thus related to the problem of identifying reality. It suggests an order disposing the things to be understood and hence is intimately bound up with the problem of the one and the many. Because the form of philosophic understanding in some sense or other needs to be adequate to the subject matter, the concept of totality thus bears upon the notion of philosophic system.

But the concept of totality is problematic in the extreme. Kant knew the concept was in trouble when he asked whether a totality of things is finite or infinite and recognized that coherent justifications could be offered for each of the opposing answers (1787, B 435–599, "The Antinomy of Pure Reason"). In the twentieth century we have recognized another grave difficulty, namely, that the claim that such and such constitutes a totality is often just a fiction, an unsupported assumption that if there are fragments there must be a whole.[1]

Because metaphysics is so central to the way around modernism, and because metaphysics is both speculative and systematic in some sense or other, it is necessary to see whether systematic philosophy truly requires that a systematic perspective hold that things are united in a totality. The thesis here is negative: system does not entail totality. Chapter 6 will present an idea of system that illustrates non-totalistic thinking. This chapter will examine the use that two major systematic philosophers, Hegel and Whitehead, made of the concept of totality. Hegel is important because he was the great genius of modern philosophy, internalizing Kant's arguments against metaphysics and then doing what Kant said could not be done, and more. When modernist philosophers say that philosophy needs to have a *new* start and establish *new* foundations, they usually mean it has to get over Hegel, or some latter-day representative of Hegelianism. The importance of Whitehead is that in many respects he is a major guide down the highroad around modernism. If he too requires a notion of totality that is unacceptable, then we must be clear how to amend his approach in that regard.

Because in a brief compass it is impossible to do a thorough study, the selective principle here will be to focus on those elements of the discussion that bear particularly on our own possibilities regarding systematic philosophy. The conclusion will be that neither Hegel nor Whitehead is able to articulate a conception of totality adequate to the use to which he put it. As a result, we can sustain conceptions of "world" and "system" only if they do not require conceptions of totality, at least so far as Hegel's and Whitehead's suggestions go. Chapter 6 will make the positive argument.

Although every philosopher has a (sometimes unwitting) selective focus when writing about other philosophers, the selective focus in this chapter warrants a further introductory remark. The agenda of this book is to develop a practice of systematic thinking that does not presuppose totality in either reality or in a system representing it. Neither this agenda nor its negation—the assertion that reality or a representative system is totalized—was the exact agenda of Hegel or Whitehead. The concern about totality is one they did not share directly. Hence the questions put to their philosophies here are ones they themselves did not exactly ask, and the responses they are represented as making are to some degree uncharacteristic of their thought. Hegel and Whitehead scholars may see the arguments here as distortions or oblique representations of the way their respective masters saw things. Yet philosophic discussion requires responding to alien questions legitimated by the questioner, not the responder. The texts of Hegel and Whitehead—even more, the arguments within their own agendas—set strict controls on what we can represent as their side of the discussion. Nevertheless, their thought must have a new look, speak in a new voice, when brought into conversation with new concerns. One element in the greatness of both of these thinkers is that their philosophies increase in interest as they are reshaped in the ongoing dialogue.

I. Hegel: Finite and Infinite

The concept of totality and its thematic use pervade Hegel's philosophy. Hegel's *thematic* use of the concept totality is the synthesis of unity and plurality, the categories of quantity. Hence for Hegel any issue concerning the one and the many brings a use of the concept of totality. In a more general sense, totality is the analogue of the synthesis or reconciliation of any positive element with what denies or extends out from that element. Following Kant's Table (1787, B 106), totality is allied with limitation (which is the synthesis of the qualitative categories of reality and negation), with community (which is the synthesis of the relational categories of substance and causation), and with necessity (which is the synthesis of the modal categories of possibility and existence). Thus for Hegel, totality is determinate or limited, inclusive or a matter of inter-relatedness, and necessary—a function of infinite spirit. (See Hegel 1833, 201–332, for one of his best discussions of this topic, including his analysis of Kant.) The analysis here will be limited to two roles for the concept, that involving the infinite-finite relation and that involved in the movement of negative dialectic. Despite the fact that much that is important will be left unsaid, those two roles complement and correct one another.

One commonly recognized aspect of Hegel's genius is his claim that, if one can set limits to a thing or domain, in some sense the setting of limits takes place from a position transcending those limits. Hence, Hegel could reject Kant's critical limitation of reason as disingenuous: the faculty exercising the critique is, if not reason, then as much like reason as the true author of the *Illiad* and *Odyssey* is like the mythical Homer, being blind himself and also called Homer. Hegel's principle is that if a thing is determinate it is determinate with respect to something outside itself. Therefore the determinateness of one thing requires those other things with respect to which it is determinate that, also being determinate, implicate others until all possibly related things are involved in what Quentin Lauer calls a "totality of interrelatedness."[2]

Lauer also points out that, because of the above argument, for Hegel it is the infinite which is the primary bearer of determinateness. No finite thing is determinate by itself, and only the infinite contains all determinations. Hegel's concept of the infinite is extraordinarily complex and problematic but the discussion here will be limited to one issue concerning the infinite and determinateness. Whereas finite things are determinate in reference to external things which bound them, by virtue of what is the infinite itself determinate? There are two main ways of responding to this question.

The first is to stress the difference between finite and infinite reason. Although it is the character of finite reason to grasp determinateness in terms of contrast—and finite objects are so to be grasped—infinite reason constitutes its own determinateness by its very movement of totaling up the finite determinations. The infinite's determinateness consists in its determinate contents. In making this point Hegel stressed in many contexts the necessity of actual knowledge of the determinate steps of spirit, not a romantic absolute like the night in which all cows are black. Denying a wholly transcendent infinite, Hegel asserted the necessary and actual character of spirit which is infinite because it is determinately finite, and finite only because it is an infinite totality of finite interrelatedness.

Now let us consider what may seem a stupid question. Is the infinite a finite or infinite totality? Put another way, noting the difference between bad and good infinites, is there a finite set of categories constituting the infinite *Geist* (Hegel 1830, Paragraph 94)? Is the chart of the Hegelian system from the back of Walter Stace's *Philosophy of Hegel* a possible enterprise? Is there a highest order of orders, the inclusive absolute order, which is the finite totality? The question these many formulations ask is stupid, of course, because it misunderstands Hegel's idea of the notion as the infinite philosophical category or category of *Geist*. An infinite category is determinate because of what it integrates or interrelates, not because of what it relates to externally. In fact, as Hegel's dialectic shows, an infinite category that still has an external neighbor is not yet fully determinate, and reason moves on to the more inclusive whole.

Stupid or not, the question seems inevitable if one is interested in totality. What if things are not fully interrelated but only fragmentarily related, with little necessity, no inclusive order, with partial and idiosyncratic determinateness? Fragmentary relatedness, however, does not appear viable for Hegel, for whom the higher notion always functions as a "third term" to integrate and transcend its relatively finite contents.

Let us examine more closely this third term, for it is at the heart of the claim that the infinite is a totality.[3] Suppose by hypothesis that the third term has no character of its own by virtue of which it integrates its contents. Suppose instead that the contents simply fit together by virtue of their own natures. In this case there really is no third term, no higher infinite notion, only the good luck of a perfect fit of otherwise independent contents. But if this is so, philosophy suddenly becomes drastically empirical, because it would have to look at each case to see whether the contents fit together. And since we know, for Hegel, that the diversity comes through the process of contradiction, the contents are highly unlikely to "just fit" together. The point of the third term, of the notion, in many instances is to reconcile what is otherwise incompatible. So we must reject this hypothesis and suppose that the third term has a determinate character of its own by virtue of which it interrelates or totals up its contents.

Consider how the character of the third term is determinate. Although its determinateness arises genetically from its function of interrelating and thereby determining its relatively finite contents, the logical status of its determinate character cannot be reduced to the aggregate determinations of its contents. Rather, the aggregate determinations of its contents call for something new, for some ordinary work to be done, for a new determination that will bring them truly into an infinite whole and fulfill their own full determinate natures. To say that the determinateness of the new element in the third term arises from its determinate contents is empty. As Hegel would argue, something actual has to happen, something particular as well as universal. If nothing happens there is no totality, only an aggregate; and even an aggregate may be impossible. Then with respect to what is the new element in the third term determinate? There seem to be two possibilities: the contents that it interrelates, or something yet external and on its own logical ontological level.

Can the new element in the third term be determinate with respect to its interrelated contents alone? No, for two reasons. First, it cannot determinately be itself over against its contents precisely because its nature comes from making them its contents. Its very function is to transform the contents into a new whole which is its own self. We are in this case referred back to the previous dilemma: the whole is either a mere aggregate or a seamless new thing, with the determinateness of the whole explained in neither case. The second reason the new element in the third term cannot be determinate with respect to its contents is that if it were it would have to be related to its contents by yet another third term. That is, the very dialectic urging that an infinite is required for the finite to be fully finite, would interpose a mediation between the determinate contents and the determinate third term that integrates them, and then mediations between all those joints, ad infinitum. Yet we know that for Hegel such a bad infinite regress is just the consequence that is supposed to be ruled out by absolute infinite reason.

It must be the case, then, that the determinateness in the new element in the third term consists in a contrast with something still external, on its own logical or ontological level. This gives determinateness to the totality of the infinite, even though it admits that the totality is only relative, not inclusive of that external thing with respect to which the third term, now the infinite absolute notion, is determinate. Hegel would embrace this solution, if reluctantly, because it acknowledges his stress on actuality. The actual achievement of the notion is determinate because it stands in contrast to the possibilities it excludes. There are two unsettling consequences of the solution, however. One is that the contrast between the actual and merely possible is a meager finite notion: the infinite is not supposed to have a possible alternative. The other is that the claim that the infinite notion is always determinate with respect to something external, and therefore always only a relative totality, commits us to a bad infinite of progression from one infinite notion to the next.

To recapitulate: infinite reason is a totality by virtue of being a third term that interrelates its determinate contents. The third term is determinate either because its contents are determinate or because of its own character. But the contents cannot be fully determinate without the new contribution of the third term. How is the third term's contribution determinate? Not by virtue of its contents, and so by virtue of contrasting with what is external to it. But if something is external, the third term is not a totality in the required respects. So Hegel's conception is problematic.

II. Negative Dialectic:
The Trick of the Modernist and Postmodernist

Let us then leave the theme of totality in the infinite-finite relation and seek to complement it with an inquiry into the role of totality in negative dialectic. In the infinite-finite relation, totality's role is to sum up or totalize its antecedents, to be the crown of dialectic, as it were. In negative dialectic, however, the role of totality is to present a situation as whole enough to negate, as something firm and complete enough to step on and away from. The totality is necessary in order to move beyond.

This point is worth stressing in connection with the dialectic of history, its paradigmatic instance for Hegel. For there to be a spiritual progression from the middle ages to the modern period, for example, the former must be sufficiently whole and integrated, a totality, for negation to be possible. True, the totalization might be accomplished only in the achievement of the successful negation. That is, the superseding stage gives the earlier a coherence it did not have until transcended. The reason or *Geist* which accomplishes the dialectical moves achieves its own actuality in the very process of negating the antecedent and fulfilling itself as a successful negation. Whereas some of its own contents might be merely accidental, they are rational because of their roles in the dialectic of negation.

If *Geist* can be modeled on the negative dialectic of history, then we have a new opportunity to address the question of the determinateness of the totality. We may say that the transcending stage is determinate with respect to the stage it transcends precisely in those respects in which it negates the possibility of the transcended stage. The actuality of the moment, then, is determinate not with respect to a possibility that it excludes, but with respect to a past actuality that it negates and subsumes. There may well be many elements in the moment that are not determinate, either with respect to the past or with respect to what is rational in the moment itself. But they might become determinate when the moment itself is totalized and negated by its own executioner. Of course the moment will be negated itself because of the contradictions flowing from the way it achieved negation of its own antecedents. But those contradictions do not reconcile themselves automatically. Movement of the spirit is labor and freedom.

Note here that the concept of totality has a different form in connection with negative dialectic than it has in connection with the infinite-finite relation. For the latter, totality is an inclusive container. For the former, the totality has reason as a selective principle. Reason, which proceeds with necessity, distinguishes within a situation between the truly actual and the adventitious (see Altizer 1967, 1977, 1980, 1985, 1990). This is such an important point that is is worth quoting Hegel, from the "Introduction" to the *Lesser Logic:*

> In the preface to my Philosophy of Law ... are found the propositions:
> What is reasonable is actual; and
> What is actual is reasonable.
> ... For their philosophic sense, we must presuppose intelligence enough to know, not only that God is actual, that He is the supreme actuality, that He alone is truly actual; but also, as regards to the logical bearings of the question, that existence is in part mere appearance, and only in part actuality. In common life, any freak or fancy, any error, evil and everything of the nature of evil, as well as every degenerate and transitory existence whatever, gets in a casual way the name of actuality. But even our ordinary feelings are enough to forbid a casual (fortuitous) existence getting the emphatic name of an actual; for by fortuitous we mean an existence which has no greater value than that of something possible, which may as well not be as be. ... In a detailed Logic I had treated

amongst other things of actuality, and accurately distinguished it not only
from the fortuitous which after all has existence, but even from the cog-
nate categories of existence and the other modifications of being. (Hegel
1830, 10 ff.)

For Hegel, totalization in reason works by way of distinguishing between
the rationally important, that is, the necessary as viewed from the standpoint of the work of dialectical negation, and the rationally unimportant
or trivial. This helps us see how totalization might be accomplished as
much in the negating of a moment as in the moment's own work of negating its antecedents.

In Hegel's dialectical systematic philosophy, totality in world or in
philosophic representation does not suppose that there is some highest
category containing all things perfectly related, but only that there is a
rational principle that totalizes the things that have bearing necessarily
on the principle itself. On the one hand this is a great advance on the
popular conception of system as total container. It expresses wisdom's
task of distinguishing the important from the trivial. We should learn
from Hegel that philosophic system means attaining to a comprehensive
view of things ordered as to their importance, with critical reflection on
the implied judgments of importance. On the other hand, Hegel's conception of reason, with its attendant conception of totality, contains a fa-
tal flaw.

Consider the people, events, and institutions that are "fortuitous"
on Hegel's view. For him they have existence, but only as appearances.
Moreover, they have no necessity as conveyed through their rational successors. That is to say in the latter instance, when the onrush of history
totalizes their moment to negate it, they are not included. The selection
of what is important does not include them. Considering the difference
they make to subsequent history, they might as well have not happened.
As Hegel said, they have the status of mere possibilities whose existence
is so accidental that history would be the same had they not occurred.
This means that the victims of history Hegel described so pathetically in
his "Introduction" to the *Philosophy of History* (Hegel 1840, 10 ff.) are
non-entities. So are the institutions that failed without a place in the
larger rational order. So are the events that seem so dear and important
to their participants but that miss the dialectic. The pathos is that those
very accidents might have been heroic elements whose personal passions
coincide with the *Geist* if the subsequent movement of history had in fact
totalized them into the rational structure of their moment. There is
nothing intrinsic to the accidents themselves giving them low value.

Rather, they are cast into limbo and forgotten because of the actual direction taken by history. Nor is it the case that the dialectic was necessitated to go the way it did. There could well have been other ways of totalizing their moment that would have given them prominence. Spirit is free in this regard, and it is at this point that spirit reduces to force. Its force consists in its power to denude things of actuality by denying them a place in reasonableness.

Even more unfortunate for Hegel's view is that there is more than one way to tell the story of history. That is, each pocket of order, if you will, projects its own perspective over the past and future, a perspective that determines which elements are necessary and actual relative to it, and which can be ignored as accidental. Hegel's reading of Western history seems plausible when reinforced by those institutions he sees as rational. But it surely is Whig history. History from the perspective of the women's movement is very different, with many of Hegel's heroes slipping into fortuitousness. Consider history of science from the standpoint of the alchemical or magical traditions. Consider the importance of European history of philosophy itself from the standpoint of Chinese scholars approaching it with the values of their own tradition.

If reason reduces to force in arbitrarily totalizing the moments of its negation, how much more arbitrary is it if there is not one reason, one *Geist*, but as many as there are pockets of order? As the history of Hegel's thought has shown, his grand historical synthesis could not withstand the creation of alternatives. Kierkegaard and Marx in their own ways preserved something of the form of Hegel's dialectic, but with a radically different story. Emerson, Nietzsche, and Peirce transformed even the dialectical form, and the non-Western thinkers whom we now must take seriously present incommensurable visions.

With regard to the coherence of system, at least in the historical sphere, we must abandon the dream of totality and necessity and acknowledge instead that, as far as we know, there are many pockets of order, sometimes interrelated, sometimes not, often irrelevant and indeterminate with respect to each other, passing with tangential connections, partially overlapping, sometimes in conflict but even then not in coherent agreement concerning what the fight is about. History has many streams, many traditions, rising and falling, entering and leaving prominence, going underground to emerge with new meanings in unexpected places, rarely with the coherence to totalize a period.

Where does this leave us with regard to the question of totality? The world seems to be not one totality but many, and even some of the many are not tightly total. Philosophic system, then, seems wholly relativized, with each pocket of order evoking its own system, its own rationale, and with no particular hope of a super-system. No wonder systematic philosophy is unpopular these days, and even seen as a threat to the integrity of individual pockets of order that might have their own rationale, their own language game.

Of course it is the modernists and postmodernists who insist that, whatever it is, metaphysics or systematic philosophy must be totalistic. This insistence itself is a totalizing of the philosophic tradition. Like Hegel's human "accidents," metaphysicians who do not totalize, who are fallibilists and committed only to pockets of order, do not register in the modernist and postmodern story. A counterargument to the modernist and postmodernist story is another story interesting enough to take seriously.

Before leaving Hegel, however, let us recall his insight that system requires a discrimination of the important of the trivial. System results from a selective ordering of things according to the forms that structure their importance. If things can be systematized, it is because the things themselves have selectively coherent importance. And if this system can be recognized philosophically it is because we have the capacity to appreciate and represent that selection of importance. But how can our pockets of order, each with its own strain of importance, be brought into a system? Is there any sense in which they can be totalized without fictions? To answer this question we turn to Whitehead, whose philosophy is built around the notion of importance.[4]

III. Whitehead: Totality in Experience

Like Hegel, Whitehead conceived the processive structure of reality to be continuous with the experiential structure of cognition and philosophy. Knowledge of nature is possible because experience participates in all the elementary structures of nature and, in a sense analogous to Hegel's, human knowing is a complication, enrichment, and fulfillment of processes extending through the world. More than Hegel, however, Whitehead stressed the point that the selective principles in accumulative processes are valuative: his theme was not the necessity of reason but the appreciative valuation of experience.[5]

The data entering experience, for Whitehead, are diverse and disjunct.[6] The activity of experiencing is to order these data so as to make up a coherent individual occasion. At least two kinds of negation are involved in experiencing: the exclusion of data from having any role in the occasion, and the dismemberment of data so as to recombine their elements in new ways. There is also positive creativity in experience insofar as novel forms arise from the recombination. Spontaneous new existence provides a subject entertaining and re-actualizing the given data. Among the creative novelties are intentions toward the future in the case of high level occasions such as are found in animal life.

Whereas it might seem as if Whitehead used the model of human experience to explain the most elementary particles, that is mere appearance. Rather, he constructed a model of elementary particles such that, by internal complexification and external combination and nesting, things such as people could be modeled, he hoped. Whitehead thus rejected Hegel's sharp distinction between nature and spirit, not because of exaggerations of spirit but because Hegel accepted too much of the mechanistic philosophy of nature for Whitehead's taste. Whitehead's project thus requires showing just what internal complexifications and external combinations and nestings are involved in the "higher" forms of experience such as the human. He did not do much of this himself and tended to leap to human functions by analogy with the simple processes modelled in single occasions. He does present extraordinary resources for that project, however.

In both the negative elements and positive creativity the main activity is the creation of orders that grade the data according to importance for the emerging occasion. Masses of data are relegated to triviality while certain other data are featured as so important that their structures set the conditions to which everthing else acceptable in experience must conform. The norms governing importance within a single actual occasion are those that have to do with that occasion becoming wholly definite, that is, determinate with respect to every possiblity and fixed in some position in an existential medium.

It might seem as if the valuing and grading that take place in a moment of process, for Whitehead, are arbitrary functions of the occasion's own need for definiteness. But Whitehead insisted (and here lies perhaps his greatest philosophical contribution) that the data entering experience are themselves achievements of value, and that therefore their own value is grasped appreciatively in the experience of them. They contribute their worth to that which they effect. Now of course the instrinsic worth of a datum might be denied by an occasion that experiences it. This is possible, however, only by dismemberment; the experiencing occasion must transmute the presented value in the datum with some substitute of lesser or different value, as when racists treat others as mere types rather than as full human beings. Distortion of value thus requires positive work, and we may suppose that only sophisticated occasions of experience are capable of it. Unsophisticated occasions in inanimate nature either reject things completely or accept them at pretty much face value. Whitehead's point here is that the value in a thing is given first by the values in the conditions that enter into it, and only derivatively and on the margins by its own creative capacity to loose and join.

The fundamental continuity of value undergirds the massive structures of importance in the world: ancient rituals of human behavior, the more ancient hills, even the highly complicated organic functions of the human body (Allan 1986). The grades of importance and triviality embodied in one thing are likely to be reiterated in those things into which it enters as a condition. Put the other way, the readiness of one thing to be conditioned by another depends on its readiness to accept much of the potential condition's expression of importance. The solidity of the world and the intricate workings of natural law express this mutual reinforcement of valuational embodiments from one domain of reality to another. The order of the world, for Whitehead, depends on the mutual resonance of valuations.

Would Whitehead say that there is a single encompassing order of the world, that the world is a totality composed of a univocal, complex supervaluation? Or might he admit that there are only pockets of order? This question must be divided into whether the world is a totality for experiencers and whether it is a totality in itself.

It is uncontestable for Whitehead that an experiencer, in a single moment, works conditioning data into a single, coherent totality. This is the bearing of all the categorial obligations, especially that of subjective harmony (Whitehead 1929, part 3, chapter 1). The structure of experience itself is the total integration of the potential contributors to experience into a world-for-a-perspective: this defines both the locus of the experiencer relative to the perspective and the rest of the more or less distant world; both are contained within the perspectival reality of the experience (see Stephen David Ross 1983). The subjective process of totalization is accomplished by integration and synthesis, by dismemberment and reorganization, and most of all by elimination of the unincludable elements. Like Hegel's moment, Whitehead's occasion can render something trivial or even non-functional which in itself is intrinsically important by what can be called, on the human scale, an "act of will" and, on the subhuman scale, "violence."

Significant experiences, however, are not single moments, but great clusters of moments united by common forms of importance, what Whitehead inadequately called "societies." We identify as human experience nothing that could happen at a moment alone, but rather continuities of occasions that involve thinking thoughts as signs, acting in context, receiving and responding to valueladen information whose own proper locus is at a distance from the experience, and so forth. People organize their experience, as Paul Weiss (1983) argued, through such temporally thick valuation structures as bodily sensitivity, responsive sensibilities, needs, desires, orientations to life, sociality, mind, will, personhood, achieved autonomy, responsibility, ego, and self.[7] Do people in this extended substantial sense organize their experience into unified totalities? The question is an empirical one and the answer is, they rarely do. One of the prime motives of philosophy is to achieve greater coherence of experience. From the temporally cumulative standpoint of a human being, the most important things in life exist in pockets of order, linked by crude metrics such as bodily, spatial, and temporal continuites.

The philosophic significance of this point is that it raises the question whether this failure of totality (1) is simply because of the feeblenes of our capacities of representation (which are so important for being able to integrate distant data) or (2) is the consequence of there being no real totality capable of being represented.

The first alternative can be considered in two steps. To begin with, our mental capacities are indeed feeble, relative to what we have every reason to believe can be known with more systematic coherence. Science is far from the end of the task, and Whitehead was sensitive to the ways in which non-scientific cognitive and artistic disciplines have unfinished work in articulating the orders and connections of orders in reality.[8] Whitehead introduces a second step regarding this question, however, namely the consideration of God as an infinite intellect. According to Whitehead's philosophical theology, God at any moment accepts all data which have been actualized up to that time within the divine experience, eliminating none. In contrast to finite occasions of experience, which are limited to the integrating forms that are given them in their experienced data, God has access to (or is) an infinite conceptuality, with access to all possible modes of integration. Therefore, argues Whitehead, there is no datum so alien that God cannot find some pattern that will integrate it with the rest, and without dismemberment or diminishment of value. Thus for God at any moment, the past is a totality. Like Hegel, Whitehead believed that totality is created for finite things by the agency of infinite divine reason.

Nevertheless, difficulties analogous to those with Hegel's view arise here for Whitehead's. Is the reference to God's infinity merely a mushy assertion that anything is possible for God, so that there can be divine totalization? No, not for Whitehead any more than for Hegel. But then whence the determinateness of the divine? There are two general possibilities. If it derives exclusively from the actual data God receives, either those data just fit together as they are or God is limited to the same powers as finite occasions. This makes the question of the coherence of the world an empirical one, and our empirical evidence is that the world is not a totality. Perhaps God is like a super-scientist, but still, whether the world is totalizable is contingent upon the world, not on God's necessary infinity. Perhaps as to the other possibility, the integrating pattern derives from God's uningressed store of eternal objects rather than from the forms that already had been ingredient in the world. How is this divinely originary pattern determinate? According to Whitehead, eternal objects in themselves are indeterminate and receive determination from God's primordial act of grading them in a comprehensive vision.[9] As graded, the eternal objects are made determinate as relations between other "things." If those other things are the elements within the actual world, then the determinate eternal objects are precisely those that are ingredient in the actual world, plus their unrealized potentialities. This is no advance upon the suggestion that the divine integrating pattern derives from the actual objects integrated. But if the things integrated by relational eternal objects are other eternal objects, then there must be an infinity of determinate eternal objects. It is no easier to conceive a bottom-most eternal object that is determinate without parts, on Whitehead's view, than it is to conceive a top-most integrating form in Hegel's dialectic of infinite and finite. In addition, if the determinate relations are infinite in a bottomward direction, then all possibilities are structurally present, and the arbitrariness in divine valuation that Whitehead affirmed, rightly, is trivialized. There could be no difference between Whitehead's divinely graded eternal objects and Leibniz's eternal possibilities to whose structural necessities his God must bow.

Not only are there paradoxes in Whitehead's claim that God imposes coherence on the disjunct actual occasions of the world, there are grave difficulties with Whitehead's overall view of God, particularly as the sides of divine envisagement and of worldly appreciation are brought together (see Neville 1980).

One last and speculative question can be raised regarding Whitehead's views on the totality of the world. With regard to finite occasions, the category of subjective unity delimits the range of data that can condition an emerging occasion prior even to its elimination of what is incompatible with its final synthesis. Are there some occasions that have reached their own actuality but cannot enter into a later thing's subjective unity? If there are, they could not even be so related to the thing as to be in its past; they would have no relation to it at all. But if there were no such things, then there would be no point to the category of subjective unity; the initial data would consist of all achieved data. Because he did stress the category of subjective unity, Whitehead did mean to say that there are some achieved occasions which are not compatible for synthesis even by elimination in a given thing's coming-to-be.

Contrary to some interpreters of Whitehead, because he held that there may be some data which do not enter any later thing's subjective unity, Whitehead meant to say that some things are actual from the perspective of no occasion except themselves (and their anticipatory antecedents).[10] Or to put the point more modestly, achieving actuality within one's own perspective is enough for actuality, regardless of other multiple locations in other later things' perspectives. On this interpretation Whitehead is a radical and irreducible pluralist, or disjunctivist. Wholly disjunct things are wholly indeterminate with respect to one another and are determinate only within their local pockets of order. Of course there would be no totality in such a world. Those who insist that achieved actuality requires existing in the perspective of some currently subjective occasion either appeal to God to sustain the otherwise fading actuality of past facts, or admit that the past becomes unreal, or say that Whitehead's system is very, very wrong.

If the world is only problematically a totality for a (problematic) God in Whitehead's system, and if it is fragmented rather than total for human beings, in what sense can we speak of a world, and in what sense can there be philosophic system?

IV. World and System

Our world is ontologically vague. Vagueness, as discussed above, is a logical term adapted from Charles Peirce, for whom it meant a sign which tolerates mutually contradictory interpretations.[11] In order to tell what the sign refers to, it is necessary to take an extra step and specify one from among the potentially contradictory interpretations. A term is vague when it requires a further specification to tell in which of several ways it is to be applied. "Vagueness" can be used in an ontological way. The world is vague in the sense that its coherence, strictly speaking, consists in the harmony it allows to be imposed by a finite subject that takes its components in perspective. A finite subject at a moment entertains a totally coherent world, but there is no way within the moment alone to distinguish between the fantasy of subjective creativity and the truth about anything in the world. To assert that a vision of the world is true or that some element of a moment's experience is true, the truth question must be framed outside the single occasion in a complex tissue of moments constituting the whole person as inquirer, and perhaps even in a whole community of inquiry (Neville 1989, chapters 1–4). Only the uncontested commonalities of a few abstract ideas provide grounds for saying there is one world for all elements of an individual's personality, or for a group of inquirers. But those bodies and abstract ideas, the sort carried in language, are vague. In order to specify them so as to refer to something in the world, they must be specified with particular concrete lines of causation that embody massively inherited importance. That is, we engage in perception, refer to the funded experience of common sense, adhere to the exact discipline of some science, or pursue a subject in depth. As soon as we take the line of some specifying discipline we leave the safe vagueness of our unified world and enter some specific world—the world of seeing here now, the world of our tradition, the world of a laboratory science, the world of a specific craft of inquiry. And of course generally there are alternatives to these specifications, any of which is compatible with the vague contours of our common world, and these alternatives might be incompatible with each other and with the ones we have chosen ourselves.

The situation is that we may have one world vaguely, but many worlds concretely. Furthermore, we suspect that people different from ourselves have concrete worlds of their own that we do not share.

Hegel and Whitehead both warned against confusing the concrete with the abstract. One version of this is the confusion of the concrete with the vague. The mistake can be made in two directions. We may begin with vague elements of commonality and believe they are concrete. Philosophers are prone to do this, especially if they contemplate charts of Hegel's system during their formative years. They are rightly criticized by artists, scientists, and working people for not being in *any* concrete world. It is more likely, however, that we begin with our favorite pocket of concrete order and believe it to be the universal order, thus denying the other pockets of order. Personal and cultural chauvinism is of this sort, mistaking a specific order for a universal order comprehending all things. Relativism is the recognition that there are fundamentally different and perhaps incommensurable orders; relativism dotes on itself too much, however, when it believes it is the last word. For, in addition to the many pockets of order, the many worlds of specific actuality, there is a vague world we have in common by virtue of our interacting physical natures and our abstract signs.

The function of system in philosophy should now be apparent. It has two parts. The first is to frame a system of categories and articulate the vague world we have in common. The great historical systems, including Hegel's and Whitehead's, are the resources for this, plus our own speculative imagination. Our system should be consistent and coherent, dialectically superior to others, or at least have advantages the others do not have. There is no reason there should be only one system, one articulation of the vague world; each has different virtues.

As Whitehead said, the system also should be applicable and adequate. But we must stress that applicability and adequacy are vague. That the applicability of a system is vague means that it requires specification in some particular order if it is to apply to actualities. To apply the vague philosophic notion of person, for instance, it is necessary to speak of the Western person, or the Chinese tradition of personhood, or the Skinnerian, the Freudian, the Kierkegaardian, or whatever. Each of these is a pocket of intelligible order, more specific than the categories of the philosophic system. One should reject those elements in a philosophic system that have no applicability in the specific orders in which we live.

That the adequacy of a system is vague means that it should be specifiable in any specific order that we have reason to respect. To put the point in reverse, if there is any pocket of order that seems important, if there is any human culture, or plausible discipline, or poetic world which cannot specify the system, then the system is not adequate. As pockets of order rise and fall in their claim to actuality, the reference set for a philosophic system changes. There can be no finality with respect to the adequacy of a philosophic system. A philosophic system is vaguely true to the extent that it is adequate and applicable.

The second part of philosophic system is the dialectic of moving back and forth between the system of categories and their potential specification in the pockets of order that seem important in our lives. This is the more extensive part of systematic philosophy, in the face of which the construction of categorial schemes seems brief. Hardly any one person can do it since the pockets of order that are important for our vaguely common world include many that are inaccessible to any one philosopher. Systematic philosophy in this sense is a cultural enterprise, stimulated by the aesthetic attractivenesss of the categories on the one hand and by the need for common critical vision on the other.

One advantage of this conception of systematic philosophy is that it advertises the importance of life with local pockets of order, legitimating the uses of intelligence that are idiosyncratic to those orders. Cultures are not to be reduced to one another. Poetry is not to be reduced to general formulation. Religions are not to be homogenized into a common mush. The various intellectual and scientific traditions are to pursue the specifics of their research enterprises so as to take advantage of advances in instrumentation, serendipidous findings, the felicities of jargon. More than non-systematic philosophies, which are likely to generalize their special orders as if they were a universal order, this conception of systematic philosophy is best friend to plurality. It stands in stark contrast to conceptions of system such as Hegel's that squeeze the multifariousness of things into the system's terms and exclude from importance the things that do not fit.

An equal advantage of this conception is that it gives shape and discipline to the task of relating our pockets of order to the vague orientations that we take to be our world and that guide our activity. A prime motive for philosophy is curiosity about whether the things that are important and intelligible for us are equally so for others, and whether we are justifed in taking them as we do. The form of a total vision is an ineluctable guiding principle, as Kant so well saw. In addition to guiding our inquiry about matters of the whole, this conception of systematic philosophy allows us to see whether and to what extent our various pockets of order are coherent, overlapping, contradictory, irrelevant, or incommensurable. Each can be translated as a specification of the system, and terms there are comparable, even if the assertions when translated into the system's common language are not coherent with one another. So systematic philosophy can provide a map through the vague world from one pocket of important order to another.

As a final summary consideration, this conception of systematic philosophy does not require a conception of totality, where that means a comprehensive coherence of the real items of the world. Neither Hegel's divine infinite reason nor Whitehead's divine infinite conceptuality is required for an ontology compatible with systematic philosophy.

Against Hegel we can say that the basic philosophic categories are not infinitely inclusive totalities but rather vague structures requiring external supplementation in order to refer to actual things. With Hegel's victims we can say that their pockets of order have an importance of their own that ought to be registered in an adequate system. Those pockets of order are not reduced to the system; rather the system is supplemented with specifications to reach out to each pocket of order. An implication of this philosophic view is that the project of determining which important pockets of order have claims upon us is thrown open to the empirical inquiry. This is a felicitous result in an age characterized by the encounter of world cultures and by the assertion of minority, third world, and female perspectives.

The view of systematic philosophy presented here is closer to Whitehead's than to Hegel's. Nevertheless it differs from Whitehead's by abandoning the conception of totality implicit in his conception of God's conditioned, consequent nature. It differs also by stressing not only the need for generalizing up to abstract categories but also the need systematically to relate to the pockets of order important for our lives. It is clearer than Whitehead about the kind of abstraction involved in systematic philosophy: logical vagueness requiring further specification in order to have real reference. Should Whitehead believe that philosophic abstractions are merely general, referring immediately to actual things, the system of categories might be taken to require a totality in its references which is unjustified by either our experience or our philosophic arguments. The most potent argument against systematic philosophy today is that, since experience shows our orders to be fragmented, any system of categories requiring them to be totalized must be wrong. That argument cannot be made against a system construed as a vague hypothesis. And despite the fragmentation, we vaguely move together in a common world that should be acknowledged and understood relative to those existentially viable pockets of order.

Although totality has seemed to be a concept essential to having a world and a philosophy of that world, in fact it is a liability (see Buchler 1966, 1978). The failure of our two great systematizers, Hegel and Whitehead, adequately to defend a conception of totality, marks the liability. By abandoning that conception, we can still sustain their great ideal of philosophic system and yet pay proper tribute to the multifariousness of the world.

CHAPTER SIX

✳

ON SYSTEMS AS SPECULATIVE HYPOTHESES

The conclusion of the previous chapter sketched a technical conception of systematic philosophy that responds to the need for metaphysics in the highroad around modernism. The purpose of the present chapter is to develop that conception more concretely.

For the first three quarters of this century philosophers were preoccupied with finding a "nature" for philosophy, something that would define philosophy as a professional discipline, as a special kind of science, or as an art with its own integrity. Of a piece with modernism in other cultural enterprises, this concern for professional integrity led philosophers to an obsession with what counts as "genuine" philosophy. The result was the outrageous tragicomedy in which each philosophic group's understanding of the very heart of philosophy was denounced as unphilosophical by other philosophers. These denunciations became the substratum of professional politics and they looked more ridiculous to the rest of the intellectual world than any debates about quantities of dancing angels on pinheads.

Like art (see Davis 1980 and Krauss 1979), architecture, literature, and other humanistic "professions," however, philosophy seems now to be fascinated to enter a postmodernist phase. This book is an attempt to minimize this fascination. Postmodernism is not the triumph of any new style but rather an abandonment of the modernist obsession for style, for defining professional discipline and integrity so as to distinguish philosophy's own essence as a condition for the practice of philosophy. But postmodernism defines itself as rejecting style precisely in the narrow sense of modernism. If philosophy is not preoccupied with getting over modernism, and over what modernism was concerned to get over, what is its shape? Among the characteristics of its shape is a bias toward systematic thinking.

Does the highroad around modernism and postmodernism mean that the question of philosophical method is dead? By no means. Only changed. Whatever philosophical tasks are pursued, the organization of the pursuit can be objectified as method and then criticized regarding its worth. This kind of methodic self-reflexivity has characterized Western philosophy since its inception and is perhaps its most lasting achievement. The relevant question raised by postmodern tendencies in philosophy is whether there are any tasks commanding philosophic attention and any correlative methods to reach them that are normative for philosophy in our time. Lacking an a priori definition of philosophy's tasks and techniques, the answer to that question must be sought by considering the things that merit philosophic attention.

The thesis here is that, with all due respect to historical irony, one of philosophy's essential tasks, although not the only one, is to be systematic, and that systematic method in philosophy is as vital and important now as it was in the eras of the great system builders. System in philosophy, it will be argued, is defined by a norm that mediates between the diverse techniques and capabilities of philosophers on the one hand and the range of justifiable and perhaps obligatory tasks on the other. Both the techniques and tasks may be defined by other considerations than systematic ones, mostly historical and *ad hoc,* differing from age to age. But system in thinking, in the ideal sense, is the general norm that measures how philosophy may fulfill its diverse responsibilities.

A cursory review of any half dozen of the great systematic philosophies, however, is enough to demonstrate that no such statement as this is sufficient to describe systematic philosophy or the methods by which it is pursued. The most obvious stumbling block is that systematic philosophers disagree among themselves about their aims and methods. In light of this, how can the above thesis be made determinate and defended? A five-step argument will be offered.

The first step will provide a relatively neutral account of what systematic philosophy is, what motivates it, and what methods seem natural to it. The account will be abstract enough to apply to all or most of the commonly recognized systematic philosophers throughout Western history, and yet precise enough to discriminate systematic philosophy from some of the practices in recent philosophy that have thought of themselves as non-systematic or even anti-systematic. The abstractness of this step in the argument, nevertheless, renders it too vague to articulate the controversial cutting edges that make the systematic philosophers most interesting. It is too vague as well by itself to give much support to the thesis that system in philosophy is a norm for adjusting philosophy's resources to its responsibilities.

The next three steps in the argument, then, will take a special form. Each will consider a special contemporary problem for philosophy with respect to which systematic philosophy must become determinate, and will argue for a particular view as to how systematic philosophy ought to do so. The arguments here will make the conception of system more concrete. Step two will consider how systematic philosophy might best contribute to the social context of philosophy, the "ongoing conversation of mankind," as Rorty calls it, though with a tougher sense of conversation than he intends.

Step three will consider how systematic philosophy avoids the imperialism of imposing its categories on a multifarious world of pockets of order. Many of the deconstructionists, for instance, have argued that any metaphysical system must commit the gross sin of logocentrism. Step three will relate this to the topic of the previous chapter, namely, how systematic philosophy can cope with the value and integrity of the incommensurate domains it systematically integrates, avoiding the unprovable (and empirically unlikely) presupposition that the world is a total system.

Step four will focus the problem of radical skepticism, asking how systematic thinking can undercut concerns that all assertions are disengaged from reality. The argument will deal with existential doubt about whether the basic images that transform natural processes into experience authentically engage the world. The answers developed in response to steps two, three, and four can be summed up in the fifth step through a discussion of philosophy's normative responsibilities. The conception of systematic philosophy will be reformulated in ways loyal to the general inspirations of systematic philosophy described in the first step, but warranted for practice today, as other conceptions of system may not be, because of its responses to social context, incommensurability, and skepticism. It will be apparent, finally, why systematic philosophy should be a tool for adjusting philosophy's techniques to its multifarious tasks.

I. Philosophy as System

Consider the following remark by Paul Weiss, doubtless the greatest system-builder of our generation.

> Since every man is unavoidably the product of his time, culture, and stud-
> ies, since at his best he is confused, ignorant, biased, limited in vision and
> insight, . . . none can ever hope to achieve a perfect, all-encompassing,
> neutral, articulate account. . . . But the effort must be made. Not only is it
> desirable to try to push back the limits within which one had unreflecting
> lived, to try to avoid arbitrarily assuming what should have been exam-
> ined, and to try to reduce the number of unreliable, derivative, unex-
> plained, and unexamined judgments that are made, but it is good to
> expose to the critical eye of others, and hopefully to one's own at some
> later time, the weaknesses as well as the promises of a philosophy, and
> thereby to alert all to what next should arrest attention. (Weiss 1977, 22)

Taken straight, Weiss's point is a truism: examine your assumptions and
judgments where you can. Who could be against this? Willfully disre-
garding reflection about assumptions and judgments can be justified
only by exceptional circumstances. These exceptions themselves require
systematic justification, and in practice nearly always receive it. As it
stands, however, Weiss's statement calls for three glosses.

First, the remarks about assumptions and judgments provide an elementary characterization of systematic method in philosophy. Assumptions, Weiss says, should be set within the widest possible context and
should be examined regarding their justification and connection with
each other. Systematic method then means to look at everything from as
many angles as possible with a way of being responsible for the connections between those viewpoints.

Truism or not, Weiss's point signals the initial and recalcitrant opposition between systematic philosophy and other dominant modes of
philosophy in America, which in this respect can be called "program"
philosophies. A program philosophy is one in which the context of a finite discussion is accepted as set by some prior discussion. Phenomenologists, for instance, are program philosophers when they undertake the
description of a certain field without critical discussion of how that process of description calls into question their original suppositions about
methods of description. Analytic philosophers often address themselves
directly to prior discussions, supplying answers to other people's questions, criticizing other people's answers and replying to others' objections to their own views. Although a legitimate form of analytic
argument is to object to someone's formulation of the issue, even this
argument is couched in terms oriented toward re-steering a previously
initiated program. Because they willingly enter a previously defined
conversation as a way of making progress, analytic philosophers can

write short articles. Of course both phenomenologists and analytic philosophers sometimes, in the long run, practice systematic philosophy; but this runs against the grain of the program orientation of those schools. On the other side, although systematic philosophers such as Weiss often seem to operate within the "program" of developing their own systematic views, they tend to write long books because any systematic project aims to be complete but self-limiting, to be called into question by the next book. Systematic philosophy is not program philosophy precisely because antecedently defined programs, including its conversational context, have to be questioned in order to be looked at from enough systematic angles.

Second, according to Weiss's statement the purpose of systematic reflection is not so much to justify one's view as to make it vulnerable to criticism. Philosophers want to be corrected, not vindicated, says Weiss. Perhaps this is not correct, at least as an empirical description of the group. Nevertheless, if we ask not from the standpoint of the speaking philosopher but from the standpoint of the listeners (including the speaker at a later time), what is important in a philosopher's presentation is how it can be assessed and corrected critically. This highlights systematic philosophy's methodic concern with self-reflexivity and putative completeness. In order to make one project vulnerable systematic philosophy steps back, objectifies it, and creates a new perspective on it. To examine a domain from many perspectives is not enough; one must also examine the perspectives from a perspective that relates them, and so on. This leads to concerns about the nature of system itself.[1] Anti-systematic philosophies reject the obligation to distance thought from any finite argument in order to gain a more self-reflexive and inclusive system. Without denying that such further perspectives can be taken, they claim that a good argument, analysis, or description can be taken simply for what it is as located within the discussion. Systematic philosophy, without denying that reflection is always at some merely finite place, claims that there is a positive obligation to step back and take responsibility for the reflection at that place.

Third, system functions within the community of discourse "to alert all to what next should arrest attention." Notice Weiss does not say (what he also believes) that the function of systematic reflection is to teach truths or justify views. Its pertinent function here is heuristic: to bring things forward, wittingly or unwittingly, that should command someone's philosophic attention. System serves to reveal what is important to consider. Lest this point be taken as a reversion to program philosophy, the following distinction needs to be kept in mind. For program philosophy, the challenges presented to a philosophy by the ongoing conversation look like problems or puzzles to be solved. (Consider the view that philosophy is therapeutic, curing conceptual illnesses.) For systematic philosophy, however, solving puzzles is but a part of its *logica docens*. Its *logica utens* aims to gain access to worthwhile perspectives on things that had not been attained before, to discover new connections and dimensions of reality that had been obscured by the unexamined implications of categories. The novelty in these perspectives is what allows a system to be called "speculative." A given system alerts the conversation to what emerges as important from its newly achieved perspective.

There is a special limitation in Weiss's language as quoted above. His distinction between assumptions and judgments may suggest to some that philosophy begins with a system whose premises are assumptions and whose inferences are judgments; this would be misleading regarding the dialectical method of systematic reflection which is always in the middle of things. Systematic philosophy is thinking toward a system, hardly ever in a system. To appreciate this consider the typical problems that legitimately give rise to the exercise of systematic method. There are at least four.

1. The most obvious move to system occurs when it is felt that a philosophic claim is historically or situationally or dialectically naive. Systematic reflection sets the claim alongside others in a larger context, exposing its assumptions and implications, relativizing and objectifying it. The reflection examines the arguments for and against the claim relative to the perspectives of its alternatives. This critical argumentation does not necessarily take the claim seriously in terms of its own argument; rather it shifts and relativizes the ground of the discussion. Philosophies that take their rise from a special domain, such as science, often needs this shift to see the limits of their claims.

2. The systematic method of responding to a claim on the claim's own ground is to treat it as part of a system, to expose its systematic presuppositions and consequences, and to probate its argumentative validity. If the presuppositions or consequences are undesirable, this may constitute an argument against the claim. The claim itself is "treated systematically" by being construed as part of a system that constitutes the logical form of its arguments. Not all arguments for claims are framed in the well-formed formulas of a system; but this is to say that not all arguments expose their own premises and implications. The desirability of doing so is illustrated in the widespread interest in formal logic and in the concern for presuppositions.

3. Perhaps the most frequent but least noticed kind of move to system occurs when the specific formulation of a philosophic claim is rejected. The critical motive is that the formulation does not *engage* the real problem either in stating or solving it. The systematic method is to seek out why it results in non-engagement or alienation and to invent new and engaging forms. Systematic method here is not a method of doubt, because the issue is not the truth of a claim which can be doubted. The issue, rather, is whether the formulation catches its subject.

4. As the quotation from Weiss suggests, beyond considering whether formulations engage their issues, whether they are critically justifiable in some justifiable'context, or whether they have acceptable formal connections, systematic method in philosophy aims to discern what is important to think about. Is the discussion at hand dealing with what it should deal with, given the context? Most actual disputes within the philosophic struggle concern not coherence, truth, or engagement but rather the basic importance of the discussion. If philosophy is responsible to external needs for wisdom, this systematic concern is all the more crucial. Although these points have been expressed as systematic responses of philosophy to itself, the positive motive for systematic philosophy is the importance of systematic results for those who want wisdom.

Systematic philosophers from Plato to Weiss would agree with the following: always seeking correction, philosophy is well advised to step back from its assumptions and to consider the worth and connections of its claims, as long as there are unexamined assumptions and claims, so that as a result of this methodical examination one can tell what to think about next. For any finite philosophical endeavor it is important to understand how it relates to historical and dialectical alternatives, to see its formal assumptions and implications, to appreciate whether it authentically engages its subject matter, and to assess its importance. The various techniques for calling these issues into question and dealing with them collectively constitute the means of systematic method. Even when a philosophy presents itself as anti-systematic, its fate in the history of philosophy is either to be ignored or in fact to be subjected to examination in these various systematic dimensions.

II. System as Fallible

The reference in the previous sentence to a philosophy's "fate in the history of philosophy" is important. While some might argue that

historical fate is adventitious to the real merit of a philosophy, others beginning with Charles Peirce, Josiah Royce, and then John Dewey have
argued that philosophies are intrinsically defined by relation to critical
communities. That is, a philosophy is a complex hypothesis proposed to
a community, the plausibility or truth of which is defined in terms of the
community's ideal examination of its case. Stephen Toulmin (1972) has
argued that at least within the realm of science one ought not construe
truth in terms of the arguments directly given for or against a theory but
rather in terms of the considerations according to which the larger community adopts the theory and according to which it puts it aside.

This point asserts the fallibilist principle that any position taken in
philosophy is internally and essentially subject to reconsideration by
subsequent philosophical arguments. Not just fate: from the standpoint
of systematic philosophy this is the heart of responsible reflection.

But as Rorty points out, most Western philosophers, especially in
the period since Descartes, have believed that philosophy's job is to establish the fundamentals upon which all other knowing is based, the
conditions for the possibility of knowledge. From the foundation thus
established, philosophy could oversee, correct, and license all other
claims to cognition (and beyond cognition, claims to morality and culture). Kant drew up the battle lines against fallibilistic philosophy at the
end of the *Critique of Pure Reason,* writing:

> Since criticism of our reason has at last taught us that we cannot by means
> of its pure and speculative employment arrive at any knowledge whatso-
> ever, may it not seem that a proportionately wider field is opened for *hy-*
> *potheses?* . . . If the imagination is not simply to be visionary, but is to be
> *inventive* under the strict surveillance of reason, there must always previ-
> ously be something that is completely certain, and not invented or merely
> a matter of opinion, namely, the *possibility* of the object itself. (B 797 f.)

Kant meant, of course, that we can define neither what an hypothesis is
in relation to its objects, nor what would count as confirmation or dis-
confirmation, without an a priori transcendental understanding of the
situation. An hypothesis about hypotheses would be circular, he
thought. By extension, we could not assess the course of philosophical
conversation without knowing foundationally how knowledge relates to
objects, or how propositions have meaning and refer.

Contrary to his intention, what Kant really did was to state a dilemma. *Either* knowledge by hypothesis is undergirded by a transcendental, certain foundation, he showed, *or* what hypotheses yield when

explicated only by other hypotheses is not knowledge, in the classical sense of being certain, but only more or less plausible hypotheses. Whereas Kant took the first horn of the dilemma, Charles Peirce seized the second horn, as claimed in chapter 1, and developed the thesis that *all* knowledge is hypothetical, including systematic philosophy. To appreciate Peirce's point, consider what is lost by his pragmatic move.

The first loss is the claim to a priori, certain, transcendental knowledge of the conditions for the possibility of experience. But this does not mean that we cannot know about the specific conditions under which specific experience is possible. It means only that knowledge of the "foundations" is not foundational knowledge in the sense that it itself is presupposed as knowledge by all other knowledge. Knowledge of the conditions of the possibility of knowledge is hypothetical and suffers the fate within the larger philosophical conversation of other broadly referring philosophical hypotheses. The allegation of transcendental status is merely special pleading for exemption from revisionary criticism.

The second loss for Kant entailed by the pragmatic move is the synthetic a priori knowledge in science and mathematics. Few philosophers today would want to defend him on that point.

What would *not* be lost by adopting Peirce's horn of the dilemma is any of the hypothetical knowledge that Kant thought himself able to justify with his transcendental apparatus. For, an ordinary hypothesis is justified according to its career in the larger historical discussion where reasons and evidences are presented for and against it and where it either succeeds or fails to make out its claim. With all his transcendental apparatus, Kant still must abandon hypotheses to that same fate, because his apparatus could never prove an hypothesis, only interpret how it relates to its possible object. To move to Peirce's perspective is to allow that some further hypothesis can make that interpretation. A systematic claim need not be, nor derive from, an a priori structure.

Nor need the claim derive from an empirical entity such as a sense datum or a *grund satz* that has a special incorrigible status as foundational knowledge. Wilfrid Sellars is correct to have said,

> The essential point is that in characterizing an episode or state as that of *knowing*, we are not giving an empirical description or that episode or state; we are placing it in the logical space of reasons, of justifying and being able to justify what one says. (1963, 169)

The "logical space of reasons, of justifying and being able to justify what one says," is the existential space of all philosophical discourse, including systematic thinking. If philosophy takes place within the logical space of reasons, it consists in assertions plus more or less worthy attempts to justify them.

An assertion is any remark or intentional action subject to assessment or justification. This point has often been understood too narrowly. A scientific description which claims to mirror what it describes is an assertion subject to assessment. But so is a hermeneutic assertion claiming to represent its object in a particular respect that itself requires further interpretation. Moral assertions too are subject to justification. In fact, any intentional action in a social context that calls for attention and is subject to being assessed regarding whether it is fitting or proper can be called an "assertion." Even certain attitudes, such as pity or admiration, are assertions subject to criticism within the logical space of reasons. Assertions assert the appropriateness of their content.

"Appropriateness of asserted content" is a good general characterization of "truth," which discourse of assessment and justification attempts to ascertain. While not all kinds of assertions play central roles in philosophy, it is good to bear in mind the variety in those that do. Besides descriptive assertions of "what is," philosophic assertions may be interpretive: they may assert the value, relevance, importance, triviality, irrelevance, debasement, silliness, pomposity, or arrogance of assertions. Philosophical assertions may be declarative, exclamatory, interrogative; narrative, aphoristic, or theoretical; even gestural like Dr. Johnson's kick, all so long as they enter the dialogue in the logical space of reasons. For an assertion to have good reasons means that a case can be made for its appropriateness as a response to its context within the overall conversation. The means for making a case are at least as diverse as those described by Stephen Toulmin in *The Uses of Argument* (1958). They can be summarized as "persuasive rhetoric" if that phrase may be taken to include rather than exclude the best of justifications.

"Rhetoric" is the name classically given to political discourse, discourse intended to move people's judgments. If politics in its most general sense is the search for justifiably appropriate ways of acting, then truth is the pre-eminent norm for politics since public ways of acting can be considered as justifiably appropriate only by considering them as overt assertions within the logical space of reasons. If one can ask whether a public action is appropriate or not, which is what rhetoric does, then one is asking whether it is a true response to situations within the logical space of reasons. Intellectually formulated verbal assertions are continuous with deliberate political actions. Peirce implied as much when he argued that beliefs remain habits of behavior until they are actively questioned within the logical space of reasons, at which point they become self-consciously intellectual. Assertions are acts within a social situation that are subject to being assessed for their appropriateness or truth in that situation. The activity of assessing such acts is the heart of political process.

Because the form of rhetoric in the search for truth is to engage the best possible reasons and justification, rhetoric is not limited to the "rhetorical" tradition that was contrasted with the philosophical tradition in the introduction above. Indeed, the distinction between the two traditions is that the rhetorical tradition aims at persuasion and the philosophical at criticizing persuasiveness by trying new angles on the truth. Where the rhetorical tradition is suspicious of references to the truth, the philosophical is suspicious of persuasiveness.

Peirce spoke of a community of investigators or inquirers, which is too narrow a conception because it too exclusively suggests the scientific community. Dewey (1927) spoke of the Great Society—great because permeated by intellect in the form of claims in the logical space of warranted assertability—but his conception assumes without warrant that society is more cohesive than it is. Rorty speaks of philosophical conversation and its relation to the great ongoing conversation of mankind, which is a bit too academic a conception, suggesting an unreal separation of talk from affairs. Perhaps we should settle for the awkward phrase, "truth-obliged society," suggesting as it does that assertions ought to be assessed according to their appropriateness, that likely they are not, and that society is defined by its obligation to truth, not by its success in attaining it.

What is philosophy's role in a truth-obliged society? That is an historically contingent question, of course. It generally has been the case that philosophy provides certain rather high level and refined services for the assessment of assertions, whether the assertions be moral, descriptive, or whatever. The topics of Plato's dialogues provide a decent catalogue of philosophy's range of contributions, including many of the intellectual techniques that currently are thought justifiable. Philosophers address not only other philosophies within the logical space they make for their arguments but also claims in nearly every other assertive domain of life.

Is there any special role for *systematic* philosophy in all this? There is, and it may be seen from the following considerations. One function of assertion is to communicate. To assert something, whether it is a statement of fact, a command, a promise, anger, surprise, or any assertive action, is to assert it as appropriate for someone in a public arena.

Whereas there may be private fantasies, it is hard to imagine logically private assertions; an assertion to oneself merely has a narrow responsive public, and the scope of its potential public depends on what it asserts.

Who is included within the public? The public might be thought to be limited to the people who are intended in that address, the people who are told the fact, commanded, or at whom one's anger is directed. But whereas one's intention may be to affect those people, the truth of the assertion lies in its appropriateness, and that appropriateness is assessable by anyone capable of entering the relevant space of reasons. The potential scope of the logical space of reasons sets the potential scope of the public. The normative public whom one's reasons for assertions are obliged to address consists in principle of all who can enter the logical space of reasons. There are other senses of privacy, to be sure, in which one is justified to keep someone from knowing about an assertion; but when the question is the truth of the assertion, assessment of the justification should be open to any who can enter the logical space.

In plain fact, however, the world's cultures are fragmented into pockets of local publics. A local public is a domain of internal intelligibility and effort within which people use their local terms to address one another. With those terms they make cases with reference to local questions, but that local public might not be commensurate with other domains of discourse. Its actual space of reasons might be incommensurable with that of other domains. They are not public to one another; they do not exist in a common public. One cultural tradition's arguments are not necessarily public to another. Natural sciences are foreign domains to the social sciences and the humanities. One political faction's judgments about what makes justifiable sense can be non-sense to another faction, for historical reasons. Without multiplying examples or kinds of foreignness, it is painfully obvious that there are many local publics that are private to each other in most of their concerns, and there are precious few if any concerning which groups or domains of assertion can enter the public discussion.

Now the special function of systematic philosophy is to create perspectives from which what otherwise would be private becomes public. In examining things from all perspectives it necessarily asks how each domain bears publicly on other domains. Since it creates new languages as bridges, and since it must examine those languages too, it asks about the descriptive, moral, political, aesthetic, and other commitments in its own public-making tools. Since the systematic bridges should be public to each of the domains bridged, the domains become public to one another; system provides the common space of reasons. Philosophy is not the only cultural endeavor that aims to make local publics more broadly public. The arts, sciences, and other humanistic disciplines all have hermeneutic functions. But systematic philosophy's unique contribution is to provide perspectives for integration that treat themselves as assertions to be assessed according to their justifiability.

Summarizing step two of the argument, systematic philosophy is the making of hypothetical assertions whose truth depends on the cases that can be made for them in the logical space of reasons, and at least one of whose functions is the political one of providing perspectives wherein diverse local publics are brought into a common public domain. Although no one seems in danger of overestimating the powers of systematic philosophy in these regards, the social need for systematic philosophy, as well as its intrinsic hermeneutic interest, cannot be denied without justifiably asserting that some domains ought to remain private relative to the larger conversation.

III. System as Tolerant

Nevertheless, the greatest postmodern or deconstructionist complaint lodged against systematic philosophy is that some domains *ought* to remain private and that systematic philosophy violates them. There is an imperialism to systematic philosophy, precisely in its political role, the complaint goes, for system is logocentric. Systematic philosophy makes falsely commensurate what is incommensurable. There are two main problems concerning incommensurability.

The first is posed by the immediate integrity of many local publics and conversational enterprizes, for instance poetry and the arts. One appreciates this integrity by entering into the local language and loses it by moving away in interpretation. Since the value of so many local publics is precisely what is destroyed when their expressions are translated into the language of a system, systematic philosophy must be destructive.

Incommensurability has been acknowledged in the strategies of twentieth-century philosophy. The response of scientific reductionism is to eliminate from the philosophical part of the discussion those elements that cannot be made to conform to antecedently recognizable criteria of publicity. If it is objected that this is philosophically blind to the genuine values achieved in local publics, the reductionist response is to reject those values as important for philosophy. Philosophy should restrict itself to what is in fact commensurable within a large community (mostly science). The opposite philosophical strategy has been adopted by some late Wittgensteinians, namely to protect the integrity of local publics by making them diverse games, each intrinsically irrelevant to the other's inner interests, but all penetrable by philosophers and others who learn the diverse games. The games are no more public to each other than is supposed in noting that a single person can play first one game and then another, or read science in the morning and poetry in the afternoon.

Systematic philosophy can object that these strategies assert a deceptive irrelevance, because one local public might have a vital interest in the assertions of another; interests are not confined to the language games explicitly used to serve them, and if poetry does not decisively have a bearing on science, science at least bears upon poetry. The culture of conservative Catholicism has an integrity over against that of liberalism, but the fact that its reasoning concerning abortion is not in the logical space of liberalism's reasons, and vice versa, is of momentous import to both sides and to many others. So long as there is a logical possibility of mutual interest, the logical space of the public should be inclusive of the local publics. Furthermore, in order even to perceive and protect some local integrity, philosophy must take up a perspective on the larger discussion of which it is a part and characterize its integrity; difference is recognized only through comparison. This line of argument commits systematic philosophy to a certain kind of abstractness of perspective that acknowledges the integrity of local publics in the same terms that makes them commensurate enough for the difference to be apparent.

But is it possible for systematic philosophy to construct such an abstract perspective? The first and second steps of the argument here characterized a philosophical system as a coherent perspective on experience. A perspective is not only a "look" at experience but an appreciative or evaluative engagement by virtue of which we attend to some things and not others. Systematic philosophy involves a selection of the important elements to keep in view, in distinction from the relatively trivial elements that can be dropped from sight. The important elements are articulated in categories that indicate their bearing upon one another in logical, causal, and other ways that make for the importance in question. This is the clue to the proper abstraction.

The move to categories itself is necessitated by the self-reflexive character of examining things from all sides. To examine something from many perspectives run through seriatim is not enough, for self-reflection asks about the relations between these perspectives. To answer, as Wittgensteinians might, that there simply is this array of perspectives which we can occupy one after another, is explicitly to reject a task of thinking about what one is doing; only rarely is there justification for philosophers to do that. Once systematic philosophy has entered the task of constructing categories self-critically, all the formal issues of generality, consistency, coherence, applicability, adequacy, completeness, and the like become elements that themselves shape the system. The great systems of philosophy, including the great anti-systems such as Kierkegaard's and Nietzsche's, are formed by the outcomes of their attempts to address these issues concerning categories. Their intellectual conclusions in and about categories constitute their perspective on the perspectives they declare important for appreciating things.

How should categories now be conceived if they are to respect the valuable incommensurability of local publics, the immediacies of diverse languages? They are abstractions that abstract from the welter of detail by constructing intellectual forms claiming to present what is important. But there are two broad senses of abstraction that Charles Peirce distinguished, and only one of them is servicable for system in philosophy. He called them "generality" and "vagueness" (Peirce 1935, CP 5.446–450, 505–506. See the discussion in chapter 1 above).

Generality in a proposition, said Peirce, consists in the proposition's referring directly to all members of a class, leaving the identification of objects to any interpreter who understands the proposition and its systematically related propositions. An abstract category is general when nothing beyond understanding the category and other categories within its categorical system is needed to tell what falls under it. Scientific hypotheses and categories are aimed to be general because it is hoped that they can be tested by particular critical experiments; an hypothesis about electrons, for instance, that is ambiguous as to what counts as an electron, would be difficult to test.

Although some philosophers may have thought that their categories should be general in the sense just characterized, that is a mistake. For it entails that everything that counts in the world is a recognizable example of the systematically defined categories. As Hegel pointed out in claiming that the rational is the real and vice versa, "the infinite variety of circumstances" must be put down to petty concerns compared with the interest of philosophy in the rational (Hegel 1821, 10 f.). Consider these words attributed to Moses, in basic ways the founding motif of Western culture: "I have set before you life and death, blessing and curse; therefore choose life, that you and your descendents may live" (Deuteronomy 30:19). Now suppose that its metaphysical commitments have to fall, directly and without intermediate interpretation, under one or several of the following categories: (Aristotle's) substance, quantity, quality, relation, place, time, position, state, action, or affection; or (Whitehead's) actual entities, prehensions, nexuses, subjective forms, eternal objects, propositions, multiplicities, or contrasts. To believe that the ontological commitments of Moses's point can be rendered directly in the language of either of those very respectable systems is preposterous. When people are told that the reality in their nuanced experience is supposed to be nothing more than illustrations of some set of categories, they rightly protest that the integrity of their localized experience would be brutalized by systematic philosophy.

Philosophical categories and propositions in systems should not be general but, rather, vague. A vague proposition is one that requires a further assertion to identify its object and give it a truth value. "The person of whom I am thinking is conceited" is Peirce's example, explicitly not mentioning that the hearer is the person intended, although suggesting it while at the same time logically allowing the speaker to deny just that. Vague categories are those into which their objects cannot be put without some further identification of objects. As a logical notion vagueness does not mean fuzzy or emotive or distracted. For, vague assertions are still determinately distinct from their logical alternatives.

The vagueness of systematic categories and assertions shows why the domains they interpret are required to be external to the categories just at the point the categories provide a means of commensurating them. For example, if the Whiteheadian system says that everything actual consists of events, and gives a formally precise definition of events in terms of its categories, a further physical theory still is required to show how the perihelion of Mercury, say, is composed of such events; it is even more complicated to show how a person is a congeries of events. Because the speculative theory of events is vague, from that theory alone it is impossible to tell how it is applicable to what the theory might be referred to explain. Consider the latter example more closely. Suppose the Whiteheadian says that a person is a complex ecosystem of events nested in a wider environing ecosystem of events. To show this, the Whiteheadian should explain how events make up a person as described by Freud; the system is better if it also can show how events make up a Skinnerian person. Unless some intermediate theory of description of persons is interpreted in terms of events, the Whiteheadian cannot indicate how a person is a system of events, and the more interpretations of persons can be described as events, the better for the vague theory of events. The vagueness in a philosophical system requires that the system be supplemented by intermediate assertions arising from elsewhere than the system in order to be applicable, to have truth value. If the system is thought to be general rather than vague, its truth values are immediate; or it distorts the integrity of its content.

If a systematic hypothesis is properly vague, than *any* plausible positive interpretive assertion about its subject matter, from whatever position within the conversation, must be capable of being expressed as an exemplification of the hypothesis in the well-formed formulas of the system (however awkward that might be for the purposes of the intermediate assertion). As supplementary, the expression of the intermediate assertion in the language of the system asserts more than is asserted in the system by itself. The truth of that interpretive assertion must be made out on its own account; it cannot be derived from the vague systematic hypothesis; neither can it be falsified by the vaguer hypothesis. If the systematic hypothesis does not show the mid-range claim to be a possibility, then there is a fault in the vagueness of the systematic hypothesis.

Whereas the test for applicability in a speculative system consists in finding *some* plausible participants in the cultural conversation whose assertions can be expressed as specifications of the system, the test for adequacy is whether *all* the plausible participants can have their important assertions so expressed. The plausibility of the philosophic system is weakened to the degree it cannot be made specific in terms of some language of assertion that has an independent basis of plausibility. If a philosophic system is supported by the specification of a now plausible assertion that later comes to be implausible, the system is not necessarily falsified; but it requires plausibility from elsewhere and it must be specifiable by whatever assertion becomes plausible in the stead of the first. Otherwise the hypothetical speculative system should be altered.

The truth conditions for a systematic hypothesis can now be summarized. A system is true to the degree all the following conditions hold when it is asserted:

1. the system is formally consistent and coherent, and
2. the system is dialectically superior to alternative systems on formal grounds, and
3. the system can be specified compatibly by all true assertions of lesser vagueness (however the truth of those asssertions is established), and
4. some plausible assertions of lesser vagueness do specify the system, and

5. if the plausible assertions are incompatible specifications of the system, no other system satisfying 1–4 would make them compatible and the system could be consistently specified by a pervasive range of assertions compatible with the falseness of one side of the incompatible plausible assertions.

There are thus four levels of discourse involved in the stipulation that systematic philosophical categories and assertions be vague. The lowest is the subject matter to be interpreted (and this may or may not itself be discourse). At the top is the system. Just above the subject matter is the interpretive language interpreting it; Freud's theory, for example. Both the subject matter and its interpretive language must be able to sustain their integrity over against philosophical language, and possibly over against alternative interpretive languages. Each interpretive language attempts to say what is important in the subject matter. Finally there is a level expressing the assertions of the interpretive language in the well-formed formulas of the system. This expression is a translation of the interpretive domain, picking out what is claimed by the system to be important, and it is also a specification of the system to assert more that it does by itself. In terms of the previous example, this level is a Whiteheadian expression of Freud's theory and an assertion of what Whitehead would say about persons if Freud's theory is true.

The system then is a vague abstraction specified by expressions which themselves abstract from the interpretive domains that abstractly respond to subject matters. Whitehead wrote that "an abstraction is nothing else than the omission of part of the truth. The abstraction is well-founded when the conclusions drawn from it are not vitiated by the omitted truth"(1938, 138). This suggests that the abstractions of a vague system are well founded when what is left out in their expression of intermediate interpretive domains does not vitiate their truth. Of course, as systematic, the philosophies should inquire into this question. Therefore, if that which a translating expression leaves out of an interpretive domain can itself be stated, and not simply restated in the old confusion with what was orignally translated, it too should be expressible in the well-formed formulas of the system. The faithfulness of the system to the subject of its own abstractions can thus be tested by using the system to say what its original translating expressions left out.

The content question in each case of assessing abstraction is whether what is represented as important really is so. The form of the abstraction dictates what can be represented as inportant *by that form;* but the form may lie about what it represents. What is important must be important in the subject from which the abstraction is made; but it is not represented there as such, or else the abstraction would be unnecessary. *That* something is important is asserted by abstractions of subjects in ways to be assessed in the logical space of reasons.[2]

We may now summarize our answer to the problem about the intrinsic value of local publics and the danger of foundering on incommensurability. That danger exists only for philosophic systems construed as general, in Peirce's sense. A vague system is not by itself a neutral langauge to which a poem, a scientific theory, and another philosophy all may be reduced. Nor can the system be substituted for any of these things. But the system provides a language such that, when the poem, scientific theory, or other philosophy are re-expressd in the system's language, the important things in them that are inexpressible do not vitiate what is expressed. The logical structure of the relation between a vague system and the local publics is an interpretive one, not one of replacement.[3] The power of the system is that it should be able to give an interpretation of the poem in relation to all else; and if what is left out of its interpretation can be stated, then the system can, through further translation, provide a perspective on that too.

Another dimension to the problem of incommensurability must be considered at this point, a yet more difficult problem than that posed by the need to acknowledge and protect the integrity of local publics. Does not the very attempt to construct a coherent, consistent, adequate, and applicable system presuppose that the world itself is a system? Yet according to the argument of the previous chapter, the more we assess our particular domains of knowledge, the more apparent are the discontinuities between things, at least so far as we know. Empirical disciplines may discover descriptive or explanatory continuities; but they may also conclude that there are none. Systematic philosophy, it might be argued, can only impose fictional continuities by virtue of asserting, in a kind of ontological argument, that its own ideal of system is mirrored in the world.[4] But there can be no a priori reason that the world is a system if we can conceive that it is not a system, fragmentary instead. And if the world is not a system at some hidden level that the philosophical system might reveal, then the unity in the system is a fiction, and the philosophy is a lying perspective.

The objection to systematic philosophy arising from this problem is plausible only if one misconceives the logical character of vague systems. A vague philosophic system does not presuppose that the world is a unity, because it may be specified both by a lower level of assertion of A, and by a lower level assertion of not-A. As Peirce said (CP 5. 447), vagueness suspends the law of contradiction in a respect. A systematic translation of Skinner's theory of mind is possible, and so is a translation in the same system of Freud's. Likely both cannot be asserted as true within the specified systematic language; but the systematic language provides univocal terms for seeing just how they are mutually incompatible. That is, the system provides a perspective for relating the two incompatible theories. The direct validity of the Skinnerian and Freudian theories cannot be determined by the system expressing them but only by other empirical considerations. A philosophic system can show just where the world is fragmentary, and it need not prejudice the case for coherence of the assertions it brings into unity of perspective. A perspective is not a mirror image or picture of the world, but a conceptual heuristic device for the making public of discourse, the expressing of assertions in terms whereby they bear upon one another.

At this point a new objection must be considered to the whole strategy of protecting the integrity of local publics and of avoiding a priori commitment to the world as a system by treating systems as heuristic perspectives. For this strategy, says the objection, fails to indicated how systems can provide knowledge of the real as real. If philosophic systems do not do this, then something else should (which would have better claim to the title of systematic philosophy).

This objection has force, for systematic philosophy is something more than the merely heuristic or pragmatic endeavor that has been described here so far. The context of our discussion to this point has treated systematic philosophy mainly in terms of its instrumentality for bringing publicity to domains within the logical space of reasons. Has it no character more nearly intrinsic or essential to itself? It does, but not as a mere assertion within the public discourse. The essential feature of systematic philosophy is a unity of vision. Beyond all the instrumental advantages of unity of perspective mentioned so far, a unity of perspective has a worth in itself. It is a worldview, an envisionment of life's important elements that orients a way of living. This value cannot be expressed in instrumental terms, for that would be to retreat to the worth of the unity for something else.

Perhaps the worth of perspectival unity can be suggested, however, by noting that it allows one to have a larger world. The experience of grasping things with a unified perspective is richer (1) by virtue of its breadth and enlarged participation. The experience is as large as the interpreted world to which the system gives formal access. Furthermore, the unity of philosophical perspective allows (2) for experiencing the world in greater depth and penetration, than would be possible without the unity. For it allows access to perspectives on dimensions of experience that otherwise would be encountered only adventitiously. System allows one to engage a thing from many sides, correlating the sides. Philosophical system thus creates a special kind of experience distinguished by the extreme breadth and depth made possible by unity of perspective.

Although this experience may be had privately by contemplative philosophers, it is actually a cultural experience, an experience for cultures containing systems. The great philosophic systems have provided more or less well-unified conceptualities or worldviews for responding to life, and as systems they are layered into our cultural experience. Plato saw things one way, Aristotle another, and Confucius a vastly different way. Our culture includes Plato's vision as part of its own structure, and it also includes Aristotle's and Confucius's. We do not have to choose between Plato, Aristotle, and Confucius as cultural resources, but can appreciate the fact that life can be seen Plato's way and also Aristotle's and Confucius' ways. In this cultural sense even anti-systematic philosophies such as Kierkegaard's and Nietzsche's are philosophic systems because they provide useful perspectives through their conceptions for responding coherently to just about everything.

This essential trait of philosophic system, its unity of perspective, cannot be called knowledge, strictly speaking, because it does not matter to the unity whether the perspective is true or false. The question of truth is not relevant to whether a unified perspective creates a systematically enlarged and penetrating experience. This is why we can take profound contemplative satisfaction in wearing Plato's vision, and also Aristotle's and Confucius's, without being much concerned to square them with one another. Each system presents its own breadth and depth, representing different things as important, and each can be appreciated for the experience it provides. The *assertion* of the perspective is an interpretive move away from enjoying the world in the perspective; assertion harmonizes the essential unity of a system with its conditional relation to the world of which it might be true. Assertion places the system contingently in the logical space of reasons. This of course is done whenever one asks whether what is experienced through a given system is really the world.

Philosophical system as a whole needs to be conceived as a conjunction of both its essential feature of unity and its conditional connections as a heuristic device for attaining publicity within the critical culture. As participating within the truth-obliged society, the system should be as true as possible; it should be considered as an assertion for which cases need to be made within the logical space of reasons. But its character as a vague hypothesis should be remembered in order to acknowledge the incommensurability and freedom of the cultural dialogue itself. At the same time systematic philosophy should be recognized as the creation of a peculiar kind of enlarged and penetrating experience that comes from unity of perspective.

At one more reflective level, however, once the relevance of truth is seen to apply to a system's conditional role in the culture, part of the essential unity of perspective is the integration of the system's public role, and truth becomes important on a higher level for unity of perspective as such. The difference between the philosophical aesthetic of enjoying Platonism one day, Aristotelianism the next, and Confucianism later, and the obligation to work out the best philosophy possible, is that the latter recognizes the necessary conjunction between systematic philosophy's essential character and conditional roles.

The third step in the overall argument has sketched a logical form for philosophic system capable of providing a unified perspective on incommensurate local publics within the larger public, heuristically making them public to one another. At the same time, that logical form is exactly what is needed to allow for the systematically essential experience of breadth and depth. For, rather than having to include and exclude, its logical form provides access to things and also perspectives on them, whatever their mutual connections or irrelevancies. The logical form of a philosophical system should not make the system replace anything in experience, or subsume it, but rather provide unified experiential access.

IV. System as Engaged

But the basic difficulty for systematic philosophy may not have been addressed yet. Despite all the hedging of system as hypothesis subject to continual probation, there has been the assumption that systematic method in fact engages important matters. It does, of course, if the truth-obliged society to which it relates and the visionary philosophic experience it provides themselves engage important matters. But perhaps they do not. There has been a gnawing skepticism since the beginning of the modern period in philosophy, symbolized in Descartes's concern to know whether there is an external world. It continues down to recent philosophers' concern to know whether there are "other minds." Although often treated as an interpretive problem of truth, to be answered by yet better argument, this skepticism arises about the whole context of argument (see, for instance, Cavell 1979). It brings in the common fear that if the truth of assertions is a matter of persuasive rhetoric, it is mere rhetoric, not foundational proof. Rorty's dismissal of skepticism as a consequence of foundationalism misses the point that skepticism is the true motive of foundationalism (Rorty 1979, 107–114). The skepticism of modernity is not to be allayed by a new systematic perspective domesticating things so that we do not have to be skeptical any more; Weiss's dismissal (in 1980, 188) of solipsism as systematically partial also misses the locus of skepticism's bite.

If skepticism cannot be dealt with as a problem for the truth of assertions or for an embracing vision, how can it be addressed? Only by indirection. Let us therefore approach it with a philosophical myth, a theory that presents itself as a fable and is regarded as such by those who do not feel the bite of skepticism. Call it the "Myth of the Natural Standpoint," to play on Husserl's term.

The Myth asserts that cognitive and other experiential elements of intelligent social life are certain complicated patterns within the order of nature. Whereas comparatively elementary causal patterns characterize inorganic and organic natural reactions, within experiential reactions the causal patterns are very special. Mere voice sounds, for instance, are combined with habits or responses developed through complicated interactions between people and cultural artifacts so as to produce intentional responses with syntactic, semantic, and pragmatic characteristics. Lower level non-intentional nature is taken up and tranformed into higher level intentional human experience. To understand human experience as a phenomenon, according to the Myth of Natural Standpoint, is at least to understand its causal genesis out of a broader non-experiential environment. "Form of life," "conversation," "life world": these phrases signify some kind of intentionalistic integrity over against the relatively simpler push-pull patterns of brute nature. So the philosophic focal point for the Myth of Natural Standpoint is to explain the shift in causal patterns that marks the passage from non-intentional to intentional nature.

The best account of this, ironically enough, comes from the great anti-naturalist, Kant, who explains the transition in terms of *imagination*.[5] Imagination is his term for special kinds of synthesizing activity which combine the brute data of non-intentional causation with intentional patterns so as to produce experience. An account of imagination from the Natural Standpoint would have to describe the syntheses that produce the texture of experience and conversation. Images, styles of images, imagery: all constitute patterns by which the brute causal outputs of the world become present in experience. The imagery consists of forms that allow certain data to be present in experience together, and other data to be excluded. Imagination works with many layers of images and many styles of imagery filtering and interpenetrating one another. For every new level of judgment there is an enabling imagery. And although some images may be brought to consciousness and subjected to critical judgment, even formed by critically deliberative artistic activity, the images function in experience prior to any critical intentional judgement. So says the Myth of the Natural Standpoint.

Without vital imaginative connection with the rest of nature nothing is accepted in discourse except its own talk, chatter without engagement in reality. Are we genuinely experiencing anything to talk about? Are we really hearing anyone else in the conversation, or even ourselves? The Myth of the Natural Standpoint locates the problem of skepticism in imagination: is the imagination properly working? what would it be for it properly to work? Better imagery engages us with that with which it is important to be engaged, while worse imagery distorts the importance of things and inhibits genuine engagement. The result of bad imagery is disengagement, alienation. The tragedy of skepticism, like Kant's tragedy of reason, is for our intentional faculties to be running their merry way in some crucial disconnection from the nature that brings intention into contact with reality.

But now, why need we say that the natural standpoint is a myth? Husserl's attack on it (1931) notwithstanding, there is a long tradition of systematic philosophy whose perspectives occupy the natural standpoint. One more case is made in favor of that standpoint if it can give an interpretation of the location of skepticism. But the reason for calling it a myth was that we must allow for the possibility that skepticism itself undermines any philosophic perspective or assertion. Perhaps systematic philosophies of the natural standpoint are themselves alienated by virtue of disengaged imagery.

There is no good reason to call the natural standpoint a myth. The question whether naturalistic systems have good imagery is a question for poetic imagination itself, not for argument in the usual logical space of reasons. It is not identical with the question whether the natural standpoint is plausible and its assertions about the locus of skepticism in the imagination are true. Whether the imagery itself is bad, whether skepticism is warranted in a given place, is a problem for poetry, the art of dealing with the imagination.

Because skepticsm is indeed a problem for systematic reflection, systematic method in philosophy must contain more than assertions obliged by truth and visions normed by unity, more even than a theory of imagination. It must include philosophical poetry, the arts of indirection, that can bring problems of imagery to light as such and repair them. The poetic arts of philosophy often are continuous with other domains of art and criticism, and philosophy has always drawn critical energy from these. To distance themselves from the argument within the logical space of reasons, which they must do in order to objectify its imaginative base, the poetic philosophic arts often employ humor and irony. Rorty (1979, 367) notes as "peripheral" the work that the poetic philosophers do, and lists Goethe, Kierkegaard, Santayana, William James, Dewey, the later Wittgenstein, the later Heidegger, and perhaps Plato. But whereas Rorty interprets them as offering arguments ouside the mainstream's logical space of reasons, at least part of their contribution is not argument at all in any usual sense but a poetic shift of imagery. What may be surprising even to these anti-systematic thinkers is that their creative address to imagination is as much a part of systematic philosophy as the construction of systems and arguments for them. For, how else could philosophy be reflective about the unexamined commitments of imagery? Perhaps this is surprising even to philosophers who identify themselves with system building.

The first step in our argument said that systematic method in philosophy is justified by the need to reflect on things from all angles, and that philosophical system is whatever results from this. If there is merit to the intervening steps, however, it should now be possible to frame a new, more determinate statement of the nature and worth of systematic philosophy. And from this we finally can ask whether, as the introductory thesis asserted, system in philosophy is a norm for mediating between the diverse techniques and capabilities of philosophers on the one hand and the range of justifiable and perhaps obligatory tasks on the other.

Step two considered how systematic philosophy best comports itself within the ongoing philosophical conversation, or more importantly within the process of a truth-obliged society. The assertions appropriate to philosophy ought to be public, it argued, and philosophy becomes public by becoming systematic. Furthermore, philosophy makes other domains public to each other by interpreting them systematically. Even philosophies and other domains that intend not to be systematic are assessed within the ongoing dialogue according to systematic criteria of adequacy, applicability, consistency, coherence, relevance, and self-referential completeness (also according to their imagery). Because the truth-obliged society is to be understood in social or political terms, and the truth of assertions is a political value, the interpretive dimension of systematic philosophy gives it an essentially social function. This dimension of systematic philosophy is rightly called "interpretive," and its overriding norm is truth.

Step three considered how systematic philosophy relates to the fact that many elements in culture are incommensurate with one another and that often their value and integrity lie in what makes them incommensurate. Why should systematic philosophy even attempt to join them in a common public? The form of systematic philosophy was then interpreted as a commensurating perspective on other things, making them commensurate *from its standpoint*. The means for constructing such a perspective is a set of categories whose reference to things is logically vague, requiring further specification by less vague domains of discourse that may be incommensurate with each other. The specification of the system's categories, however, involves translating the important elements in the less vague domains into the language of the system, thereby making commensurate within that language what is hypothetically proposed as important. The role of systematic philosophy as the search for truth is conditional upon society. The essential character of the form of a system, however, is not so much to aim for truth, prescinding from the system considered as an hypothetical assertion within the larger community, as it is to aim for a unified experience that allows for grasping the world with breadth and systematic engagement. This dimension of systematic philosophy as both public interpretation and experiential envisionment can be called "theory."

Step four addressd the radical problem of skepticsm and argued that it is an affair of the images by which experience is formed out of other natural causal processes and by which experience engages reality. Skepticism's existential locus is experientially prior to assertion and theoretical envisionment, in the very function of imagination itself. In order for systematic philosophy to address issues from all sides, it therefore must criticize cultural and philosophical imagination and become involved in creating more engaging, less alienating, images. This dimension of systematic philosophy can be called "poetic imagination."

Is there not something strange about referring to these dimensions of philosophy as "systematic," even after all this discussion? Surely there are philosophical interpreters who make no effort to be systematic in the sense described here. There are philosophers of science, of religion, of education, of art, and of a host of other extraphilosophical domains; there are ethicists, metaphysicians, epistemologists, and logicians, each of whom is comparatively innocent of the others. We cannot say that these practitioners of "philosophy as interpretive assertion within the logical space of reasons" are not philosophers because they do not care for integrating perspective. Similarly there are theorizers or system builders with a deep concern for unity of vision but with a negligible level of effort at argumentation and interpretation of other domains of experience. These include not only "religious philosophers" but also many of the great system builders such as Whitehead whose applied philosophy is comparatively superficial. Whereas system builders trade off close-grained analysis for the breadth and depth of vision, interpreters trade off orienting vision for precision and density or argument. We need not belabor the point that more poetic philosophers of indirection are unsystematic in other senses. It is possible, apparently, to be legitimately philosophical in each of these dimensions without being systematic.

This suggests yet another dimension to systematic philosophy, one that has been present since the beginning of the discussion and that accounts for the systematic quality depicted in interpretaion, theorizing, and imagination. Systematic philosophy has a self-referential *responsibility* to evaluate and redirect its own thinking. This is the heart of the description of system in philosophy as the examination of things from all angles and the examination of the perspectives involved in doing this. It is what makes philosophical interpretation take responsiblity for intepreting one thing in terms of another so that coherent responses are possible and reasons are seen in public light. It makes theory be not only broad and penetrating vision but also a servicable and true guide to life in a truth-obliged society. Philosophy's poetic imagination is not only aesthetic art but part of a larger philosophic enterprise because of the responsibility systematic thinking has for the images of culture and its own reflections. Philosophy's pursuit of systematic responsibility turns it both to the needs of wisdom in the truth-obliged society and to self-critical reflection on the norms of imaginative engagement. Weiss referred to systematic philosophy's responsiblity when he said it should alert us to what to think about next. He could have added that a system is responsible for saying *why* that should be next.

This word *dimension* indicates that systematic philosophy is involved in or determined by the norms of all the dimensions at once. Whatever its assertions or vision, a given bit of thinking involves some imagery, and it has responsibilities to make that imagery engaging. Whatever its imagery or unifying excellence, a philosophical system is still a set of assertions, at least potentially, and thus is responsible to the issue of truth. Whatever its assertions or their imagery, it is of the essence of systematic philosophy to provide a unifed vision wherein the world can be experienced in breadth and depth. And whatever it is doing de facto, systematic philosophy has an internal self-reflexive obligation to ask whether this is what it should be doing. When philosophers neglect any of these dimensions for very long, they fail to take the responsibilities that are theirs and fall back on the momentum of previous accomplishments.

Does not the actual practice of philosophy indicate the normative character of these dimensions in systematic connection? A system builder may be inspired by an inner vision and transfixed by its formal elegance. But the theory is challenged to prove itself dialectically superior to alternatives, to make sense of domains it does not mention, and to offer evidence that is needed to assert what it does. If the system builder does not respond to the challenge, other critics will pass the verdict. As for "philosophers of . . . ," are they not challenged concerning how they relate to other domains, and is there not constant pressure to state and justify the most abstract presuppositions of their interpretations? Are not all philosophers, even logicians, challenged to make contact with life outside philosophy, to tap into and respond to the imagination of their culture, and to be sensitive to the arts for this reason? We rightly condemn any sustained divorce from the forces of imaginative cultural life as sterile and academic. Do not most philosophers respond to these challenges by attempting to decide whether their challenged thoughts are responsible to the relevant norm at hand? To practice philosophy is a pluralistic enterprise, involving at once the responsible construction of theories, responsible argument making contact with other thinkers in a common public, responsible criticism and creation of imagery that engages philosophy with life, and a self-reflexive concern that these responsiblities be fulfilled in ways for which the philosophy can take responsibility.

Interpretation, theory, imagination, and philosophical responsiblity: tolerance suggests that techniques with which systematic philosophy can address these tasks are indefinitely various, still often inadequate, and instrumentally related to the tasks. System in philosophy itself is a norm that mediates between its techniques and its obligatory tasks, obliging philosophers with systematic responsibilities. This was the original thesis presented above.

Truth in systematic philosophy is the carryover into the philosophic discussion and more broadly into the interpreting civilization of the value in the multifarious world.[6] Unlike other interpretive enterprises attempting to be true, systematic philosophy by definition aims to leave nothing out. Yet its way of carrying over the value of everything is to sort things into ranks of connected structures of importance. Systematic philosophy offers a way of accepting what each intermediate interpretation finds to be of value. It carries over everything by ordering subtheories that offer guides to the worths of things not directly represented. Systematic philosophy depends upon the very multifariousness of our diverse interpretive paths to sustain access to what is only vaguely present in the categoreal consideration. In this sense, systematic philosophy is the life of curiosity within civilization. How could modernist and postmodernist philosophers ever think to delegitimate it? If systematic philosophy were missing, the multifariousness of civilization would invent it. It has.

CHAPTER SEVEN

❊

REFLECTIONS ON AMERICAN
PHILOSOPHY

The venue of this chapter is peculiarly delicate to state. Its thesis is that American philosophy has an important contribution to make to the development of a world philosophical community, and this in virtue of certain traits associated with its special American character. Precisely because of approaches that distinguish American philosophy from much of the rest of the Western tradition, it is ready to facilitate a world philosophic dialogue. Paradoxically, much of the practice of recent professional philosophy in America misses just this point. So the argument here is addressed to two groups. One is the American philosophic profession, and the point is that it should reappropriate certain important American roots in order to take part in the larger world of philosophy; this point is argued with a critique of some current professional practice. The other group consists of those already engaged in philosophy situated in the world community, either as comparativists or as representatives of philosophic traditions who aim to expand their audience.[1] The point is that they might look to the development of the classic American pragmatic and process traditions for helpful elements of a common language for world philosophic dialogue.

I. Emerson on the Range of American Philosophic Practice

Ralph Waldo Emerson delivered his Phi Beta Kappa address, called "The American Scholar," in 1837, in which he announced:

Our day of dependence, our long apprenticeship to the learning of other lands, draws to a close. The millions that around us are rushing into life,

161

cannot always be fed on the sere remains of foreign harvest. Events, actions arise, that must be sung, that will sing themselves. (1837, 45)

Emerson's foe was apprenticeship, and the usual reading of his essay believes it to be a declaration of American cultural independence from Europe. There is a point to this interpretation, though in the hands of
some it treads dangerously close to ethnic chauvinism; anyway, Emerson
abandoned that theme after his first paragraph. Let us call to mind the
plot of his actual argument.

By apprenticing themselves, human beings become partial; wholeness results only from a special kind of self-reliance that consists in responding to the right influences. Influences *can* make one whole;
apprenticeship to the things that might influence one destroys integrity.
Emerson traced this out with regard to nature, books, and action. Long
before Nietzsche and Heidegger, he wrote that wholeness of self requires that one learn from nature considered in its individual parts,
each with its own particularity, setting, and integrity. To aggregate the
parts of nature, however, and bow to their cumulative masses is to *apprentice* oneself to their material usefulness; the self then is captured by
its own selfishness, a point in which Heidegger (for instance, 1954) follows Emerson.

As to books, one discovers one's own full mind by discovering other
full minds; Emerson was clear about the importance of literary influences, and wrote especially about the need to attend to Asian literatures
and to non-canonical elements of the Western tradition. The importance of books is that they reveal the character of great minds. For such
a mind, the world comes to it as life and is returned as truth. The danger
of books, however, is that one can respond to them as dogmas rather
than as emblems of the action of mind. Hence scholars are prone to apprentice themselves to other people's programs and, thus, are fragmented within themselves.

As to action, Emerson did not promote a political program, as did
his contemporary Marx, but rather he likened action to the undulations
of nature. That is, the scholar is a natural force, thinking with wholeness
while moving through the natural circumstances, rhythms, and stages of
life. Reclusion is the dangerous apprenticeship that distorts action. Emerson closed with a consideration of the duties of the American scholar.
"The office of the scholar," he wrote, "is to cheer, to raise, and to guide
men by showing them facts amidst appearances" (1837, 55).

Taking Emerson as a guide, we may reflect on the contemporary
philosophical scene in America in terms of the distinction between

apprenticeship and the self-reliant development of intelligent living through the finding and appropriating of the right influences. Two initial observations are in order.

First, Emerson's moral polemic today would be directed against what can be called "program philosophy," the kind that identifies itself as working out or responding to the suppositions of some genius-founder. This apprentice philosophy is distinguished not so much by a dogmatic scholastic defense of its principles against all critics but by a drastic narrowing of philosophic interest to the affairs of its own program. Questions not of interest to its program, or not framed in terms commensurable to the questions of the program, are assumed, and sometimes asserted, to be unphilosophical. The style of program philosophy is to ignore and delegitimate, not to refute, its competitors. In our own time, program apprenticeship has been practised with a vengeance in high places by followers of Husserl, the early Wittgenstein, the late Wittgenstein, Whitehead, Heidegger, Merleau-Ponty, the MIT cognitive scientists, and the deconstructionists. Somewhat earlier in the century there were apprentice shops for logical positivists, Deweyan educationists, and Thomists. This is not to say that any of the figures named was or is a program philosopher; all except Husserl would have been offended by the suggestion. Yet there are or have been institutions of higher learning where admission to the profession requires apprenticeship to one or more of these programs: philosophy not so apprenticed is not recognized as philosophy or allowed to be legitimated with a degree. The institutions that eschew program philosophy and use ideas as "influences" only, are few and far between.

The second general observation is that the classical American philosophies of pragmatism and its neighbors, that followed so naturally from Emerson's own influence, are remarkably clear in sharing his vision both of philosophic self-reliance and of the importance of philosophy for life and public affairs. Yet it would be a mistake to construe this native tradition as defining in an exclusive way the range of American philosophy. From the early philosophers of the American constitution through Emerson to Dewey and Whitehead, American philosophy has been taken to be a creative innovation resulting from the absorption and transformation of many traditions originating outside of America. The most important recently, if not the most noticed, is the entry of Asian thought into the culture of philosophy. In the last twenty years enough critical editions and translations have been made that Indian and Chinese philosophies are as available to contemporary American students of philosophy as the Greek and medieval traditions of the West.[2]

In addition to Asian philosophies, the American tradition has been influenced in many important ways by European traditions represented by newer immigrations from Europe, most notably the Thomist and Neo-Thomist philosophies of Catholicism, the various kinds of analytic philosophy that flourished as critiques of idealism, the logical positivism, phenomenology, and existentialism of the thinkers fleeing Hitler, and the recent interest in the hermeneutic thought of Germany and France, including deconstruction. All of these movements have enriched the American philosophic scene in ways Emerson could not have anticipated as developments of what he knew.

II. Nature, Books, and Action

Let us turn now to the present state of Emerson's themes of nature, books, and action.

Emerson insisted that original thinkers encounter nature in its raw particularity. Charles Peirce directly followed up on this concern with his interest in nature as knowable by pragmatic science. Despite his precept and example, however, subsequent thinkers, including Royce, James, and Dewey, were more interested in the process of interpretation than in nature interpreted and, hence, reoriented the focus of philosophy from wonder at nature to solving the "problems of men," as Dewey put it. Santayana and Whitehead, almost alone in their generation, were concerned with philosophy of nature; more recently Justus Buchler and David Weissman should be added to that list.

Almost all the rest of the European-inspired parts of the tradition accepted Kant's critical philosophy that assigned the topic of nature to natural science and limited philosophy to the epistemology of philosophy of science. Therefore neither analytic nor continental forms of philosophy have contributed much to our understanding of nature. Heidegger's desperate plea to return to "things" in the *Question Concerning Technology* (1954) is a symptom more than an explanation of this. Chinese Taoist and Confucian thought is almost the only inspiration for philosophy of nature these days, which explains the great attractiveness of these Chinese traditions for responding to issues of ecological ethics (for instance, Callicott and Ames 1989). Of the Western philosophies, it appears that only Whitehead's thought offers continuing resources for philosophy of nature. Some attempts have been made to revitalize Aristotle's philosophy of nature, but without much success. Philosophy of nature remains in deep need of recovery (Neville 1989).

Thanks to Derrida, our notion of the book has been expanded to that of "text," a change Emerson would have applauded. Several texts need discussion here (most but not all of which are also books) that are influential within the range of contemporary American philosophy.

First are the texts of the philosophic profession, texts that lie in jeopardy of being taken as programs to which young philosophers should be apprenticed. Let us assume, however, that they can be taken as influences rather than programs. The texts at the dominant institutions of professional education in philosophy are still those of the analytic traditions, now developed enough to recoil upon themselves. Fortunately, the influential analytical books now are those that call into question the old narrow professional definition of philosophy. For instance, ordinary language philosophy has developed into speech-act theory that in turn has moved into linguistics, where the line between linguistics and philosophy cannot be drawn. The old desire of the naturalized epistemologists has been fulfilled by the move of philosophers into cognitive science, supported by those who two generations ago would have been interested in formal language analysis. Analytic ethical theory largely has been turned over into case-study analysis, with philosophers becoming adjunct specialists in other fields such as medicine, warfare, business, and education. Richard Rorty's neopragmatic critique of the analytic tradition's epistemological focus merely provides an external summary and legitimation of recent developments in analytic philosophy. The breakdown of philosophical professionalism in which analytic philosophy has pioneered is all to be approved from Emerson's perspective. Its only limitation is that in most cases it has not led analytic philosophers to broaden their appreciation of what else counts as philosophy, or of the history of the philosophic traditions, except insofar as these have grown out of earlier analytic practices. Robert Nozick's *Philosophical Explanations* (1981), for instance, seems like daring analytical metaphysics when in fact it is a tentative approach to a position something like Paul Weiss's, which it does not mention; nor does it mention Whitehead, the previous metaphysician at Nozick's Harvard.

The mention of history exposes another range of proper influences in American philosophy. Careful study of great thinkers remains essential for learning the complexity and depth of true philosophic thought. In addition, the last decades have seen a revival of philosophic research in the history of philosophy, and indeed the French school has taught once again the importance of reading philosophy in its historical and social context. Perhaps the most exciting developments in history of philosophy are those focusing on Chinese philosophy, developments that employ all the methods available without the strain of having to find something new in a field that has been thoroughly leached by previous scholars; one thinks of the work by American philosophers such as Tu Wei-ming, David Hall, Roger Ames, Kuang-ming Wu, and Cheng Chung-ying. Perhaps it is a lamentable fact of our situation that those who read Norman Kretzman would not also read Michel Foucault and the philosophers of China. Yet undergraduates are more recalcitrant than ever at learning what they ought *not* to read, and a great rush may be foreseen on the part of students to a comprehensive sense of the methods and topics for philosophical history and historical philosophy in the near future.

The influence of the Continental tradition, which was so focused on pure phenomenology, existentialism, and Marxism a quarter century ago, has become an extremely fruitful exploration of hermeneutics, broadly considered. On the one hand is the strict hermeneutical tradition deriving from Heidegger through Gadamer and Ricoeur, and on the other is the French structuralist tradition of Levi-Straus; both are set in critical relief by poststructural and postmodernist criticism that has given new life to Marxist thought after its political excitement died away. Another Continental tradition that was influential a quarter century ago was Thomism and Neo-Thomism, and its approach through thinkers such as Gilson and Maritain to the history of philosophy. At the moment that tradition seems submerged, but it lies just below the surface and, in this day when everyone has to critique modernity in order to be respectable, will emerge as an important contributor, along with Chinese philosophy, to an alternative to that which we are now "post." The helpfulness of the influence of Chinese and Indian philosophy has already been mentioned. Indian philosophy was focused as a world philosophy mainly in the period before independence, under the leadership of the great movement from Aurobindo to Radhakrishnan to recover the ancient tradition. The great writers in these traditions have yet to be accepted and internalized by most professional philosophers. But in this respect the professionals will have to run to catch up to thinkers in other parts of the range of American philosophy.

There are several other texts, less bookish, that properly are influential today, namely the traditional vocational consumers of philosophy, especially science, religion, politics, law, the arts, letters, and imaginative literature. Philosophy continues to be interested in the new ideas of physics and chemistry, including the recent work of Bohm and Prigogine; biology and socio-biology have become important stimuli for philosophy, and so has psychology both in its soulful approaches through the work of people like James Hillman and the bodyful approaches through cognitive science and neuro-psychology. Religion continues its customary service of forcing philosophy to provide disciplined responses to concerns about the big picture, but now also through concerns that have appropriated the ambiguities and pluralisms, even the death of God, of contemporary religious hermeneutics, as in the work of David Tracy. Bringing non-theistic religions into the picture has provided new speculative tasks for philosophy of religion. Politics and law are fields that often have been influential texts for philosophy, though that seems to be less true now than fifty years ago when John Dewey and Walter Lippmann proved philosophy has a role in public affairs. The texts of the arts, belles-lettres, and imaginative literature have been less stimuli to philosophy recently than substitutes for philosophy. One thinks of the philosophies of Ad Reinhardt, Frederick Jameson, and Saul Bellow. But this is only to say that the range of American philosophy extends far beyond the profession.

A final influence to be noticed is the non-literary texts of two sources that until recently have not registered in the American philosophic tradition, namely the experiences of non-literate and culturally suppressed people, and the problems of the natural environment. Liberation movements for women, for oppressed nations, for homosexuals, and ethnic minorities have brought to prominence experiences that hitherto have been ignored; but except for brief excursions of Marxism, philosophy has been unable to express these experiences well or to interpret them in connection with the experiences of the tradition. As to nature, the ruination of our ecology is enough to call attention to the human relation with the environment; yet this attention also falls on issues concerning the intrinsic value of nature, animal rights, and the rest. These "texts" are also appropriate influences to which American philosophy needs to make a response if it is to be whole.

Emerson's third theme, after nature and books, was action. Though only in specialized situations should philosophy feel obliged to have a political program, Emerson was clear that philosophy or scholarship is to be practised as an enhancement of the ordinary rhythms of life. Earlier in this century, when some philosophers were bent on showing that philosophy has a discipline of its own that allows it to be a science, or at least a profession, philosophy was defined as a set of techniques for linguistic or phenomenological analysis. If philosophy abandons such methodological self-definition for an orientation to its subject matter, it turns again to be a way of life. We need not fear that philosophy will collapse into religion if it is regarded as a discipline of life, although it bears a connection with what traditional religions have tried to do. Philosophy, as Dewey argued, is disciplined intelligence in the living of life. To conflate Emerson's emphasis on action with his definition of the special office of scholarship, it is "to cheer, to raise, and to guide men by showing them facts amidst appearances." Long before Emerson and Dewey, Plato made the point about guidance. The emphasis on cheering and raising is perhaps peculiarly American. The cheering and raising part of scholarship, especially philosophy, comes from this, that a knowledge distinguishing "fact from appearances" allows intelligence to come into play in life. Even when the appearances are comforting and the facts terrifying, knowledge of their difference allows the response to them to be the beginning of our self-reliance, and this is cheering in Aristotle's sense of activity in accordance with virtue. Even when the possibilities for response are limited and bleak, our aspirations can be raised to the point where our responses are whole and integral; at worst then human life is tragic. Without the philosophic distinction between "facts and appearances," life in good times as well as bad is limited to the pathetic. This is to say, human life pathetically would be apprenticed to other forces, either blindly, or by learning the algorithms of another mind. What is a computer but a faithful apprentice?

Emerson's vision has its limitations for the range of American philosophy. The individualism of his view of the heroic thinker seems quaint today. He was naive about the possibility of thinking independently from social and economic interest. He was nearly blind to the irrational forces of the unconscious and to our capacity for self-deception. And we have learned far more about the vicious limitations of technological reason in managing public and personal affairs than he could have imagined. Emerson was naive even for his own time because he was so soft on the doctrine of original sin, his contemporaries' understanding of why human powers are treacherous.

Even thinking the worst of his limitations, however, Emerson's vision retains a prophetic critical edge for our own time. The range of American philosophy, especially in its institutionalized forms, stands in jeopardy of collapsing into apprenticeships. Nature can be forgotten in our preoccupations with human freedom and interpretive reason. Our philosophies can degenerate into narrow programs, delegitimating both independent thought and other programs. Philosophers can segregate their professional lives from the rest of their action, relating to intellectual peers rather than the contexts of life itself. Like the Great Refusals of Confucius and Socrates, Emerson would say No to those apprenticeships. Philosophic wholeness and integrity requires self-reliance that seeks out proper influences rather than masters. Insofar as the range of American philosophy practises such self-reliance, its marvelous multi-fariousness, its pluralistic genius, will be able to perform the office of cheering, raising, and guiding public life through the power of insight into the distinctions between appearances and facts.

III. American Philosophy as World Philosophy

By name, American philosophy is a national or ethnic philosophy. Is it more than that? Is it a world philosophy that can have power and relevance beyond its place and period of origin? That question can be sharpened and some complex answers suggested.

Every philosophy arises out of a mixture of intellectual play and endeavor with the particular conditions of an historical culture. Ideas are not free floating but are shaped by some vague, if often faulty, relevance to situational conditions. Part of the meaning of the question of whether a national philosophy can become a world philosophy is whether the important conditions of its existential situation obtain or have analogues in other situations.

One of the famous conditions that has had an undeniable impact on American culture from the time of Jonathan Edwards to the beginning of this century has been the wilderness. The "frontier hypothesis" explains much that is unique in America, but if it were to be a main explanation of its distinctive philosophy, it would mark that philosophy as non-generalizable, for not many situations involve taming a frontier. The wilderness component of the American situation may not be a dominant condition shaping its philosophic tradition, however. Latin American and Australian philosophers addressed the civilizing of wilderness, and neither developed anything like the American philosophic tradition, or show much sympathy even today. And the two American philosophers who lived and worked, at least for a while, on the frontier, Edwards and Josiah Royce, are the least emancipated from European modes of thought of all the American "greats." The discussion shall return shortly to identify some of the real determining situational conditions in American thought and to ask whether they in fact have general application.

To juxtapose a national philosophy to a world philosophy leaps over a common intervening step, namely a multinational tradition, such as the "Western." Kant is a prototypical German philosopher whose philosophy has become central to all Western philosophy since his time. No Western philosopher can fail to come to terms with Kant's

reformulation of the tradition and with the limits he claimed for its intellectual powers. Yet it is not at all clear whether Kant's philosophy has
much interest for those whose philosophic paideia is the Indian or Chinese tradition; Plato, Hegel, and Whitehead, by contrast, clearly are of
interest to contemporary Samkhya, Vedanta, Mahayana Buddhist, and
Confucian philosophers. The question to ask about American philosophy is not whether it generalizes to a full-scale place in *Western* philosophy, but whether and under what conditions it can function as a *world*
philosophy.

Another clarification of the question of whether American philosophy is a world philosophy has to do with the matter of national style.
Related to the concrete situatedness of national philosophies is the fact
that they tend to have styles of thinking, perhaps originating with some
early founding thinkers but reinforced and reinforcing subsequent cultural developments. Thus, the ancient Greeks were creatively imaginative and speculative, the French love a play of reasoning that is easily
disconnectable from common sense, the Germans combine a love for ex-
actitude and completeness with a reverence for the contextual penum-
bra of ideas, Hispanic philosophers have a passion for relevance and
critique, while the British hate nonsense worse than boredom. By the
same token American philosophers have a pragmatic orientation, even
when they criticize, as Peirce and Dewey did, the crass meaning of that
term, or when they antedate the pragmatic movement. Benjamin Franklin and Thomas Jefferson, though not accepted as true philosophers,
embodied an engineering mentality that affects the style of American
thinkers from the early spiritual engineers such as Edwards and Emerson to the later social and intellectual engineers of the so-called Gold-
en Age.

Style is *not* something that generalizes. Indeed, for American philosophy to be a world philosophy, it would itself have to be adaptable to
the various styles of the cultures in which it would be embodied. Mahayana Buddhism exhibits its character as a world philosophy in the interesting contrasts among its Indian, Chinese, Korean, Japanese, and
American styles—Edward Conze is a very British Buddhist. To discern
the viability of American philosophy as a world philosophy, we must
be able to see its multi-style embodiments, just as we must be able to
find common or analogous situational conditions across the cultures it
might address.

One final remark is appropriate about the precision and scope of
the notion of "world philosophy." It is an approximation at best. No
comprehensive and universally shared set of philosophic terms or prob-

lems exists. Nor is it a comprehensive survey of world philosophies to cite merely those that take their rise from the axial age thinkers of China, India, and the ancient Near East. The best approximation of the notion of a world philosophy is in terms of potentiality: a world philosophy is one that can engage and has something to contribute to the work of any major philosophic endeavor in the world, East or West, North or South, elite or unprivileged. Not all the philosophies to which a world philosophy needs to be responsive are themselves world philosophies. Needless to say, much work of translation might be required before it is possible to say whether a fruitful engagement is possible.

That American philosophy is fit to serve world philosophy can be argued in six points. These points characterize American philosophy in important and essential ways, and have been developed through the 250 years of the tradition's history. Each point, in some important measure, is responsive to very general situational conditions, not merely American ones, and no point is especially dependent on the American style.

1. The trajectory of the American philosophic tradition avoided modernism, as has been argued throughout this book, and hence is not seriously defined by postmodernism, deconstruction, Rorty's conversationalism, or any other current movement designed to get over modernism. Modernism is the family of cultural responses to the panic of Europeans about the collapse of their religion and values in the face of modern science. Modernist movements in art, literature, and philosophy converge in attempting to produce cultural things that have meaning intrinsically within themselves and so cannot be made unintelligible by what happens outside them, things that are valuable in themselves, things that by needing nothing else can be foundation stones for uncollapsable culture. Phenomenology's search for the pure description, existentialism's will that precedes essence, Marxism's class solidarity, analytic philosophy's devotion to formal or ordinary language—all these are modernist in one way or another, and all have been summarily criticised under the label of foundationalism.

American philosophers have thought that philosophy is one among many other disciplines from which its margins are indistinct and that philosophy bleeds off into those others. Furthermore, philosophy is not only de facto fallible, for the Americans it is de jure fallible. As in so many other instances, Peirce made the argument traced above, that best epitomises the tradition in his critique of Kant's rejection of the method of hypothesis. Of course, there is no certainty, no foundationalism, in the fallibilist theory of knowing by hypothesis. But then, according to the fallibilist theory, there should not be. Experiential learning can bring conviction, but it establishes no claim to authority that further learning might not amend. Like the modernist movements, the American addresses the scientific world with understanding and sympathy, both domesticating it and providing a critical tool to use against it. But unlike modernisms, it does not depend on foundationalism or infallible authority. If anything characterizes the worldwide situation for philosophical thinking today, it is that nothing in any previous belief or tradition can be taken at face value, that everything needs to be supplemented by further learning in order to provide a wise understanding of our age.

2. The second point follows immediately from this. If most traditions in the world cultures are looking to adjust themselves to the demands of the scientific age, then an empirical understanding of experience is obviously relevant. As John E. Smith (1978, chapter 3) has pointed out, Hume's analysis of experience into impressions and ideas is an a priori metaphysical imposition of categories, not an observationally derived hypothesis. The Samkhya pair of *prakriti* and *purusha,* the Vedanta theory of illusion, the Buddhist Abhidharma—all are being subject to critiques of their traditional status, and they are stronger if presented as hypotheses. The American tradition has a solid commitment to learning what experience is from *learning,* not from any kind of pure reasoning. Just as Western European thought has rejected the a priori approach, most forms of Chinese and Indian thought have never expected it. America's approach here thus has worldwide relevance.

3. A third character of American philosophy, pre-eminent in Edwards and running through Emerson, Peirce, Dewey, Whitehead, and Weiss, is an appeal (with analysis) to an aesthetic theory of beauty as the cornerstone of moral theory as well as religion. Not that morals or religion are to be reduced to aesthetics, though perhaps Emerson and, today, David Hall tend in that direction. Rather, the American tradition has given an aesthetic interpretation of value, objectivist and formal. When the values are those of human relations, morals are involved, with the relativities and ambiguities of competing or incommensurable values; when the values of things, good and evil, are related to the ground of being, religion is involved. This formal and objective approach to value is embodied many ways, from the religious philosophies of Edwards, Peirce, Royce, and John Smith to the naturalisms of Dewey, Santayana, Randall, and David Weissman. But all stand opposed to the theory of value as subjective projection that led to the modernist philosophies of existentialism and emotivism. As the threatening realities of nuclear war and the destruction of the environment shove all philoso-

phies from inherited agendas to living, forced ones, an objectivist and formal approach to value seems eminently sensible for worldwide relevance.

4. The fourth characteristic of the American tradition, perhaps not as universal as the others, has often been seen as a fault by European interpreters, namely, an inability to draw a sharp distinction between the self and nature. American philosophers have seen human beings as deeply embedded in ongoing processes of nature. Indeed, parts of human beings are parts of larger processes, other parts are parts of other processes, and whether these can be integrated temporarily and flexibly according to some ideal of personal unity is touch and go. Peirce said a person is a sign, or maybe a process of interpretation over time, and this view does not allow for much inward-turning, infinite, Kierkegaardian reflection or alienation from the environment. Dewey, too, was concerned with the fragmentariness of the things important for human life, and was almost obsessed with attaining leverage over the ongoing forces of society and nature so as to make possible the enjoyment of civilization's graces. After critics for most of this century have bemoaned the inability of the American tradition to participate in the modernists' bitter joy at the collapse of Western culture, it now seems not such a bad idea simply to finesse the exaggerated self-other, subjective-objective theme. American philosophy demonstrates that Cartesianism is not the only way to grow from European philosophy. The naturalism of American thought is far more akin to the philosophic traditions of other world cultures than the European aberrations of Cartesian and Kantian scientism, and it is far more connectable with the actual practice of scientific investigation.

5. Having stressed the naturalism of American philosophy, it is important also to note its idealism, the fifth characteristic. Idealism need not be meant in any of its several technical senses, for American philosophers have held all sorts of positions in this regard—naturalist, materialist, transcendentalist, nominalist, and so forth. Rather, the American philosophers are idealists in that they believe in the usefulness of ideas, even big ideas such as beauty, truth, vision, and responsibility. From the early Puritan understanding of philosophy as a reflective tool for building cities of God on earth, through the engineering mentality of the American Enlightenment, to the Golden Age of pragmatism and process philosophy, down to the current recovery of the American speculative spirit, philosophy has been regarded as a specialized development of civilization to help guide life, living well, and living better, as

Whitehead (1929a) put it. Philosophy is not a self-justifying profession but a culture-serving profession, a profession defined by the needs of its clientele rather than by the authority of its methods. The American tradition is indeed more speculative and playful than many others because of its confidence in the usefulness of ideas to promote wise living. Because ideas are instruments, not merely treasures or inheritances, they can be taken with great seriousness and flexibility, not with reverence. American philosophy is outrageously intellectual, and that is of powerful importance when so many of the other dominant strains of Western thinking are celebrating the end of philosophy.

6. The last characteristic of American philosophy to be mentioned is its emphasis on community. This enormously complex topic cannot be discussed with any rigor here, but one important contrast may be drawn. Most traditional philosophies of community have emphasized the importance of the common inheritance and the deeprootedness of institutions. One thinks, for instance, of Gadamer's views (1975) on prejudice in hermeneutics, or the Confucian stress (Tu 1979, 1985) on filial piety. While not denying the importance of commonality, the American tradition has given greater importance to community precisely as the engagement of the Other, the Alien. One thinks of Peirce's theory of interpretation bridging the otherness of Secondness, or of Royce's philosophy of loyalty (1908) overcoming intrinsic competition. The most striking case is that of Emerson, who felicitously misunderstood Kant and Hegel and believed that the Absolute, the Transcendental Ego, or the Oversoul, unites all people each as an original, each as a spontaneous individual, a unique reflection of Soul. The people who *do not* fit into Emerson's community of great-souled people are those who merely fit into a larger solidarity. Nietzsche appreciated Emerson's celebration of genius, but failed to see that it defined a special sense of community running contrary to the super-community of the superman. The only conception of community appropriate for a world culture is one respecting the differences of traditions, prejudices, practices, and conditions. The alternative is totalitarian, as has been proved in the fascist and communist experiments of our century.

Two important qualifications need to be made to this reading of American philosophy. First, it has employed a highly selective identification of the American tradition. The important American philosophers were all of European extraction, yet those European influences that came after the Golden Age of pragmatism have been discounted in this reading. The reason is that they all were modernist after a fashion, except for the Roman Catholics, and they attempted to supplant rather than graft themselves onto the earlier American themes. The history of philosophy in America includes the near-complete suppression of the classic tradition of the Golden Age for the middle half of this century by so-called analytic and Continental philosophies; but insofar as the modernist philosophies are determinative of the American situation, they are as deserving as the pragmatists to be called Americans. The history of American philosophy also includes the small story of those thinkers who survived the suppression of the classical tradition and who now are reviving its themes, often in explicit dialogue with philosophic traditions from East Asia and India. It is that latter group, those self-consciously identifying with the pre- and para-modernist American philosophies, whose collective viability as a world philosophy has been considered here.

The second qualification is to admit to an idealized reading of the American tradition. Each of the traits singled out for celebration also has been corrupted in ways that seem typically American to the culture's critics. The theory of knowledge as hypothetical has sometimes meant that knowledge for its own sake is unimportant. The empirical approach to experience and learning has sometimes entailed a loss of historical consciousness. The aesthetic definition of value can let the critical edge of moral reform degenerate into nature-romanticism. The naturalist approach to human identity can mean a superficial culture of feeling. The emphasis on the usefulness of ideas has widely degenerated into technologizing scientism. The ideal of community as a gathering of unique and spontaneous individuals can slide into a modernist dialectic of atomic individualism versus mass solidarity. There is a truth to the popular image of Americans as thoughtless, historically ignorant, vacuously romantic, gushy, technocratic, unconnected "individuals who are all the same." Explanations abound for the phenomena named here. But none of the serious explanations is that these popular bad characteristics are the direct outgrowth of American philosophy. On the contrary, for they are precisely the characteristics that Europeans and now the Japanese are taking over from America, without the slightest understanding of the classic American philosophy. If anything, the degeneration of American popular culture has been made possible by the substitution of modernist importations that cut the culture off from its own traditional philosophic roots.

The point here has not been to praise American philosophy per se but to suggest that certain of its distinctive themes have important relevance beyond the American situation. Each of the traits mentioned addresses a situation that seems to obtain across all cultures that have begun the process of "modernization," and the American condition is just one version, perhaps a more European version than Americans like to admit, of that larger situation. To say that the American can be a world philosophy is not to say that it is the true world philosophy, only that it has important insights and thoughtforms that need to be addressed. This in itself is a significant contribution. The consideration of American philosophy cannot be separated from its professional embodiment, and to that topic the discussion needs to return directly.

IV. A Role for the Professional Philosopher

Richard Rorty has called into question what he takes to be the main outcomes of the Western philosophic tradition. How disappointing it is to be unable to locate one's own philosophic practice among either those he proscribes as foundationalisms or those he lauds as non-foundational reduction of philosophy to conversation. As has been evident from what has preceded, the argument here is that interesting and viable kinds of philosophy are speculatively metaphysical, culturally critical, and engaged with interpreting and guiding human affairs. This ideal is obviously Platonic, and its recent greats have been Charles Peirce in his later speculative and semiotical writings, John Dewey in his metaphysical writings Rorty rejects, Alfred North Whitehead, Paul Weiss, Justus Buchler, John Findlay, Robert Brumbaugh, John E. Smith, and others already discussed. For these philosophers, philosophy is often about the foundations of things, but the status of its own assertions is that of hypotheses. Thus philosophy need make no claim to be certain or foundational for other disciplines. How could Rorty have fudged this distinction: philosophy about foundations does not have to be foundational in the sense of uncriticizable formal or ordinary language, or an eidetic reduction? Furthermore, since the hypothetical character of philosophic assertions serves to guide and correct activity, as both Plato and the pragmatists showed in their respective ways, philosophy is not principally about problems of the philosophic tradition or even about the topics of the traditional conversation. It is about human personal and cultural problems and it employs the philosophic traditions as resources for wise counsel.

The purpose of this final section is to characterize in more detail just one ideal role for philosophy among the many possible, and to do so with regard to the need to achieve balance and coherence among the several variables of our topic. These variables include (1) a generic nature for a kind of philosophy, (2) special modifications of philosophy accruing to its professional status, (3) the definition of philosophic agenda by their social responsibilities or usefulness, and the peculiarities of the American situation.

The generic nature of any philosophy is not an ideal essence but an historical phenomenon. There are three great cultural traditions of literate philosophy that have converged in our time to provide orientations and resources for philosophic practice: the Western tradition arising in ancient Greece and associated with European and Islamic civilization, the East Asian tradition of China, Korea, and Japan, and the Indian tradition. At the present time the three great cultures seem mutually incommensurable to many professionals within Western philosophy. That is mere appearance, however, and can be accounted for by the exclusivistic professional training common in the Western tradition. In fact, the three great civilizations now are deeply enmeshed in cultural interactions and there is an explicit trading of philosophic ideas, especially outside the sphere of professional philosophy, say in business, religion, technological management, and social planning.

The three great cultural traditions are remarkably similar in their roots, an important fact for an historical approach to the nature of philosophy. Each emerged out of a pervasive social upheaval in the 500 years before the Common Era. In each case philosophy arose out of a mythopoeic culture as a tool for objectifying and criticizing troubled conceptualities of a religious world. In each case, also, the critical philosophic practice was put at the service of social matters or political philosophy, thus defining a new relation between religion and the rest of cultural life. In the course of their long historical evolution, each of the three great traditions unfolded root ideas and developed various ways of objectifying and criticizing their cultural world, especially through their respective versions of speculative representation and logic. Each cultural tradition also developed the topical areas of personal norms, social and political norms, epistemology, metaphysics, and critical analysis of such cultural fields as religion, education, economics, and art. The Western tradition is unique in having a long history of analysis of science.

In each tradition, East Asian, Indian, and Western, philosophy has been a specialty engaged in creatively by only a few but sometimes appreciated by the populace and influential in forming the imagination of the evolving civilization. In certain historical periods philosophers played active roles in the determination of government policy, in the guidance of religious institutions, in education, and in the internal criticism of the arts.

The generic nature of philosophy for us is what the heirs of these traditions can do today. Being an "heir" allows for many different interpretations. Generally it means at least that the intellectual resources of the traditions are brought to bear upon some critical problem that present circumstances make interesting. Even a brief survey of the three great cultural traditions reveals an extraordinary wealth of resources.

Philosophy as a profession is distinguished by the rigors of graduate training and by institutions such as books, journals, and conventions where opinions are expressed precisely and criticized by others who have been disciplined by graduate training and by the institutions of professional communication. Before the American job market became problematic we would have assumed that professional philosophy involves employment in the academy; even now philosophers who practice professionally outside the academy usually have an educational component to their work. In general, the socially responsible part of professional philosophy is to deliver the product of philosophical work, usually through the medium of liberal education, to various parts of society that would benefit by being philosophically sophisticated, though not professionally so. Often philosophic ideas are positive ways of seeing things in a special light; perhaps more often the results of professional philosophic practice are habits of thought, angles of questioning, attitudes of criticism and argument. In contrast to an unprofessional heir to a philosophic tradition, a professional is obliged to appropriate the tradition and to practise it with discipline. The job of the professional is to see that the philosophic ideas and arguments are public, and thereby subjected to all the criticisms that concerned thinkers can lay against them. Philosophy in the broadest sense is a collection of intellectual habits of thought the great literate cultures have developed among some specialists for internal critique and redirection of personal and social process; it is thus instrumental to culture while being at the same time a critic of culture, particularly of a culture's abstractions, as Whitehead said.

In contrast to the ideal of public criticism for philosophic ideas, however, much current philosophy is organized as school or program philosophy, with groups of thinkers who define their work in reference to a common project, with a special language and set of communications media, and with a sense of satisfaction that this conversation can be carried through without serious reference to those outside the school. It is true that much of twentieth-century Western philosophy, and much religious philosophy in all traditions in all ages, has had the character of school philosophy. A culture critic could argue that such self-contained, self-justifying, philosophical conversations are particularly apt for modernist culture. Postmodernists might claim that philosophy necessarily has to take place in schools because there can be no continuity of argument across different assumptions.

Nevertheless, the semi-isolated conversations of program philosophies betray the ideal of objective publicity and turn philosophy back toward the innocence of mythopoeic thought. Is this not the ironic outcome of much postmodernism? Publicity in philosophy does not mean only free communication among those engaged in a tight conversation. It means also free communication with anyone with a thought or care about the topic. If people disagree about a thesis because of different assumptions, then the dialectic must engage the assumptions in order to determine the truth of the thesis; otherwise, the discussion passes from a quest for truth to a mere sociological observation that people with different assumptions believe different things. To develop a philosophic position means not only addressing the problems arising from the prior discussion; it means as well seeking out other points of view, to determine what they might say on the topic, and addressing them. Philosophic argument would be wise not to assume continuity of assumptions or the meaning of terms with antecedents or conversation partners. On the contrary, it should assume discontinuity and take continuity as a thing to be built through the work of argument.

In short, to engage in philosophic conversation publicly means eliciting views from anyone or any perspective that might have an interest in the topic and constructing an argument that takes those views into account. This is an immense task, practically impossible in any finite case. Nevertheless the direction of professional philosophic argumentation ought to be toward those outside one's comfortable conversation group. The philosophic commonplace is correct that one should advance toward presuppositions and assumptions, not just follow out the inferential lines of argument. Program philosophy, insofar as it takes a limited project to be self-justifying for any extended period, especially insofar as it de-legitimates other approaches to the topic as unworthy of its notice, is a betrayal of the historic achievements of philosophy in all three great cultural traditions.

One moral to be drawn for professional philosophy from the sorry state of its organization into schools is that its curriculum in graduate institution should insist on solid and extensive training in the history of philosophy, the history of all three great traditions. There are two purposes for this. The first and most obvious is that it makes possible the deep appropriation of the intellectual resources that allow philosophy to be an advance on cleverness. The second is that it makes possible the appreciation of the background of more of the contemporaries with whom one ought to be in conversation.

Turning briefly to philosophy's responsibilities and usefulness to society, there have been at least four cultural functions that philosophy often has performed. The most ancient and continuous is that philosophy has guided the social definition of responsibility. Philosophy at its best has caused crucial social agents to ask whether their goals are the best ones, whether their habits serve the best goals, whether the institutions might be amended the better to embody, foster, and achieve the great values of civilization in the particularities of the circumstances. The second cultural function of philosophy has been to provide understanding of the pervasive and fundamental structures of nature and culture by representing them in articulate conceptual visions. Philosophy functions here as a speculative mirror so that people can come to terms with the broadest categories of their existence by representing them and by criticizing the representations. That there are many alternative systems of representation does not mean that each does not have its value in its place. The third cultural function is interpretive personal, social, or cultural criticism itself, the point of which is to provide an understanding of what values are involved in the situation, on what those values depend, and what their alternatives might be. The fourth social function of philosophy has been to articulate, form, and reform the cultural imagination. Philosophy thus is responsive in its way to society's needs regarding the guidance of the pursuit of responsibility, regarding a capacity to represent its world, regarding a critical assessment and interpretation of itself, and regarding the culture's very imagination.[3]

Moving from such general social responsibility to philosophy's responsibility or usefulness in the current situation, it is fair to say that certain philosophers of this century have made extraordinary contributions to society in each of the functions mentioned. For many years John Dewey was a powerful force in the dialectical conscience of American affairs and letters. Alfred North Whitehead's speculative system has been influential far beyond the arena of professional philosophy and offers a vision that makes some sense of twentieth-century Western culture in light of recent science. John Rawls's treatment of justice, though formulated as a theory, has functioned rather as a critical interpretive tool to develop the refined wisdom of the Liberal tradition. Existentialists, both European and American, have decisively impacted the artistic imagination of our time.

If we ask about the social responsibility of philosophy for the next two decades, however, those models are not sufficient guides. Four imperatives may be ventured from the above discussion for addressing social responsibility.

1. Philosophers as professionals ought to engage in cooperative discussions with non-philosophical specialists in all fields of vital development. Another way to put this is that professional philosophers should subordinate their concern to advance upon the dialectic of their own local philosophical community (though not abandoning the discipline that comes from that) in order to turn to the problems of civilization.

2. Philosophers as professionals ought to engage one another as diversely as possible, abandoning labels such as "analytic" or "Continental" philosophy except as doors to ways of thought one might not yet have explored. One's own philosophic orientation should be a perspective on all the others, not merely a continuation of an ancestral line of development.

3. Given the extraordinary interaction of world cultures and the advanced state of scholarship in translations and comparative studies that make the three great cultural traditions of philosophy available to each other, American philosophers ought to include the Indian and East Asian traditions within their discussion. Failure to do so from this point onward is only illegitimate parochialism, another kind of dreaming innocence.

4. Most important, American philosophers ought to think up better ideas. The heat of the recent discussions about philosophic pluralism comes not only from real concerns to protect or achieve proprietary interest over the major institutions of philosophic education and communication, but also from the sense that philosophy now is conceptually impoverished. This sense motivates Rorty as well. The only long-range justification for the exercise of authority within philosophy's institutions comes from the quality of one's philosophy. Philosophic imagination is stifled both by a preoccupation with school philosophy and by the political (non-intellectual) confrontation of that school project with other projects. Philosophers need to get on with their own work, relating to one another as friends who can help without supplanting, but not relating to one another as conspirators.

PART TWO

✳

POLITICS AROUND MODERNISM

CHAPTER EIGHT

*

POWER, REVOLUTION, AND RELIGION

The thesis that modernism and its negation in postmodernism is not the only development of late modernity, nor the best, applies far beyond philosophy itself. This chapter explores the thesis as it applies to some of the effects of theological ideas on political structure and action. In particular, it traces how the early modern ideas of power and narrative lead down the trail to modernism, and it argues that the covenant theology abortively broached by the early Puritans, and ruined by them in practice, provides an alternative that leads to the highroad around modernism.

Although not without precedent, ours is one of the few periods in history in which theological traditions have provided rich and aggressive leadership for social change and revolution. Beginning in the 1950s, Martin Luther King, Jr., developed the theological plan for the deconstruction of racism in America, a plan expressed in such documents as the "Letter from the Birmingham Jail." He derived that plan from the metaphysical and social theology of his Boston University Personalist teachers, who in turn were theological descendents of the New England Transcendentalists. Today Christian theology is providing conceptual guidance, and the Christian community often the personnel, for large-scale social change, even revolution, in Latin America, Africa, Eastern Europe, and Korea. From Jakarta to Marrakesh, Islamic theologies across a broad spectrum are reshaping that world. Buddhist thought is re-emerging across Southeast Asia to be the native philosophy for appropriating modernization as colonial powers leave and Marxism is revealed to be both Western and unhelpful. An important aspect of the current turmoil in China is the recovery of the theological virtues of Confucianism in the wake of the moral and economic obsolence of Mao's political Marxism, and the Christian churches are thriving. One could go on with smaller and doubtless subtler contemporary examples of the enormous revolutionary social impact of creative religious thought, reacting to volatile circumstances out of the resources of ancient traditions. There is no unanimity in the social direction of these theological influences; they embrace a spectrum from the fundamentalist right to the radical left, and the more institutionalized theologies appear to be the strongest intellectual and moral force for balancing the spectrum from the middle.

Instead of exploring the breadth and variety of these examples, however, only one family of theological traditions will be discussed here, the Christian, because of its influence in forming European modernity. The situation is paradoxical. The principal ideas in current revolutionary Christian theologies, including feminism, Black theology, and most liberation theologies, are themselves unrevolutionary modernist developments of European modern thought, the very thought against whose institutionalized culture the social revolutions are believed to be addressed. The romance of the struggle of the theological involvements, therefore, reinforces a spiritually morbid and religiously conservative line of thought within Christian theology. Theology itself needs to be revolutionized by the extraordinary circumstances of our world. A true exercise of wit, in Aristotle's sense of hitting upon the "third term," is needed to invent forms for addressing our circumstances with the wisdom of ancient inspirations and vital traditions. The highroad around modernism in the bearing of theology on politics is just such a revolution.

I. Power and Narrative

The argument to be made here begins with an interpretation of two main themes of European modernity, the idea of power and the idea of narrative or story. These are among the most important of the ideas that have shaped recent theologies of revolution, both enormously complex and intertwined in exceedingly important ways. What follows is a brief sketch tailored to the purpose of explicating the current revolution in religion.

The idea of power took its modern form from the Renaissance invention of mathematical physics.[1] There were many versions of the new physics, each with its theory of force or power. Newton's won the day and power was interpreted as inertia. A thing in motion tends to remain in motion unless deflected by some countervailing thing in motion; degree of force or power is measured by what is required to deflect inertial motion, and Newton provided a mathematical metric to express degrees of power.

The explanatory power of the new physics was so great that it displaced the older approaches. In particular, by representing both structure and change in a mathematical language, the new physics was able to ignore all reference to value in nature, and it displaced those older languages for which worth and the recognition of worth are crucial variables.

The explanatory reference to power was not limited to the topics of physics but quickly became a theme and metaphor in many other areas. Human beings, for instance, were described by Thomas Hobbes and his successors as machines whose behavior is a function of the pursuit of will, a kind of inertial force of self-continuance formed by desire, passion, or arbitrary choice (Hobbes 1651). Human behavior is subject to rational understanding when we assume that persons are impelled toward goals, consciously or not. The combination of the factors of life is comprehensible as an organization designed to accomplish a person's will, and the person's career is intelligible in terms of coping with the structures of the environment relevant to inertial pursuit of goals. Life is to be understood as the modification of inertial will by one's resources and environment. Thomas Hobbes was but one of the earliest to depict the person as an inertial machine. But even without his crude mechanistic psychology, most subsequent modern philosophers accepted the consequence of his view, that individual subjectivity is intentionally directed inertial will, whether or not that inertial direction is conscious. The brilliance of this modern view is that human behavior is thus subject to mechanistic explanation; rational analysis can be made of human behavior as the organization of means to achieve goals, and the goals themselves are understood to be set by vectors of inertial forces. Human beings are considered as problem solvers, where the problem is a function of the obstacles that stand in the way of achieving the will's goal. Problem solving is the successful exercise of power. Even the contemporary psychological functionalists and proponents of artificial intelligence such as Fodor (1981, 1983) share this view, which had been made the basis of the social sciences by Adam Smith and Karl Marx.[2]

According to the modern commitment to inertial power, the determination of the will's goal is only to be understood as the vector outcome of antecedent forces. There is no modern way to register the ancient world's concern with the merit and justification of the will's direction. Merit and justification are issues only to be raised about instrumental choices, assuming the larger inertial goals, such as the continuance of life (Hobbes's version) or the pursuit of wealth (Locke's version). Nor is there a way, within the modern conception, to register the problematic of sin, the suggestion that the direction of the will is flawed because it is formed in some serious disrelation to God or to the ultimate conditions of existence.

Political theory, too, adopted the modern metaphor of power. The social contract theory, not to say Machievelli's views, understands social structure as the organization necessary to compromise or vector together the diverse and often conflicting inertial interests of the citizens. Modern political philosophy typically does not judge primary human interests, or even primary goals, for a polity. It judges rather the efficiency and rationality of a society, particularly its government, in allowing the individuals' inertial powers to be pursued with least deflection. Most forms of capitalism assume that primary economic desires are not rational but that the secondary desires for attaining the primary ones are. A market is "free" in order to respect the subjective integrity of will itself. Freedom, in the modern sense, divorced from any responsibility more profound than service to the instruments of due procedure, is a function of the prevailing metaphor of inertial power. Chapter 10 will return to this theme.

The crude residue of the power metaphor in current concerns for social justice is to be found in the mentality suggesting that injustice consists in dominance or oppression, that is, in imbalances of power, especially the powerlessness of the poor and oppressed. Shaped by the metaphor of power, the apparent goal of justice is to give power to the relatively disempowered to seek their own interest, whatever that might be. This residue of the power metaphor abjures any attempt to articulate a true or valid interest for people, save those that are instrumental for exercising power. There are two core elements of truth in the modern conception of justice. One is that victims of injustice usually are also powerless and habitual perpetrators of injustice need power to sustain themselves. The other is that justice in some way requires power for all individuals to participate in public life, a crucial ideal for democracy. Nevertheless, the modern way of expressing these core truths, by means of the metaphor of power, excludes the consideration of the worth of ends; it legitimates only deliberation about means. Furthermore, the belief that the empowerment of the victims by itself leads to greater justice for them or for others is sheer delusion, manifested again and again in our century.

How the idea of power moved from the themes of subjectivity in the human machine and the employment of the social contract to rationalize individual power, to the social rhetoric of dominance, oppression, and empowerment, is too complex a story to rehearse here. At this point, however, we may note that European and American *religion* averted the impact of the metaphor of power up until this very century. For this, religion paid the price of being viewed by the intellectual establishment as not cognitive, not entirely rational, and something to be explained away in non-religious terms, such as those of psychology or sociology of knowledge. Exclusion from cognitive respectability has been painful to many theologians, but it has not inhibited religion from periods of great creativity and influence; the Wesleyan movement is but one case in point. Religion has, however, in our own time, suddenly adopted the mentality of the power theme.

In order to understand this it is necessary to recur to another of the original Renaissance themes, that of narrative. By narrative is meant the understanding of persons and history in terms of the interaction of individual stories. Not a chronicle of episodes nor an exemplification of persons as types, narrative in the modern sense supposes that each person's life hangs together as a meaningful unit in story form, and that narrative involves the interweaving of these stories.[3] The story of a person's life depicts the shifting direction of intentionality as life's events are met and addressed. There are many sources of the modern narrative theme, including the Renaissance recovery of ancient humanism and Luther and Calvin's recovery of Augustine's *Confessions*. William Haller (1938) has noted that the late sixteenth-century English Puritan sermons departed radically from the Everyman typology of earlier allegorical preaching and, instead, instructed their hearers that each person has a story responsible to God, a story of ancestry and conditions, but principally of the shifting intentions of the heart or will. Thus was the modern "individual" born, and Haller attributes Shakespeare's success in part to the audience prepared by Puritan preaching. Shakespeare indeed was the first master of "characterization," in which the crucial action is the interaction between persons' intentions and circumstances. He was aware of the tension between the old conception of the trajectories of nature respecting limits of due proportion and the new conception of inertial forces moving on until stopped, the power theme. Furthermore, Shakespeare was most acutely aware of the revolutionary tension between the old definition of persons in terms of type and office and the new definition in terms of intentions. Consider the bafflement of Lear upon the heath at his daughters' disrespect for his identity as father and emeritus monarch:

Blow, winds, and crack your cheeks! rage! blow!
You cataracts and hurricanoes, spout

Till you have drench'd our steeples, drown'd the cocks!
You sulph'rous and thought-executing fires,
Vaunt-couriers to oak-cleaving thunderbolts,
Singe my white head! And thou, all-shaking thunder,
Strike flat the thick rotundity o' th' world,
Crack Nature's moulds, all germains spill at once,
That make ingrateful man! . . .
Rumble thy bellyful! Spit, fire! spout, rain!
Nor rain, wind, thunder, fire are my daughters.
I tax you not, you elements, with unkindness.
I never gave you kingdom, call'd you children,
You owe me no subscription. Then let fall
Your horrible pleasure. Here I stand your slave,
A poor, infirm, weak, and dispis'd old man.
But yet I call you servile ministers,
That will with two pernicious daughters join
Your high-engender'd battles 'gainst a head
So old and white as this! O! O! 'tis foul!

King Lear Act III, Scene II

Religion in the modern era has understood well the importance of narrative for its own expression. The Protestant Reformation, the Catholic Counterreformation, and the rise of Hassidism with the reactions to it, have fostered the articulation of the individual person's story as the way of understanding identity in terms of the interaction of personal intentionality and circumstance, both social and physical. The story-formed identity, of individual and group, is what is conceived by modernity to stand in significant relation to God.

Furthermore, as Thomas J. J. Altizer has documented so thoroughly (1977, 1985, 1990), the implicit model of the story-formed self that developed for human beings was mirrored in the developing model of God as self. Just as human beings were imagined to have a depth of self of the sort that consists in and is revealed by the unfolding of a personal story, so God was thought analogously to have an interior, story-formed depth.

To be sure, there were antecedents for the personalization of God prior to the modern period. Yahweh was thought to be a jealous, personal God, insistent that Israel follow him (yes, *him*) rather than the other gods; in this the Hebrew religion bore many resemblances to Mesopotamian and Greek polytheism. As monotheism became the norm in

Hebrew thinking and Yahweh came to be conceived as creator of the world and lord of all nations, the sense of divine intentionality, with judgment, mercy, and love, was carried along. Yet the transcendence of the creator God made it difficult to sustain much of a feel for divine subjectivity, and mediators were thought necessary to convey God's intentionality. So the Yahwists appealed to Wisdom and the Logos. In early Christian thought, the humanity of Jesus, coupled with divine origins, divine authority, and uncompromised divinely begotten nature, allowed the personal characteristics of God to be wholly embodied in the actions and fate of Jesus. Apart from such particular revelations, the transcendent creator was a mystery.

In all of this early history, however, the story-form of Yahweh's history with Israel was not a matter of divine inner subjectivity but a chronicle of episodes of promise, betrayal, forgiveness, and restoration. In Augustine there was a significant beginning to the notion of subjective depth in the self, modelled on a conception of God as memory, love, and will; yet in Augustine's God those are more like principles than an unfolding story. With Thomas Aquinas the conception of God was again returned to principles, especially that of *esse*, or the pure act of existence. Only in the Renaissance and Reformation with its assorted reactions to scholastic theology did God come to be conceived as a person in the modern sense. Within Christianity, the Christocentrism of the Reformation thinkers tended to assimilate the personal qualities of Jesus as Christ to the trinitarian Godhead as a whole.

In the grand philosophy of Hegel, the culminating model of the internally developing, story-formed self, intentional and responsive to external conundra, came to define both the metaphysical principles of the universe constituting divinity and the nature of the human person. That grand synthesis (1807, 1830, 1833) incorporated even the "nature" of modern physics, defined with inertia, into the historical self of the Absolute. Hegel was first and last a theologian, and since then his work has been the orienting point for nearly all European theology.

The Hegelian synthesis summed up a more pervasive cultural assumption of modernity, that history is to be viewed as a story of progress. Its form is a story of the episodes in which the powers of the morally superior prevailed over other powers, over the vicissitudes of nature and disease, over the limitations of humans' ability to travel and live outside their niche, over ignorance, barbarism, parochialism, and irrational violence. The most common current focus of the idea of progress is that we now are living in a dramatic narrative in which the powers of right and justice are in contest with those of political and economic oppression: progress hangs in the balance as we righteous ones struggle to make the story come out for justice.

The Hegelian synthesis of course did not last. The narrative side abandoned the rigors of scientific understanding for wild imagination, and the scientific side thought of the narrative form precisely as imaginative, romantic fiction. Marx was the last major thinker of the European world to attempt to wed narrative to science. In retrospect we view most of the nineteenth century of European and North American culture to be a war between science gone to scientism and romanticism gone to bourgeois aggrandizement of the ego. Their sometime marriage resulted in effective imperialism. More often they were two independent, incompatible, and equally foundational themes for organizing and understanding culture, both crucial for the construction of the modern Western world.

II. The End of Narrative and Power

By our own time, both modern projects have come to an end, beginning with the narrative form for understanding either self or God.

Freud in his way, and Marx in his, pointed out that certain very important elements in a person's story are functions of analogues of inertial forces, not of intentional motives for which a story of responsibility can be told.[4] Therefore, persons are not to be understood as having story-form identities, but rather as having identities construed on the analogue of vectors of forces. The powers of these intrapersonal forces shape the social story as well. And they lead to a cheap counterfeiting of the true achievements of the deep story-formed self. Perhaps the great ironic symbol of our time is the person walking down the crowded street with the SONY Walkman, listening to the immediately accessible language of the blues made public, encapsulated in the deepest psychic feelings of the private world. The psychic depth that supposedly comes from the extended story of a person before God in the world is transmogrified into a momentary and repeatable feeling, immediate and exempt from criticism, expressed in a public medium that reduces the individual to Everyman with the Blues, alone again with no historical relations.[5] Altizer says the fate of the individual in our time amounts to an abandonment of the Judeo-Christian historical identity and an acquiescence in the Buddhist no-self.

The grand conception of God as the Absolute Self similarly became implausible. Among the reasons are the continuing problems of theodicy: this is not the kind of world an absolutely good, knowing, and powerful God would create; the First World War held a mirror to European culture and what was seen was not the Israel of God. Meanwhile, liberal theology undermined the sense of personal relation with a personal God, anxious to make religion compatible with the inertial-power worldview of modern science and to enlist religion in the improvement of a progressing but far from perfect world. By no means is it necessary, or even common in the world's religions, that religious life means a person-to-person or I-thou relation with God; but it had meant that in modern Christianity and in much of modern Judaism. That became impossible in the twentieth century. At most, recent popular Christianity entertained a person-to-person relation to a ghostly Jesus, usually in the garden when the dew is still on the roses. When, in the 1960s, Altizer, Rubenstein, van Buren, Vahanian, and others repeated Nietzsche's claim that God is dead, some Christians and Jews complained, for nostalgic reasons; but hardly anyone else cared. The other religious people knew that the God of the Great Self was a misrepresentation, and that a new representation must be found if religious communities are to sustain themselves.

The fate of the physics of inertial power in the twentieth century was to choke on its own success. Since Francis Bacon, science saw itself as the engine of technological control over human destiny, and maintained the fiction of general progress until technology's own instruments were used to put an end to the illusion of progress and teach once more the ancient doctrine of original sin (Reinhold Niebuhr 1949). The great theoretical achievements of the twentieth century, those conceptions that showed the theories of Newton and his peers to be local special cases of a far vaster truth, gave rise to nuclear destructiveness that completed the joining of the vast elements of nature with the unnatural passions of Lear's older daughters. What is physics now but a paradigm (Kuhn 1962) negotiating its way through a thoroughly political contest of intellectual and economic dominance?

The combined critique of power and narrative lies in the deconstructionists' use of the notion of logocentrism (for instance, Derrida 1976). Their claim is that Western culture since Hellenic times has been formed by a few dominant ideas or patterns of ideas, of which the themes of inertial power in physics and of narrative are examples. The dominant ideas constitute a logos that centers the culture and gives it meaning. For the logos to be meaningful, it has to be determinate and exclusive. Its meaning consists precisely in those alternative ideas or perspectives that it excludes. And because the dominant idea of a culture excludes from purview the real alternatives to its way of centering reality, it is incommensurable with regard to them and cannot defend itself as superior. In the end, every candidate for the logocentric idea is arbitrary, incommensurate with its alternatives, and no better or worse than the others. Most deconstructionists, being Marxists from nostalgia, recommend the non-dominant perspectives, or at least insist that they be placed alongside the dominant ones. No cultural structure can legitimate itself on the deconstructionists' view, however, because any structure depends on being centered around certain exclusive ideas. The practice of deconstructing the dominance of any logocentric candidate is thus presented as an intrinsically necessary subversive task for any society. Hence the high moral tone of most deconstructionist writing, despite its obligation to treat any moral idea as logocentric. Deconstruction becomes the voice of philosophic truth and cultural honesty when ideas themselves are viewed under the aspect of their power alone, regardless of their truth or interest.

In the current theological contributions to social revolution, these ideas of modernity have two principal embodiments, both but partial truths and largely mistaken. The first is the supposition that the most important characteristics of people regarding justice are the power relations that hold among them and that these are distributed according to social class. The second is the intepretation of the situation of justice and injustice in our time as part of a cosmic narrative of progress, now at a crisis point, where the powers for empowering the victims must overcome the powers of the oppressors. Individuals within the drama are defined by the narrative itself, not by their individual circumstances; they are responsible by virtue of being on one side or another, not because of what they do. The third embodiment, arising from deconstructionist themes, is that, once the follies of the reduction of justice to power-dynamics and of individual life to participation in a cosmic narrative are recognized, real life has no historical or actual commitment but is like a free-floating, critical, gnostic angel. Against each of these elements of modernity in contemporary theology, a far more revolutionary counterproposal needs to be laid.

III. The Road of Covenant Theology

Without denying that people do fall into various classes and that sometimes these are mediators of large-scale structures of power, an alternative, early-modern conception of the human social condition needs to be reconsidered, namely that people are related to one another by an ontological covenant. The idea of covenant has deep biblical roots and has had several theological revivals. One of the most important was the covenant theology of the Puritans who attempted, and disastrously failed, to establish the "city set on a hill" in New England. Their failure was a function of an inability to define a human authority to accomplish what their theory required of a divine authority.[6] Despite the failure of the earlier model, it was an alternative to the branch of modernity that went through the liberalism of Locke to the Kantian version of the Enlightenment and on to modernism. The version to be proposed for our current thinking differs from the Puritan model and has five main characteristics. Each of these constitutes an hypothesis, or part of a unifed connected hypothesis, about the human condition (Neville 1991b).

1. First, as covenantal, relations among human beings are to be recognized as more than "natural," where "natural" means what birds, snakes, lions, and lambs might do by virtue of their inertial will. Specifically, a covenantal relation according to this hypothesis includes, in addition to the natural elements, two kinds of representations. Each individual acts in reference to representations of himself or herself as a member of the covenantal society. In addition, there are representations of certain relations among people, between individuals and social institutions, and between both of those and the rest of nature, that are normative and ought to be respected as such (Weiss 1983, chapter 2). These representations, both of self in social roles and of norms for social life, are conventional in the sense that they are subject to the developmental contingencies of history. Yet the former are constitutive of what it is to be a person: persons are beings that integrate representations of themselves with their responses to other things. The latter are norms identifying some of what is valuable and how the values of certain things oblige us. Although the margins of such norms as reflected in the Ten Commandments and the Golden Rule are historically variable, they express observations about worth and obligation that appear to be universal across cultures.

2. Second, the covenantal character of human life, according to this hypothesis, is ontologically constitutive. That is, the conditions of self-representation and responsiveness to representations of value are intrinsic parts of being human. In the old theological language, although animals were created merely naturally, human beings were created by means of the covenant. God prepared the natural garden of Eden for Adam, whom he imported from the outside. Adam was made to name the animals, creating conventional language, and to accept a caretaker role with regard to nature. He was biologically divided down to human

proportions and presented with Eve, another person, relations with whom were essential to being human. The consequence of acknowledging that the covenant is ontologically constitutive is that, although it can be broken, it cannot be ignored. We can misrepresent ourselves and can deny or distort our appreciations and obligations, but we are then in self-deceit and sin, not free of the covenant. Here are the seeds of a far subtler analysis of injustice than the simple view that the wrong people have the power.

3. Third, as creatures in covenant, people relate to one another by both natural and institutional media. They participate in various natural systems of metabolism and environmental interaction, and they play roles in economic, domestic, political, ethnic, artistic, and religious systems. No individual, however, is reduced to one or all of these systems, but has essential features for relating himself or herself to them so as to be responsible. The idea of responsibility is crucial to the covenantal understanding of human life. Whereas according to the class analysis typical of modernism an individual is an abstract token or counter in a concrete class struggle, according to the covenantal analysis a person's participation in a social structure is but one part of the individual's reality. That reality likely offers openings for the exercise of the person's responsibility. Whereas on modernist-modernity's power-analysis a person is either a victim or oppressor—that is, passive or active with respect to power—on the covenantal analysis a person is nuanced in many ways with respect to activity and passivity, and in very many ways is responsible for how to relate to environing systems that in turn relate to other people and nature.

4. Fourth, because every person, indeed every natural thing and social system, is a center of worth and value, according to the hypothesis, and because each thing enjoys that value because of the many relations in which it stands to other things, morality is essentially ambiguous and fragmentary (Neville 1987a, chapters 1, 3, and 10). A person may be good in the economic system but wicked politically. An event might be a triumph for some of the actors but a disaster for others. Of course we should always choose the greater good where discernable, and avoid the greater evil; often the moral course is quite clear, especially with regard to the commonly recognized elementary values. Nevertheless, the best of actions will have evil consequences too, no project will ever be completely finished, no life ever fully self-realized. Everything is fragmentary, incomplete, and excellent according to a kind of local snapshot. This is part of what finite existence means. Therefore, no single cosmic story can be told. And, although it is often quite clear in the proximate

view how to tell good from evil people and the better from the worse course, we know that in the long view the judgments will get more complex and perhaps even reverse. The depiction of moral life as a cosmic drama is a bourgeois illusion, an idolatrous expansion of the local to divine proportion.

5. Fifth, because the covenantal status of human beings is in the nature of things, the way we are created, and because we ruin it by deceit and sin, and because that ruin perverts nature and our institutions, and because even our virtues are ambiguous and fragmentary, we are thrown back on the Creator for forgiveness and fulfillment. Divine infinity bears our sorrows and sins, loves those we strive to destroy for the greater good, completes our partial lives, and embraces our days in a vaster life that trivializes your death and mine. Or if there be no God, the ambiguous fragmentariness of finite reality is as absurd as Camus said, and it is unintelligible that there be a world at all. Without faith, one might despair in that contingency. Regardless of despair, the broken covenant constitutes us in a truth about how to represent ourselves and obliges us to respect the irreconcilable worths of things.

To sum up, the covenant hypothesis sees human beings as constituted by representations of self and of moral matters, as well as by natural elements; it treats the covenant as ontologically constitutive of human existence; it analyzes social institutions and the natural environment as elements relating individuals but not exhausting them so as to dissolve personal responsibility; it appreciates the fact that finite life is both ambiguous and fragmentary; and it gives thanks for that finite creation as such, hoping for fulfillment in the divine. Perhaps it is becoming apparent how this conception reconnects the current situation with the historical depths of the Judeo-Christian past. Before exploring that, however, it is important to take another look at the conception of history as narrative.

The second modern theme embodied in most Christian theology fueling social revolutions is the myth of cosmic narrative. Admittedly, the belief that one is devoting oneself to a great cosmic cause, with the movement of history behind one's puny efforts, is a great motivator. It ranks with other theological views suggesting that martyrdom in a holy war gets one straight to heaven, regardless of sins. Yet like the other it is a great lie. There is no cosmic narrative, rather a great many small narratives interwoven, with overlapping and sometimes contradictory significance. Nor is the fictional narrative told about the West true, that it is a steady progress from paleolithic to primitive to bronze age, iron age, literate age, antiquity, feudalism, renaissance, modernity, enlightenment, high technology, to us. Even the use of technology waxes and wanes. The moral qualities of Western civilization are dappled with black spots, many of which are of our own time.

Most particularly we are self-deceived to think that our moral efforts, which have also been great in the twentieth century, are part of an historic struggle between good and evil. We may indeed minimize racism and gender prejudice in North America, change the social roles of women to give them due advantage, and restructure the international economic system so as to support those now in poverty with means of their own and with human dignity. We may disarm the nations possessed of the power to destroy beyond their right, and establish policies of international law, properly enforced, so as to inhibit war. Yet if we do so it should be by a million piecework efforts, not by a juggernaut movement that destroys everything in its path to the goal. And even those small efforts will be destructive as well as constructive.

Is there an alternative to the grand narrative for understanding our historical situation? Nothing with the integrity and simplicity of a story. Rather, the ambiguities of the covenant are our best hope. Each person, each creature and system in nature, each organization and institution in society, has a complex worth of its own. Each is indeed lovely, and as the theological tradition puts it, is loved by God just in being created. When, therefore, we strive to eradicate the AIDS virus, defeat the Nazis, undermine oppressive wealth, eliminate means of nuclear defense, incarcerate people prone to violence and abuse—all good things to do—we should do so with a consciousness that all those people and things also are lovely and holy creatures. From their perspective, our efforts are destructive if not wicked. Therefore, all our moral efforts ought to be hedged round with an appreciation of the intrinsic loveliness of the entirety of creation, including perhaps especially those things inimical to health and justice as we best define them. This is but to say that, given the realities of the covenant, we should love all things even as their creator does: the theological language is most accurate.

IV. Covenant as Revolution

This returns our reflection to Martin Luther King, Jr. The linchpin of King's social theory was that nothing should be done that could not be done in love toward those people and institutions that stood in the way. He recognized that massive, institutionalized, social evils exist and that a mass effort must be focused to remove them. He did not acquiesce in inaction because of the complexity of the moral issues. He did not fear to speak many languages to many different people, articulating their roles in the struggle. Yet he did not allow the struggle to be seen as one between classes of people, in which people were defined by their class for good or ill. The struggle was against evil aspects of institutions in which people were caught up in some parts of their lives. Even those institutions had their comforts: King was more at home in the South of the United States where he was a "nigger" than in the North where he was an "educated Negro." The strategies he developed from Gandhi's non-violent activism were pragmatic ones. Perhaps he would not have held to them in all circumstances. Yet they were normative because in his circumstances they allowed for the pursuit of justice with love for all and an appreciation of the costs of one's particular good.

A deeper appreciation of the covenant lies in King's life. The reason for his activism was occasional: that is, the opportunity for addressing racism was occasioned by the events leading up to the Montgomery bus boycott and the forces that rallied round for generalizing the struggle. No manifest destiny here. No grand story. Merely a rectifying of this particular wrong. And his dream was for freedom and community, not victory. Furthermore, his strategy supposed that the events are never finished so as to constitute a story; there is always more to do, and successes can only be partial. Finally, he understood that martyrdom is not justified by the subsequent success of your cause, because it is almost impossible to tell what success would consist in. Rather, the sacrifice of a life is justified by its excellence as received into the infinite life of God. Just as there is no excuse for shirking moral action because it is ambiguous and unending, so there is no guarantee that the right shall triumph in one's own story. Failure, even inevitable failure, does not detract from the excellence of one's efforts because that excellence, like everything else lovely, has its true home in the infinite Creator.

Rather than the motive of a cosmic narrative in which we line up with the triumphant powers of goodness, we should take a more local commitment to the goods we can see to be obligatory in our own part of the world. Where real causal connections can be made, we expand the scale of moral efforts. But where they are postulated by myth, we should abjure them as the devil's temptations to do damage beyond the reach of our love.

The covenant conception of history has an important implication for learning. Instead of seeking terms of analysis that block individuals into classes, or into *dramatis personae* in a large narrative, we need social analyses that identify the various ways in which persons participate in many different systems, how they are responsible in that participation, and how the values of things are altered as they are passed through the various systems. A great failure of most current analysis is that it abets the ideological simplifications of class struggle. Each one of us must balance the merits of one social cause against the deficits its pursuit has in other areas. Just about all of life is a balancing of competing claims, none of which we can satisfy. Yet they all make sense as elements in our position in the covenant.

The third embodiment of the power and narrative themes of modernity is in deconstruction, and it is a paradoxical embodiment. On the one hand, the deconstructionists are preoccupied with power and have adopted a fairly simple Hegelian view of the negative dialectic in narrative form. On the other hand, the preoccupation of all modernity with power and narrative is itself a prime example of logocentrism and so subject to deconstructive criticism. As has often been remarked, deconstruction will eventually deconstruct itself and cease to exist.

The mode of being of critical consciousness, then, associated with deconstruction, is what earlier was called a "free-floating, critical, gnostic angel." That is, the deconstructionist can identify with no social form because each is arbitrary and logocentric. Actual effort, indeed revolutionary effort, can be expended to ablate an oppressive form; yet not connected to a real community, that critical effort has no historical actuality of its own. Deconstruction looks upon embodiment much the way the gnostics did.

The alternative to gnostic deconstruction is a critical consciousness that accepts the finitude of historical ambiguity and limited perspective. It sees the finiteness of the critical perspective as itself part of creation and has the courage to judge from within that basis. Furthermore, such finitist critical consciousness begins with a fundamental identification with the covenant: criticism is a form of love, appreciating the loveliness of all things but suggesting ways of overcoming unnecessary subordination of the importance of one thing to another. Paul Tillich, who may yet turn out to be the theological genius of the twentieth century, characterized this courage to embrace the ambiguous and fragmentary and to go on with moral and spiritual life, as the essence of faith (Tillich 1952). Our grand stories of progress have failed. Yet the creation is as rich and obligatory as ever. One has faith when one accepts all this and takes responsibility for critical consciousness and moral action within the limits of one's corner of the garden. If deconstruction is the culmination of the age of modernity in one of its branches, modernism, then its theological fault is faithlessness.

True faith is the mature acceptance of the finite conditions of the covenant and the courage to live up to one's excellence within the limits of one's lights. Perhaps this language is too individualistic. Like the faithlessness of deconstruction and its siblings, faith is corporate courage as well as individually located. Religiously motivated social movements of our time have often been expressions of corporate courage. As St. Paul said, we need to encourage one another. The courage is fake, however, when it is mere identification with success and progress. The faith is real when it acknowledges the limits of the finite and the distance between that and the infinite. Part of that distance is that our efforts all must fail in some respects, and our own lives will be incomplete no matter how long and powerfully we live.[7]

It was claimed earlier that theology needs concepts more revolutionary than the merely modern and modernist themes that stimulate many of the current social revolutions. Let us recapitulate and reflect on the argument.

First, revolution in the modernist sense has been conceived as a dialectical negation, a rejection of the old in favor of forms that negate it. To the contrary, a more radical revolution is one that breaks open the present to accept the past and move toward a better future. The theological idea of the covenant defended here in fact is a retrieval of an ancient theme that leads straight to the future goal of a community of mutual respect. Theology has impoverished itself when it has rejected the language of its tradition. Instead it must recover that and reshape it to the critical advantage of the present.

Second, the idea of covenant requires abandoning the tired modern idea that people are seekers of inertial self-interest. They rather are complex creatures participating in many different systems, most likely misrepresenting themselves in their participation and perverting the true worths of things. People are not just selfish, as modernism suggests, but in fact destructive of the self and of the entire community of persons, society, and nature that constitutes the human creation. This is sin, not immaturity, illness, selfishness, or frustration at self-realization. That our problems are those of sin, not mechanical malfunction, is truly revolutionary for the modernist age but merely a playing out of the modern directions of the Puritans.

Third, moral action and social change ought not to be conceived as devices aimed to fulfill oneself or one's group. There is nothing to suggest that fulfillment is possible except at the expense of most of one's environment and even of most of the dimensions of one's life. Rather

than fulfillment, we should seek excellence in that part of the coven-
anted creation local to our actions, accepting the fact that excellence is
itself limited, fragmentary, and perhaps also vicious on its dark side. Our
aim at social justice should be justice, not success with our plans. Hence
the revolutionary motive power in justice is love, not the anger of
struggle.

Nothing said here about the idea of covenant as an analysis of the
human condition, nor about the finite and non-teleological approach to
social action, nor about faith in the worthiness of virtue, is particularly
new. Its novelty comes only in its use as a para-modernist critique of
modernism and postmodernism. In the actual social revolutions and
changes now being guided by theological reflection the covenantal
terms are present alongside the other themes of modernity. Perhaps the
other modern themes are stronger: they surely determine the rhetoric
in most instances. Yet the covenantal themes are both closer to the rhetorical roots of Western theological tradition and are far more realistic
about the human condition. People are not just power machines, and
the grand narrative, particularly that aspect depicting progress, has
been given the lie by history. For theology to be truly revolutionary,
it must first revolve to its origins and repossess its early insights. Then
it can guide the volatile forces of change with nuance, realism, and
true faith.

The temptation at this point is to proceed to a justification of theological faith. But that is not the present task. The next chapter will delve
more deeply into the problem of class analysis in economics, and the one
following will pick up the Puritan vision of freedom and responsibility.

CHAPTER NINE

✳

BEYOND CAPITALIST AND CLASS ANALYSIS

I. The Need for New Theory in the Social Sciences

The invention of mathematical physics during the European Renaissance successfully united the modes of quantitative and qualitative thinking so admired by the Greeks. Plato had hoped that all things could be understood in terms of numbers, or ratios; his famous but lost lecture on the Good was supposed to represent value mathematically.[1] Aristotle, by contrast, developed Plato's suggestions about classification in the *Statesman* and elsewhere into the theory of genera and species, a mode of understanding that relates to the qualities of things. Aided by Descartes's invention of analytic geometry and by the physically descriptive powers of Newton's (and Leibniz's) calculus, early modern physics was able to give mathematical descriptions to classes of things. To put it another way, descriptions were preferred that could be quantified in the language of a universal metric. For the early modern philosophers, to be a physical object is to be measurable. This view about astronomical and microscopic bodies became the model for theoretical understanding of just about everything in the early modern period, and down to today in some strands of modernity.

When it was generalized beyond the immediate application in physical mechanics, however, the mathematical model had the disastrous effect of excluding valuational thinking from theoretical status. Since the early modern period, politics, ethics, aesthetics, and normative aspects of philosophy of education, art, and religion have had a nearly impossible time defending themselves as properly cognitive in light of the Renaissance or "modern" mode.[2]

The social sciences have been in a particularly embarrassing bind, vacillating between a hypocritical positivist claim to value-freedom and a social engineer/religious prophet's claim that all theory should be frankly biased to serve some ideology. The former seemed to dominate the academic social sciences in the North Atlantic community through most of this century, partly because of the prestige of Max Weber and other great theoreticians of value-free social sciences. The latter have recently become more popular, in part through the internal recognition that even value-free social science serves some specific interests, in part through the increasing influence of social sciences from the Marxist traditions, particularly those of the Third World. In fact they represent a dialectic within modernism: either social science is pure, objective, grounded research, or it is merely the expression of personal or class interest. Most forms of postmodernism incline to the latter stance because of the association of deconstruction with Marxism.

New paradigms of thinking that reconstruct a proper relation of valuation to quantitative and qualitative analysis are imperative before the obviously value-laden subjects of the social sciences can be approached with appropriately formed theories.[3] The social sciences cannot be theoretically framed areas of discourse until a new paradigm of theory is adopted. The highroad around modernism in this respect, of course, is to understand social science theories as hypotheses subject to correction. Because hypotheses have a history, they doubtless have reflected the interests of classes and persons, probably with confusion and inconsistency. The point of vital social science is to understand and correct for these biases where they are inappropriate. Within a social science theory, not only do values need to be articulated and recognized but the truth of the theory depends in part on properly representing what is really valuable in the subject matter. The discussion of this chapter presses the issue in the context of economic theory. If indeed a valuative paradigm for social science theory is required, then the conceptual apparatus of economic theory should display and explain the values involved in its subject matter.

Two qualifications to the notion of value need to be mentioned at the outset. First, by "values" in this context is not meant only the values commonly identified as economic, such as use, exchange, or labor value. Economics also contains within its subject matter the historical and civilizational values of economic arrangements, values vis a vis the environment, values in the impact of the economic system on other social systems such as the law, religion, politics, social and class structure, and gender relations; and most particularly the values embodied in the different economic roles of producer, consumer, manager, and so forth; the values these roles have in and for the individuals who play them relative to their degree of wealth, power, social standing, ambitions, and inherited cultures.

Second, except in special circumstances, "value" does not mean the "idea" by which a person or group estimates the actual value of something, as when we speak of the "values" a person or culture stands for. That is a second-order value, a representation of something as valuable. Rather, value in this discussion means *the worth achieved in the thing itself,* the first-order value. That people in a society can come to value certain things and represent those values to themselves in a second-order way as "values" is itself a first-order value that needs to be achieved in any organized society. A proper theoretical understanding should indicate how an economic system disposes worths in its diverse values and explain to whom, in what ways, and by what means it achieves that.

Most approaches to economic theory, such as the Marxist and Liberal capitalist, in part recognize this need to attend to values. Both Adam Smith and Karl Marx put forward their own theories as socially valuable. But in larger part, the ways by which the major economic theories highlight specific values is usually implicit and underground. An opposing theoretical perspective is often needed to point out that a given theory's structure highlights some values and obscures others, thereby serving some parochial interest. Overall, it is, alas, fair to say that our major theoretical approaches to economics obscure rather than display and explain the values in their subject matters. The reason for this is that both Liberal capitalism and Marxism, as well as socialist and mixed economies, share the metaphysical assumptions of modernism that separate facts from values, believing that theories should explain only the facts.

Process philosophy and pragmatism have provided alternatives to these metaphysical assumptions, alternatives that recognize facts as achievements and embodiments of values and that can offer new directions to economic theory. The purpose of this chapter is to explore the highroad's "axiological requirements" of a proper approach to economic theory, building on a base of pragmatism and process philosophy; "axiology" was discussed in chapter 3 above. The classical American philosophies of Whitehead and Dewey broke the ground; if extensions, modifications, and criticisms of their theories need to be made in the course of extending the highroad around modernism, that is only a tribute to their revolutionary importance. Of course there are many requirements besides the axiological ones for a viable economic theory, requirements that economists will recognize far more readily than the axiological ones. The axiological argument, however, may be the beginning of a dialogue between economics and metaphysical philosophy.

To argue for an axiological dimension to economic theory is of course to call for a restructuring of the conceptual apparatus of social science. But it is also, and more fundamentally, to make a metaphysical point. The reason that Marxist, capitalist, and other modern Western analyses deal with values in such restrained ways is the limitation of their metaphysics. By metaphysics here is meant the broad range of vague, abstract concepts that are assumed when an economic theory formulates its own assertions, concepts about the nature of being a thing, of relation, causation, space-time, change, and so forth. These metaphysical notions are *informally* vague in the sense that they can be assumed without examination and without even the consciousness that they are assumed at all. The metaphysical notions are *formally* vague in the sense discussed above that a more specific level of theory must be added to them before they can be applied to concrete phenomena. Causation is such a vague notion, and it needs specification as economic causation (according to one theory or another, e.g., Marxist historical materialism), material mechanics, psychological motivation, or some other, before we can apply it. What happens in practice, of course, is that we slip in some specifying theory usually unnoticed. The specifying, relatively concrete theoretical levels are also vague, though less so; they too need to be specified by more particular levels of analysis, perhaps including appeals to paradigm individual cases. Hidden metaphysical assumptions, and hidden ways of parsing these in specific applications, are the original "false consciousness" or ideology, though not necessarily with (hidden) malevolence intended.

II. Liberal Capitalism and Marxism: Rejection of Market and Class

Although both liberal capitalism and Marxist theories share that part of the metaphysics of modern philosophy (rigidified in modernism) asserting a separation of facts from values, there are important metaphysical differences between them. A brief exploration of those differences is in order, first, to illustrate the level of abstractness at which philosophy can provide a non-modernist alternative in economics and, second, to formulate criticisms justifying the need to move beyond those forms of economic analysis to an axiological one.

Throughout this chapter ideal types or extremes of Marxist and liberal theory are discussed rather than the more prevalent socialisms and mixed economies. The justification for this is that usually the intent is to discuss the structure of the theory as such. Where these ideal types as stated by Marx and Locke, say, have been compromised, one way of understanding the compromise is to say that the form of the theory itself is at fault. Indeed, it shall be argued that each side has been compromised precisely to be able to acknowledge the values that are central to the other but that cannot be registered within the ideal type at hand. The adjective *liberal* is frequently attached to *capitalism* to indicate that the subject of discussion is the particular kind of capitalism associated with the rise of liberalism in Western Europe. In a looser sense, capitalism could be applied to any economy with a market system, money, and the practice of lending for investment; China's economy for thousands of years has alternated between such capitalism and a more strictly land-based agrarian barter system.

Marxist analyses often criticize the liberal capitalist mode of production for dehumanizing people in two steps. First, wage labor—the meaning of labor in a theory emphasizing price, supply, and demand—recognizes nothing more of individuals than their capacity to be place-holders in an impersonal economic system. Second, a captialist economy steals from wage laborers the due rewards of their labors.[4] Expressed in metaphysical language, according to the Marxist critique the personal lives of individuals are externally related to the economic system in capitalism, and irrelevant to it so long as the individuals are capable of playing the system's roles. Marxism understands capitalism to pay no attention to people's religion, for instance, or ethnic background, or personal concerns, except insofar as these get translated into strictly economic variables such as productivity and consumption. The metaphysical basis of this critique of capitalism within Marxism is Marxism's own belief that these "personal" elements are all themselves a function of the economic variables; Marxism simply prizes different economic variables.

On the other hand, the Marxist critique notes that the economic system does have a deep effect on people's lives and thus is internally related to the individuals within it. Capitalism thus presupposes at the metaphysical level an asymmetrical relation between individuals and the economic system, in the Marxist view, the system is internal to the individuals whereas the individuals are external to the system. This is unjust on the one hand, Marxists say, because individuals are at the mercy of the system and exploited in their labor, and unstable on the other hand because the system is essentially untouchable by human wit and blindly runs according to its own evolving laws, tending (according to classical

Marxism) toward overexpansion and crash. These two points, the injustice of exploitation and the instability of economic forces, are combined in a mechanistic metaphysics that developed from early modern physics down through modernism. By virtue of blind economic forces, persons are thrown into social classes as distinguished according to ownership of the means of production. There is no merit or justice that justifies some persons in being owners and others in being wage laborers or peasants. Furthermore, the inertial will of each class to advance its own strictly economic interest puts them in a conflict of powers. The metaphor of power as a vector of physicallike forces is crucial to the Marxist argument. The step is simple from saying that the system throws classes into a kind of warfare to saying that justice consists in advancing the cause of the weak, as if there were only a matter of supporting power on one side. With respect to the values of things, the asymmetry in relations between individuals and the economic system determines that the individuals must internalize the abstract values of the economic system but cannot re-embody their own human values in the system: the system is strictly impersonal.

The opposing metaphysical critique capitalism would make is that Marxist theory mistakenly assumes symmetrical relations between individuals and the economic system, internal in both directions. That is, the personal element is now supposed by the Marxists to be incorporated into the system through joint management and communal ownership, and the system, now made personal, is incorporated back into each individual.[5] Symmetrical internal relations would constitute both sides as mere analytically distinct elements in a totalitarian whole, according to capitalism. Value in Marxist theory would belong to the totality, the state or collective, and not to individuals, as capitalism thinks necessary. For individuals to be valuable in themselves, according to capitalism, they must be somewhat external to the economic system. Whether and where they enter the economic system must be external to the system itself, a matter of the individuals' choice.

The metaphysical reason for capitalism's insistence that individuals remain somewhat external to the system is its deep commitment to a particular theory of what it is to be a thing, a theory perhaps naively but influentially articulated by Locke. Locke's explicit statement of the economic consequences of his metaphysics of property is in Chapter 5, "Of Property," of the *Second Treatise of Civil Government* (1690). The metaphysical underpinnings of the theory that to be is to be an owning of properities is in his *Essay Concerning Human Understanding* (1700), Book II, in which he criticizes the older theory of substance and develops his own.[6] To be a thing, for Locke, is to be a possessor of properties, not to be some underlying substratum that does the possessing. A person, on this theory, exists in the owning of personal things, primarily one's acquired experiences and body, secondarily one's labor and the fruits of it, and finally in one's powers over one's ownership as exercised in transferring title, buying, and selling. Capitalism's culture can admit that an economic system is internal to a person's nature, but only as the medium through which the person exercises ownership, which is both self-expression and self-control. By the same token, the system itself does not include the individuals because it is only the *medium* of transferring ownership, not ownership itself. Only individuals can own, and the system, not being an individual, is a personally neutral set of relations. Value, within the capitalist metaphysics, is a function of individual willingness to buy and sell, on the one hand, and of the system's provision of reciprocal willingness to sell and buy, on the other. The system itself has no intrinsic values, only the function of relating individual wills so as to fix value.

While capitalism assumes that individuals always want to buy or sell something or other, the nature of the commodity is metaphysically less important than the fact that the transaction is an instance of change in ownership. Except for vital necessities in the abstract, systems other than the economic determine the content of what people want insofar as that is not affected by its relevance to the virtues of ownership itself.

The language of internal and external relations is somewhat alien to liberal capitalism for which relations are paradigmatically those of possession and transfer of possessions. The metaphysical reason for Marxism's sharp attention to internal and external relations has to do with its conception of identity and change. In general agreement with Hegel, Marxist analysis interprets the identity of a thing in terms of how it has internalized things so as to overcome oppositions and in terms of how it alienates things and thus stands in further oppositions. From this perspective an isolated individual could hardly claim to have achieved ownership of anything but his or her own brute nature. Both human socialization and ownership of goods are achieved not by the dialectical activities of isolated individuals but by a complex social process. Values are to be determined not by exchange alone but by the various factors of achievement overcoming alienation within the social process. A person's work takes its value less from its contributions to the person's own existential definition than from the roles it plays in the dialectic of the situation. What one notes about the value of something in a Marxist analysis is its factual character as overcoming certain oppositions or alienations and falling into certain others, not the nature and degree of worth.

We need to move beyond a capitalist economics of production limited to the values demanded by a metaphysics of ownership. Without questioning the worth of the individual liberty upon which Liberal capitalism insists, the metaphysics of ownership is simply too partial to give an adequate account of personal life. The Marxist criticism of capitalism's brutality is generally well taken, to judge from experience. The relatively powerless people in most capitalist situations are made to conform to such appaling conditions that their freedom to trade their goods or labor is worth too little. The powerful, on the other hand, become seduced into believing that they are fulfilled by the successful playing of economic roles alone, and all other domains of life get shoved into the private sphere or diminished entirely, resulting in boredom and alienation.[7] An economic theory that improves upon capitalism requires a metaphysical foundation that, expressing more generally the nature of individual life in terms of the many connections, systematic or otherwise, people typically have with the world. In particular, an improved metaphysics must be able to represent not only how economic values are responsive to the sense in which people are what they own, but also how economic and other values impact upon all the typical dimensions of human life.

We need also to move beyond the Marxist economics that relates individuals to the economic system by treating them as members of an economically defined social class. Although Marx and Marxists have never said that individuals are nothing but ciphers in their social class, they have often indicated that the other dimensions of human experience are somewhat blindly run by the dynamics of class roles; hence, the therapeutic emphasis on class solidarity. Yet people take part in many systems, and in unsystematic connections, besides economics. No matter how powerful one's theory of social class, it is unlikely that any one set of variables defining social class would give a complete coordination of all the social systems to which a person belongs. Marxist social analysis and prediction have run afoul uncoordinated ethnic systems in Russia, vivid religion in Poland, the American assimilation of unionism to the love of lodges rather than to revolutionary politics, and so forth. The concept of social class, then, is inadequate both for a total definition of human life and for a far-reaching determination of how people relate to an economic system. For, any such relation can be mediated by religion, ethnicity, or any number of other systems or historically particular conditions with which economic participation must be integrated. What is required of an economic theory improving upon Marxism is a meta-physics showing that individuals can be members of many systems at once, that these memberships bind the people together in some ways but not all ways, and that the values transferred along the various systems present both necessities and opportunities for the ways in which they can affect the people involved.

A reminder is in order here that the focus of this discussion is on the axiological requirements of an economic theory. Other require-ments, not discussed, have to do with understanding how not to go broke, how to relate effort to resources, and how to supply basic needs. Our explicit concern about the nature of economic theory should not blind us, however, to some of the practical tests of theory, tests both Marxism and liberal capitalism have failed.

The overwhelming and nearly worldwide rejections of govern-ments with Marxist economic policies from 1989 to 1992 stems from at least two failures of Marxist theory. The first is that the theory simply does not take into account the proper market variables, with the result that Marxist policies in the economy reduce wealth rather than increase it. Perhaps the failure represents a neglect in finding proper motivation for enterprise, as capitalist critics of Marxism have argued. Marx, of course, believed that his policies required an increase of wealth that could be shared and that a centralized state-owned economy would ac-complish that.

The second failure derives from the first, namely, that with de-creasing wealth the pressure increases on the government to maintain a fair distribution system. Rejecting a market system of distribution, a Marxist economy must give tyrannical powers to government, and peo-ple after a while cannot tolerate the totalitarianism to which hard-pressed tyrants are forced. Although a Marxist government is supposed to be the people as a whole, as represented temporarily by the Commu-nist Party, in fact the increased pressures on the government to distrib-ute increasingly scarce goods creates a new class of bureaucrats. That class is just as oppressive in practical terms as the class of capitalist own-ers. An improved economic theory needs to identify the variables that Marx missed.

Similarly, liberal capitalism has not been able to systain itself, even though its revolutions have been gradual and undramatic. Although some capitalist ideologues might argue for a perfectly free market, none in fact expects or would even want it. Trade unions have long been rec-ognized for their value in giving workers a share, and interest, in the in-stitutions at hand for economic prosperity. Whereas Marxists have thought people divide automatically into owners and workers, in nearly every advanced capitalist economy individuals are both: every employee with a pension plan is a stock or bond holder. Furthermore, most advanced capitalist economies employ transfer payments, such as in a graduated income tax, to move money away from the sectors that earn it through direct enterprise to sectors that do not profit directly from the economic institutions at hand. At some level the justification of transfer payments is to strengthen the overall economy by helping the poor come to be able to participate for the profit of all. At a more basic level, however, the justification for transfer payments is to bring benefit to those who deserve to be helped irrespective of the economic institutions. The economic institutions simply are not adequate for distributing wealth to all who deserve it on humanitarian grounds, no matter how much better these institutions are than alternatives. So capitalist economies have been modified both by government and by various private institutions such as churches and other groups to distribute goods on more than market considerations. This proves, among other things, that capitalist economics is not adequate as a normative theory about how to distribute wealth. It also shows that the economic is not the only system operative in a society.

III. Metaphysics of Social Analysis

Three metaphysical topics bear particularly upon the suppositions that lie behind social analysis. The first has to do with how to conceive things and the ways they work. Lockean liberal capitalists believe things are substances constituted by what they possess and Marxists believe things are driven by the dialectics of power; both conceptions are metaphysically mistaken and, because of this, misconstrue the relation of values to individuals and social systems. An alternative to "substance" and "power" needs to be developed. The second metaphysical topic is the participation of individuals in social and natural systems and the effects of those systems on individuals. The dialectic of internal and external relations in Marxism and liberal capitalism is not an adequate account. Of particular importance is the ways the values of things are affected and transformed by participation. The third topic is freedom and limitation. Marxists minimize the former, and have been thrown out of office. Capitalists deny the effects of systematic limitation on those unable to invest profitably, and exaggerate the place of freedom. Both the Marxist and capitalist views of freedom and limitation are neglectful of the real character of the values of things, believing instead that value is only to be bestowed on things by human projection or will. Many other metaphysical topics bear upon the construction of social scientific theories, but these are among the most important.

1. Concerning what things are and how they work, both the Lockean substance theory and the Marxian dialectics of power have been rejected by process philosophy and classic American pragmatism in their redirection of the development of modernity. Whitehead's most important and noticed contribution was his new model of causation and substance. As discussed earlier, he proposed to say that a fundamental actuality, which he called an "actual occasion," comes into being by prehending or including as its own material stuff the actual entities of the past.[8] All of the actual occasions in the emerging occasion's past are taken up initially; but the process of coming-to-be, "concrescence," sorts out some to eliminate and some to keep, and among the latter dismembers and recombines them until a singular, definite, individual integration of them is achieved. The new entity then is the integration that includes the past entities as modified by the integration plus the emerging entity's own contributions involved in the integration. The emerging entity depends upon the previously realized actualities in its past for the conditions to which it must conform and the resources out of which to make itself. Its own unique contribution is the existential power of integration, resulting in what Whitehead called "subjective form." Once the entity fully emerges, its subjective existential power ceases and its achieved actuality is objectified so as to be available to condition future entities.

In complex entities of the sort comprising human experiences, the means of integration include composite rearrangements of conditions so as to constitute consciousness and what Whitehead called "presentational immediacy." This allows for the envisionment of a spatio-temporal field with a future and with objects at a distance, both of which can figure in the integration process.

The revolutionary importance of Whitehead's view is that both existence and causation are functions of creativity in the present, creativity that takes up the past within the limitations set by the past and makes it presently real in modified form, adding to the reality that had been achieved in the past. At a stroke, then, Whitehead provides an alternative around the view, as old as Aristotle, that the reality of the present is merely the unfolding of the past or the continuation of past substance. Although the past provides the raw material, on Whitehead's view, and thus sets limitations on what the present can and cannot do, the force of present existence and of causal change consists in present creativity presently making up something out of the past resources. Thus both the substance metaphysics of Locke's continuity of possessions and the dialectic of power in Marx's theory of persons in economic systems are revealed to be mere metaphors for specific kinds of limitation the past can put on the present. Whether the present in fact takes those metaphors seriously depends on what it does within the limitations; and exactly what the limitations are becomes an empirical problem for investigation, not an a priori metaphysical assumption. The shift from the older metaphysical models to Whitehead's allows many things that had to be assumed as given in the nature of things to be reconsidered as open for investigation, and possibly for change.

According to Whitehead, as has been discussed earlier, an actual entity is an achievement of value. It includes all the values of the entities that it has integrated (as modified in the integration) plus the values emergent in the having of those values together in just that way. What Whitehead stressed is that the entire actual entity, value and all, enters into the subsequent entities it conditions. If the subsequent entity dismembers it so as to distort or lose its value, that is the responsibility of the particular subsequent process. On the initial metaphysical level every entity contributes its achieved intrinsic value to the entities it conditions. The conditioned entities may have some limitations as to what elements of value may be retained and re-objectified in their own nature, and they may have some choice about that. But the massive stability of nature consists in the regularities and continuities of values transmitted through multiple lines of causation. This conception of nature as the structured transmission and revaluing of values is the beginning of a cosmology that surmounts the fact-value distinction in modern metaphysics.

There is a decisive limitation to Whitehead's idea of actual occasions, namely that they are momentary. For him, only the present is fully real, and the past and future have reality only insofar as embodied in the present.[9] His view cannot give an account of an individual that is temporally thick, with a past, present, and future dynamically shifting with the date; the closest approximation to such an individual is a particular aggregate or society of occasions with highly personal order. The genius in Whitehead's conception, however, is that he shows how causal efficacy and value enter into any present moment of decisive actualization. His point holds good whether the relevant past is another individual or an individual's own past.

To balance out the momentariness of process philosophy's theory of atomic occasions we can turn to pragmatism's theory of habit. For Peirce, as described above, and for Dewey as well, reality is a welter of processes, interweaving, colliding, separating, and altering one another. Each process behaves habitually until it happens upon circumstances for which it has no appropriate habit, and then it changes to meet the affairs at hand. The metaphysical model of habits is quite apt to describe both individuals and systems of social institutions and nature. For a system or individual to modify a habit is not for it to change everything but only those ways or working that need to be changed in order to respond to the environment. Also, changes can be understood precisely as responses to the environment, not as mechanical unfoldings of previously set algorithms or the dialectics of power, nor as the adventitious setting of will by fancy and whim.

The pragmatic theory of habit has its own limitation, namely, that its theory of continuity does not allow for a significant distinction of the present (in which change takes place) from either the past (which is finished) or the future (which is mere possibility). By itself, pragmatism suggests a universal malleability with little room to understand the guilt and tragedy of mis-taken or missed opportunities. Pragmatism's weakness, however, is process philosophy's strength. The atomic theory of the present in Whitehead provides exactly the corrective needed by pragmatism. Through creative concrescence in the present moment, things modify their habits in response to circumstances, exercising what freedom is allowed by the limitations of those circumstances.

In order to integrate pragmatism and process philosophy at this point, a more comprehensive metaphysical system is needed that expresses the following distinction. In every thing or process, in every individual, institution, or system of society or nature, the thing relates to other things by virtue of its conditional features, and it integrates its conditional features to maintain or achieve its own identity by virtue of its essential features. Thus some moments in the past of an individual or a system are essential parts of that thing and, thus, give it moral commitments and essential continuity of identity; some moments in the thing's future are also its own future, in contrast to the future of other things affected by its actions, and those states of its own future have more bearing and provide temporally thick identity. Although things are responsive to both their own past and other things in the past, and to their own future and other things in the future, their identity is tied essentially to the former in each pair and, conditionally, to the latter. Only by virtue of the continuity of a changing but temporally thick identity can we understand the interaction of individuals and systems.[10]

2. The mention of interaction of individuals with systems recalls the second metaphysical topic, participation. The older substance model thought of things in terms of their possession of properties, but that

model has difficulties accounting for how properties relate things. On the metaphysical theory presented here, an individual participates in many systems, playing roles in each. Some of the systems are natural, such as the metabolic; others are social, such as the economic, political, educational, or religious. Each of the systems contributes conditional features to the individual. Some of those conditional features are necessary, such as the economic. Others may not be necessary but only adventitious, such as membership in the Boy Scouts or Girl Scouts. Most social systems are intertwined in causal ways; *if* you are to do well in the economic system, *then* it pays to get deeply involved in the educational system. Some systems combine both natural and artificial elements; again, the economic system of food production and distribution illustrates this. Most human participation in systems, even the natural ones, is affected by participation in cultural or semiotic systems.

The systems essentially provide roles for things to play in them. Conditionally, the systems consist of the things actually playing the roles. The economic system thus depends upon people to be producers, distributors, consumers, and so forth. In certain respects, the systems are affected only by the individuals acting according to the systematically defined roles. But sometimes the specific character of the participants affects the systems themselves. Some scholars, taking their clue from Max Weber, (1904–1905; 1951) have hypothesized that people participating in Calvinist or Confucian religious systems will play roles in economic systems quite differently from people whose religious participation is Roman Catholic or Mahayana Buddhist, developing a stringent work ethic. Thus not only do different kinds of individuals transform the systems in which they participate differentially, so also systems themselves modify each other. Changes in weather modify the economy; changes in economy modify education; changes in education modify religion; religion in turn modifies all the others—even the weather, according to some beliefs.

These various kinds of participation of systems within systems and individuals all need to be modelled in social science theory. But what is most important to model is how the values of things are transformed when they come to participate in and perhaps to modify systems and persons. A grass has one value in a prairie ecosystem, another as providing grain for bread in an economic system, another as providing pleasure as an ingredient of whiskey in systems of leisure and celebration, and yet another as contributing to drunken driving in a transportation system. A society with no automobiles does not have to worry about drunken driving, nor does a society that does not make alcoholic drinks.

The importance of this point is that social science theories need to display how social systems affect the values in individuals and in nature, as well as in themselves and each other. Capitalism has been unable, through its elementary categories, to understand how the economic system affects the value of people's lives in ways other than those displayed in production and the market. Marxism has been unable to represent in its elementary categories the ways in which the various values in the other systems in which people participate lead them to participate differentially in the economic system. Both of those economic theories have been unable to develop any but the crudest moral evaluation of economics. Social sciences need to be able to represent the nuanced interactions of individuals and systems that provide the content and context for moral issues.

By virtue of the metaphysical fact that the value of something is a function of its objective character (as in hot sun being good for corn in July), persons, social systems or institutions, and natural systems all lay obligations upon us. As will be argued in the next chapter, any time something with value might be affected by our actions there is an obligation to do the best by it. In the previous chapter it was suggested that a covenant theology is the best description of the human condition. That can be filled in a bit more at this point. A covenant theology can say that people are created to be obligated to the values in one another in the various systems of nature in which they live and in the institutions and systems of their social interactions. Not to be properly attentive to the values in those three realms is to be in conflict, indeed contradiction, with the created status of being obliged (see Neville 1991b, chapters 3–6).

3. The third metaphysical topic is freedom, also implicit in the discussion of the other two topics. Process philosophy has argued in the terms of its theory that, within the limits set by the conditions it prehends, an entity might be able to integrate them in more than one way. Included among the conditions are the systems in which an individual participates; there may be more than one way to integrate participation in the economic, religious, and educational systems at hand. The ways differ from one another not only structurally but in the values to which they give importance. One option might keep certain of the past values intact, perhaps even enhancing them by their surroundings, while paring down other past conditions with their values to subordinate instrumental roles and eliminating yet other past conditions entirely. An alternate option for integration might have a quite different arrangement of what is valuable. With respect to a given conditioning value, this

is what Whitehead called (1929, 240–255) "valuing up" or "valuing down."

We employ natural regularities and use craft to increase them in order to gain control and limit freedom in some other things; freedom of alternate integration is the last thing we want in the machines we use, for instance. Where the past conditions are partially indeterminate in how they can be integrated, perhaps not all kinds of indeterminacy are helpful to human freedom. The past conditions have to be indeterminate with respect to the important choices for the emerging individual, and this requires being quite determinate with respect to those processes that set up the important choices. For instance, physiological and social systems, insofar as they enter an occasion of choice as conditions, must be stable and regular if the emerging occasion is to deal effectively with them.

Although each conditioning element enters an occasion with its own intrinsic value, that value must be modified in order to be integrated with the values of the others, and the modifications might be diminishments as well as enhancements. Where nature is tightly organized according to rigid law, values tend to be transferred intact because the conditions limiting one entity are pretty much the same as those limiting the other entities. But in human affairs where there seems to be a wide range of free play and non-integration, the values of the past can be transformed radically as they pass through agents and institutions. Questions of justice and morality have to do with the transformation of values in process of transmission.

As the pragmatists have long argued, the amount and kind of limitation on choice is an empirical matter. Peirce's rejection of the hypothesis that necessity must be presupposed for science to be possible (discussed in chapter 1 above) lays open the field for an empirical study of freedom. Kant was surely correct that freedom must be possible in order for morality to be obligatory. With our metaphysical hypothesis, we can see how to ask just how free, and in what respects and ways a person is free. The same question can be asked for a social system or institution with some internal guidance organization.

IV. On the Structure of Social Theory

With these new metaphysical assumptions, assumed by hypothesis now, we may see several crucial elements for the understanding of society, and especially of economic systems.

1. We have remarked several times that social science theories ought to be able to represent or model how individuals, social systems, and economic systems participate in one another. More particularly, we have noted that what needs to be represented is how they change one another. The issue is not how static structures interact but how their interactions structurally modify the individuals and systems.

Finally, what is most important to represent is how the values of things are transformed in these interactions. The reason for this is not the ideological one, that social sciences ought to be useful for making moral progress in society. The reason, rather, is that things are objectively valuable, and that the truth about them includes the truth about their worth. The most important truths are those having to do with the changes in value that things undergo as a result of their interactions.[11]

2. Such natural joints, distinguishing one social science from another, have to do with the essential integrity of different social and natural systems. (We may deal with the natural systems insofar as they bear upon social systems, as they do in ecological, agricultural, and other concerns.) This is to ask whether there are certain phenomena that are systematically related essentially, such that other phenomena may play roles as conditions but are not essential. Can economics be defined as the cluster of value-achievements or changes involved in producing and distributing commodities? Education as the cluster of systematic practices for transmitting knowledge and habits cultally and acquiring better knowledge and habits deliberately? Religion as the systems of rituals, cosmologies, and spiritual practices that constitute people's responses to the fact of existence? Government as the system of institutions for regulating the distribution and use of power? These are all empirical questions about whether some standard definitions in fact demarcate genuine differences between systematic connections.

According to our metaphysical hypothesis, no social scientific theory devoted to one system, for instance the economic or the political, needs to be reductive in the sense of ignoring or diminishing the importance of the others, as Marxism needs to subordinate most social causation to the economic. Rather, a theory oriented to one system can represent the other systems in terms of their conditional contributions to the primary one under study. If there are systems of systems—which may not be true, for there is no reason to think that systems have to relate according to the systematic connections of yet more inclusive systems—then there might be inclusive social science theories. There is no a priori need to believe that there ought to be an inclusive social science theory, because there may be only various systems reacting to one another according to their own dynamics, without the intervention of higher order systematic rules. The theory being discussed here is a theory about theories, not about social phenomena.

3. The previous point can be rephrased as whether there are specific values at stake in economic phenomena that can be understood systematically and other values at stake in politics, religion, government, and the rest. In addition, social science theory needs to understand how those values relate to human individuals and what values are essential to human beings as such. Earlier we took note of Paul Weiss's hypothesis (in *Privacy,* 1983) that there are essential epitomies of the human: sensitivity, sensibility, need, desire, orientation, sociality, mind, resolution, autonomy, responsibility, and the ego (see also Neville 1987a, chapter 7). If these, or some similar list, are in fact what are essential to develop and foster in human life, each social and natural system can be examined for how they help or hinder them. Each of these epitomies can be understood as a structure internal to individual persons by virtue of which the conditions of life are integrated, including the social and natural systems in which the people participate.

It is necessary for economic theory (or any social science attentive to the transmission of values) to identify the relevant classes of essential features constituting the human. The example of morals, employing all the epitomies, is a fairly obvious one. Its obviousness comes from our Western theme of contractual obligation as defining the human, a theme as old as Sinai if not Noah's Landing. What are the additional structures built up through growth, maturation, and learning that constitute the human? Although embodied at every moment of a person's life, these structures exist only with temporal thickness; they build on one another hierarchically, and they interpenetrate, affecting one another both essentially and conditionally as circumstances dictate.

4. A limitation should be noted on all this discussion. The discussion has been principally of the nature of social systems and the systematic nature of individuals: synchronic topics. Yet as Marx stressed, economic systems themselves are in process of historical evolution, as are all other social systems; perhaps the development of the essential human epitomies is also historical. A full social science account cannot be only synchronic but requires a genetic or diachronic dimension as well, dealing with the stages of development of each of the important kinds of individuals and institutions. In addition, it must build in references to particular historical events determining the shape of economic conditions. Social science theory must represent the particulars of history as well as the systematic structures of their phenomena. The special

theoretical shape discussed here treats history insofar as it bears upon transformations of the values in systems and individuals.

We may expect the development of a value-oriented economic theory to suggest radical changes in economic policies once the worth of transactions is better known. The values of production are too abstract, and capitalism is thus a distorting ideology. The values of the interest of social classes are also too abstract, and Marxism thus is another distorting ideology. Both kinds of value, however, those of production and those of social class, are sufficiently important to justify the development of an appropriate economic theory and to put in place the analytical mechanisms to allow it to provide data and guide policy.

Nevertheless, the reason for the development of a value-oriented economic theory, or any other social scientific theory, is not so that it presents values for ideological manipulation. Rather the reason is that that is the way things are: value-laden. To make wise policies about what ought to be done, we need to have theoretical tools for analyzing what is at stake and how things work that are neither themselves the result of ideology nor constructed so as to emulate some other kind of science. The reality of value-laden social phenomena must measure our ways of representing them.

CHAPTER TEN

✳

FREEDOM, TOLERANCE, AND THE PURITAN ETHIC

The previous two chapters have alluded to conclusions about freedom and responsibility that are not the expected ones for a late-modern liberal. As remarked in chapter 8, they are more characteristic of what a late-sixteenth-century Puritan might have thought if shown the history of the world through the latter years of the twentieth century. The Puritans pointed to the development of modernity in a way that goes around modernism, and their inspiration will guide the argument of this chapter explicitly, and the next implicitly.

I. The Principle of Universal Public Responsibility

The concerns of this chapter and the next arise from a basic assumption to be advocated for political theory that will be called the "Principle of Universal Public Responsibility." This Principle, stated in an abbreviated formula, maintains that

> *every person in a social group, subject to certain qualifications, is responsible for all the group's public obligations.*

The Principle of Universal Public Responsibility stands in obvious contrast with the parallel assumption underlying the liberal tradition, namely, that any personal responsibility for the public good derives from the offices of the social contract, and that apart from the contract no one is responsible for public matters, only for their own private interests. When the social contract breaks down or its forms become incompetent to handle the demands of public obligations, the liberal assumption is that obligation to the public good evaporates and only private interests remain. The Principle of Universal Public Responsibility, deriving from the Puritan sensibility that preceded the rise of British liberalism, says, on the contrary, that when the contracted social orders break down, the socially constructed division of labor with regard to public obligation evaporates and primary responsibility returns to everyone, subject to certain qualifications.[1]

To use the old-fashioned language, the Principle of Universal Public Responsibility asserts that in the state of nature everyone is responsible for all public goods of the group, whereas in the state of civil society that responsibility is divided and assigned artificially to special agents as defined by the contract or laws and customs. Privacy and freedom *from* public responsibility, thus, are artifacts of civil society according to the Principle of Universal Public Responsibility. When the working forms of civil society break down or are in jeopardy, the privileges of privacy and freedom from public responsibility take second place to primary responsibility to public obligations. Because privacy, leisure, and attendant freedoms from having to attend to all public obligations are great goods, there is a powerful motivation to sustain and improve socially constructed orders. Yet the bite of the Principle of Universal Public Responsibility comes when society is in trouble. Instead of a collapse into an amoral chaos with little or no public responsibility—the implication of the liberal assumption—the Principle of Universal Public Responsibility points out the activated responsibility of everyone for the good of the social group as a whole. Although it is not possible fully to justify this Principle here, it will be explained in order to express important concerns about its implications for freedom, tolerance, and commitment.[2]

1. The first point to note is that the Principle assumes that nature and society contain real goods that can be discerned and related to possible action in order to be secured. This assumption has not been common in the modern era. The liberal contractarian theory from Hobbes and Locke to Rawls has assumed on the contrary that there are no real goods that can be known and pursued and has turned instead to a polity based on human wants and interests.[3] Indeed, the very strategy of placing responsibility exclusively within the social contract arises from the assumption that public goods are constructions resulting from agreements about how to pursue personal wants and interests. The liberal assumption about the value-neutrality of nature and society conforms to other metaphysical assumptions of the mathematical science of the modern era about the separation of facts and values. There are many

reasons to dispute that liberal assumption, but they will not be engaged here beyond what has been said earlier (see also Neville 1981, chapters 1–4; 1987a; and 1989).

2. The second point in explaining the Principle of Universal Public Responsibility concerns the definitions of social good and public obligation. If goods are real and discernible, the content of the social good is of course an empirical matter. Most social goods are negative, for instance, the preservation of the peace, the alleviation of suffering, pain, hunger, oppression by others, and the like, although many social goods are positive, such as privacy and leisure for personal excellence, enjoyment of the fruits of the earth, the development of various human relationships, the arts and other benefits of civilization, and a spiritual attunement to the earth and ultimate things. Then there are the various social institutions that are good because they secure or foster the others: for example, educational, judicial, religious, communal, and athletic institutions.

What makes these goods social rather than merely personal is that their achievement by some one or few people benefits the rest. The key to this is the web of interconnections in social causation, interconnections with a wide variety of forms.[4] In a crude sense, the social group benefits from the health and security of individual members because they then can make their own contributions to the group as better producers of food, goods and services, nurturers and teachers of the young, warriors, and the like. Of course in an overpopulated society, the opposite may seem to be true; nevertheless, control of population is one of the goods a society is obligated to respect and attend to. As to the members of the society, the whole society benefits from their health, prosperity, and capacity to contribute to the common good. Jefferson and others have made these kinds of interconnections more sophisticated in their argument for universal education: a democratic nation needs an educated citizenry. Deeper kinds of interconnections are revealed in empathy and sympathy for the experience of others: starving people in Ethiopia, tortured people in totalitarian jails, all diminish us who are well fed and free.

The social goods may be called "obligations" because their worthiness demands that something should be done, or abstained from, in order to achieve, secure, or protect them, other things being equal. The last phrase means that actions taken or abstained from have costs, and the goods need to be weighed against those costs. Utilitarian considerations are by no means the only ones that bear upon determining the costs of attending to social goods.

The mere normativeness of social goods, however, only determines the public obligation that something should be done about them. "Someone should do something about that!" It does not determine who has the obligation. Public obligation, which is normative and general, should be distinguished from personal responsibility, which consists in a personal subject being under an obligation. To be responsible is to have one's moral character determined in part by an obligation. Liberalism can recognize general public obligations, but it relates those to individuals whose responsibility it is to fulfill them only by means of the social contract. Therefore, when the social contract goes seriously awry, all of the then-obvious public obligations such as keeping the peace and securing the economy may fail to have anyone responsible for them. The Principle of Universal Public Responsibility says that precisely because of membership in the social group, all individuals, with certain qualifications, have responsibility for all social obligations. Liberal polity would be satisfactory only when everything is copasetic; such a time has not yet been recorded in history. The Principle of Universal Public Responsibility addresses the situation when at least some people are ill served by the obtaining social structures.

3. The third point in explaining this principle is the qualification to universal responsibility. There are at least two kinds of qualifications that can deactivate, as it were, all or part of a person's responsibilities to the public good: natural disabilities and social limitations. By "natural disabilities" are meant those having to do with being too young or old, with disabling trauma or defects of birth or disease, and with being incompetent or removed from the action in ways that could not have been helped by planning or preparing differently earlier. Lurking behind all these natural disabilities that qualify one's responsibilities is the primary responsibility to be ready for responsibility if at all possible.

By "social limitations," the second kind of qualification of universal responsibility, is meant the array of arrangements that divide up responsibilities to make culture efficient, finitely teachable, and capable of achieving more goods and avoiding more evils by virtue of cooperation and division of labor. Of course a wholly unorganized society, with everyone attempting to fulfill all social obligations (if ever there could be such universal virtue) would be total chaos.[5] All societies in their traditions and living cultures have social roles for rearing children, for attending to economic matters, to domestic chores, to defense and peace, for settling disputes, and the rest. This is not to suggest that the intentionality behind the development of social roles is for the sake of efficiency in fulfilling social obligations. On the contrary, the intentionality in most societies is part of the tissue of the overall culture whose center is often religious or patriotic. Yet the division of labor regarding the social goods is what relieves each individual of having activated responsibility for all of them. By reason of whatever intentionality, most people have deactivated responsibility for most public obligations, usually on the condition that they have activated responsibility for certain specific responsibilities, often those for which they are specially fit or trained, and in the fulfillment of those few responsibilities act as surrogates for others.

Civilized societies do not divide labor exclusively according to inherited cultural roles. In addition there are explicit social constructs of leadership and other institutions for managing social organization itself, the matters of government, polity, and law of which the early contract theorists thought. Most issues of channeling responsibility for public obligations concern these explicit social constructs. And they are the ones that so often go wrong, so that the responsibilities they are supposed to handle in fact revert back to everyone.

4. The final point about the Principle of Universal Public Responsibility has to do with defining the social group. In accordance with the terms in which social benefit was described above, a social group is constituted by the causal interactions of people with one another, usually through the joint manipulation of material and cultural processes. The group is more or less tight according to the kind and density of the causal social interactions. With a few exceptions, the social group in our time is worldwide in many important respects. The divisions of people into separate nations, or separate language and cultural groups, are (among other things) divisions of labor, and their legitimacy needs to be tempered by judgments about whether they serve the achievement of the public social good. To the extent that nationalism, say, inhibits rather than promotes the worldwide social good, it is a detriment to the fulfillment of each person's responsibility. Because of the global network of social interactions, the group whose good most of us are responsible for seeking is a worldwide community. The goods of that worldwide community that provide universal public obligations are those having to do with the causal processes in terms of which the worldwide community is constituted. There is a worldwide economic system, for instance, and in economic terms each individual has global responsibilities; there is no worldwide ethnic culture, and therefore no one has responsibilities for the good of all ethnic groups as such.

What are the implications for social polity that flow from the Principle of Universal Public Responsibility? Let us question three implications: What kind of social commitment is required to exercise universal responsibility? How can that commitment, if it is universal, be prevented from overreaching itself so that one person takes it to be a personal responsibility to coerce another person to conform to the first person's definition of responsibility? Is there a sense of freedom that is native to universal public responsibility, or is freedom reduced to artificial protections against having to fulfill all responsibilities? These are the topics of Puritan commitment, tolerance, and freedom.

II. Puritan Commitment

In contrast to the liberal conception of atomic individualism, which has been roundly criticized over the past 150 years, the Principle of Universal Public Responsibility implies that people ideally are individuated through fulfilling their connections with the things that have normative bearing on their lives. That is, people are individuated in a factual way by being responsible for the particular context in which they relate to the universal range of obligations. And they are individuated ideally by the extent to which they fulfill those responsibilities. The modes and degrees to which people positively address their responsibilities give individuating content to life. The more tied into the context in normative ways, the more one's individuality is fulfilled. Individuation comes with commitment to the normative tasks of one's context, and through that context to the normative tasks of the social group. This may be called the "Corollary of Individuation through Commitment."

It might seem as if this is the wrong inference to draw from the Principle of Universal Public Responsibility. For, if everyone is responsible for all public obligations, except insofar as a socially constructed division of responsibility deactivates some responsibilities, then is not everyone the same as far as responsibilities go? And then the contextual differences between people would be relatively trivial except insofar as they coincide with the social division of responsibilities. So whereas the liberal polity assumes that people are essentially different because of their different contexts and only contractually united in a system of responsibilities, the Principle of Universal Public Responsibility seems to trivialize the differences of context.

To answer this objection we need to remember that the keystone of the Principle of Universal Public Responsibility is the network of causal social relations by virtue of which individuals participate in a social group and in the group's activities regarding interactions with material and cultural processes. Involvement in the network is what transforms a general social obligation into the personal responsibility of individuals. The network of social processes is historically, geographically, and personally particular. Each person is particularly defined by the diverse implications of the network for the various positions the person occupies. If there were no responsibility involved, we might say that the person is individuated only as the particular unique congeries of all the network's implications for the person's positions. But since many of those implications place the person in relation to social goods that give particular responsibilities, the person is not just a complex set of roles but a partially self-creating or affirming individual. For, it is through being responsible for particular things and committing oneself to fulfilling those responsibilities that one becomes an individual in the full sense. Being responsible gives one a moral soul, and how one fulfills those responsibilities, for better or worse, gives one a moral character.

The particularity of one's individuality comes from the fact that responsibilities are always contextual. That is, one is responsible for the more general social obligations such as keeping the peace, voting for governmental leaders, paying taxes, and so forth, because one's particular social context is causally connected with those general obligations. One also has more proximate responsibilities to one's job, local community, religious and civic organizations, family, and so forth. Proximate responsibilities are not merely means for fulfilling more general ones nor are the general responsibilities for the sake of supporting the proximate affairs; there is a reality to social obligation at all levels of generality. Yet it is through the causal structures connecting proximate affairs with more general ones that all individuals have responsibilities for the most general obligations.

In good times there is a division of responsibility such that dealing with proximate responsibilities virtually fulfills all one's activated responsibilities save those served through tokens such as taxes. In these good times, government responsibility is activated only for officials for whom holding office is a proximate responsibility. But bad times reactivate people's responsibilities for a wide range of goods, many far from their local context. The leisure of deactivated responsibilities is diminished. Yet the obligatoriness of even the most remote and general social good falls upon the diverse individuals because of the diverse particular ways in which the context of each of them is networked with the larger group. One is a citizen in general and a parent of particular children, both at once with concomitant responsibilities; yet the reason both provide responsibilities is that they are causally connected.

The virtue arising from recognition of this ground of responsibility is commitment to the good of the social group, that is, commitment to fulfilling responsibilities in all the contexts in which one participates, general and proximate. Because that commitment is the substance of one's pursuit of moral responsibilities, it is the trait that underlies moral character. Commitments are always particular because even general responsibilities, such as to peace in the world, are always mediated by the particularities of more proximate contexts that bear their own responsibilities.

The people in the West who recognized the individuating function of commitment best were the early Puritans. They understood that each person is an individual in the eyes of God, with an individual salvation to be fulfilled by relating rightly to every part of the person's social context—to family, community, work, and country. Even though many of the Puritans entertained a deterministic metaphysics, they thoroughly understood that salvation means changing bad laws and social conditions that make life hard for people. Their social revolution was for the sake of improving the lot of all the individuals (or those they could recognize) whose salvation was at stake.

But then their revolution was a terror: bloody, coercive, and utterly contradictory in effect to the aim of bringing a kingdom of God on earth. Nearly everyone in England sighed with relief when the restoration of Charles II brought in moral relaxation and liberal tolerance. We have only to remember the Salem witch trials, the excesses of the Great Awakening, or the potential tyranny of the so-called Moral Majority, to know that in certain crucial respects, Puritanism is a very bad thing. The Puritans seemed better suited to being critics safely kept out of office. What is wrong with Puritan commitment?

III. Tolerance

The formal difficulty with Puritan commitment can be stated rather simply. If I am responsible for everything, then I am responsible for seeing that you fulfill your responsibilities. If that merely meant that I would help you, there would be only a grateful situation. But it can also mean that I must define your responsibilities because they are part of my responsibilities, and force you to work because that is part of my work. The usual existential implication of the Puritan polity was that everyone is an authority over everyone else. Since this cannot work, power politics, mediated in the Puritans' case by a religious ideology, decides whose authority is really authoritative. The authoritative authorities then are responsible not only for the social good but for the moral character of everyone else.

In small part, the difficulty here is with knowledge of the good. Although it has been argued above that there are natural goods and that they can be discerned, their discernment is difficult and partial. Even with the best of will, people can genuinely disagree about what is obligatory and what to do about it. In principle, this is not an insuperable problem, however, because individuals in disagreement can recognize that they must refrain from insisting on their opinions until the issues of moral discernment have been clarified enough for cooperative responsible activity to be undertaken. The next chapter shall thematize this issue under the topic of leadership. The chief difficulty is not disagreement in knowledge but disagreement in will or conscience. Conscientious Puritans believed they must insist upon their conscience.

The way out of the dilemma is to deny social authority in its strong sense altogether. And the way to make that denial is to recur to a valid insight of *both* Puritanism and liberalism, namely, that each person is the responsible author of his or her own actions and influences. The *seat* of responsibility is in the individual subject, just as the *content* of responsibility is in the objective goods that are obligatory to serve. The Principle of Universal Public Responsibility joins the objective content of obligation to the subjective seat of responsibility. It implies that one person cannot, logically, spiritually, or metaphysically, exercise another's responsibility. Since the excellence of individuation involved in developing one's virtues in fulfilling responsibility is one of the greatest goods encountered in civilized experience, East and West, there is a deep and pervasive social obligation on everyone to encourage the development of responsibility in others. Negatively put, the abridgment of someone else's responsibility is a deep evil. More precisely stated, the abridgment of someone else's responsibility, when that person is indeed capable of being responsible, is merely violence against that person; it cannot be a substitute proxy for that person's responsibility.

The moral of this is that tolerance is a fundamental political virtue. Tolerance has primary and secondary levels. At the primary level tolerance is the explicit allowing of space for other people to engage their responsibilities and to achieve a moral character appropriate to their success or failure at that engagement. At secondary levels tolerance is adjusting to the ways, perhaps idiosyncratic, inefficient, and costly to others, by which others approach (or avoid) their responsibilities. Secondary tolerance is putting up with ways of life or approaches to problems we might never approve for ourselves, for the sake of allowing others to engage their obligations on their own responsibility. Contrary to the practice of the Puritans, therefore, the Principle of Universal Public Responsibility enjoins the practice of tolerance at both levels. Tolerance is not a minor virtue, like politeness. It is a fundamental political virtue arising from recognition of the nature of responsibility as subjectively seated in responsible individuals.

There are at least three circumstances in which we generally recognize that tolerance comes in conflict with other obligations, circumstances of emergency, of cooperation, and of sin.

In circumstances of emergency one or more persons can perceive that the tolerance of another person's secondary ways of exercising responsibility, or even primary space to act responsibly, will lead to disastrous results. We tolerate Grandma's slow, cautious driving, for to deprive her of it would be severely to limit her life options; but we grab the wheel when she is about to make a stupid mistake. When a community's safety is threatened by invaders, we limit tolerance by conscription of human and material resources according to the plans of our leaders. Even in these cases, however, it is an empirical matter whether the danger in continued tolerance outweighs the cost of denying the others the tolerance to pursue their responsibility in primary or secondary ways. When President Reagan was shot and Secretary of State Haig said "I am in charge here," it was deadly wrong of him to undermine the constitutional authority of Vice President Bush, even if it were true that Haig would be far better than Bush in a real emergency. When Admiral Poindexter and Lt. Colonel North thought that the legal political process would lead to a disastrous foreign policy and instituted an illegal process of undercover government, they were mistaken to believe that their emergency outweighed the value of constitutional government. But we can imagine scenarios in which the reverse judgments might be made, when the legal government simply fails its obligations and when Grandma really ought to be prevented from driving, for her own sake and the safety of others. The judgment of when an emergency obtains that justifies limiting tolerance is the moral responsibility of each participant in the affair, and that judgment may turn out in retrospect to be mistaken, or everlastingly controversial. In a well-ordered society, with a finely tuned system of allocating activated responsibilities for determining when such an emergency obtains, there is a due process for making the determining decision. We can be satisfied in such a society that the "right" decision is simply what the Supreme Court, or the President, or the Congress decides. But some emergencies of large scale call that due process into question. In no circumstance does the judgment that an emergency obtains fail to be the responsibility of the participants, with moral consequences for all.

The need for cooperation is a circumstance that can limit tolerance, as when all hands are needed to row the boat out of danger. On a superficial level, cooperation can be understood pragmatically. Many of the fundamental obligations of a society require cooperation and, hence, a tailoring of ways of addressing responsibilities to the patterns of the cooperative enterprise. In a society with automobile traffic, traffic laws appropriately limit driving practices. In a society with a need for defense, welfare entitlements, and the rest, tolerance of how individuals spend their money is appropriately limited by taxation and contracts.

On a more fundamental level, however, cooperation is intrinsic to the human condition because much of what makes us human is the use of signs and meaningful actions and gestures. Most of what we do is "significant," and most of what we are is the result of attaining to the ability to participate in the social system of significant things. Therefore, we are already cooperative in our being and practices, and bare participation in the social system itself is a massive qualification of what otherwise might be conceived as unlimited tolerance. Because a high degree of cooperation is already assumed by the mere fact of participation in the social system, tolerance has come to mean not tolerance of ways of pursuing responsibility but tolerance of deviations from the normal expectations and ways of interpreting and sending social messages. Popular tolerance is of eccentricity. To admit that tolerance involves special cases of making room for eccentricity is to acknowledge that the potential field of tolerable ways of life has already been severely limited by elementary participation in the social system.

The circumstance of "sin" is the greatest test of tolerance. By sin is not meant here the whole Puritan Christian doctrine of original fall and corruption of mind and will, but the simple fact that nearly everyone sometimes and some people much of the time act in ways that deliberately deny their responsibilities.[6] The problem is not that they are klutzes, or that their way of fulfilling responsibilities is unnecessarily costly to the rest of us; the problem is that they do evil, that they act so as to undermine their own responsibilities and interrupt the means by which we attend to ours. All too often, the sinner is ourselves. Can sin be tolerated? The Puritan said no, and from this judgment stemmed the terror of Puritan authoritarianism. Yet the answer must be yes, sin must be tolerated, although it is everyone's responsibility to ameliorate the public consequences of sin as much as possible and to prevent them where predictable. Society should demand of people a minimal degree of responsible behavior, for instance, not stealing, murdering, raping, or committing mayhem, as a condition for admitting them to various privileges of social participation such as the right to socialize with others or be around other people's property. Beyond punishment for crimes, punishment that respects the responsibility of the perpetrator, society can protect itself against future criminal action if it has very good reason to believe the person cannot act responsibly. This of course requires scrupulous attention to due process to guard against special interest in the judgment about the nature of crime and in the characterization of the alleged criminal's responsibility. We also need to be alert to the deficiencies of due process itself that might come from its control by special interests. In addition, we must recognize, as Martin Luther King, Jr., argued, that sometimes responsibility for the public good obliges people to criticize, attempt to change, or disobey a social structure that seriously inhibits their pursuit of responsibility; this is not sin in any sense, but a courageous attention to responsibility. In general, the application of the notion of tolerance in circumstances of sin is to tolerate the sinner because evil is rewarded in an appropriate moral character but not to tolerate certain rights of participation in society that need to be earned by demonstrated responsible behavior. Persons have no right to the fruits of sinful action.

IV. Freedom

Either as an individual virtue or as generalized into social policy, tolerance is a negative good. It is fundamental to the Principle of Universal Public Responsibility because it is an essential corrective to the Corollary of Individuation through Commitment. Each person's commitment must be tolerant of the other's commitment, or failure of commitment, because not to be tolerant is to mistake the individual subjective seat of responsibility.

Beyond tolerance, is there no positive virtue of freedom, as liberalism has argued in its very essence? There is, though it is a complex ideal with many dimensions. Let us reflect on four: political freedom, personal freedom, social freedom, and spiritual freedom.

1. The heart of political freedom is the obverse of tolerance. That is, no person or government can logically or metaphysically have the right to abridge a person's authorship or responsibility for what the person is and does. Positively put, governments and people ought to acknowledge the inalienability of authorship and responsibility. The reason for this is not the liberal one, that people are free unless there is

a contractually valid law inhibiting that freedom. It is rather the recognition that people are naturally responsible for the public good, and that their authority for their own actions is inalienably their own. Enjoyment of political freedom in this sense does not mean that one's actions or liberties cannot be curtailed for the public good, if the needs of the social good so demand. On the other hand, what the structures of society determine in the matter might be mistaken: the public good might not require the curtailment of the actions in question. This is to say, the political legitimacy of regulating individuals' actions for the public good is not identical with the content of what the political structure decides. A political decision might well be an illegitimate one, one not justified by the needs of the public good. Procedural legitimacy does not guarantee moral or even political legitimacy in the larger sense. A totalitarian government that tortures its enemies according to a clear law is not politically or morally legitimate for all its due process. Political freedom, in the restricted sense used for the term here, means the recognition of the subjective seat of responsibility and authorship of actions and the respect for such actions unless the public good requires their inhibition.

2. The personal dimension of freedom, often confused with the political, consists of at least four aspects. The first is freedom to act. Negatively, this means external liberty, not being inhibited in action by nature, society, or government; this sense of freedom is closely tied with political freedom. Positively, this aspect of personal freedom means capacity or ability to act, which requires culture, training, education, experience, and practice, often specifically related to a field of action. This is the aspect of freedom that Hobbes, Spinoza, and Edwards focused upon. Secondly, personal freedom involves the ability to choose among alternatives. On the one hand, this means having real options for choice and, on the other, the capacity to make choices, a capacity again dependent upon knowledge, experience, and practice. Failure to have the freedom to choose among alternatives means that, despite the freedom to act, there is no special responsibility that can be assigned to the actor rather than the actor's antecedents. Responsibility requires that the actor as chooser make the crucial difference. The third aspect of personal freedom is the freedom to choose according to standards; uncontrollable random choice can make the actor causally responsible but not morally responsible. The fourth aspect, closely related, is the freedom to criticize standards for choice and to take responsibility for using the standards one does. This is responsive to Kant's problematic about the sense in which responsibility is giving oneself a law.

3. The personal dimension of freedom is abstract relative to actual life, and it needs to be understood in conjunction with the social dimension of freedom. This also has four aspects: opportunity, social pluralism, integral social life, and political participation. For freedom of opportunity, society needs to provide access to the media of social participation, it needs to make clear and available what might be valuable to people, and it needs to foster engagement with culture that turns a naked opportunity into a prized real option. Social pluralism is that aspect of society allowing space for privacy, for ways of doing things and fulfilling responsibility that are not pre-empted by the needs for conjoint action in the service of the public good. Only by organizing society into deactivated responsibilities and channeled activated ones is it possible to make room for the privacy that genuine creativity requires. Social freedom also requires a social structure that makes integral life possible. This is not problematic in a monolithic society denying privacy and social pluralism; in a pluralistic society it is difficult to find individual integrity. Social freedom also, of course, requires avenues of participation by which people modify their social environment. Democracy is the great family of ideas about how to structure the governance of society so that people's responsibilities to the public good are congruent with their powers for affecting social conditions. All of the aspects of the social dimension of freedom are themselves important parts of the social good and constitute obligations for which individuals are responsible in various ways according to their particular contexts.[7]

The spiritual dimension of freedom has to do with the attainment of spiritual excellence or perfection. This has a negative side, freedom from sin, ignorance, or stain, and a positive side, the achievement of high levels of spiritual power and experience, which include the transformation and integration of other dimensions of freedom. The spiritual dimension of freedom is extraordinarily interesting in its own right, especially as it affects the notion of individuation discussed above.[8] But for the most part, with one exception, the spiritual dimensions of freedom are not internal to the political affairs governed by the Principle of Universal Public Responsibility. That one exception has to do with guilt. By virtue of the Principle of Universal Public Responsibility, we have more responsibilities than we can possibly fulfill. Even if society were ordered with utter perfection, so that each person had responsibilities neatly in keeping with that person's powers, and each person fulfilled those responsibilities perfectly, and all the social obligations were tied to the individuals whose responsibility they were, the situation would not last. Someone would be born when the stars are out of alignment, as

Plato said, and the perfect social structure would be unprepared and thus disfunctional. Or someone would sin, leaving a hole in the network of responsible actions. The realistic situation is that much of the time we fail at the responsibilities we undertake and neglect responsibilities we hope are being cared for elsewhere; and even if we do not do that, others will, so that someone else is given new responsibilities. There is thus inevitable failure, and we, being subjectively responsible for it all, are guilty. Religions address that guilt or failure. In the Christian tradition, the belief that guilt is not our regular state is the sin of pride, the sin of thinking we are infinite and perfect like God. Redemption, or enlightenment, or the attainment of true sageliness, is the religious way to cope with the human condition brought to light by the Principle of Universal Public Responsibility.[9]

This chapter has tried to explain and make plausible a political principle that cuts reality more nearly at its natural joints than the competing assumptions of the closely related liberal tradition. The Principle of Universal Public Responsibility emphasizes positive responsibility over individual freedom as the basis for justifying political orders. It points out that the true nature of human life is to be contextually and socially defined, and that virtue consists in commitment to fulfilling responsibilities in and to that context. The grave danger in this approach is its incipient authoritarianism, which can move as far as totalitarian terror. For this reason, an obligation to tolerance is intrinsic to the Principle of Universal Public Responsibility, for that obligation is commanded by the need to respect the fact that each person is subjectively responsible for the public good, responsible in ways that others cannot displace. Freedom, then, in its political, personal, social, and spiritual dimensions, especially the political and social, is an achievement of cultural order and a great good we are obligated to serve. Freedom is not "natural," like responsibility, but a product of civilization. No one needs to defend responsibility: we are responsible whether or not we accept the fact and attempt to do well by it. But freedom has been dearly bought and is in constant danger of decay. Its protection is the social good on which our own culture has pinned its identity and excellence.

CHAPTER ELEVEN

✳

LEADERSHIP, RESPONSIBILITY, AND VALUE

The Principle of Universal Public Responsibility introduced in the previous chapter requires that general public obligations be channeled to specific responsibilities for individuals if chaos is to be surmounted and obligations effectively met. In a well-ordered society, this channeling is done by social habits, law, and institutional structures. But well-ordered societies are rare. Therefore leadership is involved to direct the channeling of responsibilities. Leadership differs from the sovereignty of the king (Hobbes) and the sovereignty of the legislature (Locke) because both of those senses of sovereignty are defined by well-ordered social structures. They are of the essence of the modern social contract theory. Leadership is required when the social structures are missing or malfunctioning. If one rejects the modern liberal social contract theory, as was done in the previous chapter, then leadership is seen to be extraordinarily important, not a mere adventitious necessity in a pinch. The highroad around modernism needs to understand the role of leadership as something different from the role of "posited" social office.

Leadership is a role (1) obligated by social conditions, (2) deriving from the reality of value, and (3) demanding the exercise of courage. Plato, Confucius, and the author of the *Books of Samuel* enunciated these interlocked themes early in the axial age, and they require fresh reflection in every age.

That the bearing of value and courage on leadership is a metaphysical theme and not merely a topic for political philosophy or Weberian sociology is to be expected, given the previous argument of this book. The claim that metaphysical considerations are intrinsic to moral and political philosophy is by no means innocent; nor does the fact that they will be treated here as essentially related mean that it is finally justified to do so. The French intellectual left, for instance, believes that

239

moral and political philosophy are possible only if they are sharply distanced from metaphysics. But then, what the French left means by metaphysics is a severely circumscribed reading of the Western tradition; the above reading of that tradition, and of the Chinese tradition of "moral metaphysics," does not represent them as often having forms susceptible to anti-metaphysical attack. Furthermore, the positive results for moral and political philosophy derived from Continental anti-metaphysical polemic are meagre, indeed usually only highly reflected versions of Marxism (a splendidly logocentric nineteenth-Century metaphysics).[1]

Plato, in the *Republic*, couched the question of leadership in terms of the responsibility of a special class of citizens who are outstanding in reason, and well educated in its exercise, whom he called "philosophers."[2] Their responsibility is to provide leadership for a state containing at least two other kinds of citizens, appetitive people and spirited people. In Plato's analysis, the appetitive people are those who appreciate value or worth in things and work to produce it. Spirited people are disciplined to conserve the value enjoyed or produced, and their virtue in this regard is courage. Leaders, for Plato, must have strong appetites and tempered courage; they are not to be educated exclusively in intellectual ways but also in the ways of timing and practical administration.[3] He never understood leadership to be defined by the problematics of power alone but by those of the good. His dialogue, the *Statesman*, just as much as the *Republic*, emphasizes the combination of reason with artful practice, and its discussion of normative measure, in distinction from standard measure, repeats the essential connection of leadership with the good.[4]

Beginning with Plato's analyses of value as appreciated and produced and of courage as the virtue whose excellence is the conservation of value, we may expose certain metaphysical roots of the problem of leadership. The conditions of Plato's time were, in important respects, different from our own, and the contemporary problems of leadership shall be posed, finally, in terms he might find strange. We live in a time and place in which the virtues of democracy are so proved and taken for granted, despite the intrinsic difficulties of which Plato warned, that they are an essential part of any viable political equation. Included among these virtues are the equality of rights of individuals to make claim upon the state, the inalienability of real authority from individuals to sovereigns, consent of the governed, and a universal imperative to participate in public life.[5] To understand democracy in the modern sense one must look more closely at the early modern social contract theorists. The twentieth century has witnessed a sea change in suppositions about democracy, however; roughly, the transformation has been from an atomic individualism in democratic life to a participatory conception that emphasizes the importance of medium-scale social structures and institutions that mediate between individuals and society and the state at large. Another aspect of the sea-change has been the final abandonment of the early modern attempt to justify a serious kind of political authority. Although the nature and extent of the sea-change is only now becoming clear, mainly through observations of the ways in which African, Asian, South Asian, and Latin American nations are relating to democracy, a pivotal figure in the change was John Dewey.[6]

I. Value

There are many dimensions to value, as has been evident in previous chapters. That to which philosophers have most often given attention is the formal dimension, which Plato treated principally in the *Phaedrus* and *Philebus.* Formally, something is valuable because it is a harmony of parts. Each part contributes to the value of the whole because of the relations in which it stands to other parts; change those relations and the value of the whole is destroyed or altered. Like the inscription on Midas's tomb, a collection whose parts can be rearranged any which way has no value as a whole, whatever the value of the parts individually.[7]

Plato recognized that the formal is not the only dimension of value and considered the contribution of that which takes on form to the concrete worth of things. He gave several accounts, calling it the "indefinite" in the *Phaedrus* and the *Philebus* and the "receptical" in the *Timaeas.* Plato's dialogues about virtues or human values such as courage, friendship, love, beauty, and justice, are rarely about the formal properties of those norms. Rather they are imaginative experiments asking what various components need to be formally united under the norm. This surely is true of the *Republic,* in which the various aborted attempts to define justice formally are put in context by a surrounding discussion of what is relevant to take into account regarding justice.

Neither the formal nor the material dimensions of value concerns leadership here as much as does the attractive dimension. By attraction, value elicits and moves eros, as Plato set forth in the *Republic,* the *Symposium,* and the *Philebus.* Plato's idea of eros subtly differs from most modern versions. Freud's theory of eros summed up the modern period's attempt to define human behavior according to underlying analogies with inertial motion. For Freud, eros is a drive with inbuilt pressure seeking an object to give it release. After union with that object, there is a sudden relaxation in pressure; but it builds up again in time and needs new release. Freud's theory is a wholly modernist development of the early modern idea of power. Plato, by contrast, said that the value in the object itself creates the erotic drive. In the *Phaedrus* and again in the *Symposium* he explored how physical beauty in lovers elicits the passionate drive for sexual union. The result of each union is hardly a temporary diminishment of the drive but an escalation of eros to a higher level, to friendship, to concern for the other's welfare, to truthfulness, justice, to procreation of a virtuous society through the deepest kinds of education.[8]

In the *Republic* (at 507–8) Plato suggested that the Good is the creator of the world, of the invisible and the visible, and of the grounds for knowledge and of opinion. With some change in vocabulary, he elaborated this in the *Philebus* (at 23–24) in his theory of the good as "the cause of mixture" that puts the right form or "limit" in the right "indefinite" set of potential components to be ordered. The mixing of form and the ready-to-be-formed is to be understood as taking place for the good of achieving a specific value. In several important senses, Alfred North Whitehead (1933), Paul Weiss (1958, chapter 2), and Robert Brumbaugh (1961), in our century, have developed this metaphysical idea of goodness or ideality as the ground of definiteness. The concern here is not with the metaphysical generality of the claim but with the special function of valuable things in creating the content of human life.

Plato was right, in the *Philebus*, to suggest that every natural process achieves the specific value of harmonizing its components into the mixture defining its identity. Each of its components, in turn, is a mixture exhibiting an achieved value, and so on back. Our world, thus, is a vast melange of processes, each of which has a value and many of which affect the values of others as they interact with or enter into them as components (Neville 1989, part 2).

The pragmatists, in turn, were right to call attention to the valuative character of human experience. Everything encountered, including the processes internal to life, elicits some kind of valuative response, erotic or anti-erotic. In cases where these valuative responses reach consciousness and are subject to further reaction by means of representations, we tickle out language that channels valuation into simplifying abstractions. At some point, where experience is interwoven with representations, we gain some control over valuative responses. Do we appreciate the values of things correctly? Are our representations of those valuations good ones? Perhaps the most important question is how can we integrate one valuation with another so as to order our own cumulative experience. As these questions are asked, representations of alternatives are formulated and we imaginatively construct ideals with which to judge the valuations, their representations, and their mutual integration. Much of what we commonly recognize as human experience consists of emotional and cognitive processes developed to construct ideals for valuing well, for representing those valuations evaluatively, and for determining integrated habits in which to respond to what is appreciatively valued.

There are many ways of classifying the ideals that shape the levels and dimensions of human life, such as Paul Weiss's epitomies discussed above.[9] Whatever the schemes, they exhibit personal and social processes to be attempts to achieve some approximation of ideal integrations of things antecedently valued and perhaps explicitly prized. All this is to say, with Plato, that, given the felt worths of various things, the imagined or perceived *ideals* for how to integrate and make compatible their enjoyment create the *actual* human processes that pursue that integration. The ideals of human life elicit the erotic responses in which the physical structures, habits, and self-reflexive representations of the higher human traits and characters consist.

The plot of this argument so far, which has only been a brief sketch of an hypothesis resting largely on the authority of Plato, exposes the suppositions that the things of the world all have specific values and that many of these can be appreciated by people. It points to the conclusion that, with the appreciation of these various goods, human processes are developed to enjoy and correct that appreciation, and to integrate our various elementary and higher level valuations. As processes of enjoyment, criticism, and integration, these human traits take on worth of their own and are subject to some control according to further imagined ideals.

The values of things are intrinsic to their own attainment of integration and, hence, are not dependent upon being appreciated except in certain instances. The concern here, however, is indeed with their appreciation and with the role of leadership in the organization of society so as to allow people to be faithful to what is of value. Of course, human beings do not appreciate everything of worth, only those things to which they have access. Furthermore, they represent the valuation only of a small portion of the things they value and, hence, recognize but a small portion of their valuative responses, and that in a highly filtered form. Even the limited part of our recognized valuative responses is still important, however, and it guides our thought about ideals and how they stand with respect to actual and possible processes.

II. Courage

Plato characterized the normative human response to the specific worths of things, given their enjoyment or pain, to be their conservation. The spirited part of the soul, the will, the drive toward personal integrity, aims to conserve the positive values appreciated and to destroy those things whose negative worth inhibits or threatens the positive. In Plato's society, as figured in *Republic* 429–430), the soldiers are the conservators of the society's attainments from external and internal enemies. Although the process of conservation might itself be fruitful of many new things, especially under the guidance of the philosophic guardians, the essential contribution of the courageous is conservation.

At the outset, we may note that, when two or more ways of directing a social process are possible and one is better than another, it is better to pursue the better way than the worse. This simple truth signals elementary obligation. Without specifying whose obligation it is, the sheer fact that one way of developing a process is better than another entails that the better ought to be pursued.

In public affairs, the normative differences are often negative. Poverty ought to be eliminated or its effects ameliorated. Unfair distribution of harms ought to be amended. Steps should be taken to protect society against foreign enemies, against natural disasters, and against the breakdown of those institutions that enhance the social values as they stand. In some instances, of course, public obligations are positive. We can imagine better institutions than we have, especially in the service of education, culture, and the arts. We surely can imagine a more just society in the distribution of goods and services. Public obligations exist simply because of the fact that processes can be controlled somewhat for the better or worse. But the fact of obligation does not specify whose responsibility it is to pursue the obligation. We just say that "someone ought to do something about that."

At this point it is important to draw attention to the contrast between the classical modern sense of community and the "revised democratic sense" cited from Dewey above. The classical modern view assumed either a chaotic state of nature or an organized community with strong authority structures. On that view, an appeal to individual responsibility in the face of public obligation, such as is being made here, reinforces a strident individualism. Furthermore, on that view an individual who exercises responsibility is justified by, or endowed with, authority in some strong sense. An appeal to individual leadership in the context of the early modern view of community lends itself to authoritarianism. On the revised democratic view of community, individuals are defined in large part by their relations with others and especially with social institutions. There never is a pure state of nature, only social groupings with various kinds of institutional organization, working well or ill, relevantly or irrelevantly, according to the needs of the society and the excellences of the civilization. "To do something about" a public obligation is thus rarely an individual heroic act but rather the mobilization of people, usually structured in various connected institutions, to "do something" jointly. Leadership is required when the ongoing social processes are not sufficiently mobilized to attend to the obligation.

The next step in the philosophic argument is to determine personal responsibility to fulfill a general social obligation (see Neville 1987a, chapter 3). How does public obligation become the personal responsibility of particular individuals? Although the distinction advocated here between obligation and responsibility might seem arbitrary from the point of view of the language, the real distinction signified is truly important. *Obligation* derives from the *objectivity* of publicly important values, which means that some developments are better than others whether or not anyone recognizes them and regardless of whose responsibility it is to do something about it. (This is not to say that all processes can be ranked in value or even that they are commensurable; *some* processes can be ranked, however.) *Responsibility*, on the other hand, is deeply tied to *subjective personal identity*. A responsibility is an obligation that defines a particular individual's moral identity.

The transition from public obligation to personal responsibiltiy is a lacuna in much current political philosophy.

Plato, and the ancients more generally, undertook to facilitate the transition by means of assigning responsibility according to fitness of type. In the *Republic* Plato argued that public need for defense and for sophisticated leadership should promote the development of cultural classes of people whose responsibility it is to address those needs. If one were born and trained a warrior, defense is one's responsibility in time of need; that sense of military noblesse oblige continues to spark a living mythology in some parts of New England and the Old South today in the United States. The aristocratic ideal of Plato and much subsequent culture, however, could not and did not much survive the egalitarianism of early modern European capitalist society. Who can believe now that personal responsibilities are attendant upon membership in a class when class membership shifts frequently according to merit and factors irrelevant to the responsibilities?

The social contract theory of early modern European philosophy provided a distinct alternative to the aristocratic theory. Although several versions of the contract theory were put forward, they agreed that without civil society in a state of nature there are no responsibilities, save perhaps to oneself. Hobbes argued in the *Leviathan* (1651, chapter 14), that in the state of nature there is a natural impetus to seek one's own welfare but no significant normative obligation to do so. Locke, in the *Second Treatise of Civil Government* (1690), allowed that there are normative natural rights in nature having to do with one's own body and property but no norms binding one's conduct to that of another, except in civil society. And of course there are no public obligations because there are no values save those generated by egoistic desire. Hobbes was the genius of the social contract movement in seeing that the theory allowed human beings and their goods to be understood in analogy with the Newtonian theory of inertia: egoism is the human analogue of a body in motion continuing in that motion unless deflected by other bodies in a vector of forces. The social contract theory promised to provide a value-free approach to the normative aspects of human life, value-free in much the sense sought by later social science, and that early modern physics had attained.

The function of the social contract is to define both public obligation and personal responsibility. The public obligations are those defined by the contract in its own justification, including keeping the peace and enforcing legal contracts, and supporting the institutions that serve those ends. Personal responsibilities are then of three sorts. The most general sort comprises the responsibilities of citizenship attendant upon everyone with acknowledged citizenship. The least general are the responsibilities of fulfilling the terms of specific legal contracts and of presumed social contracts such as the responsibilities of parenthood. In between are the responsibilities attendant upon holding office in the civil society; these middling responsibilities define the moral individual insofar as the individual plays a role to which the social contract or its authorized agents determine responsibility for an obligation.

The social contract path to transmitting public obligations to individuals as personal responsibilities takes a strikingly different direction from the classical path of assigning responsibility according to social class or personal type. In the social contract perspective, there need be no recognition of real, natural, or objective goods for individuals or societies, save, on some theories, the good of maintaining personal momentum. Rather there is the recognition of will or desire and of the rational need to maximize the efficiency with which anyone's or everyone's will can be realized in concert with others. Here is a true egalitarianism of causally interconnected but morally autonomous wills, morally autonomous because empty with regard to normative values beyond those specified in the contract and the laws created by it. In principle, and within the limits set by the needs of peace and the enforcement of legal contracts, according to the social contract no one's will is to be respected in a privileged place over anyone else's. Thus everyone is equal in dignity and protected by due process. Over nearly four hundred years of effective application, the moral force of the social contract theory has been enormous: the establishment of judicial institutions where justice is fairness, the undermining of the institutions of slavery, the exposure of discrimination against women and other circumscribed groups as denials of the fundamental definition of citizenship, the support of positive measures such as public education and affirmative action hiring policies to provide individuals with competitive access to exercise their will in the social system, and in general the enhancement of the recognized worth and conditions for freedom.

Alisdair MacIntyre (1984) has provided an effective internal critique of the limitations of the social contract theory and its moral tradition. Two points need to be made here in order to support the belief that the social contract theory by itself is inadequate and that another approach must be sought to tie public obligation to personal responsibility.

First, the studied indifference in the social contract theory to publicly normative goods other than those defined by the contract is deeply mistaken if, in fact, there are such publicly normative goods. Although John Rawls (1971, part 3) has made a heroic effort to include a normative theory of goodness in what amounts to a neoclassical social contract theory, few people believe that the theory of goodness is intrinsically related to his formal social contract theory of justice. The reason for the studied indifference lies in the pervasive sense in early modern times that value-free mathematical science provides the prime analogate from which other senses of cognitive endeavor must find analogous justification. We now can understand the modern fact-value distinction to be a general hypothesis. Whatever its worth as a methodological hypothesis for science, as an hypothesis about the general nature of things, including the concerns of human life, the fact-value distinction is implausible.

Ethical considerations about personal virtue, as MacIntyre has shown, and about social excellence, as Paul Weiss (1986) has shown, can

have implications for social policy over and above those justifiably arising from the social contract. Religion, the arts, and other dimensions of
culture make similar normative claims on policy. Indeed, even the values
that have come to be appreciated through the enculturation of social
contract theory itself—for instance, those of freedom, tolerance of personal differences, and advancement by merit—likely have grounds
deeper than social contract theory alone. If the values of things are intrinsic to them and practically discernable by our intelligence, then the
normative limits of social contract theory are a profound impoverishment of what society should recognize to affect its public obligations.
Consequently, the scope of the personal responsibility that social contract theory ties to public obligation is equally impoverished. The poverty is noted in the common observation that our lives seem privatized
except when we vote, pay taxes, go to court, or, with blessed infrequency,
go to war.

The second point about the limitations of the social contract theory
is that it ties personal responsibility to public obligation *only in good times.*
This is a sad irony, for the theory itself arose in a very bad time as a justification for imposing government on what was perceived as brutal natural anarchy. In bad times, however, public officials fail to do their work
or do it badly. The persons holding those offices can then separate
themselves from the role and thus slough off responsibility. If no one
holds the office, no one has responsibility for public affairs. In bad
times, the enforcement of legal contracts and other matters of justice is
weak or unfair. When the civil society does not enforce the contracts,
they become non-binding, or only partly so, since their capacity to bind
the responsibility of the contracting parties derives from the effectiveness of the judicial and penal system in enforcing fair compliance. In
bad times, the effectiveness and legitimacy of the contracted civil society itself, and of its government, weakens and fades. People then can reject the responsibilities of their own citizenship by rejecting citizenship
itself, either by moving or by taking up rebellion. In bad times, public
officials can will themselves out of personal responsibility, contracting
parties can will themselves out of the responsibilities of contract, and
citizens can will themselves out of the general responsibilities of supporting the social contract. Thus, in the very hour of need, the vastly
increased public obligation to do something binds no persons to the responsibility of doing it. Any tie to the public obligation can be rejected
by willing oneself out of the contract, returning to a state of nature.

In ironic consequence, social contract theory does not justify the
responsibility to enter civil society and take up public obligation; rather

it is an ex post facto justification of a strong and effective government already in place that keeps the peace and monitors the legal contracts. Although most of the nations of the Earth today have adopted parliamentary democracy as the putative form of government, most governments fail to be effective and fair. So in most instances affairs are determined by vectors of power struggles masquerading as democratic process. That is but the state of nature as Hobbes described it. Even in favored North America, so rich in the democratic traditions of social contract, we have seen in our time the rejection of the legitimacy of government and, thus, of personal responsibility to it by minority groups for whom the contract has indeed not worked fairly. The social contract, by its own principles, is not then normative for them and is supported only by other groups whose interests it serves. Here is not true civil society but, rather, in this respect, a state of nature. Personal responsibility for public obligations, in contract theory, is limited to those whose interest is served by the social contract, and their relation to the others can be a mere conflict of interest as much as mutual participation in civil society. Social contract theory does not demand courage.

However well the social contract practices of liberal democracies work in many instances, there is nevertheless a need to tie public obligations to personal responsibility in a different way from that of the contract tradition. For, when things go bad, that is just the time for personal responsibilities to become acute, not for them to be dissolved in a convenient return to nature. How can the values giving content to public obligations be conserved, in Plato's sense, when it is no one's responsibility to do so, or even to think beyond personal interest? Thrasymachus understood the implications of social contract theory, even if he underestimated its benevolent effects in most instances.

The previous chapter proposed an hypothesis to reconceive the relation between human nature and the values ingredient in nature and society. Suppose that, subject to certain qualifications, the moral identity of every individual is constituted by personal responsibility for *all* public obligations to which the individual's actions might make a difference. This is the principle of universal public responsibility. The only qualifications to this principle are those that would define a person as other than a moral agent, for reasons of being too young, too infirm, insane, mentally deficient, or otherwise not morally competent. Except for these qualifications, everyone in a causally connected society is responsible for all public obligations. This is the exact reverse of the social contract view that in a state of nature no one is responsible for anything except possibly his or her own interests.

The reverse analogy with the social contract theory cannot be extended far, however, for there is in fact no good distinction between a state of nature and civil society. That distinction was rendered important for social contract theory because it denied that nature contains any tie between obligation and responsibility; an artificial civil society is required precisely to institute that tie. In historical fact, there have always been social institutions and, within recorded history, there has always been government with some publicly defined roles. There has been historical differentiation of responsibilities by age, class, gender, skill, mutual agreement, and other considerations.

The historical differentiation of society points up the next crucial step in the hypothesis. Although every morally competent individual is responsible for all public obligations, in fact society differentiates social roles so as to divide up the responsibilities in more or less efficient ways. Various structures of social organization thus deactivate most of the responsibilities of any given individual, leaving that person with the active responsibilities of his or her few roles in the overall structure. The more efficiently the various public obligations are attended to, by effective differentiation of personal responsibilities, the better the society in that respect.

In a very good society, in very good times, public obligations are fulfilled effectively, and each individual rests with all personal responsibilities deactivated save those few that by fortune, talent, interest, and training the person can fulfill with the excellent virtue that leads to happiness and glory.

Insofar as a society is not so structured as to meet its public obligations efficiently, personal responsibilities that might otherwise be deactivated become active. Far from escaping personal responsibility for public obligation, in bad times those responsibilities become active again. Rarely do all such personal responsibilities become activated in a wholesale way. Rarely is a society all bad, with no public obligations fulfilled. But where the society's structures seriously fail, everyone is responsible to do something about it. When a society's legitimate political processes lead to a deeply immoral war, or to the oppression of certain groups, or to the denegration of learning and the arts, or to any other serious failure of the values that require public conserving, it is everyone's responsibility to do something about it.

What is true of the society as a whole is true as well of a segment of a society that has its own public obligations and its own constituency with personal responsibility for them. When an educational system breaks down, it is the active responsibility of everyone in that system, educators, potential students, and the parts of society affected by the breakdown, to do something about it. The contours of responsibility are determined by the causal connections that bind societies and segments of society together. The looser the causal ties, the looser the responsibility. An understanding of the real causal connections in society and its parts is crucial for understanding the scope and direction of universal responsibility for public obligations.[10]

The question of leadership has now been thrust upon us. When times are bad and the given social structures come to fail crucial obligations, how do the myriad of individuals whose responsibilites are suddenly activated determine what to do? Everyone trying to do everything, even supposing the plausibility of such a universal acceptance of personal responsibility, would be chaos. Efficiency could hardly be possible. Incompetence would impede effective work. An overriding obligation is to invent new social structures to channel active responsibility to the service of the public obligations and to deactivate the vague responsibilities of the vast majority. Here lie precisely both the role and importance of leadership.

Dewey provided technical language to make the point. He defined the "public" as the group of people affected in one way or another by the consequences of a set of transactions. They thus have an interest in controlling those consequences. But without recognizing those interests and organizing to do something about them, the people are an impotent public. Leadership is required precisely to bring the circumstances and interests to attention and to create the organizational structures that make the public effective. Leadership thus is the initiation of cooperation.[11]

Before turning directly to the consideration of leadership, it should be acknowledged that even in the worst of times, with wholly ineffective social structures, the chaos of universal personal responsibility accurately reflects the fact that their moral identity requires people to do the good where it can be done, even if the means are in confusion. Because of the social confusion, they might not in fact be able to fulfill their responsibilities; yet by virtue of the objective need of the goods at stake, they are morally identified by those responsibilities. The chaos of universal personal responsibility contrasts with the chaos of the social contract theory's state of nature. The contractarian view of the state of nature survives on the fiction that there are no objective goods at stake, or that, if there are, they have no morally binding relation to persons. If the goods fail to bind persons morally, then persons have no moral identity. But suppose to the contrary that there are objective goods that do bind persons morally. Can a structural lapse of civil society then deprive persons of moral identity? No. It can only deprive them of the means to satisfy their responsibilities efficiently. Our moral identity is determined by how well we serve or fail the active responsibilities that are our lot.

III. Leadership

In a case of the failure of social structures to address public obligations with an efficient division of activated and deactivated personal responsibilities, everyone causally bound to the difficulty ought to take up the task of establishing leadership.

Leadership differs from the exercise of office in several ways. First, the exercise of office carries whatever authority the office grants, whereas leadership has no intrinsic relation to authority. Second, the exercise of office involves the pursuit of activated responsibilities that are defined in part as tokens that deactivate the responsibilities of others. Because of the successful exercise of the office of school superintendent, for instance, most of the people in the community do not have activated responsibilities for the management of the school system. Leadership does not necessarily deactivate anyone else's responsibilities to the matter at hand, although it might give them specific form. Third, the activities of an office are principally those of management, that is, of seeing that the officially prescribed structures work. The activities of leadership, by contrast, are those that institute new structures that address public goods that were not otherwise being addressed well. Many official jobs do have specific and circumscribed elements of leadership included as potential specifications of official responsibilities.

The concept of authority that extends beyond the definition of a public office is highly problemmatic. Most strong senses of political "authority" are mistaken and the concept in its strong versions should be abandoned (Neville 1987a, chapter 8). Perhaps the best polity should be called "big government anarchism," "big government" because of the frequent obligations to amend large-scale social structures.

In the case of unsatisfactory social structures, *two* universal responsibilities are activated. First, everyone in the relevant group is responsible for the public obligations. Second, because the means to address the first universal responsibility are confused, everyone in the relevant group is responsible for establishing leadership to form servicable social structures. Whereas responsibility on the first level is to the obligations at hand, defined by the various and sometimes conflicting public goods, responsibility on the second level is to the community as such: It is to form a community with social structures dividing personal responsibilities so as to handle the primary obligations. Leadership is directed at the exercise of responsibilities on the second level, responsibilities to form or improve a civil community itself.

As the establishment of social structures that assign roles of activated responsibilities to some people and deactivate the responsibilities of others, leadership requires the distinction of leaders from followers. That is, persons in a moderately well-ordered society lead in certain areas and follow in others, and the leadership regime, as it were, determines the roles of leading and following. In a society of failed structures, everyone is obligated to be a leader in all respects. How can the initial distinction between leaders and followers be determined if that distinction is itself the result of leadership?

The answer, of course, is that the leaders make that distinction by their very activity, creating a community of leaders and followers, and other social structures, in the exercise of successful leadership. An unsuccessful leader can fail in many ways; the most intrinsic is a failure to gather sufficient support to establish leadership. Lest we exaggerate the practical difficulties of this paradox, three mitigating circumstances should be noted immediately. First, because leadership is usually hard work and risky of one's status quo, most people will not attempt to assume it even when it is a universal responsibility; so in practice the competition for leadership is usually narrowed to a few, not necessarily the best few. Second, in most sociopolitical traditions, especially democratic ones, there are habits of *shared* leadership. Nothing requires that leadership be an individual matter, though only individuals have personal responsibility for seeing that adequate leadership is exercised. Leadership can be undertaken by a committee or by a group with procedures for making decisions and taking action jointly. The worse the times, the less likely are the habits of joint leadership to be effective. Third, rarely if ever are times so bad that all social structures are inoperative. Rather, only certain institutions will have broken down or are effective in improperly selective ways, as in the instance of a school system that serves some ethnic groups well but not all, or that serves the self-image of secular rather than religious people while ignoring a complex history. In these circumstances of partial breakdown, initial delineations of the distinctions between leaders and followers often come by analogy or reaction from the intact structures. Rarely would there be complete indifference as to whom to look to for leadership or followership, even if failure in practice forces a modification of the initial distinction.

This tentative conclusion, that leaders make themselves, is a disappointment to democratic modernist sensibilities, although Dewey would have understood it perfectly. With the modernist sensibility we would rather have a procedure that determines leadership and justifies the other people in deactivating their second level responsibilities for leadership. We would like to think that leadership arises cooperatively, out of a shared perception of its need. We like consensus processes that give rise to a shared approval of divisions of activated and deactivated responsibilities. But crises in leadership are likely to be precisely those occasions in which the habits of cooperation and consensus fail to operate. In bad times, leadership is often unpleasant and lonely, but no less obligatory for all that. Such an undemocratic outcome should recall us with an uneasy conscience to Plato's antidemocratic view of leadership, to which we shall recur shortly.

First, however, we should attempt to be clearer about how a leader establishes leadership, admitting that there are a great many "styles" of leadership, some pleasant and some unpopular. There are two sides, with shifting responsibility. A leader must present or elicit from others a regime and plan, or their analogues, with channeled activated responsibilities for everyone relevant, that can be construed by everyone relevant as justifying the deactivation of their own universal responsibilities for leadership. Regimes and plans are dynamic, of course, unfolding and reversing in developing ways. Rarely is a leader the sole author of a plan. Further, success at establishing leadership does not entail success at accomplishing the tasks relative to public obligations for which leadership is undertaken in the first place. Nevertheless, in order to establish leadership, there must be an idea for dividing personal responsibilities that is sufficiently plausible to give everyone in the relevant public the confidence that, by following the proffered lead, their own personal responsibilities can be divided into the active ones called for in the regime and the deactivated ones that the regime's plan addresses some other way.

The second side to the establishment of leadership is not the leader's responsibility at all, supposing that the regime and plan have been put forward, but the responsibility of the potential followers, or of persons who are leaders in some respects but in other respects followers. In bad times, when the public obligation for leadership is a universal personal responsibility, not everyone has the responsibility to try to *be* a leader. Rather, the universal responsibility is to *establish leadership*. If no other candidates come forward, then that double responsibility devolves upon each individual. But the primary responsibility is to the establishment of leadership, which might very well mean to make oneself an effective follower. Hence, there is a deep responsibility on the part of potential followers to identify leaders, to support them in establishing the authority of direction, and to play the active roles assigned in the leaders' regime and plan. The classic model of the reluctant leader, Cincinnatus called from his plow, is as honorable as the model of a leader who has sought the role. In contrast to Plato's assignment of responsibility by class, in a democracy everyone has the responsibility to establish leadership in bad times, and that responsibility can be fullfilled through the roles of leader or follower, so long as public obligations are addressed. Often the establishment of leadership involves complex roles that are leading in some ways and following in other; furthermore, those roles are intimately involved with institutions such as political parties, *pro bono publico* groups, coteries of friends, and the like. The universality of responsibility to establish leadership is what participatory democracy comes to in bad times.

A follower aims to identify a leader that is worthy of support. That worthiness has at least three parts, as Plato suggested: Discernment, courage, and guiding rationality.

Discernment is the capacity to recognize, appreciate, and understand the various goods involved in public obligations. These include elementary goods such as the necessities of human life, the value of the environment, and so forth. They include also the goods in social institutions that organize our responses to the elementary goods, institutions of government, the judiciary, religion, education, and economics.

Discernment in leaders requires two parts. One is a passionate and catholic appetite for the good, a depth of appreciation that is not parochial or limited to class perception. Leaders ought to have such big appetites that their own personal gain is lost in the passion for the goods to be sought.

The second part of discernment is vision, a capacity to see how the goods fit together, how the competing needs and goals might be reconciled. Most particularly, a vision for leadership must be able to discern what is important, to set priorities, and to understand how the various kinds of goods relate with respect to importance. Plato might have associated vision with reason, rather than with appetite; surely vision requires an appetite formed both by imagination and by critical assessment of the representations of how the world's goods are related. But the association of vision with appetite rather than directly with reason is justified by the fact that the vision, because of its worth in integrating the public goods to be served, becomes itself an object of appetite. A leader must have passionate commitment to the vision as such.

Courage, as Plato knew, is the virtue that internalizes the discerned goods and organizes a person's activities so as to conserve them. Where social structures have broken down, conservation is not a conservative return to an old situation but the invention of new means to divide personal responsibilities to fulfill the public obligations. Courage is not merely the will to serve the public goods, but the development of a psychically integrated character dedicated to them. As Plato wanted to train his warriors in gymnastic and dance, so leaders need the physical and spiritual disciplines necessary for the ability to act well in response to true obligations that have been taken to heart. Indeed, the metaphor of the heart means the development of a psychic structure of integration that responds to things in terms of organized activity. Because leadership requires so much elicitation of cooperation, so much stimulation of others to contribute, and so much of the capacity to articulate one's vision in diverse languages, the paths of gymnastic and dance are perhaps too circumscribed to be effective. But whatever the paths to preparation for leadership, they constitute a discipline as stringent as the warrior's.

Guiding rationality is the facility to achieve vision in the circumstances. As Plato pointed out, such rationality requires the sciences necessary to understand both the situation and the vision, and to determine means to get from the former to the latter. He also pointed out the need for timing, for political savvy, for persuasiveness, and for judging when enough is enough. Without discernment and courage, guiding rationality might seem mere technocratic reason, the cunning of Ulysses rather than the understanding of Plato (Whitehead 1929a). In leadership, however, discernment and courage cannot be absent from guiding rationality. All three are required to form a regime and pursue a plan. In combination, their harmony also can foster a self-consciousness about the role of leadership itself in bad times, its foibles and corruptions.

IV. A Confession, a Caveat, and a Homily

This chapter calls for three brief concluding remarks, in the forms of a confession, a caveat, and a homily.

The confession is to the moral idealism of the view of leadership espoused here. Based on a metaphysics of intrinsic value in public matters and of the public obligation and personal responsibility this entails, leadership has been prescribed as the responsible, though ideal, response to a failure in social structures. That leadership is an ideal is no guarantee it would be recognized widely as such. Indeed, some people take leadership to be inextricably bound up with paternalism or authoritarianism. Moreover, as a form of moral idealism, this approach stands opposed to the modern view that politics is all a matter of the pursuit of power, not goods. In late years, even the self-interest of groups has been reinterpreted as their empowerment to do their will rather than as a content objectively worthwhile as their interest. Ironically, even Marxist criticism has come to this transformation of value to power, ironic because Marx was such a moral idealist. To be sure, many customary political visions are but ideological defenses of the interest of groups adept at generating commanding visions. In this era we must take special pains to discern the different, sometimes competing, and frequently alienated interests of groups whose intrinsic character and merit are not taken into account in the dominating visions. The metaphysically sound response to special interests is to see them as legitimate in their context and in need of reconciliation with other goods in such ways as not unfairly to subordinate them to the goods of the majority or larger whole. The legitimate interests of special groups, of course, require the empowerment of those groups to attain and enjoy them—not for the sake of the power as such but, rather, for the sake of the merit of the group's own self-interest.

The caveat is a twofold warning. Beware of tyrants disguised as leaders and beware of believing that true leadership in bad times can be very effective; or if it is effective, beware of believing that effectiveness is an unalloyed good. Leadership requires support, and when people take on roles to make a leader's regime and plans effective, that constitutes enormous power. Power corrupts and many people who begin as good leaders moulder into tyrants. Given the human talent at self-deception, often the new tyrant is the last to know about the fall.

Even with powerful support, however, leadership cannot be expected to overcome the enormous social forces whose blind inertia (the small truth in the modern metaphor of power!) seems to wreck our most auspicious chances. Furthermore, the fickleness of followers is surely as great as the readiness of leaders to become tyrants. Competition among leaders can weaken them all. Our knowledge of how things work and of what is good and important is partial, indeed miniscule, as we see in the often disastrous consequences of effective leadership played out in projects of social engineering.

Most dangerous of all, the vast numbers of factors that must be brought under control in order to achieve even the slightest increase in public good, such as raising the employment or literacy rates or giving all ethnic groups the access to advantages enjoyed by a few, seems to require totalitarian measures. The danger that leaders will succeed may be as great as that they will fail. Freedom is one of our most cherished and hard-won goods, yet it seems so fragile when integrated with the massive needs of distributive justice.

The homily is that, despite the dangers, despite our fairly sure knowledge that we will fail or, perhaps worse, that we will succeed, it is a universal personal responsibility to establish leadership when it is needed. The universal responsibility arises from the fact that leadership can make a difference to the worth of things constituting our social and physical environment. Because there are real goods at stake in the way we act or fail to act, each person has a responsibility for the establishment of leadership. We ought not hide in a garden protected by a high fence, nor ought we crouch behind a wall until the storm blows over. Only during storms is leadership required. The rest is merely good office.

Like Plato's, ours is a stormy time, though for its own reasons. Western cultural certainties have collapsed, and the non-Western alternatives are themselves collapsed certainties. Worldwide communication has made the previously accepted enjoyment of privilege untenable. Groups whose worth and needs have not registered in the customary visions of the divisions of life now demand their say, and rightly. The interlocking economic and political systems of the Earth make universal distributive justice an ideal that cannot be denied without arbitrary prejudice. Old hurts and special ambitions keep parts of the world in a seething state of near-war. The public obligation to establish leadership in all this is undeniable.

And it is the responsibility of each person to contribute to that establishment, recognizing with more than a bit of irony that our pursuit of responsibility may be as flawed as the rest of the human condition. Such is the way of finite life in a world with infinite density of goods and obligations. The contemporary flight from leadership, the antagonism to hierarchy, and the celebration of the *privacy* of appetite, vision, courage, and reason, constitute a vast metaphysical mistake. The error is to suppose that goods are not truly real and that personal responsibility can be met without the courage to cleave to those goods. Metaphysical wisdom in this instance is a call to public practical reason.

CHAPTER TWELVE

✳

TECHNOLOGY AND THE RICHNESS OF
THE WORLD

The reader who is also a student of American culture, or who knows that the development of a world philosophical conversation is happening through the dialogue among world religions, will have noticed a curious restraint about religious topics in this volume. Given the importance of religion in American culture, beginning with Jonathan Edwards, its first great philosopher, given the role religion has played continuously in recalling philosophy to the large issues of metaphysics, and given that John Dewey, the most secular of philosophers, affirmed religion as a universal trait (1934), how can we avoid the theological *topos*? Of course, the theological theme has underlain the entire argument here, beginning with the epigram from Peirce at the head of the introduction and continuing with the moral metaphysics of covenant first elucidated in chapter 8.

Religion for modernism has been seen either as simply impossible superstition or as requiring a foundational new start, as in fundamentalism or Barth's neo-orthodoxy. Postmodernism by and large simply rejects religion as organized logocentrism. The way around modernism, therefore, can well afford to postpone its blatant religiosity until the differences between modernism and the highroad around it are marked out. Those differences have now been explored in several areas.

Four themes have been important in American religious culture as moving it around modernism: the idea of God as creator (as in the quotation from Peirce), a reverence for the divinity in nature, an appreciation of the moral character of all creation (as in the idea of covenant), and a positive concern for technology. These themes are interwoven in a typically American way through a discussion of technology and the

259

richness of nature. The discussion, not unexpectedly, provides the opportunity for the most straightforward presentation of metaphysical ideas in this book.

The Biblical convertibility of swords into ploughshares and spears into pruning hooks suggests that the morality of technology lies directly in the uses to which implements might be put. When Plato discussed instruments and craftsmen, it was to highlight the fact that technological expertise requires a specialized understanding of the real nature of the matter at hand, even if that expertise could not be generalized to philosophic scope. Thus in the ancient roots of our civilization technology was viewed at worst as morally neutral and its habitual employment was a source of learning the natural joints of nature and the good.

Of course modern technology is more problematic. Leonardo da Vinci, whose technological imagination surely equalled Thomas Edison's, Alexander Graham Bell's, and Buckminster Fuller's combined, had a bleak vision of the consequences of technology. In his *Atlanticus,* 1495, for instance, he propounded a riddle, the answer to which is "metals."

> There shall come forth out of dark and gloomy caves that which shall put the whole human race into great afflictions, dangers, and deaths. To many of its followers, after great troubles, it will offer delight; but whoever is not its supporter shall perish in want and misery. This shall commit an infinity of treacheries, prompting wretched men to assassinations, larcenies, and enslavement; this shall hold its own followers in suspicion, this shall deprive free cities of their liberty, this shall take away the lives of many people, this shall make men afflict upon each other many kinds of frauds, deceits, and treacheries. O monstrous animal, how much better were it for men that thou shouldst go back to hell! Because of this the great forests will be deprived of their trees and an infinite of animals will lose their lives.

Metal is the source of the machine technology Leonardo did so much to design. As depicted in the riddle, it shall afflict the whole race, being active where humankind is passive though treacherously seeming the opposite; it will educe the full range of human sins and destroy the natural environment.

The later Romantic reaction to "nature dead," in Whitehead's phrase, included an attack on technology as tools for the murderous dissection. Whitehead's analysis in *Science and the Modern World,* (1925, chapter 5), argued that modern technology, symbolized by the Charing

Cross Railway Bridge, made possible the accomplishment of human purposes without regard for the massive depth of the context; hence technology and the instrumental pursuit of human purposes lose coherence with the whole of life and become violent and ugly. Heidegger's *The Question Concerning Technology* (1954) argues that the culture of modern technology leads us to view the world exclusively as if it were a set of resources for our own use. The world then loses the status and richness necessary to command any profound uses, and our culture thus exhausts itself in useless passions.

These general points are hardly new, and many recent studies have drawn useful distinctions among various technologies and analyzed their differential effects. Less attention has been paid to the nature of the world that is impoverished by technology. That is the topic here. How should we conceive the "richness of the world" that technology threatens or destroys?

I. Natural Richness Denied

Why has the topic of the natural richness of the world been neglected? That is a complex story. First of all, Kant's philosophy destroyed philosophy of nature, substituting for it two disciplines: physical science itself and philosophy of science, an epistemological enterprise. By virtue of its dependence on the methodology of the controlled experiment, modern physical science is sufficiently allied with technologies of control as to be subject to the standard criticisms applied to technologies in many respects. Since philosophy of science accepts the scientific articulation of the world to be the principal or only kind of knowledge, the nature of the world prior to or apart from scientific analysis just doesn't register. One of the consequences of the Kantian philosophy is that discussions of the "richness of the world" are relegated to metaphysics, mysticism, or symbolic theology. These three allegedly non-cognitive domains are sources in themselves for skepticism about knowing the richness of the world. The next several points will inquire whether they are in fact non-cognitive.

Second, regarding the metaphysical articulation of the nature of reality as densely rich, Kant was but one of several forces that have tended to delegitimate that discipline. Despite the demise of logical empiricism, in our own time phenomenological positivism, Rorty's neo-pragmatism, and deconstructionism all conspire to suggest that metaphysics is not only intellectually illegitimate but immoral as well, an imperial, coercive imposition of a "transcendental signifier" on a truly less organized world, to use the jargon of Derrida's deconstructionism (Derrida 1976). This is a new version of Kant's claim that metaphysics is transcendental illusion.

Nevertheless, all these criticisms are beside the point in that they assume falsely that metaphysics must be a set of ideas that alleges to "determine objects," as Kant said, to be a mirror or reading off of the forms of things. The criticisms also assume that since metaphysics is about the most basic and general traits of existence, it must be certain and foundational for all other kinds of knowledge if it is anything at all.

These assumptions have been deminstrated to be false with regard to metaphysics as it has been practiced for the last century by pragmatists and process philosophers. Beginning with Peirce (to recapitulate our argument), metaphysics has been conceived within the context of interpretation: a metaphysical idea is an hypothesis that interprets a subject matter, subject to the variety of tests appropriate for hypotheses of such great generality. Even well-established hypotheses are by no means certain. And metaphysics is foundational only in the sense that it is sometimes *about* foundations. By no means is metaphysics itself a foundation upon which other knowledge is to be built. Indeed, the very complexity of testing metaphysically general hypotheses means that they are highly vulnerable to the vicissitudes in all the other kinds of knowledge called in to probate them. So, metaphysics as hypothetical inquiry about "generic traits of existence," in Dewey's terms, is by no means subject to an attack on certainty and foundationalism.

Third, there is deep suspicion about talk of the infinite depths or richness of the world because such discussion seem so intuitive or mystical. The authors who have evoked the mystery and majesty of the world are poets. Many take it to be a criticism of the later Heidegger that his evocation of the world relative to technology is "poetic." The poets and poetic philosophers, such as Emerson and Thoreau as well as Heidegger, "do not write clearly," where that means being able to correlate their references to discriminable objects. The richness of the world is never satisfactorily represented in a finite set of terms, and the fact that depths shine through depths suggests that representation in names or definite descriptions may be misguided from the start. Poetic speech evokes *experience* of the richness of the world. So do religious meditations and lifestyles close to nature; these do not help allay criticisms of the non-cognitive status of claims about the world's richness.

What should allay criticism, however, is that metaphysics can step in to provide clear interpretants of those intuitive or mystical experiences. An intuitive feel for nature (or for nature and culture together, for that matter) is holistic and it registers levels of depth. Yet it is internally differentiated by the interpretations it harmonizes within its own texture. Therefore, intuition is not certain, however aesthetically "right" it feels subjectively.[1] The degree of plausibility in its cognitive claims depends entirely on the merit of the interpretation internal to the intuitive process. There are, of course, many symbols that interpret intuitive experiences of the sort in question here. Those provided by metaphysics can be made clear, well-defined, checkable in many contexts other than the intuitive ones, and thoroughly public. The quality of an experience (intuitive or not) depends not only on the reality encountered but on the store of interpretive resources brought to it. If metaphysics provided the only interpretants for intuition or experiences of the nature-mysticism sort, they would be impoverished by their abstraction. Fortunately, interpretants of metaphysical generality can be integrated with interpretants from as many symbolic domains as address the scope of the experience. These are the sources of the poetic imagery expressing nature-mysticism.[2]

Fourth, in a move parallel to the delegitimation of metaphysics, theology has been criticized as a cognitive discipline and relegated to the study of symbols. Without accepting that criticism, it is worth pointing out that theology is indeed, among other things, the disciplined appropriation and development of religious symbols (Neville 1991a). It allows us to bring into the discussion of matters such as the "richness of the world" the appropriate funded experiences of the great religious traditions. We thus have access to the traditions of the world as God's creation, as created in and by the Logos, as well as to the traditions in India calling up nature as the dance of Siva, as the infinite faces of Krishna, and to the Chinese traditions of the Tao. By themselves, these symbols are uncoordinated and controlled only by the particularistic communities using them. Or, more often in today's world, by the communities that abandon them for the bits and bytes of technology. When integrated under the guidance of metaphysical ideas, however, these symbolic theological expressions can be ordered as testimony for an understanding of the richness of the world. Metaphysics, intuition of the nature-mysticism type, and symbolic theology thus are mutually reinforcing tools for approaching the topic of the richness of the world.

A fifth and last reason for the neglect of that topic is that in the contemporary situation many people believe the "richness of the world" is sufficiently expressed by the mere acknowledgment that no one set of categories or representations constitutes an exhaustive description. As Popperian philosophy of science has argued, descriptive theories can be falsified but not positively verified. Verification is of the indirect sort that indicates that the theory identifies aspects of the nature of the subject matter that are differential in a controlled experiment, or more generally that make a difference to what can be done and observed in active experience. In principle there is no limit to the number of theories that can be verified this way, though each might be incommensurate with the others. We employ those theories our culture appreciates, that we fancy ourselves, or that are particularly useful for identifying what is important for our purposes. Derrida's emphasis on "differance" simply pushes this notion so far that there is little point to distinguishing the descriptive process from the reality described. The moral regarding the richness of the world is that the world is capable of sustaining an indefinite, if not infinite, number of descriptions, each from its own angle. The difficulty with locating the warrant for the richness of the world on the meta-level of richness of description is that, though valid as far as it goes, the point is not helpful regarding technology. Since technologies themselves greatly affect the descriptive schemes with which we regard the world, they can easily suggest that, of the indefinite number of descriptions, only those abetting technology should count. Indeed, even the plausibility of the hermeneutical strategy itself presupposes that the world can be conceived as interpretable in an indefinite number of ways.

Therefore, relative to technology, it is worthwhile to attempt to articulate the infinite richness of the world "on its own terms." These terms, to be developed in the following pages, are metaphysical and theological, and they serve to interpret the experience of the "whole world" that people feel is threatened by at least some forms of modern technology. The discussion of the reasons for the neglect of the topic of the richness of the world has, backhandedly, presented the methodology for discussing it, that is, metaphysics related to religious symbolism.

II. Infinite Density: An Ontological Vision

The infinite density of the world is a theme represented in a great many metaphysical systems. In Whitehead's for instance, any actual occasion is a synthesis of an infinity of prehended antecedents, with each of the antecedents given some particular valuation. For Spinoza, *natura naturans* is the infinitely deep productivity of God's self-nature, and the known attributes of *natura naturata,* thought and extension, are but two of an infinite number. In Leibniz's world, each monad is a determinate reflection of an infinity of other monads. Even Aristotle's system, conceived long before the theological motif of an infinite God imaged in an infinite-and-finite world, allows that substances have a finite essence but an infinity of contextualizing accidents. Where these systems differ is less in the acknowledgment of infinite complexity in finite things than in the account each gives of the kinds of relations among the elements that form the whole. Whitehead's are temporally causal, Spinoza's eternally causal, Leibniz's reflective like mirrors, and Aristotle's environmental.

To provide a viable contemporary account, it is necessary to operate at a level of very great abstraction, greater than in those theories just mentioned. The reason for this, as argued in chapter 6, is that the abstract account must be able to be illustrated in *any* more specific account of the natural world that has some plausibility, from the particle physicist's to the Dakota Indian's to the landscape painter's to the musical composer's. Peircean "vagueness" is the capacity of abstractions to be made specific or be illustrated in each of several conceptual or symbolic systems on a less abstract level, systems that might be wholly incompatible with one another. In addition to being specifiable in the terms of the less abstract systems just mentioned, a metaphysics appropriate for discussing "the world" threatened by technology needs to be specifiable by the relevant religious or theological symbols.

Two principle hypotheses, referred to throughout this book, will be put forward to describe the richness of the world at a level of metaphysical abstractness. (1) The first is that to be determinate is to be a harmony of essential and conditional features created ex nihilo by an indeterminate ground. It follows from this that, because the essential and conditional features are themselves determinate, they too are harmonies, and so on down and around, infinitely. Whereas the first hypothesis is pure ontology and says little about the layout of the world, the second thesis is more cosmologically descriptive. (2) It is that the world is a process of subprocesses that each separately and all collectively illustrate four categories called by Plato (in the *Philebus*) the Unlimited, Limit, Mixture, and the Cause of Mixture. Each of these four is a special slant on the world's richness, and each expresses something necessary about existence as such. Furthermore, each of the four has been thematized in religious or theological symbols. Thus, the first hypothesis says that the world is created as infinitely rich, and the second says something about that in which infinite creation consists.

The first hypothesis, that to be a finite thing is to be a harmony of essential and conditional features, has a metaphysical and an ontological dimension. The metaphysical dimension is a description of determinate identity. The "argument" in the metaphysical description is that, on the one hand, to be determinate is to be determinate with respect to something else. Hence, there must be conditional features relating a determinate thing to those other things with respect to which it is determinate. On the other hand, a thing must have an essential character of its own to give it standing relative to other things; without essential features a thing would collapse into its relations with others and, thus, could not even sustain those relations. By acknowledging only conditional features, we would be reduced to a monistic metaphysics of internal relations, with Bradley's result of internal lack of differentiation (Bradley 1897). By acknowledging only essential features we would be reduced to an atomistic pluralism of diverse things not at all related to one another. By acknowledging both essential and conditional features we rest with a metaphysical pluralism in which things require one another without being reduced to those requirements.

That things are *harmonies* of features means that at the highest level of integration, the top level features just fit together dyadically. If they were harmonized by some higher "third term," their essential features over against each other would be lost. Therefore that top level harmony is what Whitehead called a "contrast," an immediate togetherness of several things. This contrast is thus always finite; it is a "this and not that," and is determinate by virtue of what it excludes as other possible relations among its top level constituents. The contrast-character of the top level in any thing also applies to any lower level; finite definiteness is achieved by harmony as contrast. Yet, because any contrast requires that each of its components be a harmony, any contrast is infinitely deep. That is, each harmony contains essential and conditional harmonies that themselves contain essential and conditional harmonies ad infinitum. A determinate thing thus is both finite and infinite: finite in its contrastive nature and infinite in its components. If one were to make this metaphysical hypothesis specific by applying it to the Whiteheadian cosmology, for instance, the data prehended would be conditional features and thus infinite in the stretch back through time, whereas the subjective forms giving new individual definiteness would be essential features and the bearers of finitude for each new occasion.

The ontological dimension of the hypothesis about harmony appears when we ask how two or more harmonies can be together. As a function of cosmological causation, or cosmological relations, they condition one another by their conditional features. Yet, because the conditional features of a thing would be indeterminate without the thing's essential features, mutual conditioning would not be possible were there not a more profound level of ontological togetherness. In the ontological context of mutual relevance, even the essential features of different things must be together. In order to prevent the representation of the ontological context from eliminating real plurality by turning the essential features into mere conditional ones, the ontological context cannot itself be determinate. If it were, it would be a containing "third term." The ontological dimension of the hypothesis, therefore, is that the ontological context of mutual relevance is the ontological creating of the determinate things ex nihilo. There is no determinate creator apart from the creating, only the creating itself, resulting in the world of mutually determinate but irreducibly plural things. The language of "creation" obviously arises from the Western theological tradition; the point is expressed also in Lao tze's distinction in the first stanza of the *Tao Teh Ching* between the Tao that can be named (the mutually determinate world of the ten thousand things) and the Tao that cannot be (the indeterminate ground of the named Tao).

The ontological dimension of the hypothesis about harmonies thus gives a non-temporal vector character to the world. Any determinate thing, or set of mutually determinate things, has a character of its own. But that is contingent on the creating of the mutually determining order of which it is a part. Within the orders of the world there are obviously temporal vectors—early things causing or conditioning later things. Temporal vectors are cosmological, however, as constituted by conditional relationships. The ontological vector is non-temporal and unites without blending both conditional and essential features of things. One must be careful not to represent the non-temporal ontological vector character of the created world by means of temporal symbols, such as *totum simul* or everlastingness. All representations of ontological contingency or the ontological vector character of things must be properly "eternal."

The ontological dimension brings a new element of infinity to the world. The infinity of the metaphysical dimension of things consists in their infinite internal complexity, topped by contrastive finitude. The infinity of the ontological dimension is the infinite inclusiveness of the vectoral togetherness of all things in the determinateness of any one. To be finite is thus to be "with" an infinite creation. Each thing is infinitely deep metaphysically and infinitely "associated" ontologically. Because of the ontological vector character of the association, an individual thing's identity is in one sense indifferent with respect to whether it refers to its own finite character or the inclusive character of the whole. "That am I," "Tat tvam asi," is an experience of mystical union expressed in many different ways and cultures. It recognizes the mutual requirement of finitude and infinity in the determinate world.

III. Infinite Density: A Cosmological Vision

The second hypothesis, calling upon Plato's four categories, is a specification of the first. If the first is metaphysical tending toward ontology, the second is metaphysical tending toward cosmology, and can be called a "Primary Cosmology" (Neville 1989, chapter 6). Each of the categories is definite by virtue of exhibiting essential and conditional features. To be an *actual* determinate thing is not only to have essential and conditional features, but to have (1) some that provide Limit or patterns, (2) some that provide the Unlimited or subprocesses that are to be ordered by patterns, (3) some that determine Mixture or the definite haecceity of existence, the set of contrasts constituting finite nature, and (4) some that are the Cause of Mixture, the balance or fit of the thing with other things and with its own components.

(1) Let us suppose, as is surely the case, that nearly all of the things in the world are processes, whose components are other processes, and that themselves are run through larger processes. "Things" thus denotes an enormous spectrum of kinds of processes. Viewed as a matter of pattern, some things have tight organic integrity, such as biological organisms, whereas others are organized more loosely into events, specific causal vectors, situations, cultural artifacts, social intitutions, etc. Our culture tends to name things according to their pattern and according to the roles they play in other patterns.

(2) Things can be analyzed from the standpoint of their components as well. A situation, for instance, has to be able to pattern together enduring individuals, social habits, pervasive moods, historical crises, institutions of many sorts, climatic conditions, and many other factors. An enduring individual such as a human being has components as diverse as its internal organ systems, as biological systems such as the metabolic in which it participates but that extend far beyond it, as semiotic systems of language and gestures in which it participates with other people, as roles in social systems, as stages in maturation, as historically defined factors, as particular relations with place and persons, as personal purposes and goals. Because so many things are mutually determined, a person is a component in a situation in one set of ways, whereas the situation is a component in the person's life in other ways.

To analyze any one thing is to see it as containing a variety of components organized according to patterns that deal with that variety. Furthermore, each component is itself a harmony of components, of bewildering variety on down and around. Each component of a harmony has something of a career of its own, according to the nature of its own process. Sometimes a component is wholly dependent for its very possibility on being harmonized with the other components of the thing at hand, as a person's economic livelihood depends on being integrated with other factors in an economic system. In other cases, a thing's components have a great deal of independence and the harmony of the whole must respect the laws of the components, as physical or chemical elements always behave in their set ways when combined into physical and social objects. In all cases, if one takes away in analysis the overall pattern of a harmony, its components are to that extent then "unlimited," and will either cease to be possible, change radically, or go their own way irrespective of the thing under analysis. Any level of pattern or order is thus fragile with respect to the coherence of its components. There may be other factors in the environment that guarantee a certain order, but that order is thus dependent on the environment. From the standpoint of any given harmony, its fragile identifying order is constantly in jeopardy to the separate, usually blind, processes that are its components and context. The Unlimited is not pure lack of order but the relative chaos resulting from lack of a specific order. Depending on the kind of patterns in each level of components, a thing has levels of relative stability and relative instability, and these levels can be of diverse kinds. As Plato recognized, no form or pattern can last for long because the components of the complex formed are constantly changing.

Regarding the components of an harmonic process, it is one-sided only to fear their potential for destruction of the organizing patterns. The other side is that the quasi-independence of the careers of many components are the source of vitality and novelty. This is not metaphysical creativity or spontaneity, but rather the force of freshness and change that comes from the fact that any process is itself but the temporary coherence of many other processes, each going its own way. Whereas the inevitability of change always means that any order is only temporary, it need not mean that change is always for the worse. No system can be so totalitarian that some birth at wrong season can't break it and improve it (to play with Plato's image in *Republic* VIII).

(3) As a Mixture, a concrete process is to be understood not only according to its patterns and components but also according to its existential definiteness. Within process there is a temporal passage that effects transformations of things through the three temporal modes. The future is an organization of possibilities, utterly vague in the infinite

yet-to-come and progressively more specific relative to the present as the possibilities have to be possible outcomes of present changes. The present is the temporal mode of changes in which fixed past events are altered to become new things according to the proximate possibilities for the moment. The conclusion of a present moment is a completely determinate state of affairs, which is thereby past. The past consists of all finished changes, coordinated in the structures and matrices of the spatial and causal vectors of forces. There are thus three senses of alteration in the mix of processes. The future alters the structure of possibilities as it faces different present states. The present is existential change, altering possibilities into actualities. The past alters by the accretion of more actualities, extending the lines of actualized causal influence.

Possibilities are disjunctive but lack the force of the excluded middle, as Paul Weiss (1958, proposition 2.13) has argued. That is, my possible posture five minutes from now is "sitting-or-not-sitting;" "not-sitting" has to be determinate on its own to be a real alternative (i.e., have its own essential features), so the possible posture is "sitting-or-standing-or-lying-down-or-walking-etc." That inclusive possibility has to be actualized some way or another (assuming that the other possibilities for things allow me to be around in some posture) but five minutes from the event each of its internal disjuncts can still be actualized. Because the real possibility is the inclusive disjunct, the principle of excluded middle does not apply to the possibility itself. At the point of actualization, the disjuncts must be made determinate and all the internal alternatives but one must be excluded. In one sense, actualization is the elimination of all vagueness, of all alternative specifications, from possibility.

The determinateness of possibility comes from the definiteness of actuality, not from some eternal grab bag of forms. The future in itself, apart from its connection with the present, is pure formal unity, utterly indeterminate without some plurality to form up. The differentia come from the possibilities having to be relevant to actual things. If there were no animals, there would be no possibilities for posture; if there were only snakes, the posture possibilities would include lying down and crawling but not sitting, standing, or walking. Because the determinateness of possibilities derives from actuality, it is a mistake to think of actual entities as merely complete definite selections of universals, with every universal either "in" or "out" (this is Kant's conception). Rather, actualization is the making definite of possibilities, the achievement of complete haecceity, of existential individuality.

A universal is a common nature; it retains some vagueness even when it is embodied in an actuality that participates in it. All descriptions of the usual sort involve reference to the common natures that get actualized, but usually without mentioning that the real actualized thing is not just the common nature but an haeceity even more specific than that. The exception to common description is in morals. If Chang had the real possibility of robbing the bank or not robbing the bank, and actualized the robbery, forever after he is the one who robbed the bank but could have done otherwise. Similarly Chang actualized the possibility of having a button nose; but not just any button nose—it is exactly "this" shape. An accumulation of qualifications of "button nose" can describe Chang's nose more accurately but cannot exhaust it, since each descriptive predicate is a common nature and is embodied in some even more specific way in Chang's actual face. Chang's actual face includes both the common nature "button nose" and the specific embodiment of it, Chang's haeceity, just as his actual moral character includes both "robbing-and-not-robbing-the-bank" and "actually robbing." Chang's full existential being cannot be completely described because he is more than the sum of his common natures.

The existential depth of actualization of individual haecceity is not reducible to the possibilities of the future or to the patterns of the past. Rather, both of those depend on the conjunction of future, present, and past in actualization. Existential philosophy and theology have recognized the importance of this, for instance, as expressed in Tillich's notion of the depths of Being. Often, however, existential thought has focused on the passage from possibility to actuality in the present without attending to the essential features of future and past. At any rate, the concrete reality of Mixture has to do with processes of actualization, with definite individuality.

Because there are many processes in the Mixture of affairs, there are many scales to time, and these have various coordinations. The scale according to which a mountain range is actualized through a collision of continental plates is different from the scale of a human being's maturation, from the diurnal rhythms of everyday life, from the development of an idea in conversation, from the degeneration of an atomic structure in radioactive decay. The remarks made above about the interweaving of components in a harmony are complicated by the different time-scales of actualization. To think that the world as a whole proceeds moment by moment, where "moment" means the tick of some kind of astronomical or physical-particle clock, is a gross abstraction, sometimes helpful to physicists and trainmen, but often mischievous. The mischief lies in its

obscuring the richness of the interplaying temporal structures of the
various processes of the world; the mischief consists in the ruination of
processes that require a complex sense of balance, such as education or
care of an environment that is used for immediate needs.

(4) The Cause of Mixture is the category apparent in the last point.
Plato characterized it as balance, proportion, measure, and the like. It is
the normativeness involved in conforming all things, all processes, to
bring out the values in possibilities to be actualized. Each possibility has
the flat value of being a way of actualizing its components together. Yet
the richness of the world consists in the greater harmony of the values of
all the ongoing processes, adjusted to each other so as to maximize the
values in each. Because of the Cause of Mixture, the various processes of
the world are the Tao, the Way of integral movement. Each process is
what it is not only in terms of its essential and conditional features, displayed in the career of its actualization, but also in its place in the larger
movement of things.

It is unlikely that any good sense can be made of the notion of "the
whole of things." Kant's arguments against "totality" are good ones. Yet
when we think of everything we can imagine together and enlarge that
imagination as much as possible, we approach a kind of aesthetic perspective on value. The aesthetic perspective is almost not a perspective
at all; it is the consideration of any given thing—however arbitrarily de-
marked—as possessing and displaying its value in its world. From an
aesthetic point of view, each thing is the center of its own world. The
Cause of Mixture is the coordination of all things in an aesthetic way,
giving each its due at its own standpoint. Those "standpoints," of course,
are processes with their own temporal scales, related to the environment
of other processes with their temporal scales. Morality, in contrast to aesthetics, requires a fixation on some one finite set of perspectives, taking
the array of environing processes as subordinate in value to the values of
the defining set of perspectives, e.g., the values of human civilizations.
The aesthetic Tao of process is, to use Whitehead's phrase, "a little oblivious as to morals."

The reality of the Cause of Mixture, of the whole of process, is not
apparent except in refined experiences, as in nature mysticism, religion,
"the peace that passes understanding."[3] It is the most obvious place
where misplaced technology interferes with the integrity of the world.
Yet the Cause of Mixture is that dimension of reality most difficult to
describe, because its description consists in showing what value is
achieved by having the mixture of processes adjusted this way rather

than that. The difficulty is in attaining the "infinite perspective" from which the values of the alternatives can be compared.

IV. Richness as the Infinite in the Finite

The senses of "richness" articulated by the two metaphysical hypotheses are implicit in the above remarks and, perhaps, even obvious. It remains to make them explicit and connect them with the religious symbols that embody them in our concrete culture. At the same time we can reflect on the class of technological "dangers" associated with each. In general, by "richness" is meant a finite something that contains or reflects an infinity of somethings, an infinite "contrast," or an "actual infinite." The following six points spell out some of what this can mean.

1. *Infinity of eternal identity.* According to the first hypothesis, the identity of a thing consists in its essential and conditional features. By virtue of the latter, it is connected with an infinity of other things cosmologically; the significance of this will be brought out in the senses of infinity associated with the Primary Cosmology (points 3–6 here). By virtue of being a *harmony* of essential and conditional features, a thing's identity is dependent on being together with all other things with respect to which it is determinate with their essential features. This ontological togetherness underlies all temporal kinds of togetherness and is the basis for identity as such. It is properly eternal and is the community of identity of all things.

The Indian religious traditions, perhaps more than other traditions, have developed the theme of the underlying ontological unity of all things, the mutuality of identity. Yet even in the theistic traditions there have been mystical strains that experience an internal dialectic in which the individual's true identity is not the differentia exhibited in the plurality of the world but rather the positive force of the divine. That force is equally expressed in all other things, and there is thus a commonality of identity that yet respects the differences of one thing from another. If God is our true identity, then we enjoy that identity in other things as well. For there to be finite identity as such, there must be the mutual identity of all.

At the deepest level, technology can be taken to be a disrespect for identity as such, denying the mutuality of identity by subordinating "others" to use. This is the profoundest truth in Heidegger's concern about taking the world simply as resources. The problem is not that if we do not respect others our own identity is threatened. The problem rather is that if we do not respect others, or ourselves, identity as such is

betrayed. The infinite reality of the finite as such is betrayed by instrumental thinking that does not acknowledge the infinity of togetherness
in the identity of the thing used. Of course this does not mean that we
cannot use things or think instrumentally; that is part of the real identity of all living things depending on an environment. What it means is
that we need to attend reverentially to the things we use so as to acknowledge their identity and the fact it is in complete solidarity with our
own and that of the world a such. The Native Americans, who rever-
enced the buffalo while slaughtering them and using every part, had the
right attitude toward the eternal infinity of things. Kinds of technology
that prevent this reverence, that require forgetfulness or gallows humor,
destroy our attunement to this sense of "richness of the world."

2. *The infinite contingency of the finite.* The vector character noted in
the ontological context of mutual relevance, in eternal identity, presents
another sense of infinite richness. That we or the world exist does not
proceed from antecedent determinate principles. There is no formed
potential for divine creation in some God, nor a disposition to ontological fecundity in Mother Nature. There is simply the eternal act of ontological creation, eternal because of the eternity in ontological identity.
Temporal things are among the creatures, and so ontological creativity
manifests itself in each particular moment of change. Yet the modes of
temporality are not in time and, hence, are together in eternal ways.

The shock of contingency, and sense of dependence on an ontological ground, have been registered in the religious traditions with symbols of creation. In most such traditions, the conception of the creator
has been associated with conceptions of local gods, generalized perhaps
to a cosmic God. Yet the experience of contingency has motivated a dialectical search for an interpretant that does not attribute determinateness to the creator. The Neo-Platonic tradition first in Islam, then in
Christianity and Judaism, funded a conceptual search for symbols of
simplicity and unity in the Godhead. Without the theistic association of
the ground of contingent reality with an individual god, other traditions
have readily symbolized the infinity of ontological contingency. The
Buddhist doctrine of the emptiness of form is perhaps the most obvious,
the dependence of finite being on ontological non-being (see, for instance, Waldenfels 1980, or Nishitani 1982). The relation between the
Tao that can be named and the one that cannot, in Taoism, and the gen-
erativity of *jen* in Chu Hsi's theory of *jen* also illustrate the point (the
texts are quoted and discussed in Neville 1991a, chapter 7).

The spiritual content of the shock of contingency is, at the very
least, wonder and thankfulness. To the extent technology gives us the

sense that we control things, that we are the authors of things, it blights that spiritual content. Of course, we do control what we control; but that is to be analyzed into our powers for affecting the forces of the world. We are indeed authors of our deeds and have moral responsibility because of that, but we are not authors of the ontologically contingent context of our actions. There may be many causes of the loss of wonder and thankfulness for existence. Technology is among them when and as it suggests that we depend on ourselves, obscuring the fundamental contingency of things.

3. *The infinity of order.* Immanuel Kant found the sublime in the starry heavens above and the moral law within, and he was surely right to do so. The heavens above symbolize the fact that any finite order with which we identify our place is itself part of a larger order, which is part of a yet larger, and on without end. The moral law within symbolizes that the value we make is nested within an infinity of other worthy orders, all affected by the rightness or wrongness of what we do. Indeed, the very discovery of the hermeneutical structure of understanding—that things can sustain an indefinite number of interpretations, each with its point—indicates the infinity of order or Limit in any finite thing. Moreover, as Plato emphasized, no order by itself is adequate for either the existence or the representation of a finite process because the process is always on the way to some other order.

The idea of a creator imposing order on the world, both structural and moral (if those are distinguished) is about as universal an element of mythology as any. Indian, Chinese, Semitic, Greek, and Norse mythology express that element. It is the symbolic theme behind the Sky God, the gods of thunder and lightning, as well as the more complex divinities of monotheism. Frequently, the imposer of order is one god among many, or one aspect of a more complicated monotheistic god, or a symbolic figure in a non-theistic tradition such as Confucianism or Buddhism. As an expression of Limit, the divinity of order-making is part of what it must mean to be ontologically contingent.

Many thinkers have observed that modern technology is this patriarchal dimension of culture run wild. Technology is the imposition of (human) order over nature that has its own, less finitely ordered, state. There is a great truth to this. Yet order itself has its infinity that can be distorted by the technological imposition of human order. Human orders, the goals of technology, are precisely the ones that do not ordinarily register the infinite nestings of the world's orders. Ecological mistakes are mistakes about the real orders of things. Moral mistakes are mistakes about the real structures of value. The traditional critique of technology, as in Roman Catholic thinkers of anti-modernity, is usually a valid critique of a technology's distortion of the infinity of orders.

4. *The infinity of the Unlimited.* It seems redundant to say that the Unlimited is infinite, but the obvious redundancy is a mistake. The Unlimited is not pure lack of order but the separate integrity of the components of any given ordered thing. A thing is a harmony of its components, each of which is a harmony of its components, on down and around. This is an obvious case of "actual infinity," where the finiteness comes in the fact that the harmony itself is a contrast, indeed perhaps a contrast with haecceity.

The religious symbolism for the infinity of the unlimited often has to do with nature, with Mother Nature, the Earth Mother, the creative procession of subprocesses, with accidental birth out of season, with powers of causal vectors that stampede blindly through the delicate orders of human society. From the standpoint of a patriarchal culture, the religious recognition of the Unlimited smacks of the demonic, of forces that are disrespectful and destructive of imposed order. In religious cultures that balance the yang and yin, Siva and Shakti, there is an appropriate recognition of the infinity of components in definite process and of their partially independent powers that are oblivious to higher orders.

Insofar as technology inculcates pride in human order, nature takes her revenge. Our wells fill with soap suds, our skies with smog, and our psyches with trash. Soon we cannot taste pure water, see clearly, or have real feelings. Where technology must assume that the lower order components do not count, our experience is impoverished by being limited to the recognized components. Yet the very being of those high level components depends upon their infinite depth of internal components. The limited experience of things then becomes the experience of a mask. The reality behind the mask will get its revenge.

5. *The infinity of Existence.* Actual things include not only their common natures, their vague possibilities made specific, but also their exact haecceities. Just as having order and having components are elements of contingent ontological creation, so is the fullness of actual existence. There is a strange coincidence of opposites in the infinity of finite existence. In the very achievement of final individual definiteness there is an infinity of detail: any universal feature is specified further in actuality. The Scotist poet, Gerard Manley Hopkins, revelled in the haecceities of things, dappled beauties shining forth like shaking foil.

From "I Am That I Am" through Thomas's conception of the world as participating in God as Act of *Esse* to Tillich's and Buber's existential conceptions of Being, the infinity in finite existence has been a theme of Western religions. In Islam, the Sufi tradition has elaborated the same theme. The Taoist emphasis on particularity, the Confucian on filiality, the Buddhist on suchness, express the point in other ways.

Technology can threaten the richness of the world in this sense when it takes things according to their types and manipulates them according to the separate natures of their components. The former is a function of the abstractions involved in Cartesian objectivity. The latter is a function of a mechanistic metaphysics. Twentieth-century existentialism is a proper protest against the technologism of modernity precisely in its rejection of the reduction of things to their orders (types) and components (mechanisms). With one exception, this sin of technology is the most important for it pervades our whole culture. And it has a multiplier effect in conjunction with the other threats of technology. Reducing things to their orders, technology also can misconstrue the true orders of things. Reducing things to their components, technology can obscure the infinite depths of components. The result is a cultural world that is like a child smashing around a china shop while in a dream. This compounds technology's threat to wonder, thanks, and the sense of the infinite togetherness of identity. The one more important sin of technology arises in consideration of its threat to the Cause of Mixture.

6. *The infinity of harmony in the world.* All religions thematize the problem of finding a Tao, a path that leads one (or one's people) into harmony with the whole, however the whole is conceived. The conception of the whole is extremely problematic. On the one hand is the problem mentioned above with the notion of totality as such. On the other is the problem of imaging connections among things on a scale large enough to be relevant here.

"Harmony" is perhaps the best word to describe the comprehensive connections because it connotes both the interdependence of the various components of the world and also their independence: their intrinsic values are to be enhanced by their juxtapositions in harmony with other things. Yet harmony has unfortunate connotations as well. Clearly the deep processes of nature are often violent—exploding masses, colliding stars, destructive transformations of environments, and the like. On the human scale it has seemed in nearly every part of the world that sometimes the path of righteousness requires one to fight. As is made clear by the Earth Mother's violence on the one hand and the Sky God's call to arms on the other, the harmony of the whole cannot be all sweetness and light. Religions have recognized this paradox. The peace that passes understanding is incomprehensible because it includes the endurance of crucifixion. Arjuna's encounter with the comprehensive faces of

Vishnu resulted in his resignation to the duty to slaughter his mentors and relatives. The sense of the whole is a deep mystery transcending moral considerations, as God remarked to Job out of the whirlwind.

From the abstract position of metaphysics we can note that the Cause of Mixture requires a reconciliation of ontological identity with cosmological connections. That is, the harmony of the whole requires that the integrity of all things' harmony with essential features be recognized in the cosmological relations to be established among them. Thus the Cause of Mixture commands a kind of piety that may have the appearance of morality. It is deeper than morality, however, because it demands an aesthetic appreciation of the worth of each thing from its own standpoint and a positioning of oneself so as to harmonize with those interacting but independent worths. Because of the vast array of overlapping time scales of actualization, people in various religious traditions tend to view the task of this appreciation as one of finding and attuning to a center. There is no real cosmic center, of course. Nor does the relevant piety entail that one treat one's own standpoint as privileged. Rather, the appropriate center is one of personal harmony with things such that one's own position is irrelevant, and the center can be moved or expanded anywhere.

One more aspect of the mystery of the whole needs to be mentioned. Whereas it appears that finding one's center and pursuing one's way along the path are matters of grave individual responsibility, paradoxically the view from the path enlightens one to the sense that the deep rhythms of things are what count and that one's personal agency is a trivial puff. More strongly, the path involves surrender to ontological grace, to the generative movement of the Tao, to the spontaneity of Buddha Mind. Too much emphasis ought not be put on the common themes in obviously different religious symbolic traditions; yet there is a common reinforcement of the mystery of the infinite harmony of the world.

The greatest sin technology can commit is to suggest, because of the enhanced powers it delivers up to the human will, that the world is not ultimately mysterious. That sin has the ancient dignity of being the sin of pride. It leads to a profound misapprehension of what is real and good and, very quickly, to a diminishment of the potential of human life. Perhaps, in the great harmony of things, human life is due to be diminished, like a bacterium that in flourishing chokes itself out. Perhaps sin itself is but the mortality of our species as inflexibility was the death of the dinosaurs; surely the Calvinists were right, that sin is bigger than we know—a profounder phenomenon than immorality. Nevertheless, we are indeed finite creatures with an infinite content in an infinite world, in at least the ways specified here. As finite, our visions, actions, and goods are limited, and our moral obligations stem from the reality of our finite nature. We are not gods whose taste is purely aesthetic and therefore transcendent of morality. Aestheticism itself is the greatest sin of pride, the ascription to ourselves of a godlike capacity. Consequently, we should sin not. In particular, we should circumscribe our technology so as to prevent it from diminishing the richness of the world.

The arguments of this last section have been less in the nature of a conclusion and more of a project proposal for further research. Six senses of "infinite richness" have been sketched and correlated with religious symbols to reinforce their cultural significance. It remains to pursue those symbols systematically, to see how the differences among the various traditions from which they are drawn really imply different nuances in the general point symbolized. It remains also to identify just what kinds of technology, in what contexts, lead to the diminishment of each sense of richness. By focusing on the potential threats technology poses to the richness of the world, the argument here has fallen into the common habit of assuming that technology is monolithic and bad. On the contrary, certain technologies can put us into closer touch with certain aspects of infinite richness, with the starry skies above if not the moral law within. The scheme presented here offers a potential for appreciating as well as depreciating various kinds and aspects of technology. For the argument to be moved to the position to do that, however, the present consideration of the richness of the world would have to be supplemented by a parallel discussion of the nature of human behavior, experience, and purpose—another topic. Perhaps enough has been said here to indicate something of the richness of the world.

The richness of the world is a theme that needs to be made self-referential, in an ironic way, to the argument of this book. The point has been urged from many angles that modernism is not the only outcome of modernity and that the modern tradition is rich enough to include the contribution of American thinking to a highroad around modernism. The defense of that highroad has often been polemical, exaggerating its uniqueness and its virtues, glossing over its silly parts and attacking modernism with too little appreciation of modernism's virtues. The defense of the highroad is defensive, by necessity, because modernists and postmodernists would close down travel upon it and deny its existence by ignoring it. If the way around modernism has been represented as a broad and richly connected highroad, in contrast to the narrow rut worn by the schoolish majority of North Atlantic thinkers, that may be acknowledged to be hyperbole generated by polemics.

In fact, there are doubtless many roads around modernism-postmodernism, not just the one described here. Furthermore, the game of totalizing modernism cannot be played seriously for very long, because that would be directly counter to the pluralism of the highroad described. There are many modernisms and quasi-modernisms. Furthermore, although this book has represented the highway as connecting with other cultures than the Western in the making of a world civilization, it has not acknowledged either the variety or vitality in those others.

We should end, then, by noting that the situation of contemporary culture is itself a thing of infinite density, to which an indefinite number of finite responses need to be made in cognizance and cooperation with one another.

NOTES

Introduction. Why Speculative Philosophy Should Not Shut Down

1. For an excellent sympathetic analysis of deconstruction, see Culler 1982, especially chapter 2. For an historical analysis of recent literary theory, where deconstruction has its home, see Lentricchia 1980.
2. Although not as famous as his *Principia Ethica*, 1903, G. E. Moore's *Some Main Problems of Philosophy* (1953; lectures originally given 1910–1911) was probably more indicative of the vast influence of his simple view of common sense. Among Russell's influential early books are *The Problems of Philosophy*, 1912, *Our Knowledge of the External World*, 1914, and *Mysticism and Logic*, 1918.
3. Logical positivism was itself a diverse movement. Perhaps the collection, *Logical Positivism*, edited by A. J. Ayer, 1959, is the most helpful representative. It also contains a fine bibliography. Ayer's *Language, Truth, and Logic*, 1936, is still the classical popularization of the positivist program. J. O. Urmson's *Philosophical Analysis: Its Development Between the Two World Wars*, 1956, is a fascinating history of the movement written by a participant at a time when most of the founders were still alive.
4. See the fascinating criticisms of Heidegger running throughout Jacques Derrida's *Of Grammatology*, 1976.
5. The ironic connection between left-wing Marxism and the right-wing appreciation of Nietzsche in recent philosophy was pointed out by Allan Bloom 1987, 141 ff. Bloom's rather racist condemnation of the Germans for this cannot be sustained. However, the revelations of the Nazi past of Paul de Man, the noted postmodern deconstructionist critic, indicates that the connection between left and right is not always ironic or accidental.
6. Whitehead took some pride in avoiding the whole philosophic world that derived from Kant. See his *Process and Reality*, 1929, xi–xii. See also George Lucas's fine study, *The Rehabilitation of Whitehead*, 1989, especially chapter 5.
7. Perhaps Derrida's clearest statement of the nature of logocentrism and of his deconstructionist program is an essay "Structure, Sign, and Play in the Discourse of the Human Sciences," in Macksey and Donato 1970.

8. The thesis that reality measures our representations in some way is the thesis of my book, *Recovery of the Measure* (Albany: State University of New York Press, 1989) in which I provide both a theory of interpretation and a cosmology or theory of reality that together show both how representations are elements of reality, not extra-existential "mirrors," and how reality is their measure.

9. Within a demonstration such as that described here there is an inevitable tension between attempting to make a case for a tradition and a contemporary community of discourse, on the one hand, and the author's own version within that community, on the other. Readers can sort through the tension in part 1 by reference to the footnotes citing the author's own works; part 2 presents the author's own views explicitly, with footnote references to the larger debate.

Chapter 1. Charles S. Peirce as a Non-Modernist Thinker

1. References to Peirce's writings are by citation of *The Collected Papers of Charles Sanders Peirce*. CP refers to the *Collected Papers*, the next number refers to the volume, and the number after the period refers to the paragraph which is numbered in the text. The present citation is to volume 5, paragraphs 213–163. This citation system was designed by the original editors, Charles Hartshorne and Paul Weiss. Indiana University Press is bringing out a more complete edition of Peirce's writings, but not enough has been published at this date to be useful here. The Harvard edition contains only philosophical papers, broadly defined; the Indiana edition will contain scientific and other papers in addition to the philosophic, and these are far more numerous.

   For secondary introductions to and studies of Peirce, I recommend principally the works of John E. Smith who treats him in the context of American theology: 1950, chs. 1–2; 1961, ch. 4; 1970, ch. 5; 1978; 1983, ch. 1. See also Boler 1963, Buchler 1939, Colapietro 1989, Moore & Robin 1964, Murphey 1961, Potter 1967, and Wiener & Young 1952.

2. See Derrida's discussion of speculative grammar as semiology or grammatology in 1976, 48–50.

3. Under the gun from postmodernist critics, the former is Derrida's *signifier* and the latter his *signified;* the former is Rorty's *mirror* and the latter his *nature.*

4. For an excellent account of Peirce's theory of signs in reference to individuals, particularly selves, see Colapietro, 1989.

5. *Simplicity* is not an innocent term. See Peirce's discussion of Ockham's razor at CP 5.60.

6. For a splendid interpretation of Peirce on religion, see Raposa 1989.

7. As long as ethics is recognized as not being a matter of vital importance or in any way touching the student's conscience, it is, to a normal and healthy mind, a civilizing and valuable study—somewhat more so than the theory of whist, much more so than the question of the landing of Columbus, which things are insignificant not at all because they are

useless, nor even because they are little in themselves, but simply and solely because they are detached from the great continuum of ideas. (C.P.1.669)

8. In regard to the greatest affairs of life, the wise man follows his heart and does not trust his head. This should be the method of every man, no matter how powerful his intellect. . . . Common sense, which is the resultant of the traditional experience of mankind, witnesses unequivocally that the heart is more than the head, and is in fact everything in our highest concerns . . . ; and those persons who think that sentiment has no part in common sense forget that the dicta of common sense are objective facts, not the way some dyspeptic may feel, but what the healthy, natural, normal democracy thinks. And yet when you open the next new book on the philosophy of religion that comes out, the chances are that it will be written by an intellectualist who in his preface offers you his metaphysics as a guide for the soul, talking as if philosophy were one of our deepest concerns. How can the writer so deceive himself? (CP 1.653–654)

9. In fact, Peirce wrote:
   . . . the hypothesis of God's Reality is logically not so isolated a conclusion as it may seem. On the contrary, it is connected so with a theory of the nature of thinking that if this be proved so is that. (CP 6.491)

10. Let a man drink in such thoughts as come to him in contemplating the physico-psychical universe without any special purpose of his own; especially the universe of mind which coincides with the universe of matter. The idea of there being a God over it all of course will be often suggested; and the more he considers it, the more he will be enwrapt with Love of this idea. He will ask himself whether or not there really is a God. If he allows instinct to speak, and searches his own heart, he will at length find that he cannot help believing it. (CP 6.501)

11. In his logical works, Peirce has a technical distinction between vagueness, as tolerant of contradictory specifications requiring further choice, and generality as immediately specifiable (CP 5.447–450, 505–506). This is not the use of *generalization* to be found in his discussion of agapasm and of the notion of God.

Chapter 2. Alfred North Whitehead and Romanticism

1. Most process philosophers, for instance the majority of those who publish in *Process Studies*, treat Whitehead as a contemporary or as a timeless position to be defended, rejected, or modified. George R. Lucas, Jr.,'s *The Rehabilitation of Whitehead* treats him as an historical figure, not as a position within intellectual history but as an historical philosopher addressing problems of his age that overlap but differ from ours, partly forming our problems.

2. The literature explicating the technical ideas in Whitehead is vast. The standard systematic commentary is Christian 1959; a briefer and more focused commentary is Kraus 1979. Also of interest is Lewis S. Ford's (1984)

fascinating analysis of the compositional history of Whitehead's ideas prior to *Process and Reality.*

3. For an insightful analysis of specialization in culture, with a discussion of Whitehead's view, see William Sullivan's "The Civilizing of Enterprise" in Neville 1987b.

4. See Rorty's marvelous discussion of the " 'not really a philosopher' ploy," 1979, 370.

Chapter 3. Metaphysics in the Twentieth Century

1. Once appreciated for its originality, this conception is not without its difficulties. The definition of *objective reality* in terms of the roles played by a thing in the things that apprehend it is really a development of Descartes's conception of objective reality in distinction from formal reality. Formal reality, for Descartes and his medieval predecessors, is the reality a thing has in itself. Kant denied that any kind of formal reality can be known and that, therefore, the empirical world is *only* the way things might appear to knowers. Although Whitehead is not consistent on this, he can be read as a Kantian with a metaphysical twist. Whitehead sometimes said that when a thing completes its becoming and loses the subjective immediacy of the coming-to-be of its droplet of present time, it ceases to be and has reality only in subsequent things that prehend it; Charles Hartshorne follows this line of development. At other times Whitehead acknowledged that the past has a reality of its own and that what Descartes would have called "the formal reality of finished actual occasion" lies in the past. The interpretive issue is complicated because Whitehead held that God necessarily prehends everything that is past and sustains those objects without diminishment within the divine experience; because things are enhanced by the connections God gives them, without diminishment, their career within God includes everything they would be outside of God plus extra richness. Thus Whitehead neglected to be clear about what things in the past might be without God. For many reasons, Whitehead ought to have said that things in the past and future have reality appropriate to those temporal modes and to have clearly rejected the claim that existence means present existence. One reason within his system is the following: A thing changes only in the present and, when it has achieved full, definite actuality, satisfies the urge to concrescence and becomes past; having become fully actual and fixed, the thing cannot change any more and, hence, cannot pass out of existence. The past is the sum of things that have become actual. This has been explored at length in Neville 1989, chapters 9 and 10.

2. Another important distinction between Buchler and Whitehead is that the former is essentially interested in the epistemological route to metaphysics. Natural complexes are defined by means of "discrimination." Whereas Whitehead took the notion of prehension from Berkeley's theory of apprehension, he so naturalized it that the implausibilities of Whitehead's system come in making his categories of mentality look anything like ordinary experience.

3. The subtitle of *Process and Reality* is *An Essay in Cosmology.* He usually calls his system metaphysical and relates it to other metaphysical systems.

4. For an elaborate defense of this thesis, as well as my basic criticisms of Whitehead on all aspects except time, see my *Creativity and God: A Challenge to Process Theology,* 1980, especially chapter 3. For criticisms of his theory of time, see my *Recovery of the Measure,* 1989, especially chapters 9 and 10.

5. He develops this at greatest length in *Modes of Being,* but it forms the basic structure of his later philosophy which distinguishes basic realities that conjoin to form the world in which things appear. For the later philosophy, see *Beyond All Appearances* (1974) and *First Considerations* (1977). I myself develop the distinction as one between essential and conditional features, Neville 1989, 1992.

6. I have argued this controversial thesis in *God the Creator* (1992) and *Recovery of the Measure* (1989).

7. This argument concerning harmony as value is explored at length in Neville 1974, chapter 3, and 1989, chapter 7–8. As a special emphasis in American philosophy it goes back to Jonathan Edwards.

8. For a more specific analysis of the tradition that separates facts from values and believes the latter are projected onto things by mind, see Neville 1981, chapter 1; for an analysis of the idealist argument concerning the Absolute, see Neville 1992, chapter 1.

9. Specifically, the problem in Weiss's account of value concerns a certain ambivalence in his writings about whether possibility or the future is everywhere and always value laden, or whether only certain possibilities are valuable. The former gives him a stronger theory, as I argue in "Achievement, Value, and Structure," 1987c. For my related critical analyses of Weiss, see Neville 1970, 1978, 1987c.

10. This treatment of value as a harmony of complexity and simplicity goes back to Leibniz, say, in the *Monadology.* For my more extensive treatment of it see 1974, chapter 3, or 1989, chapter 7.

11. For this extremely important historical point, important especially in light of the wholly different approach Rorty urges toward the pragmatists, see Dewey's essay "Peirce's Theory of Quality," "Qualitative Thought," and "Having an Experience," all collected in Richard Bernstein 1960.

12. See the quotation from Rorty in note 9 of the introduction above from his 1982, 213–214.

13. Unless specified in the text here, consult the works (listed in the bibliography) of the authors discussed in these concluding paragraphs.

14. See the brilliant introduction to the 1968 edition of Royce's *The Problem of Christianity* by John E. Smith, who begins this way:

> Royce's idealistic philosophy has often puzzled philosophers, historians, and students of American thought. The fact is that his systematic form of idealism stood in a peculiar and ambiguous relation to the the philosophical currents of his time. His question, on the one hand, for a systematic view of reality and for absolute standards both in thought and conduct set him at variance with the pluralism and open-endedness of the pragmatism represented first by Peirce and James and later by Dewey. On the other hand, the voluntaristic element in Royce's thought—the stress on the expression of the individual human will

which he learned from Schopenhauer—kept his position in touch with the dominant belief that knowledge is intimately related to human purposes and must always be connected with action. The perplexing fact is that Royce emphasized the will and rejected the so-called pure intellect without seeming to come any closer to the pragmatic philosophy of his contemporaries. Perhaps the main reason for the difference of opinion is found in Royce's lack of sympathy with the functional approach. Royce, as an idealist, sought for internal connections between things; he was always dissatisfied with what James called "working" conceptions aimed at showing how distinct elements operate together without further insight into why this should be so. (Royce 1968, 1)

15. I, too, am part of this group.
16. See also Neville 1982, 1987a, 1991a.
17. See the symposium on Smith's philosophy with contributions by Andrew J. Reck, Smith, and myself, cited as Reck 1986.

Chapter 4. Contributions and Limitations of Process Philosophy

1. There is the Center for Process Studies at Claremont and the Society for Studies of Process Philosophies. Lewis S. Ford and John B. Cobb, Jr., have long edited the distinguished journal, *Process Studies*.
2. As mentioned in the introduction, Richard Rorty's *Philosophy and the Mirror of Nature* (1979) barely mentions Whitehead, and then only in connection with panpsychism; he presents process philosophy neither as an option nor as an enemy of the Edifying Conversation. Richard Bernstein's *Beyond Objectivism and Relativism* (1983) is more neglectful. Lucas, 1989, is a welcome antidote.
3. My own position is that of a philosopher deeply influenced by process philosophy but, neverthless, with an agenda of my own.
4. My conception of irony here is greatly influenced by David L. Hall's *Eros and Irony* (1982a). Not only does Hall develop his conception of irony with reference to Whitehead, he also has an extraordinary discussion of order, an important topic in this chapter. Hall is interestingly mistaken, I believe, in associating irony too much with an aesthetic attitude. Irony rather is the essentially religious attitude balancing a divine aesthetics of immediate closeness to each thing as the center of its world with a moral attitude that accepts the finite place of human priorities; see Neville 1987a.
5. Paul Weiss was the first to take a decisive step beyond Whitehead's metaphysical cosmology to a metaphysical ontology. As early as *Nature and Man* (1947) and thoroughly thematized in *Modes of Being* (1958), Weiss forced the ontological question by dialectically reformulating empirical generalizations to show the necessity of a certain set of modes of being which together account for the complexity of the world and of the metaphysical categories themselves, including their own togetherness. Although I don't always follow Weiss's solutions myself, I do follow him beyond Whitehead's speculative philosophy to ontology. I have discussed this at much greater length in *Creativity and God* (1980), chapter 3.

6. My own suggestion for the ontological question is the hypothesis that determinate things are created ex nihilo as mixtures of orders and components; see my 1989, chapters 5–6; 1991a, chapter 1; 1991b, chapters 3–4. The components are other determinate things which themselves are further mixtures, and so forth. Causal elements and diversities of temporal and spatial positions are complicated kinds of ordering elements and diversifying components. To the extent things condition one another, either symmetrically or asymmetrically, the creation has a mutual togetherness to it, but not one that is to be understood as unity rather than diversity: creation constitutes a "context of mutual relevance" for things different enough to be potentially related or unified with one another. The creation itself can be termed "divine," in deference to the Western ontological tradition, and it has a kind of trinitarian structure: creation as the source on which all determinate being depends, creation as the product created, and creation as the act of creating. But what we *cannot* say, according to the logic of "ontological creation of all determinate being," is that the creator is determinate apart from creating. The only determinateness in divinity is what was just mentioned: being creator of this world, being the world as created, and being the creating. If theism means belief in a God as having determinate character over against the world, perhaps apart from creation, then this hypothesis is non-theistic.

   The dialectical nature of the creation hypothesis is that, in answering the question Why this world?, it points toward the creative action or decision. As a hypothesis it has a hypothetico-deductive as well as dialectical use. In a hypothetico-deductive use it would "explain" this determinate world, or any determinate world, as an instance of "being created;" but its generality makes it of little interest. In its dialectical use, however, it allows us to acknowledge, perhaps stand in awe of, the radical contingency of the ontological situation: this diversity of things, ordered just so. The acknowledgement is also attentive to the creative power in the fact *that* this complex world exists. What satisfies a dialectical approach to the ontological question is a locating of the decisive creativity of things, whereas what satisfies a hypothetico-deductive approach to metaphysics is a statement of first principles. Speculative philosophy needs both in order to address the ontological question.

7. It was for the sake of accounting for continuous action on others, among other interests, that prompted Paul Weiss in *Reality* (1939) to work out a new substance theory over against Whitehead's conceptions. See particularly chapters 7 and 8. David Weissman's *Dispositional Properties* (1965) subserves the same motive.

8. The modification is to call "nonessential" features "conditional" features.

9. I have attempted in part to remedy this by the multivolume series, *Axiology of Thinking*, the first volume of which is *Reconstruction of Thinking* (1981) and the second *Recovery of the Measure* (1989).

10. Weiss himself does not see his work as complementing Whitehead's but insists on emphasizing the latter's atomism in ways that prohibit recognition of the valid connective character of prehension; see Weiss 1983, pp. 107, 253. In *Reality* (1939, 207–210), Weiss accuses Whitehead of escaping the fallacy of simple location only to fall into the fallacy of essential completeness." Be

that as it may, I do not present Weiss as a corrective and complement to Whitehead in order to associate him with a name he won't like, but to argue that the metaphysically revolutionary impulse of process philosophy needs to be broad enough to build on Weiss's contributions.

11. For an explication of Whitehead's theory of value, see Neville 1974, chapter 3, and 1989, chapter 7).

Chapter 5. Hegel and Whitehead on Totality

1. One way of understanding the ontological argument is to take it to claim that parts imply a whole. Idealistic descendents of Kant, such as Josiah Royce, often argued that we must presume whatever is necessary to complete something before us so that it is fully intelligible. A refutation of this kind of ontological argument is to point out that some incomplete thing might not belong to anything completing it, incompleteness being the state of things; put another way, the thing may not be fully intelligible, according to certain canons of intelligibility, which is the point at issue. Richard Rorty criticized Paul Weiss along this line in his remarks in Weiss's *First Considerations*, 1977, pp. 206f. See also Weiss's reply immediately following. Michel Foucault makes a strong case for the empirically grounded fragmentariness of things in *The Archaeology of Knowledge*, 1976.

2. I have learned much on the present topic from Lauer 1974, 1976, 1977, and 1982.

3. The dialectical argument that follows here is a short revision of the one I developed extensively in *God the Creator* (1992), chapter 1. In the discussion of Hegel in that account I limited myself to treating him insofar as he could be construed as saying that being is determinate. The present argument supplements that with a discussion in the next section of the process of negative dialectic.

4. "Importance is the initial and dominating concept of Whitehead's *Modes of Thought*, 1938, especially chapter 1, "Importance." Chapter 4, "Perspective," is also pertinent to the discussion below. The general problem of the ontological function of value pervades Whitehead's work, as mentioned before; see, for instance, *Process and Reality*, 1929, part 2, chapters 3–4, and *The Function of Reason*, 1929a. On the problem of importance in divine perspective, see *Science and the Modern World*, 1925, chapter 11, "God."

5. This theme pervades the references in the previous note. But it finds its most striking exemplifaction in Whitehead's polemic against theologies that represent God as necessitating power. God's proper relation to the world, according to Whitehead, is to appreciate it and reciprocally to represent for the world's appreciation a poetically moving set of worthy possibilities. See for instance 1929, part 5, or 1926.

6. The following discussion of Whitehead's theory of actual occasions, experience, value, and determinateness arises from his technical discussion in 1929, part 3, on categorial obligations. It expands the discussions in chapters 2 and 3 above. I have given my own technical critical discussion of his view

in Neville 1974, chapters 1–7, and in 1981, chapters 3–4; my alternatives to his view are in 1989, chapters 5–12. The discussion in the present text attempts to minimize relatively private technical terms.

7. See also Florence Bradford Wallack 1980, where she suggests how occasions themselves may be temporally thick, in fact very long. The dimensions of human reality listed and analyzed by Weiss are not single long occasions but enduring, organically developing structures.

8. The mention of representation in science should call to mind the fact that science is not mere modelling but also interpreting according to the leading principles and biases of its intruments, basic conepts, and habits. The point is best explored by Patrick Heelan in various writings, particulary *Space-Perception and the Philosophy of Science,* 1983. One might think that acknowledgment of the hermeneutical circle obviates the question of totality and eliminates the possibility of system. The former is not so, however, for one of the main insights of hermeneutics is the global orientations of hermeneutic stances; the systematic issue is the merit of the particular stances. The latter is not so, because the systematic suppositions of a hermeneutic process need to be interpreted and that interpretation is by means of a system used as a complex sign.

9. Lewis Ford presents a fine analysis of this complex idea in his "The Non-Temporality of Whitehead's God," 1973. For a debate about the bearing of this point on ontology, see my "Whitehead on the One and the Many," 1969–70. See Lewis Ford's "Neville on the One and the Many," 1972, and my rejoinder, "Response to Ford's 'Neville On the One and the Many'," 1972. Revised versions of of the debate which unfortunately downplay the importance of eternal objects, are to be found in Ford and Kline 1983, chapters 12 and 13. A more extended version of my side of the debate is my *Creativity and God,* 1980, chapters 2 and 3 (although chapter 3 is rather much the same as chapter 12 in the previous reference).

10. Charles Hartshorne is chief among those who believe as the truth and as Whitehead's doctrine that the satisfaction of an occasion entails that it must be prehended by a successor occasion, at least by God. My own view is that in truth and most often in Whitehead an occasion's satisfaction makes it available for subsequent prehension; but whether it is a real potentiality depends upon the successor occasion's subjective unity. For a discussion see Charles Hartshorne, John B. Cobb, Jr., and Lewis S. Ford, 1980, and my 1981b.

11. "Vagueness" is discussed throughout Peirce's writings, as mentioned in chapter 1 above. See for instance his "Issues of Pragmaticism" and "Consequences of Critical Common-Sensism" in Peirce 1934, CP 5. 447–450 and 505–506. Of extremely great historical interest is the fact that Hegel gave exactly the same analysis of vagueness as Peirce, but drew the opposite moral from it. See his *Lesser Logic,* 1830, paragraph 9, where Hegel says (in Wallace's translation): " . . . the Universal or general principle contained in it, the genus, or kind. . . . is, on its own account, indeterminate and vague, and therefore not on its own account connected with the Particulars or with the details." Hegel notes that such vague universals do not allow of necessity in philosophy and so rejects them as an adequate starting point. Peirce agrees

about necessity and affirms "vagueness" as essential to the empirical character of philosophy. See chapter 6 below, and Neville 1981, chapter 2.

Chapter 6. On Systems as Speculative Hypotheses

1. Weiss's own answer to this question, generally put, is a highly sophisticated theory of five basic and irreducible Finalities, each of which conditions the others. Each nodal point of conditions conditioning conditions provides a perspective for grasping something, and then the map relating perspectives is provided by the theory of the interplay of the finalities. This account is itself part of his system; see his 1974, 1977. Robert S. Brumbaugh, another systematic philosopher, argues on the contrary that any perspective on the system of perspectives must be outside the system, calling for a yet more inclusive system ad infinitum; see his 1961.

2. For a more extended statement of this point in conjunction with a theory of representation, see Neville, 1989.

3. The logical character of "specification" calls for a detailed formal analysis that would be inappropriate in this text. Marshall Spector (1978) has provided an exemplary analysis of the concept of the reduction of one theory to another. He shows that the operative notion should be one of replacement: the concepts in one theory reduce those in another theory when they can replace them. But the replacement is just what is denied in the concept of specification or translation. When a poem, for instance, is translated into the language of a philosophical system it is not replaced, but rather interpreted regarding what the system says is important in it.

4. Richard Rorty makes just this argument against Weiss in his commentary in Weiss's *First Considerations*, 1977, 206 f.

5. I argue this at length in 1981, part 2. Kant's discussion is in the "A Deduction" of the *Critique of Pure Reason*.

6. For a technical discussion of truth as the carryover of value, see Neville 1989, chapter 3.

Chapter 7. Reflections on American Philosophy

1. David Dilworth's *Philosophy In World Perspective: A Comparative Hermeneutic of the Major Theories*, 1989, is a highly sophisticated and self-conscious illustration of the first sort of world philosopher; Wu Kuang-ming, with his *Chuang Tzu: World Philosopher At Play*, 1982, is an example of the latter sort, claiming that his Taoism is not *only* a Chinese philosophy but a philosophy with a claim to truth that should be acknowledged or at least engaged by anyone. The discussion in the text below cites many other examples.

2. This has not been recognized by the American Philosophical Association which until very recently did not acknowledge non-Western thought as philosophic on its program. Nevertheless, the satellite societies to the American Philosophical Association's Eastern Division sponsoring discussions of Chinese and Indian philosophies have often been far better attended than official program units. In the American Academy of Religion, by contrast, the

program units treating various Indian and Chinese, as well as Islamic, philosophies dominate the overall program and have for years. American *professional* philosophy has perhaps defined itself too narrowly so as to exclude many of the world's greatest philosophic traditions.

3. The systematic integrity of these four functions of thought—pursuit of responsibility, theorizing, interpreting, and imagining—is defended at length in my *Reconstruction of Thinking*, 1981, and in *The Puritan Smile*, 1987a.

Chapter 8. Power, Revolution, and Religion

1. This discussion of power in early modern science develops in a new way the thesis about mathematical physics as the source of the distinction between facts and values that I elaborated in *Reconstruction of Thinking*, 1981, chapter 1. For the metaphysics of early modern physics, see Burtt 1932; for the bearing of this on religious ideas in the early modern period, see Klaaren 1977.

2. The brilliance of Max Weber was to invent the idea of the "ideal type," the individual who stands typically for all within a group of individuals and who can be understood as responding rationally to circumstances in terms of some purpose or goal antecedently determined and modified by the adventures of pursuing it.

3. David Tracy has analyzed and devastatingly criticized the idea of the single story in his *Plurality and Ambiguity*, 1987. For a treatment of stories as individuating people, see my *The Puritan Smile* (1987) and *Behind the Masks of God* (1991a), chapter 8.

4. Freud's way was with the hydraulic model of the libido, modified in many forms through his career but never wholly abandoned. Marx's was his commitment to the priority of the economic motive.

5. This image is extrapolated from the concluding discussion of jazz in Thomas J. J. Altizer's *Total Presence*, 1980, 107–108.

6. See my discussion in *The Puritan Smile*, 1987.

7. This conception is argued at greater length in my *Theology Primer*, 1991b.

Chapter 9. Beyond Capitalist and Class Analysis

1. See Whitehead's lecture, "Mathematics and the Good," in Schilpp 1941.

2. This historical remark is the thesis of my *Reconstruction of Thinking*, 1981, chapter 1. In that book I argue for the project of reconstructing paradigms of thinking so as to include valuational elements, in the spheres of imaginative, interpretive, theoretical, and moreal or responsibility-pursuing thinking; the book also presents reconstructed models for imagination in some detail.

3. Even the physical sciences falsely prescind from the values in their subjects; but, for them, the urgency of a reconstruction of thinking in an axiological directectly seems not so great. Nevertheless, environmental disasters and the threat of nuclear war have forced scientists to ask value questions, even if the terms of their scientific discourse are not framed to ask or answer them well. Furthermore, the recent work of Patrick A. Heelan, 1983, has shown that not

only scientific theories and the use of instruments are structured by interpretive frameworks but also that our very perception is so structured. The questions then must be asked of physical sciences: Do hermeneutical suppositions screen out the resident values in natural objects? What modes of theory, practice, and perception would be responsive to the nature, presence, or absence of values in things? What cultural values guide our experience and understanding of scientific objects?

4. In addition to the classical works of Marxism, this discussion generalizes from more recent works such as Ralf Dahrendorf, 1959, and Robert C. Tucker, 1969. On the present point concerning justice, see Tucker's second and third chapters.

5. The popular capitalist critique of Marxism as totalitarian and statist is rank among American politicians. It is stated more subtly by Paul Samuelson (1989), an advocate of a mixed economy, in his enormously influential text book, *Economics*. Marxism does indeed tend toward totalitarian statism at just this point, as I argue in *The Puritan Smile*, 1987a, chapter 3.

6. See also David Hume's *Treatise of Human Nature*, 1739, book 3, part 2, chapters 2–6. Adam Smith's discussion is not metaphysical. But he does suggest that the universal human propensity to "truck, barter, and exchange" is either "an original principle in human nature" or, more likely, "the necessary consequence of the faculties of reason and speech." The latter suggestion says more about reason and speech than about economics. See *The Wealth of Nations*, (1789), book 1, chapter 2.

7. For a more systematic discussion of the ways by which variable access to social media affect the boundaries of the public and private, see my *Cosmology of Freedom*, 1974, chapter 9.

8. The phrase "actual entities of the past" is redundant in most senses. When an entity has fully emerged as actual, it no longer has subjective immediacy and exists as past for any entity that can grasp it.

9. As discussed above and in Neville 1989, chapter 9, Whitehead was somewhat ambiguous about this, although his disciple, Charles Hartshorne, holds to it strictly.

10. This theory of continuity of identity within suppositions that do not include metaphysically continuous substances is developed at length in my *Recovery of the Measure*, 1989, chapters 11 and 12. Continuity of identity through time is there called "discursive" identity, in contrast to momentary or atomic identity.

11. I would go so far as to say that truth itself is the carryover of the value of the matter interpreted into the interpretation of it, as qualified by transformation into the biological character of the interpreter, the culture and economic systems forming the interpretive signs, and the purposes of the interpreter. This has been defended at length in Neville 1989, chapter 3.

Chapter 10. Freedom, Tolerance, and the Puritan Ethic

1. The Principle of Universal Public Responsibility does not occur in Puritan writings, so far as I know, but is a political principle I derive from the Pu-

ritan sensibility, or from the sensibility of some Puritans. On the Puritan sensibility see William Haller, 1938. By Puritans I mean mainly those in Britain, the ones who lost out to, or became, liberals after the restoration of King Charles II. For an account of what happened after the collapse of English Puritanism, or rather after its disastrous ss ss ss success in the Protectorate of Cromwell, see Christopher Hill (1984). For a study of the continuity of Puritan and liberal cultures, see Edmund Leites (1986). For a more elaborate discussion of the contemporary advantages and dangers of recurring to Puritan thought, scouting around liberalism as it were, see my *The Puritan Smile* (1987); see chapters 8 and 9 for a more detailed discussion of authority and the distinction between the public and the private than is contained in the present text.

2. The political philosophy from which the Principle of Universal Public Responsibility comes is expressed and defended in my 1974 and 1987a.

3. This remark is not entirely fair to Rawls. See his discussion of the good in chapter 7 of *A Theory of Justice*, 1971. Nevertheless, both his "thin" and "thick" theories of goodness have to do with rationality and subjective enjoyment or desire, not with the intrinsic value of things or their worthiness to be enjoyed or desired. The intent of his contract theory is to make judgments of intrinsic goodness of natural and social things unnecessary; they are replaced by ingenious procedures and an analysis of rationality and desire.

4. For a brilliant philosophical analysis of social associations and connections, see Paul Weiss's *Toward a Perfected State*, 1986.

5. Perhaps the most serious attempt to envision such an unorganized state was made by the early Taoists. See Norman J. Girardot 1983.

6. For a more precise approach to sin, consistent with what is here, see Neville 1991b.

7. The paragraphs about the personal and social dimensions of freedom partly summarize *The Cosmology of Freedom*, 1974, parts 2 and 3 respectively.

8. On spiritual freedom, see my *Soldier, Sage, Saint*, 1978a.

9. The discussion of the religious element guilt is detailed in my *The Puritan Smile*, 1987a, chapter 10, "Responsibilities in Conflict."

Chapter 11. Leadership, Responsibility, and Value

1. I support the careful recovery of metaphysics from its Continental enemies as articulated by Richard J. Bernstein in the preceding Presidential Address to the Metaphysical Society, "Metaphysics, Critique, and Utopia," 1988. Bernstein, however, identifies metaphysics as defined by its opponents and does not much honor the work of actual twentiethth-century speculative and systematic metaphysians, ignoring, for instance, Samuel Alexander, George Allan, Henri Bergson, Brand Blanshard, Bernard Bosanquet, F. H. Bradley, Robert S. Brumbaugh, Justus Buchler, Nicholas Capaldi, Cheng Chung-ying, Julia Ching, John B. Cobb, Jr., Benedetto Croce, William Desmond, John Dewey in his speculative moments, Jude Dougherty, John Findlay, Lewis S. Ford, David L. Hall, Errol Harris, Charles Hartshorne, Irwin C. Lieb, Gabriel Marcel, Brian John Martine, Kitaro Nishida, Edward Pols, John Post,

Josiah Royce, George Santayana, Kenneth Schmitz, Charles Sherover, John E. Smith, Tu Wei-ming, Carl G. Vaught, Alfred North Whitehead, Paul Weiss, David Weissman, and many more who are publishing important metaphysical work today and often to be found at meetings of the Metaphysical Society of America. For some brief samples of current metaphysics, see my *New Essays in Metaphysics*, 1987b, or watch who publishes in *The Review of Metaphysics* and *The Journal of Speculative Philosophy*.

2. The summary discussion is in *Republic* IV, 427d–434d.

3. Plato's distinction of the soul into three parts, mirroring social classes, has been enormously influential, from Augustine to Dewey. For a popular exposition, see Robert S. Brumbaugh's *Plato for the Modern Age*, 1962, 85–90. For a sophisticated analysis of the structure of the argument of the *Republic*, see Brumbaugh's new *Platonic Studies of Greek Philosophy*, 1989, chapters 1–5. For a systematic analysis of the three elements of soul and of their education, see my *Soldier, Sage, Saint*, 1978, chapters 1–4.

4. *Statesman* 283e–284c. See Seth Benardete's commentary in *The Being of the Beautiful*, 1984, 3.113–119.

5. This is, of course, an incomplete and internally controversial characterization of the virtues of democracy. I have discussed these and others, in forms I believe defensible, in *The Cosmology of Freedom*, 1974, part 3. The particularly difficult matter of distinguishing public participation from private life is discussed in *The Puritan Smile*, 1987a, chapters 8–9. See also the discussion in William Sullivan's *Reconstructing Public Philosophy*, 1982.

6. For the best theoretical statement of his "revised democratic theory," see *The Public and Its Problems*, 1927. His best statement of the difference between his own theory of democracy and that of the early moderns is *Liberalism and Social Action*, 1935. Because the chief contrast between early modern and revised democratic theory has to do with participatory engagement rather than individual freedom, the best text to explore the practical significance of participation is Dewey's early *Democracy and Education*, 1916. A fascinating partner to Dewey's work was Walter Lippmann in his *The Phantam Public*, 1925, which directly occasioned *The Public and Its Problems*, and in his more systematic statement, *The Public Philosophy*, 1955. Sullivan's title, mentioned in the previous note, pays direct homage to Lippmann's book and to Dewey's *Reconstruction in Philosophy*, 1920.

7.   A maid of bronze I stand on Midas' tomb,
    So long as waters flow and trees grow tall,
    Abiding here on his lamented grave,
    I tell the traveler Midas here is laid.

Phaedrus 264d. Hackforth translation.

I have examined Plato's formal theory of value in *The Cosmology of Freedom*, 1974, chapter 3.

8. See especially Diotema's speech reported by Socrates in the *Symposium*. The contrast between Plato's and Freud's theories of eros is a central theme of Rollo May's *Love and Will*, 1969.

9. I have argued (1974, 214–217) that the social ideals can be classified under four heads: I. Personal Values, including brute wants and likes, ideals organizing brute wants and likes, personal preferences over those ideals, life styles organizing preferences, preferable life styles, and ideals relating preferable life styles to the environment; II. Interpersonal Ideals, including economic values, ideals for interactions conveying culture, ideals for interactions developing good taste in preferences, ideals for interactions developing "human" qualities in preferable life-styles, and ideals for interactions that structure the social situation; III. Public Ideals, including ideals for social arrangements distributing qualities, costs and benefits of private interactions, ideals of institutions supporting these arrangements, and ideals of procedures; and, IV., Social Order Ideals, including ideals of social institutions in general, ideals of social balance, and ideals of civilization.

10. See my *The Cosmology of Freedom*, 1974, for a detailed analysis of this. It is, of course, the main message of John Dewey 1927, about the importance of empirical learning in political philosophy.

11. See Dewey's *The Public and Its Problems*, 1927, chapters 3–5. My agreement with Dewey does not go so far as to accept the "interest" theory of value he employs in this book. Fortunately, in most of his other books he defends a thoroughly objective theory of value.

Chapter 12. Technology and the Richness of the World

1. On the fallibility of intuition, see my "Intuition," 1967. The argument there is that Peirce's theory of interpretation, contrary to his claims, requires a kind of intuition, but a fallible kind.

2. By "nature-mysticism" I mean not only pantheism and romantic evocations of nature but any mystical approach that sees nature holistically and as being or bearing the divine. The ontological aesthetics of the Tao in Confucianism and Taoism, for instance, would count as nature-mysticism, as well as much else.

3. See Whitehead's discussion of Peace in *Adventures of Ideas*, 1933, chapter 20.

BIBLIOGRAPHY

Allan, George
>   1986 *The Importances of the Past.* Albany: State University of New
>   York Press.
>   1990 *The Realizations of the Future: An Inquiry into the Authority of
>   Praxis.* Albany: State University of New York Press.

Altizer, Thomas J. J.
>   1967 *The New Apocalypse: The Radical Christian Vision of William
>   Blake.* East Lansing, Mich.; Michigan State University Press.
>   1977 *The Self-Embodiment of God.* New York: Harper & Row.
>   1980 *Total Presence.* New York: The Seabury Press.
>   1985 *History As Apocalypse.* Albany: State University of New York
>   Press.
>   1990 *Genesis and Apocalypse.* Louisville, Kentucky: Westminster/
>   John Knox Press.

Austin, J. L.
>   1956 *Ifs and Cans.* London: Oxford University Press.

Ayer, A. J.
>   1936 *Language, Truth, and Logic.* London: Gollancz.
>   1959 *Logical Positivism.* Editor. New York: The Free Press.

Berger, Peter L. and Thomas Luckmann
>   1966 *The Social Construction of Reality.* Garden City, New York: Dou-
>   bleday.

Bernardete, Seth
>   1984 *The Being of the Beautiful.* Chicago: University of Chicago
>   Press.

Bernstein, Richard J., editor
1960 *John Dewey: On Experience, Nature, and Freedom.* New York: Liberal Arts Press.

Bernstein, Richard J.
1967 *John Dewey.* New York: Washington Square Press.
1971 *Praxis and Action.* Philadelphia: University of Pennsylvania Press.
1976 The Restructuring of Social and Political Theory. New York: Harcourt Brace Jovanovich.
1983 *Beyond Objectivism and Relativism: Science, Hermeneutics, and Praxis.* Philadelphia: University of Pennsylvania Press.
1986 *Philosophical Profiles: Essays in a Pragmatic Mode.* Philadelphia: University of Pennsylvania Press.
1988 "Metaphysics, Critique, and Utopia," *Review of Metaphysics,* 42 (December 1988), 255–273.

Berthrong, John H.
1993 *All Under Heaven: Transforming Paradigms in Confucian-Christian Dialogue.* Forthcoming.

Bertocci, Peter A.
1970 *The Person God Is.* London: George Allen & Unwin.

Blanshard, Brand
1939 *The Nature of Thought.* In two volumes; London: George Allen & Unwin.
1961 *Reason and Goodness.* London: Allen & Unwin.
1962 *Reason and Analysis.* London: Allen & Unwin.
1974 *Reason and Belief.* New Haven: Yale University Press.

Bloom, Allan
1987 *The Closing of the American Mind.* New York: Simon and Schuster.

Bohm, David
1980 *Wholeness and the Implicate Order.* London: Routledge & Kegan Paul.

Boler, John F.
1963 *Charles Peirce and Scholastic Realism.* Seattle: University of Washington Press.

Bradbury, Malcolm, and James McFarlane, editors
1974 *Modernism: 1890–1930.* Pelican Guides to European Litera-

ture. Altantic Highlands, N.J.: Humanities Press, 1978. Original edition; Middlesex: Penguin.

Bradley, F. H.
  1897 *Appearance and Reality.* Second edition; Oxford: Oxford University Press; first edition, 1993.

Brightman, Edgar Sheffield
  1940 *A Philosophy of Religion.* Englewood Cliffs, N.J.: Prentice-Hall.

Brumbaugh Robert S.
  1961 *Plato On the One.* New Haven: Yale University Press.
  1962 *Plato For the Modern Age.* New York: Collier.
  1982 *Whitehead, Process Philosophy, and Education.* Albany: State University of New York Press.
  1984 *Unreality and Time.* Albany: State University of New York Press.
  1989 *Platonic Studies of Greek Philosophy: Form, Arts, Gadgets, and Hemlock.* Albany: State University of New York Press.

Buchler, Justus
  1939 *Charles Peirce's Empiricism.* London: Kegan Paul, Trench, Trubner & Co.
  1955 *Nature and Judgment.* New York: Columbia University Press.
  1966 *Metaphysics of Natural Complexes.* New York: Columbia University Press.
  1974 *The Main of Light: On the Concept of Poetry.* New York: Oxford University Press.
  1978 "On the Concept of 'The World'," *Review of Metaphysics,* 31/4 (June 1978), 555–579.

Burtt, Edwin Arthur
  1932 *The Metaphysical Foundations of Modern Physical Science.* Revised edition; New York: Humanities Press; first edition, 1924. Republished; Garden City, N.Y.: Doubleday, 1954.

Cahoone, Lawrence E.
  1988 *The Dilemma of Modernity: Philosophy, Culture, and Anti-Culture.* Albany: State University of New York Press.

Callicott, J. Baird, and Roger T. Ames, editors
  1989 *Nature in Asian Traditions of Thought: Essays in Environmental Philosophy.* Albany: State University of New York Press.

Cavell, Stanley
1979 *The Claim of Reason.* New York: Oxford.

Chang, Chung-yuan
1963 *Creativity and Taoism.* New York: The Julian Press. Reprinted; New York: Harper & Row, 1970.

Cheng, Chung-ying
1991 *New Dimensions of Confucian and Neo-Confucian Philosophy.* Albany: State University of New York Press.

Christian, William
1959 *An Interpretation of Whitehead's Metaphysics.* New Haven: Yale University Press.
1964 *Meaning and Truth in Religion.* Princeton: Princeton University Press.

Cobb, John B., Jr.
1975 *Christ in a Pluralistic Age.* Philadelphia: Westminster.

Cohen, Robert S., Richard M. Martin, and Merold Westphal, editors.
1985 *Studies in the Philosophy of J. N. Findlay.* Albany: State University of New York Press.

Colapietro, Vincent M.
1989 *Peirce's Approach to the Self: A Semiotic Perspective on Human Subjectivity.* Albany: State University of New York Press.

Culler, Jonathan
1982 *On Deconstruction: Theory and Criticism after Structuralism.* Ithaca: Cornell University Press.
1986 *Ferdinand de Saussure.* Revised edition; Ithaca: Cornell University Press.

Dahrendorf, Ralf
1959 *Class and Class Conflict in Industrial Society.* Stanford: Stanford University Press.

DaVinci, Leonardo
1495 *Codex Atlanticus,* fol 370r. Cited in *The Unknown Leonardo,* edited by Ladislao Reti. New York: McGraw Hill, 1974, p. 287.

Davis, Douglas
1980 "Post Everything," *Art In America* 68/2 (February 1989), 11–14.

Dean, William
    1986 *American Religious Empiricism.* Albany: State University of
        New York Press.
    1988 *History Making History: The New Historicism in American Reli-
        gious Thought.* Albany: State University of New York Press.

Derrida, Jacques
    1976 *Of Grammatology.* Translated by Gayatri Chakravorty Spivak.
        Baltimore: The Johns Hopkins Press.

Desmond, William
    1986 *Art and the Absolute: A Study of Hegel's Aesthetics.* Albany: State
        University of New York Press.
    1987 *Desire, Dialectic, and Otherness: An Essay on Origins.* New Ha-
        ven: Yale University Press.
    1990 *Philosophy and Its Others: Ways of Being and Mind.* Albany: State
        University of New York Press.

Dewey, John
    1916 *Democracy and Education.* In *The Middle Works of John Dewey,*
        volume 9. Edited by Jo Ann Boydston. Carbondale: Southern
        Illinois University Press, 1980.
    1920 *Reconstruction in Philosophy.* New York: Henry Holt.
    1925 *Experience and Nature.* In *The Later Works of John Dewey,* vol-
        ume 1. Edited by Jo Ann Boydston. Carbondale: Southern Il-
        linois University Press, 1981.
    1927 *The Public and Its Problems.* In *The Later Works,* volume 2. Ed-
        ited by Jo Ann Boydston. Carbondale: Southern Illinois Uni-
        versity Press, 1984.
    1929 *The Quest For Certainty.* In *The Later Works,* volume 4. Edited
        by Jo Ann Boydston. Carbondale: Southern Illinois Univer-
        sity Press, 1984.
    1934 *A Common Faith.* New Haven: Yale University Press.
    1935 *Liberalism and Social Action.* New York: Capriborn, 1963.

Dilworth, David A.
    1989 *Philosophy In World Perspective: A Comparative Hermeneutic of the
        Major Theories.* New Haven: Yale University Press.

Edwards, Jonathan
    1746 *A Treatise Concerning Religious Affections.* Edited by John E.
        Smith. New Haven: Yale University Press, 1959.

Emerson, Ralph Waldo
    1837 "The American Scholar," in *The Complete Essays and Other Writings of Ralph Waldo Emerson*. Introduction by Brooks Atkinson. New York: Modern Library, 1940.

Farrer, Austin
    1959 *Finite and Infinite: A Philosophical Essay*. Second edition: London: Dacre Press. First edition, 1943.

Feldstein, Leonard
    1978 *Homo Quaerens: The Seeker and the Sought: Method Become Ontology*. New York: Fordham University Press.
    1979 *The Dance of Being: Man's Labyrinthine Rhythms: The Natural Ground of the Human*. New York: Fordham University Press.
    1984 *Choros: The Orchestrating Self: Lamentation and Celebration*. New York: Fordham University Press.

Findlay, John N.
    1974 *Plato: The Written and Unwritten Doctrines*. London: Routledge & Kegan Paul.

Fodor, Jerry A.
    1981 *Representations*. Cambridge: Massachusetts Institute of Technology Press.
    1983 *The Modularity of Mind*. Cambridge: Massachusetts Institute of Technology Press.

Ford, Lewis S.
    1972 "Neville on the One and the Many," *Southern Journal of Philosophy* 10/1 (Spring 1972), 79–84.
    1973 "The Non-Temporality of Whitehead's God," *International Philosophical Quarterly* 13/3 (September 1973), 347–76.
    1978 *The Lure of God*. Philadelphia: Fortress.
    1984 *The Emergence of Whitehead's Metaphysics: 1925–1929*. Albany: State University of New York Press.
    1987 "Creativity in a Future Key," in Neville, ed., 1987b.

Ford, Lewis S., and George L. Kline, editors
    1983 *Explorations in Whitehead's Philosophy*. New York: Fordham University Press.

Foucoult, Michel
    1976 *The Archeology of Knowledge*. Translated by A. M. Sheridan Smith. New York: Harper & Row.

Frankenberry, Nancy
    1987 *Religion and Radical Empiricism.* Albany: State University of New York Press.

Gadamer, Hans-Georg
    1975 *Truth and Method.* Edited by Garrett Barden and John Cumming. New York: The Seabury Press.
    1976 *Philosophical Hermeneutics.* Translated and edited by David E. Linge. Berkeley: University of California Press.

Gilson, Etienne
    1940 *The Spirit of Mediaeval Philosophy.* Translated by A. H. C. Downes. New York: Charles Scribner's Sons.

Girardot, Norman J.
    1983 *Myth and Meaning in Early Taoism: The Theme of Chaos (Hun-Tun).* Berkeley: University of California Press.

Gouldner, Alvin W.
    1970 *The Coming Crisis of Western Sociology.* New York: Basic Books.

Gracia, Jorge J. E.
    1988 *Individuality: An Essay on the Foundations of Metaphysics.* Albany: State University of New York Press.

Griffin, David Ray, editor
    1988a *The Reenchantment of Science: Postmodern Proposals.* Albany: State University of New York Press.
    1988b *Spirituality and Society: Postmodern Visions.* Albany: State University of New York Press.

Hall, David L.
    1973 *The Civilization of Experience: A Whiteheadian Theory of Culture.* New York: Fordham University Press.
    1982 *The Uncertain Phoenix.* New York: Fordham University Press.
    1982a *Eros and Irony: A Prelude to Philosophical Anarchism.* Albany: State University of New York Press.

Hall, David L., and Roger T. Ames
    1987 *Thinking Through Confucius.* Albany: State University of New York Press.

Haller, William
    1938 *The Rise of Puritanism.* New York: Columbia University Press. Reprinted; New York: Harper, 1957.

Harari, Josue V., editor
1979 *Textual Strategies: Perspectives in Post-Structuralist Criticism.* Ithaca, New York: Cornell University Press.

Harris, Errol E.
1987 *Formal, Transcendental, and Dialectical Thinking.* Albany: State University of New York Press.
1988 *The Reality of Time.* Albany: State University of New York Press.

Hart, Ray L.
1968 *Unfinished Man and the Imagination.* New York: Herder and Herder.

Hartshorne, Charles
1948 *The Divine Relativity.* New Haven: Yale University Press.
1962 *The Logic of Perfection.* LaSalle, Ill.: Open Court.
1970 *Creative Synthesis and Philosophic Method.* LaSalle, Ill.: Open Court.

Hartshorne, Charles, John B. Cobb, Jr., and Lewis S. Ford
1980 "Three Responses to Neville's *Creativity and God*" *Process Studies* 10/3-4 (Fall–Winter 1980), 73–88.

Harvey, David
1990 *The Condition of Postmodernity.* Oxford: Basil Blackwell.

Heelan, Patrick
1983 *Space Perception and the Philosophy of Science.* Berkeley: University of California Press.

Hegel, Georg W. F.
1807 *The Phenomenology of Spirit.* Translated by A. V. Miller from the fifth edition; Hegel himself produced only the first edition. Oxford: Oxford University Press, 1977.
1821 *The Philosophy of Right.* Translated by T. M. Knox. Oxford: Oxford University Press, 1942.
1830 *The Logic of Hegel.* Translated by William Wallace from the third edition of Hegel's *Encyclopaedia of the Philosophical Sciences;* first edition, 1817. Second edition; London: Oxford University Press, 1892.
1833 *The Science of Logic.* Translated by W. H. Johnston and L. G. Struthers. In two volumes; London: George Allen & Unwin, 1929. The translation is of the fourth edition; Hegel himself

prepared only the first and second editions before his death, and it is the second edition, published two years after his death, whose date is given here.

1840 *Reason in History.* Translated by Robert S. Hartman from the second edition of Hegel's "Lectures on the Philosophy of History," edited and published by Hegel's son, Karl, in 1840 from classroom lecture notes.

Heidegger, Martin

1927 *Being and Time.* Translated by John Macquarrie and Edward Robinson. London: SCM Press, 1962.

1929 *Kant and the Problem of Metaphysics.* Translated by James S. Churchill. Bloomington, Indiana: Indiana University Press, 1962.

1954 "The Question Concerning Technology," in *The Question Concerning Technology and Other Essays.* Translated by William Lovitt. New York: Harper & Row, 1977.

1959 *An Introduction to Metaphysics.* Translated by Ralph Manheim. New Haven: Yale University Press. Also Garden City, N.Y.: Doubleday Anchor, 1961.

1973 *The End of Philosophy.* Translated by Joan Stambaugh. New York: Harper & Row.

Hill, Christopher

1984 *The Experience of Defeat: Milton and Some Contemporaries.* New York: Elisabeth Sifton Books-Viking.

Hillman, James

1975 *Re-Visioning Psychology.* New York: Harper & Row.

Hobbes, Thomas

1651 *Leviathan.* New York: Dutton, 1950.

Hocking, William Ernest

1912 *The Meaning of God in Human Experience.* New Haven: Yale University Press.

1918 *Human Nature and Its Remaking.* New Haven: Yale University Press.

1926 *Man and the State.* New Haven: Yale University Press.

Hume, David

1739 *a Treatise of Human Nature.* Edited by L. A. Selby-Bigge. Oxford: Oxford University Press, 1888.

Husserl, Edmund
   1931 *Ideas.* Translated by W. R. Boyce Gibson. New York: Macmillan. German original, 1913.
   1938 *The Crisis of European Sciences and Transcendental Phenomenology.* Translated by David Carr. Evanston: Northwestern University Press, 1970; German edition, 1954; last draft by Husserl, 1938.

James, William
   1909 *A Pluralistic Universe.* New York: Longmans Green.
   1911 *Some Problems of Philosophy.* New York: Longmans Green.
   1912 *Essays in Radical Empiricism.* New York: Longmans Green.

Johnson, Paul
   1991 *The Birth of the Modern: World Society 1815–1830.* New York: Harper Collins.

Kant, Immanuel
   1787 *Critique of Pure Reason.* Translated by Norman Kemp Smith. London: Macmillan, 1933.

Klaaren, Eugene M.
   1977 *Religious Origins of Modern Science.* Grand Rapids: Eerdmans.

Kolb, David
   1986 *The Critique of Pure Modernity: Hegel, Heidegger, and After.* Chicago: University of Chicago Press.

Kraus, Elizabeth
   1979 *The Metaphysics of Experience: A Companion to Whitehead's Process and Reality.* Albany: State University of New York Press.

Krauss, Rosalind
   1979 "John Mason and Post-Modernist Sculpture: New Experiences, New Words," *Art in America* 67/3 (May/June 1979), 120–127.

Krettek, Thomas, editor
   1987 *Creativity and Common Sense: Essays in Honors of Paul Weiss.* Albany: State University of New York Press.

Kripke, Saul A.
   1980 *Naming and Necessity.* Cambridge: Harvard University Press.

Kuhn, Thomas S.
   1962 *The Structure or Scientific Revolutions.* Chicago: University of Chicago Press.

Lachs, John, editor
> 1967 *Animal Faith and Spiritual Life.* New York: Appleton, Century, Crofts.

Lachs, John
> 1987 *Mind and Philosophers.* Nashville: Vanderbilt University Press.
> 1988 *George Santayana.* Boston: Twayne.

Lauer, Quentin, S.J.
> 1974 *Hegel's Idea of Philosophy.* Revised edition; New York: Fordham University Press; first edition, 1971.
> 1976 *A Reading of Hegel's Phenomenology of Spirit* (New York: Fordham University Press.
> 1977 *Essays in Hegelian Dialectic.* New York: Fordham University Press.
> 1982 *Hegel's Concept of God.* Albany: State University of New York Press.

Leahy, David G.
> 1980 *Novitas Mundi.* New York: New York University Press.

Leites, Edmund
> 1986 *The Puritan Conscience and Modern Sexuality.* New Haven: Yale University Press.

Lentricchia, Frank
> 1980 *After the New Criticism.* Chicago: University of Chicago Press.

Levi-Strauss, Claude
> 1963 *Structural Anthropology.* Translated by Claire Jacobson and Brooke Grundfest Schoepf. New York: Basic Books. Reprinted; Garden City, N.Y.: Doubleday, 1967.

Lieb, Irwin C.
> 1971 *The Four Faces of Man.* Philadelphia: University of Pennsylvania Press.

Lippmann, Walter
> 1925 *The Phantam Public.* New York: Harcourt Brace.
> 1955 *The Public Philosophy.* Boston: Little, Brown.

Locke, John
> 1690 *Two Treatise of Government.* Edited by Thomas I. Cook. New York: Hafner, 1956.
> 1700 *An Essay Concerning Human Understanding.* Edited by Alexander Campbell Fraser from Locke's fourth edition. Oxford: Oxford University Press, 1894; republished by Dover, 1959.

Lucas, George R., Jr.
  1986 Editor of *Hegel and Whitehead: Contemporary Perspectives on Systematic Philosophy*. Albany: State University of New York Press.
  1989 *The Rehabilitation of Whitehead: An Analytic and Historical Assessment of Process Philosophy*. Albany: State University of New York Press.

MacIntyre, Alisdair
  1984 *After Virtue*. Second edition; Notre Dame: Notre Dame University Press.

Macksey, Richard, and Donato, Eugenio, editors
  1970 *The Structuralist Controversy*. Baltimore: Johns Hopkins Press.

Magliola, Robert
  1984 *Derrida On the Mend*. West Lafayette, Indiana: Purdue University Press.

Martin, Richard M.
  1983 *Mind, Modality, Meaning, and Method*. Albany: State University of New York Press.

Martine, Brian John
  1984 *Individuals and Individuality*. Albany: State University of New York Press.

May, Rollo
  1969 *Love and Will*. New York: Norton.

Mead, George Herbert
  1938 *The Philosophy of the Act*. Edited by Charles W. Morris, with John M. Brewster, Albert M. Dunham, and David L. Miller, of mainly unpublished papers; Mead died in 1931. Chicago: University of Chicago Press.

Moore, Edward C., and Robin Richard S., editors
  1964 *Studies in the Philosophy of Charles Sanders Peirce, Second Series*. Amherst: University of Massachusetts Press.

Moore, G. E.
  1903 *Principia Ethica*. Cambridge: Cambridge University Press.
  1953 *Some Main Problems of Philosophy*. New York: Macmillan.

Murphey, Murray G.
  1961 *The Development of Peirce's Philosophy*. Cambridge: Harvard University Press.

Neville, Robert C.

1967 "Intuition," in *International Philosophical Quarterly,* 7 (December 1967), 556–590.

1969–70 "Whitehead on the One and the Many," *Southern Journal of Philosophy* 7 (1969–70), 387–393.

1970 "Paul Weiss's *Philosophy in Process,*" in *Review of Metaphysics,* 24 (December 1970), 276–301.

1972 "Response to Ford's 'Neville On the One and the Many'," *Southern Journal of Philosophy* 10/1 (Spring 1972), 85–86.

1974 *The Cosmology of Freedom.* New Haven: Yale University Press.

1978 Review of Paul Weiss, *First Considerations, Review of Metaphysics,* 31/3, (March 1978), 495–496.

1978a *Soldier, Sage, Saint.* New York: Fordham University Press.

1980 *Creativity and God: A Challenge to Process Theology.* New York: The Seabury Press (now Harper and Row).

1981 *Reconstruction of Thinking.* Albany: State University of New York Press.

1981a Review of Paul Weiss, *You, I, and the Others,* in *International Philosophical Quarterly,* 21/2 (June 1981) 211–216.

1981b "Concerning *Creativity and God:* A Response," *Process Studies* 11/1 (Spring 1980), 1–10.

1982 *The Tao and the Daimon.* Albany: State University of New York Press.

1987a *The Puritan Smile.* Albany: State University of New York Press.

1987b Editor, *New Essays in Metaphysics.* Albany: State University of New York Press.

1987c "Achievement, Value, and Structure," in Krettek, 1987: 124–144.

1989 *Recovery of the Measure.* Albany: State University of New York Press.

1991a *Behind the Masks of God.* Albany: State University of New York Press.

1991b *A Theology Primer.* Albany: State University of New York Press.

1992 *God the Creator.* New edition; Albany: State University of New York Press. Original edition; Chicago: University of Chicago Press, 1968.

Newman, Charles

1985 *The Post-Modern Aura: The Act of Fiction in an Age of Inflation.* Evanston, Ill.: Northwestern University Press.

Newman, John Henry
    1852 *The Idea of the University.* New Impression; London: Longmans, Green, and Co., 1902.

Niebuhr, Reinhold
    1949 *The Nature and Destiny of Man.* One volume edition; New York: Charles Scribner's Sons.

Nishitani, Keiji
    1982 *Religion and Nothingness.* Translated by Jan Van Bragt. Berkeley: University of California Press.

Nozick, Robert
    1981 *Philosophical Explanations.* Cambridge: Harvard University Press, 1981.

Odin, Steve
    1982 *Process Metaphysics and Hua-yen Buddhism.* Albany: State University of New York Press.

Peirce, Charles Sanders
    1931–1958 *The Collected Papers of Charles Sanders Peirce.* Volume I, 1931, Volume II, 1931, Volume III, 1933, Volume IV, 1933a, Volume V, 1934, Volume VI, 1935; edited by Charles Hartshorne and Paul Weiss. Volume VII, 1958, and Volume VIII, 1958a; edited by Arthur W. Burks. Cambridge, Mass.: Harvard University Press. Citation by volume and paragraph number, e.g., CP 2.226, *Collected Papers*, Volume II, paragraph 226.

Pols, Edward
    1967 *Whitehead's Metaphysics: A Critical Examination of Process and Reality.* Carbondale: Southern Illinois University Press.
    1975 *Meditation on a Prisoner.* Carbondale: Southern Illinois University Press.
    1982 *The Acts of Our Being.* Amherst: The University of Massachusetts Press.

Post, John F.
    1987 *The Faces of Existence: An Essay in Nonreductive Metaphysics.* Ithaca: Cornell University Press.

Potter, Vincent G., S.J.
    1967 *Charles S. Peirce on Norms and Ideals.* Amherst: University of Massachusetts Press.

Prigogine, Ilya, and Isabelle Stengers
1984 *Order Out of Chaos: Man's New Dialogue With Nature.* New York: Bantam Books.

Putnam, Hilary
1978 *Meaning and the Moral Sciences.* London: Routledge & Kegan Paul.

Radhakrishnan, Sarvepalli
1967 *Religion in a Changing World.* London: George Allen and Unwin.

Raposa, Michael L.
1989 *Peirce's Philosophy of Religion.* Bloomington: Indiana University Press.

Rawls, John
1971 *A Theory of Justice.* Cambridge: Harvard University Press.

Reck, Andrew J., Robert C. Neville, and John E. Smith
1986 "John E. Smith as an Interpreter of American Philosophy: A Symposium," in *Transactions of the Charles S. Peirce Society,* 22/3 (Summer 1986) 239–288.

Ricoeur, Paul
1974 *The Conflict of Interpretations.* Edited by Don Ihde. Evanston, Illinois: Northwestern University Press.

Rorty, Richard
1979 *Philosophy and the Mirror of Nature.* Princeton, N.J.: Princeton University Press.
1982 *Consequences of Pragmatism.* Minneapolis: University of Minnesota Press.

Rosenthal, Sandra B.
1986 *Speculative Pragmatism.* Amherst: University of Massachusetts Press.

Ross, James F.
1969 *Philosophical Theology.* New York: Bobbs-Merrill.

Ross, Stephen David
1981 *Philosophical Mysteries.* Albany: State University of New York Press.
1983 *Perspective In Whitehead's Metaphysics.* Albany: State University of New York Press.

1989 *Metaphysical Aporia and Philosophical Heresy.* Albany: State University of New York Press.

Royce, Josiah
 1899–1901 *The World and the Individual.* First and Second Series. New York: Macmillan. Reprint with an introduction by John E. Smith; New York: Dover, 1959.
 1908 *The Philosophy of Loyalty.* New York: Macmillan.
 1918 *The Problem of Christianity.* New York: Macmillan. Reprinted with an introduction by John E. Smith; Chicago: University of Chicago Press, 1968.

Russell, Bertrand
 1912 *The Problems of Philosophy.* London: Home University Library.
 1914 *Our Knowledge of the External World.* Chicago: Open Court.
 1918 *Mysticism and Logic.* London: Longmans.

Samuelson, Paul
 1989 *Economics.* With William D. Norhaus. Thirteenth edition; New York: McGraw-Hill.

Santayana, George
 1942 *The Realms of Being.* Three volumes in one; New York: Charles Scribner's Sons.

Schilpp, Paul Arthur
 1941 *The Philosophy of Alfred North Whitehead.* The Library of Living Philosophers. New York: Tudor.

Schorske, Carl E.
 1980 *Fin-de-Siecle Vienna.* New York; Alfred Knopf; also New York: Random House/Vintage, 1980.

Sellars, Wilfrid
 1963 *Science, Perception and Reality.* London: Routledge & Kegan Paul.

Sherover, Charles M.
 1989 *Time, Freedom, and the Common Good.* Albany: State University of New York Press.

Smith, Adam
 1789 *The Wealth of Nations.* Edited by Edwin Cannan from Smith's fifth edition. Sixth edition; London: Methuen & Co., 1950; original Cannan edition, 1904.

Smith, John E.
   1950 *Royce's Social Infinite: The Community of Interpretation.* New York: Liberal Arts Press.
   1961 *Reason and God: Encounters of Philosophy with Religion.* New Haven: Yale University Press.
   1968 *Experience and God.* New York: Oxford University Press.
   1970 *Themes in American Philosophy: Purpose, Experience, and Community.* New York: Harper & Row.
   1973 *The Analogy of Experience.* New York: Harper & Row.
   1978 *Purpose and Thought: The Meaning of Pragmatism.* New Haven: Yale University Press.
   1983 *The Spirit of American Philosophy.* Revised edition; Albany: State University of New York Press.

Smith, Wilfrid Cantwell
   1981 *Towards a World Theology: Faith and the Comparative History of Religion.* Philadelphia: Westminster.

Spector, Marshall
   1978 *Concepts of Reduction in Physical Science.* Philadelphia: Temple University Press.

Stout, Jeffrey
   1981 *The Flight from Authority: Religion, Morality, and the Quest for Autonomy.* Notre Dame: University of Notre Dame Press.
   1988 *Ethics After Babel: The Languages of Morals and Their Discontents.* Boston: Beacon.

Sullivan, William
   1982 *Reconstructing Public Philosophy.* Berkeley: University of California Press.

Tillich, Paul
   1952 *The Courage To Be.* New Haven: Yale University Press.

Toulmin, Stephen
   1958 *The Uses of Argument.* New York: Cambridge University Press.
   1972 *Human Understanding.* Princeton: Princeton University Press.

Toulmin, Stephen, and Allan Janik
   1973 *Wittgenstein's Vienna.* New York: Simon and Schuster.

Tracy, David
   1987 *Plurality and Ambiguity.* San Francisco: Harper & Row.

Tu Wei-ming
    1979 *Humanity and Self-Cultivation: Essays in Confucian Thought.* Berkeley: Asian Humanities Press.
    1985 *Confucian Thought: Selfhood as Creative Transformation.* Albany: State University of New York Press.

Tucker, Robert C.
    1969 *The Marxian Revolutionary Idea.* New York: Norton.

Urmson, J. O.
    1956 *Philosophical Analysis: Its Development between the Two World Wars.* Oxford: Clarendon Press.

Waldenfels, Hans
    1980 *Absolute Nothingness.* New York: Paulist Press.

Wallach, Florence Bradford
    1980 *The Epochal Nature of Process in Whitehead's Metaphysics.* Albany: State University of New York Press.

Weber, Max
    1904–1905 *The Protestant Ethic and the Spirit of Capitalism.* Translated by Talcott Parsons. New York: Charles Scribner's Sons, 1958.
    1951 *The Religion of China.* Translated and edited by Hans H. Gerth. New York: The Free Press. From articles published at various times in Weber's life.

Weiss, Paul
    1939 *Reality.* Princeton: Princeton University Press.
    1947 *Nature and Man.* New York: Holt.
    1950 *Man's Freedom.* New Haven: Yale University Press.
    1958 *Modes of Being.* Carbondale: Southern Illinois University Press.
    1959 *Our Public Life.* Bloomington: Indiana University Press.
    1961 *The World of Art.* Carbondale: Southern Illinois University Press.
    1962 *History: Written and Lived.* Carbondale: Southern Illinois University Press.
    1964 *The God We Seek.* Carbondale: Southern Illinois University Press.
    1969 *Sport: A Philosophic Inquiry.* Carbondale: Southern Illinois University Press.

1974 *Beyond All Appearances.* Carbondale: Southern Illinois University Press.

1977 *First Considerations.* Carbondale: Southern Illinois University Press.

1980 *You, I, and the Others.* Carbondale: Southern Illinois University Press.

1983 *Privacy.* Carbondale: Southern Illinois University Press.

1986 *Toward A Perfected State.* Albany: State University of New York Press.

Weissman, David

1965 *Dispositional Properties.* Carbondale: Southern Illinois University Press.

1977 *Eternal Possibilities.* Carbondale: Southern Illinois University Press.

1987 *Intuition and Ideality.* Albany: State University of New York Press.

1989 *Hypothesis and the Spiral of Reflection.* Albany: State University of New York Press.

Whitehead, Alfred North

1925 *Science and the Modern World.* New York: Macmillan.

1926 *Religion in the Making.* New York: Macmillan.

1929 *Process and Reality: An Essay in Cosmology.* New York: Macmillan. Cited in the Corrected Edition edited by David Ray Griffin and Donald W. Sherburne; New York: Free Press, 1978.

1929a *The Function of Reason.* Princeton: Princeton University Press; republished, Boston: Beacon Press, 1958.

1933 *Adventures of Ideas.* New York: Macmillan.

1938 *Modes of Thought.* New York: Macmillan.

Wieman, Henry Nelson

1946 *The Source of Human Good.* Chicago: University of Chicago Press.

Wiener, Philip P., and Frederick H. Young, editors

1952 *Studies in the Philosophy of Charles Sanders Peirce.* Cambridge: Harvard University Press.

Winfield, Richard Dien

1988 *Reason and Justice.* Albany: State University of New York Press.

Wittgenstein, Ludwig
    1922 *Tractatus Logico-Philosophicus.* London: Routledge & Kegan Paul.
    1953 *Philosophical Investigations.* Translated by G. E. M. Anscomb. New York: Macmillan.

Wood, Robert E.
    1990 *A Path Into Metaphysics.* Albany: State University of New York Press.

Wu, Kuang-ming
    1982 *Chuang Tzu: World Philosopher At Play.* Chico: Scholars Press.
    1990 *The Butterfly as Companion: Meditations on the First Three Chapters of the Chuang Tzu.* Albany: State University of New York Press.

*

INDEX